Viking-Age Transformations

The Viking Age was a period of profound change in Scandinavia. As kingdoms were established, Christianity became the encompassing ideological and cosmological framework and towns were formed. This book examines a central backdrop to these changes: the economic transformation of West Scandinavia. With a focus on the development of intensive and organized use of woodlands and alpine regions and domestic raw materials, together with the increasing standardization of products intended for long-distance trade, the volume sheds light on the emergence of a strong interconnectedness between remote rural areas and central markets.

Viking-Age Transformations explores the connection between legal and economic practice, as the rural economy and monetary system developed in conjunction with nascent state power and the legal system. Thematically, the book is organized into sections addressing the nature and extent of trade in both marginal and centralized areas; production and the social, legal and economic aspects of exploiting natural resources and distributing products; and the various markets and sites of trade and consumption.

A theoretically informed and empirically grounded collection that reveals the manner in which relationships of production and consumption transformed Scandinavian society with their influence on the legal and fiscal division of the landscape, this volume will appeal to scholars of archaeology, the history of trade and Viking studies.

Zanette T. Glørstad is Associate Professor in the Department of Archaeology, Museum of Cultural History, University of Oslo, Norway.

Kjetil Loftsgarden is a research fellow in the Department of Archaeology, History, Cultural Studies and Religion, University of Bergen, Norway.

Culture, Environment and Adaptation in the North
Series Editors:
Rane Willerslev and Sean O'Neill, Aarhus University, Denmark

Culture, Environment and Adaptation in the North constitutes a space for the production and dissemination of new insights on societies in the northern regions of the globe, including Scandinavia, and Scotland, Iceland, Greenland, Canada and Alaska to the West, and Finland, the Baltic countries, northern Russia, Mongolia and Siberia to the East. Loosely defined by latitude, the North is also distinctive in the tight connections of environmental, historical, geopolitical and cultural conditions that have characterised its regions, from prehistoric times to the present day. Northern regions have held enormous natural resources that have attracted peoples at various historical periods, with their large reserves of oil and gas forming the primary focus today – with all that this entails for environmental, social and cultural challenges. This series produces cutting-edge, anthropological, sociological and geographical knowledge of northern adaptations in relation to the natural and societal environments of the northern regions.

Viking-Age Transformations
Trade, Craft and Resources in Western Scandinavia
Edited by Zanette T. Glørstad and Kjetil Loftsgarden

https://www.routledge.com/Culture-Environment-and-Adaptation-in-the-North/book-series/ASHSER1431

Viking-Age Transformations
Trade, Craft and Resources in
Western Scandinavia

Edited by Zanette T. Glørstad
and Kjetil Loftsgarden

LONDON AND NEW YORK

First published 2017
by Routledge

2 Park Square, Milton Park, Abingdon, Oxfordshire OX14 4RN
52 Vanderbilt Avenue, New York, NY 10017

Routledge is an imprint of the Taylor & Francis Group, an informa business

First issued in paperback 2018

Copyright © 2017 selection and editorial matter, Zanette T. Glørstad
and Kjetil Loftsgarden; individual chapters, the contributors

The right of Zanette T. Glørstad and Kjetil Loftsgarden to be
identified as the authors of the editorial material, and of the authors
for their individual chapters, has been asserted in accordance with
sections 77 and 78 of the Copyright, Designs and Patents Act 1988.

All rights reserved. No part of this book may be reprinted or reproduced or
utilised in any form or by any electronic, mechanical, or other means, now
known or hereafter invented, including photocopying and recording, or in
any information storage or retrieval system, without permission in writing
from the publishers.

Notice:
Product or corporate names may be trademarks or registered trademarks,
and are used only for identification and explanation without intent to
infringe.

British Library Cataloguing in Publication Data
A catalogue record for this book is available from the British Library

Library of Congress Cataloging in Publication Data
A catalog record for this book has been requested

ISBN: 978-1-4724-7077-5 (hbk)
ISBN: 978-0-367-08547-6 (pbk)

Typeset in Bembo
by Swales & Willis Ltd, Exeter, Devon, UK

Contents

Preface and acknowledgements		vii
Abbreviations		x
List of contributors		xi

**1 Viking-Age economic transformations:
the West-Scandinavian case**   1
DAGFINN SKRE

**PART I
Trade and traders**   29

2 Approaching trade in pre-state and early state societies   31
EIVIND HELDAAS SELAND

**3 The use of silver as a medium of exchange in
Jämtland, c. 875–1050**   42
OLOF HOLM

**4 Domestic and exotic materials in early medieval
Norwegian towns: an archaeological perspective
on production, procurement and consumption**   59
GITTE HANSEN

5 The price of justice and administration of coinage   95
FRODE IVERSEN AND SVEIN H. GULLBEKK

vi *Contents*

PART II
Production and resources   109

6 **The extensive iron production in Norway in the tenth**
   to thirteenth century: a regional perspective   111
   OLE TVEITEN AND KJETIL LOFTSGARDEN

7 **Viking-period non-ferrous metalworking and urban**
   commodity production   124
   UNN PEDERSEN

8 **Soapstone vessels and quernstones as commodities**
   in the Viking Age and Middle Ages   139
   IRENE BAUG

9 **The Uplands: the deepest of forests and the highest**
   of mountains – resource exploitation and landscape
   management in the Viking Age and early Middle
   Ages in southern Norway   160
   KATHRINE STENE AND VIVIAN WANGEN

PART III
Sites of trade   189

10 **A view from the valley: Langeid in Setesdal,**
    South Norway – a Viking-Age trade station
    along a mercantile highway   191
    ZANETTE T. GLØRSTAD AND CAMILLA CECILIE WENN

11 **Heimdalsjordet: trade, production and communication**   212
    JAN BILL AND CHRISTIAN LØCHSEN RØDSRUD

12 **The *skeid* and other assemblies in the Norwegian**
    'Mountain Land'   232
    KJETIL LOFTSGARDEN, MORTEN RAMSTAD AND
    FRANS-ARNE STYLEGAR

13 **The urban hinterland: interaction and law-areas**
    in Viking and medieval Norway   250
    FRODE IVERSEN

   Index   277

Preface and acknowledgements

The centuries between AD 700 and 1100 are characterised by profound changes in economic reasoning and organisation. This period saw the emergence of markets, towns and a coin economy, as well as a substantial increase in the rural production of marketable goods. The exploitation of outfield resources takes place simultaneously with an expansion in the diversity as well as the magnitude of craft production. Production was reorganised and increased dramatically in scale; products became much more standardised and were intended for long-distance trade. A central feature of these developments is thus the essential, but often overlooked, increase in the use of resources and raw materials from uncultivated areas. Thereby, remote rural areas were linked to a wider market, developing a strong interconnectedness with towns and marketplaces. This book attempts to examine these developments not as isolated events but as interlocked phenomena, and thus bring forward economic research on the Viking Age.

To stimulate such an approach, the Centre for Viking-Age Studies (ViS) at the Museum of Cultural History, University of Oslo, organised the conference *The Power of the Market* on 4–6 December 2013. The conference sought to draw together the variety of ongoing research related to Viking-Age economics in West Scandinavia, and move towards a shared platform for debate and research.

The ViS group, which has been the editorial board for this book, wanted to move beyond the conference proceedings format. Thus, following the conference, some of the contributors were invited, inspired by the discussions during the conference, to develop their contributions for this publication. The contributions address disparate topics, and their discussion of economy is not always explicit. Still, the theme of the conference resonates in all the chapters. Although they cover developments roughly within the geographic area of present-day Norway, we believe some general aspects to be relevant for the rest of Scandinavia and indeed beyond, and this volume has aspirations to encourage up-to-date discussion on empirical, theoretical and methodological issues pertaining to the transformations of the Viking-Age economy and its social ramifications.

viii *Preface and acknowledgements*

The anthology is divided into three main parts, set off by the introductory chapter 'Viking-Age economic transformations: the West-Scandinavian case' by Prof. Dagfinn Skre, the leader of the ViS group. Skre provides an overview of the *Stand der Forschung* in terms of trade, production and consumption in the period, as well as connecting them to the main economic transformations in western Scandinavia, and examines the pertinent theoretical considerations embedded in the analysis of these economic processes. The three main themes of trade, production and consumption form the basis for the rest of the volume, where each of the three parts retains a sharp focus on theoretical as well as empirical aspects and challenges within each subject. In Part I, 'Trade and traders', the theoretical platform that underlies the understanding of the early trading system is discussed, followed by case studies examining the nature and extent of trade in both marginal and centralised areas, and the social preconditions and agencies of the case in question. Part II, 'Production and resources', explores the social, legal and economic aspects of exploiting natural resources and landscapes in uncultivated/mountain areas, and examines the mechanisms behind the distribution of both luxury items and everyday products. Part III, 'Sites of trade', aims to present a more nuanced picture of the wide variety of meeting points and markets in the period, where some represent various specialised functions, while others can be characterised as multifunctional. A key theme presented is the significance of the extensive interconnectedness between legal and economic praxis, where the growing importance of the rural economy and monetary system is seen in conjunction with nascent state power and the legal system.

The terms designating these prehistoric periods in Scandinavian do not always correspond to the terminology used on the Continent and in the British Isles (Table 0.1). In Scandinavia, the term *Late Iron Age* covers the time interval c. 550–1050, including the period known in Norway as the Merovingian Period and in Sweden as the Vendel Period (c. 550–800), as well as the Viking Age (c. 800–1050). The Viking Age is furthermore often loosely divided into the early and late Viking Age, with the boundary between the two set at around 900 AD. The term *Early Middle Ages*, which is the preferred designation for this period in international research bodies, is in Scandinavia reserved for the time after the Viking Age AD (1050–1150), followed by the *High Middle Ages* (AD 1150–1350) and the *Late Middle Ages* (AD 1350–1520s/1537). The end dates of the Middle Ages mark the national political restructuration and introduction of the reformist church during these years, in Sweden and Norway respectively. In addition to the clarification given here, the terminology and the designated time frames of the periods are specified in the chapters.

We are grateful for the financial support allocated to the ViS group by the University of Oslo for continued work to develop national and international networks, and promote a progressive research scope. We are also thankful for the generous sponsoring the conference received from the 'Agrarian Network' funded by the Norwegian Research Council's programme *Forskning i Felleskap* ('Joint Research'). We would furthermore like to thank the Archaeology

Table 0.1 An overview of the overarching time designations used in European history c. 550–1500, compared with the corresponding general period designations used in Sweden and Norway

AD	Continent & UK	Norway and Sweden	Archaeological era, Scandinavia
550	Early Middle Ages	Merovingian Period/ Vendel Period (SE)	Late Iron Age
600			
650			
700			
750			
800		Early Viking Age	
850			
900			
950			
1000	High Middle Ages	Late Viking Age	Middle Ages
1050			
1100		Early Middle Ages	
1150			
1200		High Middle Ages	
1250			
1300	Late Middle Ages		
1350			
1400		Late Middle Ages	
1450			
1500			
1537			

Section at the Department of Archaeology, Conservation and History (IAKH), University of Oslo, as well as the Department of Archaeology, History, Cultural Studies and Religion (AHKR), University of Bergen, for supporting the conference, and the postgraduate students Marie Amundsen and Torbjørn Preus Schou, who provided invaluable help with the workshop.

Oslo, 30 May 2016
Zanette T. Glørstad and Kjetil Loftsgarden

Abbreviations

C	King Christian IV's Norwegian law code of 1604. Hallanger, Fr. and Brandt Fr. 1855 Kong Christian den Fjerdes norske Lovbog af 1604/efter Foranstaltning af Det akademiske Kollegium ved Det Kongelige Norske Frederiks Universitet udgiven af Fr. Hallager og Fr. Brandt. Carl Werner, Christiania.
DN	*Diplomatarium Norvegicum*, eds. C. C. A. Lange, C. R. Unger *et al.* 1847–1990. P. T. Mallings Forlagshandel, Christiania/Oslo.
Egs	*Egilsoga* translated by Leiv Heggestad, 1950. New edition 1994 by Magne Heggstad. Norrøne bokverk 15. Det norske samlaget Oslo.
F	*Frostatingelova* translated by Hagland, J. R. and Jørn Sandnes, J. 1994, Oslo.
G	Gulathing Law. Eithun, B., Rindal, M., Ulset, T. 1994. *Den eldre Gulatingsloven*. Riksarkivet, Oslo, Norway. 208 pp.
Hkr	*Heimskringla, utgave Kongesagaer/Snorre Sturluson*, translated by Anne Holtsmark and Didrik Arup Seip (1979), Norges kongesagaer 1–2. Oslo.
L	Taranger, Absalon 1915: *Magnus Lagabøtes Landslov*. Cammermeyers Boghandel. Kristiania.
KLNM	Kulturhistorisk Leksikon for Nordisk Middelalder – fra vikingtid til reformasjonstid I–XXII, 1956–78. København.
NgL	Norges Gamle Love I–V, 1846–95. Christiania.

Contributors

Irene Baug Postdoctoral Fellow – Department of Archaeology, History, Cultural Studies and Religion, University of Bergen, Norway

Jan Bill Professor – Department of Archaeology, Museum of Cultural History, University of Oslo, Norway

Zanette T. Glørstad Associate Professor – Department of Archaeology, Museum of Cultural History, University of Oslo, Norway

Svein Gullbekk Professor – Section for Numismatics and Classical Archaeology, Museum of Cultural History, University of Oslo, Norway

Gitte Hansen Associate Professor – University Museum of Bergen, Norway

Olof Holm Editor – The Riksdag Library/Centre for Medieval Studies, Stockholm University, Sweden

Frode Iversen Professor – Department of Archaeology, Museum of Cultural History, University of Oslo, Norway

Kjetil Loftsgarden PhD Research Fellow – Department of Archaeology, History, Cultural Studies and Religion, University of Bergen, Norway

Unn Pedersen Associate Professor – Department of Archaeology, Conservation and History, University of Oslo, Norway

Morten Rammstad Researcher – Section for Cultural Heritage Management, University Museum of Bergen, Norway

Christian Rødsrud Adviser/Archaeologist – Department of Archaeology, Museum of Cultural History, University of Oslo, Norway

Eivind Heldaas Seland Researcher – Department of Archaeology, History, Cultural Studies and Religion, University of Bergen, Norway

Dagfinn Skre Professor – Department of Archaeology, Museum of Cultural History, University of Oslo, Norway

Kathrine Stene PhD Research Fellow – University Museum of Bergen, Norway

xii *Contributors*

Frans-Arne Stylegar Director – Varanger Museum, Norway

Ole Tveiten Area Planner – Vestre Toten municipality, Raufoss, Norway

Vivian Wangen PhD Research Fellow – Department of Archaeology, Museum of Cultural History, University of Oslo, Norway

Camilla Cecilia Wenn Archaeologist – Department of Archaeology, Museum of Cultural History, University of Oslo, Norway

1 Viking-Age economic transformations

The West-Scandinavian case

Dagfinn Skre

The economic turn

The title of this book reflects the last few years' increased interest in the profound economic transformations of post-Roman northern Europe: the emergence of coinage, markets, towns, and mass production. The many publications within this field of research reveal a diversity of approaches to past economies; some study them within a narrow sphere of economy, while others apply a broad societal approach. Which is the most adequate and productive approach to these complex phenomena? To what extent may we rely on general theories when analysing economic phenomena, and to what extent should the various cultures and societies in question be taken into account? Is 'economy' a field in its own right, or does the singling out of economic actions and relations from other types of human dealings and interactions prevent us from understanding these aspects of human life?

Since the 1970s the societal and cultural approach to past economies has dominated, primarily inspired by the works of Karl Polanyi (1944: 142, 1957, 1963, 1968), Moses Finley (1973), and George Dalton (1975, 1977). Their theoretical strand, substantivism, has been enormously influential in both historical and archaeological research on early medieval northern Europe (Seland this vol.). Substantivism has been contested repeatedly in terms of theory, but, with the exception of some scholars adhering to classic economic theories (formalism) as well as some attempts to employ historical materialism, no coherent alternative has been applied in research on early medieval economic issues (for a comprehensive overview of alternative approaches, see Oka and Kusimba 2008).

In the last few years, however, several scholars in the field of Viking studies have explored theoretical alternatives and applied them in their research, beginning with Ingrid Gustin's *Mellan gåva och marknad* ('Between gift and market', 2004) and Søren Sindbæk's *Ruter og rutinisering* ('Routes and routinising', 2005). In Insular research the edited volumes *The Long Eighth Century: Production, Distribution and Demand* (Hansen and Wickham 2000) and *Markets in Early Medieval Europe* (Pestell and Ulmschneider 2003) have been particularly influential. One may perhaps speak of an economic turn in early medieval studies. Although economic issues had been investigated continuously through

2 Dagfinn Skre

the post-Second World War era – in Viking studies, probably most diligently and creatively treated by Johan Callmer (e.g. 1976, 1982, 1991, 1994, 1995, 2002, 2007) – the four mentioned books and other contemporary and subsequent publications have brought scholars of more diverse backgrounds into the field. In addition, they have connected the discussion of economy more explicitly to other current empirical and theoretical debates.

The new complexity of approaches is evident in Eivind Heldaas Seland's contribution to this book; he employs a number of analytical models and concepts to explain various aspects of trade in pre- and early-state societies. Pursuing a pragmatic and eclectic methodological and theoretical strategy in Seland's vein seems more viable than waiting for a full, coherent theory on premodern economy to be produced (see also Oka and Kusimba 2008). The economic history of humans is of course too diverse for any single theory to cover all variations in time and space. High-quality results emerge when scholars allow their theories and methods to be shaped by the reality of the societies and phenomena under study, adjusting their models as suited for the task at hand (Elster 2007: 447–8). This represents the likeliest path by which we can expect theoretical innovations in economic studies to emerge in the future. (For a related approach within sociology, see Swedberg 2014.)

My own contribution to this development has been to suggest that Polanyi's evolutionary model should be abandoned in favour of a view of past economies as consisting simultaneously of a variety of transaction types and circumstances of production. Correspondingly, Polanyi's idea of the economy as socially embedded should be fused with an understanding that economic considerations are a part of the human disposition. Throughout history, people have acted as simultaneously economic and social agents. Depending on the situation and circumstances, humans might perform one type of agency at the expense of the other. How these human inclinations are played out at specific times and places cannot be deduced from general theories, evolutionary or other, but calls for empirical investigation. I have proposed the term 'post-substantivism' for approaches along these lines (Skre 2008, 2011a, 2015, in prep.).

In this introductory overview of the economic upsurge in Viking-Age western Scandinavia, the main emphasis is on economic agency. Social agency receives less attention here.

Viking-Age economic transformations

In Scandinavia, the Viking Age – in this context c. AD 750–1100 – is a period of transformations. Towns were founded and became numerous, three kingdoms were established, Christianity became the dominant religion, production thrived, and long-distance contacts, peaceful and hostile, brought Scandinavian societies into closer and more regular contact with each other and the rest of Europe. By 1100 the Iron Age communities, polities, and cultures of Scandinavia had been transformed profoundly and irrevocably.

Few scholars have attempted to grasp the interconnectedness of these transformations; exploring any single transformation is more than enough for most of us. Those who have discussed a combination of them have relied heavily on written evidence; hence they focus on the two transformations that are best testified in the texts: Christianisation and state formation (e.g. Bagge 2010). Consequently, they mainly treat the latter part of the period: the tenth and eleventh centuries. In addition, due to the nature of the written records, these studies are skewed towards a top-down perspective on societal and cultural structures and processes. Although sagas, skaldic poems, law codes, cadastres, and diplomas also contain information on everyday life and commonplace occurrences, they say more about the activities, perspectives, and interests of social elites than about those of other groups. By contrast, the materiality of the archaeological record invites the building of interpretations from the ground up, complementing the top-down perspective of the written record. Thus, by consulting the archaeological record, a new range of transformations can be studied, one connected more closely to the social and economic agency of the broader population. Among the aspects of Viking-Age society brought within closer reach by a combined exploitation of written and archaeological evidence is the economy.

Within the economic sphere, the following transformations are particularly prominent:

- Production of marketable goods: While artisanal *unica* production was previously the norm, in the earliest Viking Age, artisans also began producing series of identical items. In parallel, a rather different type of production, based in domestic raw materials such as iron, soapstone, and whetstone, was taken up or reorganised for trade over long distances. In the late Viking Age such production rose to industrial proportions. In the same period quernstone and reindeer antler production was converted from satisfying local and regional needs to producing commodities for overseas trade.
- Long-distance trade: Trade within Scandinavia and beyond increased significantly in the earliest period and again around the turn of the millennium. Goods from Arab, Frankish, and Anglo-Saxon lands were brought to Scandinavian consumers.
- Urbanisation and markets: Seasonal markets had existed in southern and southeastern Scandinavia since the early first millennium AD; the establishment of seasonal markets continued there throughout the period. In the earliest Viking Age, the first four nascent towns were established. None endured into the post-Viking period; however, numerous new towns were established from the turn of the millennium onwards.
- Monetisation: In the early Viking Age, silver bullion and coins were introduced as means of payment. By the end of the period, the three Scandinavian kingdoms had well-functioning monetary systems.

Why did these transformations happen, how were they connected, and what wider societal and cultural significance did they have? An ample range of

4 *Dagfinn Skre*

studies is necessary to answer such questions; this book is a step in that direction. The title of the book suggests that the expansion of the market sphere within certain aspects of the Scandinavian economy played a role in Viking-Age transformations. The idea behind the conference (see the Preface), and indeed behind this book, was to foster an economic perspective on Viking-Age Scandinavia – specifically on commodity production and the role of markets. Several important aspects of economic life discussed in various chapters of this book are not dealt with here. Thus, the scope of this book, and certainly of the study of Viking-Age economic transformations, reaches beyond what is discussed in this chapter.

Subsistence, commission, and commodity production

The production of commodities differs from production under the other two types of circumstances of this period: subsistence and commission. While commodities are intended to satisfy the needs of some unknown consumer, subsistence production is intended for consumption by the producer and the household. Production on commission is intended to satisfy the wishes of the person who commissioned the item.

Only a selection of commodities is included in this overview, namely those produced in western Scandinavia (roughly present-day Norway) that features prominently in the archaeological record. There are two reasons for their high numbers and general occurrence: first, they are everyday utensils or ornaments for the populace, and second, they are less prone to decay than are other commodities known to have been produced. For instance, stone and iron products have been found in abundance, while antler and walrus-ivory products have only been preserved under favourable conditions, fur and hide have been documented only in exceptional cases (Wigh 2001: 120–3), and hardly any products such as rope and tar have hitherto been successfully identified.

Thus, the commodities discussed in the following were not necessarily those that had the highest economic and practical significance for producers, traders, and consumers of that period. Rather, given the heterogeneous composition of tradesmen's shiploads in premodern times, they may be seen as gauges, or proxies, for the chronology and geographical scope of trade activities that no doubt have covered a much more diverse range of commodities. Because overseas trade of the commodities in question primarily was directed at southern Scandinavia – that is, medieval Denmark – evidence from that area is involved in the discussion.

Commodity production for local, regional, and intraregional trade

Prior to the Viking period, the only known large-scale commodity production directed at long-distance trade was that of iron in the Early Iron Age (c. 400 BC–AD 550; Stenvik 2003; Tveiten and Loftsgarden this vol.). The following two centuries (c. AD 550–750) saw little or no commodity production for long-distance trade. Artisans and craftsmen in the sixth and seventh centuries seem to have been producing on commission, while other types of production appear to have been predominantly directed at subsistence, and perhaps local or regional trade.

Artisanal production

Among artisans, serial production of identical items was taken up in the mid-eighth century in southern Scandinavia. Artisans that worked with imported raw materials, *in casu* metal-casters (Pedersen this vol.) and glass-bead makers, were the first to develop serial production. Possibly, the knowledge of this style of production was spread via the Frisian trade networks that brought these raw materials into Scandinavia. While serial products are more likely to have been presented to the consumer as finished products, the precise shapes and ornaments of *unica* items would probably be the result of discussions between the artisan and the person who commissioned them. Thus, the taking up of serial production may indicate that the production process had become more detached from the consumer and that in some transactions the contact between producer and consumer was limited to the act of exchange. As concluded by Pedersen (this vol.), there is good evidence that production on commission was upheld in parallel to serial production. The introduction of serial production added a new aspect to artisanal production and trade.

Several types of artisans bought their raw materials, some from regional, others from long-distance trade networks. Smiths, comb-makers, and shoe-makers would obtain iron, antler, and leather locally or from the not-too-distant interior, while non-ferrous metalworkers and glass-bead makers would have to rely on long-distance trade. Remains from non-ferrous metalworking are found in sites where consumers ventured – towns, seasonal markets, and aristocratic manors – indication that products were sold by artisans to consumers, rather than in bulk to traders for resale. This was probably the case for most artisans. Consumers may have arrived to markets and towns from far afield. This is indicated by the substantial distribution of artisanal products to regions many hundreds of kilometres from the nearest production centres, for instance to northern Norway (Eldorhagen 2001) – some 1,200 kilometres from the ninth- to early tenth-century town Kaupang as the crow flies, more than 2,000 kilometres by sea. Although some artisanal products will probably have been produced and sold on smaller sites along the coast, many will have travelled that great distance after being purchased from the artisan in a market or town in the south.

The pattern is rather different in towns established in the late Viking Age. While artisans in the early towns appear to have produced goods for people in a vast circumference, those in the later towns seem to have supplied mainly the town's own inhabitants. Regarding the artisanal production, the towns established in the late Viking Age were 'consumer towns' (Hansen this vol.),

6 *Dagfinn Skre*

while the early towns were 'producer towns'. The main reason for this difference is probably that the later towns housed staff that administered royal and ecclesiastical interests in the hinterland, while the early towns had few or no such functions.

Rural production

Turning to rural production, Iron Age farms were never fully self-sufficient. No single household could extract their own iron, quarry their own whetstones, soapstone vessels, and quernstones, breed their own horses, or produce all the hide and wool they may have needed. To be able to obtain such goods, some production of goods intended for exchange will always have taken place on every farm.

The demand for such necessities may for the most part have been satisfied through local and regional trade. The increase in rural commodity production through the Viking Age made commodities from regions and towns far afield available to most people (see below). However, some types of production were not raised to that level until after the Viking period. This appears to be the case for the dominant output from rural production: foodstuffs.

It has been generally assumed that only to a very low degree were bulky foodstuffs transported over longer distances in Viking-Age Scandinavia, neither for trade nor for other forms of acquisition. This assumption is based on two circumstances. First, settlements are founded where cultivation is possible – most densely in the most fertile regions. This implies that in general, people settled where they could live from the land. This also goes for towns; the near hinterland will have supplied townsfolk with food. Second, most foodstuffs have high volume and weight, and therefore demand better means of transport than were available – at least in the early Viking period.

However, long-distance trade in foodstuffs has received little scholarly attention; among the few examples is research on evidence from excavations in the four early Scandinavian towns. In the ninth century, plant remains and animal and fish bones from Kaupang (Vestfold, c. 800–930) did not indicate long-distance trade in stockfish, meat, or cereals. The latter two were probably acquired from the hinterland and fish from the sea close by (Barrett et al. 2007: 303, 308). Similar results have been obtained in Birka (central-eastern Sweden, c. 770–970), as well as Ribe and Hedeby (Jylland, c. 704–850 and 804–1070 respectively; Lepiksaar et al. 1977; Wigh 2001; Enghof 2006; Mikkelsen 2006; Robinson et al. 2006). Still, it remains an open question whether agrarian products with high value and low volume, such as butter, hide, and wool, were produced to be traded over long distances in the early Viking Age.

Although long-distance bulk trade in foodstuffs cannot be verified in the four Viking-Age towns, aristocratic lifestyles and local exchange may have contributed to the development of a market for foodstuffs and to the very idea that food could be produced for trade purposes. A greater volume in the transport and trade in foodstuffs occurred at the very end of the Viking Age,

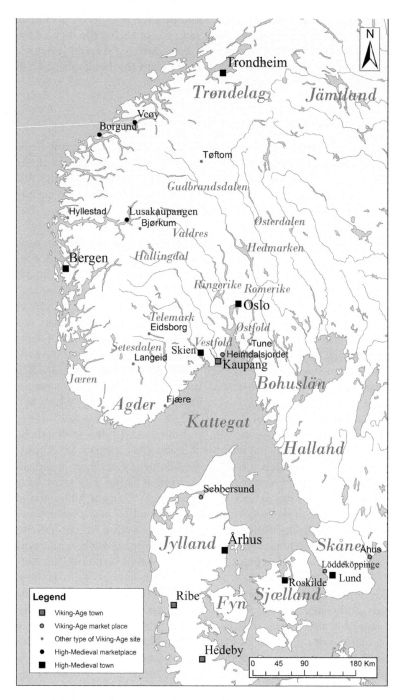

Figure 1.1 Sites and regions mentioned in the text.
Source: Map by Kjetil Loftsgarden.

8 Dagfinn Skre

when ecclesiastical institutions and royal administrative seats were established in the new towns of that period. An early example of such trade may be the exceptional find in the late tenth-century Viking fortress Fyrkat in Jylland of large quantities of pure rye, possibly originating from the Baltic-Slavic lands (Helbæk 1977).

Commodity production for long-distance trade

Viking-Age rural commodity production for long-distance trade was based on mineral, botanical, and zoological resources of the woodlands and alpine regions. The large volume of these types of production as well as the distribution of the products indicate that the production was directed mainly at long-distance trade. Nevertheless, local and regional consumers also had access to these products.

The introduction of mass production and long-distance distribution took place at different times for the various types of commodities. The evidence for mapping these variations stems from production sites and from the remains of commodities in the archaeological record. Numerous excavations and detailed analyses have produced evidence that allows more precise assessment of chronology, production volumes, and patterns of distribution than was possible only 25 years ago (e.g. Steuer 1987). Production sites, some of them containing evidence on the chronology, volume, and organisation of the production, are well mapped for iron (Larsen 2004; Rundberget 2012; Tveiten and Loftsgarden this vol.), quernstone (Baug 2013, this vol.), soapstone (Skjølsvold 1961; Baug 2011, this vol.), and reindeer hunting (Mikkelsen 1994; Stene and Wangen this vol.).

The precision with which objects can be provenanced varies substantially. On the one hand, the easily identifiable Eidsborg whetstones are known to have originated from within a few square kilometres in upper Telemark (Askvik 2008), and the quernstones made of a certain garnet mica schist have been traced to quarries within an area of approximately 15 square kilometres in Hyllestad by the mouth of the Sognefjord (Baug this vol.). On the other hand, the production of whetstones from the dark fine-grained schist has not hitherto been located more precisely than to the geological formation where this type of rock occurs – the Caledonian belt covering the western Scandinavian coastland southward to Jæren (Askvik 2008: 7–8). Although some progress has been made in developing methods for provenancing iron (Færden 1990b; Buchwald 2005), there is still a long way to go before that material can be securely traced back to reasonably small areas of origin. Better progress has been made in developing methods for provenancing soapstone items (Jansen 2015; Baug this vol.), as well as for identifying the animal species from which the antler in combs and other objects has been taken (ZooMS, Ashby 2009; Holstein et al. 2014; Ashby et al. 2015). Although the latter only point to the general areas where the various species occurred in the Viking Age, it is a great step forward to be able to distinguish between antlers from local red and roe deer used by

Ribe's comb-makers and those from reindeer antler imported from the alpine Scandinavian Peninsula. The application of isotope analysis and aDNA offers hope for further refinement of antler provenancing.

The early period (c. AD 700–950)

Contexts suited for precise dating of early Viking-Age commodities are sparse. The most significant in western and southern Scandinavia are the well-stratified and find-rich urban deposits in Ribe and Kaupang. The finds from Hedeby are also noteworthy due to their wide variety and large quantity; however, the method of excavation employed there has rendered the chronology of find contexts less precise. The high quantity in these towns of commodities associated with long-distance trade adds to their relevance for assessing the chronology and extent of trade in the early Viking Age.

Although indications of transit trade (coming in and going out in bulk quantities) of iron into Frisian trade networks have been found in early ninth-century Kaupang (Skre 2011b: 431–4), soapstone and whetstone transit trade in the early towns appears to have been sparse (Baug 2011: 332; Resi 2011a: 393; Skre 2011b: 419–20). Still, the inhabitants' needs for these products will have created a substantial demand (see below).

Regarding the distribution of commodities in rural areas, finds in settlements and graves are the primary bodies of evidence. However, only in exceptional cases do these contexts supply datings within a timespan of less than a century, a range too imprecise to address some of the research questions discussed here. In addition, objects laid down in graves were selected for that purpose, and do not necessarily reflect the material culture of everyday life. For instance, soapstone vessels were in frequent use in rural areas in the ninth century, but rarely occur in graves before the tenth (Stylegar 2007: 80–1). For these reasons, distribution of commodities in rural areas can be discussed in less chronological detail than their distribution in towns.

The dark, sometimes purple whetstones of fine-grained Caledonian schist appear to be among those early commodities from western Scandinavia that were traded over long distances, although the start date is not securely fixed. The west-Scandinavian origin of this rock is well testified (see above), although Viking-Age quarries have not yet been identified (Mitchell et al. 1984; Askvik 2008: 7–8). The stratigraphic information from Hedeby does not supply precise dates; nevertheless, it seems evident that this type of whetstone is present from the early ninth century (Resi 1990: 44–7). They are present in early ninth-century Ribe deposits, but their possible late eighth-century presence there remains uncertain due to the lack of petrographic analyses (Feveile and Jensen 2006: 140). The rock occurs in the earliest deposits at Kaupang – they date from around AD 800 – and in large quantities through the ninth century; the relation to Eidsborg schist there is 4:1 (N = 1,017:257; Resi 2011a). In Hedeby, the relation is 3:1 (N = 7,374:2,419; Resi 1990: 17). The early date of trade in this type of whetstone as well as their large quantities throughout the

10 *Dagfinn Skre*

Viking Age merits a fuller investigation of the history of their production, trade, and consumption. From the eleventh century onwards, the fine-grained dark whetstones are far fewer; for instance, in deposits from twelfth-century Bergen the relation is 1:3 (N = 23:74; Hansen this vol.). In eleventh to fourteenth-century deposits from the excavations in Oslogate 6 in Oslo, the dark-schist whetstones are outnumbered by Eidsborg whetstones by 1:12 (N = 28:350; Lønaas 2001: 15–16).

The breakthrough in antler provenancing has shown that in the 780s and 790s comb-makers in Ribe used reindeer antler; the raw material must have come from alpine regions in southwestern Scandinavia. Follow-up analyses of finds from Kaupang and Hedeby, as well as from the towns established in the late Viking Age (see below), will certainly result in additional information on this type of commodity production and trade. At this time, production volumes were moderate, and commodity production for long-distance trade probably represents only a fraction of the yield from reindeer antler production.

Slightly more recent than the earliest long-distance trade in antler and dark-schist whetstone is the introduction of trade in soapstone vessels. This rock can be found in most of western Scandinavia as well as in Bohuslän and Halland on the western coast of present-day Sweden. A small number of vessel shards have been retrieved in Ribe in deposits from the last three to four decades prior to the cessation of the well-stratified deposits there c. 850, simultaneously with the first occurrence of soapstone items in Kaupang. In Hedeby, vessel shards are plentiful, but dates are less precise. Evidently they appear in the ninth century, and thenceforth in large quantities until the end of the Viking Age (Resi 1979; Baug 2011, this vol.). Soapstone items found in rural Denmark follow the same general chronology and occur in similar volumes (Sindbæk 2005: 137–42).

The later period (c. AD 950–1100)

Around the turn of the millennium furnished burials disappear from the archaeological record in western Scandinavia. Moreover, very few rural settlements from the subsequent period have been excavated. Thus, an overview of commodity production and distribution must be based on excavations of production sites and urban deposits. In Scandinavia, a second wave of urbanisation began in the mid-tenth century (see below), and the well-excavated deposits from Oslo, Bergen, and Trondheim in particular supply ample evidence for mapping the urban distribution of the commodities discussed here.

From the mapping and analysis of production sites, it is evident that the production of iron (Tveiten and Loftsgarden this vol.), quernstones (Baug this vol.), and reindeer antler (Mikkelsen 1994; Stene and Wangen this vol.) increased significantly from the mid-tenth through the eleventh century. For the latter two commodities, this increase in production output was accompanied by technological innovations (see below).

As for the early period, the difficulty of reliably provenancing most types of products prevents an assessment of the extent of their distribution. Reliable results have been obtained only for Hyllestad quernstones, which began turning up in the late tenth century in Hedeby and other sites south of Kattegat (Baug this vol.). Soapstone vessels and Scandinavian whetstones continued to occur frequently in Hedeby in this period, but the lack of a precise chronology there prevents an assessment of whether import volumes changed. Reindeer antler constitutes only approximately 0.5 per cent of the antler there (Ulbricht 1978). In Lund, only a slightly higher percentage of the antler – about 2 per cent – is assumed to be from reindeer (Christophersen 1980).

While well-dated contexts from this period are sparse south of Kattegat, some indications of commodity production may be found in Norwegian towns that were established in the late Viking Age (c. 950–1100). In late tenth- to eleventh-century Trondheim reindeer antler dominated, although Lena Flodin (1989) supplies no figures. In eleventh-century Oslo combs from reindeer antler occur in fairly large numbers (Wiberg 1977, 1987). Bone from reindeer is frequent there as compared to bone from other types of game (Lie 1988). Reindeer antler is found in Bergen from c. 1100 onwards (Hansen this vol.).

Iron objects are numerous in Oslo in the same period (Færden 1990a). Gerd Færden's (1990b) chemical analysis of the iron in nails indicate that in the period 1000–1250 Oslo received iron from a diversity of areas, mainly from the Uplands (inner eastern Norway; Stene and Wangen this vol.), but possibly also western Sweden. Additionally, whetstones of the two types discussed here appear in the eleventh to twelfth-century deposits in Oslo (Lønaas 2001).

Technological innovations

Both the early and late wave of increased commodity production appear to have been accompanied by technological innovations. The production of soapstone vessels began when such vessels first appeared in Kaupang, Ribe, and Hedeby. At that time, the production of soapstone vessels in Scandinavia had been abandoned for five to six centuries (Pilø 1990). Unlike, for instance, quernstone and iron, it appears that the production of soapstone vessel as commodities for long-distance trade was not preceded by an initial phase of production for local supply, but was directed at long-distance trade from the outset.

Somewhat earlier, iron production was reorganised. During the eighth century, a new type of furnace replaced the old slag-pit furnace, and iron extraction started up in more remote areas (Tveiten and Loftsgarden this vol.). Probably, this shift was connected to the taking up of production for long-distance trade. One of the new production areas was the Østerdalen valley in the Uplands, recently intensively surveyed and analysed by Bernt Rundberget (2013). He found that production there was taken up on a modest scale c. 700, then expanded and intensified through the tenth and eleventh centuries, reaching a maximum between 1100 and 1250. In total, some 130,000 tons were

12   *Dagfinn Skre*

produced there over c. 600 years. Perhaps 10 per cent of that was produced before 1100 (Rundberget 2013: 253–6), with an annual average throughout the Viking Age of approximately 30 tons. Considering that this is one of five to six production regions in the Uplands, the total annual Viking-Age production was far beyond local needs – particularly in light of its location in woodlands and mountains far from the lowlands where population density was greatest (Tveiten and Loftsgarden this vol.: Figure 6.2).

In the late Viking Age, new quarrying techniques were introduced in the Hyllestad quernstone quarries; that is, at the time when long-distance quern-stone trade was taken up. While the earlier quarries in Hyllestad were what Baug calls shallow quarries where stones were 'cut along the cleavage plane', a technique of deep quarries was introduced around the turn of the millennium. In deep quarries stones are 'quarried in piles, one under another, leaving tall, carved walls, sometimes with a step-like shape' (Baug 2013: 58–9, 149–50). This technique was better suited for producing a larger number of quernstones of uniform diameter within a confined quarry area.

Large-scale reindeer trapping systems were introduced in the eleventh to thirteenth centuries; the yield from reindeer hunting consequently multiplied. The former technique of hunting with bow and arrow was complemented by extensive fencing systems designed to trap entire herds of animals, or to lead them into pitfalls (Mikkelsen 1994: 110–11). The fencing system near Tøftom, Dovre, demanded a highly refined organisation of the hunt (Mikkelsen 1994: 104–8), and probably also of the collection of antler after the annual shedding. Furthermore, the new techniques required a higher input of labour as well as arrangements for managing resources and avoiding and resolving conflicts (Stene and Wangen this vol.). Finds of antler in towns increase for the same period (Mikkelsen 1994: 142–72); however, the recently developed methods for secure identification of animal species have not yet been applied to this material.

Urbanisation and seasonal markets

In Viking-Age Scandinavia, towns and markets came into being during two periods. In the first period, c. 700–810, Ribe, Kaupang, and Hedeby were established, as well as seasonal markets like Sebbersund by Limfjord, Löddeköpinge by Øresund, and Heimdalsjordet by Sandefjord (Skre 2008: 337–8; Bill and Rødsrud this vol.). In the second period of urbanisation, c. 950–1100, towns such as Århus, Roskilde, Lund, Skien, Oslo, Trondheim, and Bergen were established (Hansen this vol.). While all the early towns were located within a zone spanning medieval Denmark and Vestfold, which at the time was probably under the authority of the kings of the Danes (Skre 2007), the later towns also include the western coast of the Scandinavian Peninsula in the urbanised Scandinavian zone.

Towns established in the early Viking Age appear to have had a modest role in supplying their hinterland with imported goods of the types discussed

Viking-Age economic transformations 13

here. The occurrence of soapstone in Hedeby's and Ribe's hinterland is much sparser than, for example, in the rural regions in northern Jylland and along the coasts of Kattegat (Sindbæk 2005: 141–2). The trade of soapstone to these latter regions appears to have been independent of towns. The same goes for west-Scandinavian whetstones, which have a fairly even distribution in Jylland (Sindbæk 2005: 142–5).

How, then, did consumers in rural areas gain access to necessities such as soapstone vessels, iron, and whetstones? For Jylland, Sindbæk (2005: 142) suggests that soapstone vessels were distributed by occasional trade between fishermen and farmers in the area. Rather, it seems reasonable that the high density of soapstone finds in the Limfjord area is due to its inhabitants acquiring them at the seasonal Sebbersund market in the eastern part of the fjord, where trade began in the early eighth century and persisted into the twelfth. It is one of a number of seasonal market sites in southern Scandinavia, of which several originated in the eighth century (Skre 2008: Fig. 9.1). Some sites are large, for instance Löddeköpinge and Sebbersund (Christensen and Johansen 1992; Svanberg and Söderberg 2000), while others are small landing places and beach markets (Ulriksen 1998; Dobat 2007). Contrary to the towns, long-distance trade goods are typically few or none in finds at market sites; the craftsmen working there largely made use of local raw materials (Sindbæk 2005: 76–8, 87–97). Accordingly, these markets were not nodes of the long-distance trading network but rather seasonal market sites of essentially intraregional significance. In rural Scandinavia, trade in everyday necessities such as soapstone vessels, iron, and whetstones perhaps occurred at such seasonal market sites and in local and regional trade networks rather than in towns (Loftsgarden et al. this vol.).

Until now, only one market site from the early Viking Age has been identified in western Scandinavia: at Heimdalsjordet in Vestfold, only 14 kilometres as the crow flies northeast from Kaupang (Bill and Rødsrud this vol.). Nonetheless, finds there include more objects from far afield than do the finds from Sebbersund and Löddeköping. The numbers of hack-silver pieces and weights are much higher, and Sebbersund has no finds of Islamic coins, while Heimdalsjordet has 174 – even more than have been found at Kaupang. Conversely, compared to Kaupang, the paucity of, for example, Continental pottery and artisanal products made of imported raw material, such as glass beads, indicates the dominance of local and regional over long-distance trade at Heimdalsjordet. These features can be found at two sites in the Danish realm of that period, the so-called nodal markets Åhus in Scania and early Ribe before permanent settlement occurred there, apparently in the late eighth century (Skre 2008: 336–8). However, as Bill and Rødsrud (this vol.) emphasise, the character and activities of the Heimdalsjordet site as well as its relation to nearby Kaupang and to other Scandinavian market sites warrant further exploration.

Due to the paucity of securely identified seasonal Viking-Age market sites, it remains an open question as to when such markets were established in western Scandinavia beyond Vestfold. Pre-950 grave finds of weights and weighing equipment indicate that markets from that period may have existed in Fjære in

14 Dagfinn Skre

Agder, and possibly in Tune in Østfold (Pedersen 2008; Glørstad and Wenn this vol.); however, no market sites have been identified in the vicinity of the graves. This situation is bound to change, though. The Heimdalsjordet site was identified through a combination of archaeological methods, most importantly metal-detecting and geophysics. When the wealth of finds discovered by private metal detectors the last few years have been systematised and analysed, new market sites may turn up. Nevertheless, a possible outcome is that market sites did not exist in western Scandinavia (except for Vestfold) until the twelfth century. The numerous tenth- to eleventh-century coin hoards along coasts and waterways (see below) may indicate that in most of Viking-Age western Scandinavia trade took place in contexts other than markets.

The west-Scandinavian market sites that have left substantial cultural deposits appear to have been established in the twelfth century, although a couple of them were church sites in the eleventh. They are Lusakaupangen in Sogn, Borgundkaupangen in Sunnmøre, Veøykaupangen in Romsdal, and Vågar in Lofoten. More elusive are the small market sites referred to in medieval and more recent sources (Loftsgarden et al. this vol.). Can some of these be of a Viking-Age date? Such sites have not produced any evidence indicating a Viking-Age date, and those that have, such as Bjørkum in Lærdal (Loftsgarden et al. this vol.), have not produced evidence that clearly defines them as market sites.

Turning to the towns established in the late Viking Age, these had – at least in the thirteenth and fourteenth centuries – a more prominent role than the early towns in providing their hinterland with commodities brought in from the types of production sites discussed here (Baug this vol.). For the period before c. 1150, however, this issue is difficult to assess; the evidence from rural settlements is scant from that period. Moreover, although substantial high-quality excavations have been undertaken in several west-Scandinavian towns since the early 1970s, detailed chronological analyses of the huge amounts of artefactual material from their first 100–200 years are few (Hansen this vol.).

Also, the late Viking-Age towns may have had a more prominent role than the early towns in transit trade (Hansen this vol.). This appears to be the case at least for Skien, where a high number of Eidsborg whetstone blanks have been identified in the early deposits (Myrvoll 1992). Skien was established in the late tenth century at the mouth of the valley and water system that runs from Eidsborg approximately 95 kilometres inland to the coast. The production and overseas trade in Eidsborg whetstones expanded in this period, and may have been one of the reasons for the establishment of the town.

Trade routes and monetisation

Ancient sea routes

One of Irene Baug's main results from her survey of quernstone finds in urban and rural contexts in western Scandinavia is that, although they were quarried

Viking-Age economic transformations 15

much further from Oslo than the Hyllestad stones, quernstones from Saltdal dominated in Oslo. Conversely, although ships carrying either Saltdal or Hyllestad quernstones would sail along the same route from Sogn to Agder, Hyllestad quernstones were most numerous in Hedeby and other sites south of Skagerrak (Baug this vol.).

When such results appear for several types of commodities, a better understanding of the dynamics of late Viking-Age production and trade may be obtained. For example, Baug observes that long-distance trade patterns established in the early Viking Age, such as for soapstone vessels and whetstones, persisted through several hundred years and came to include other types of commodities. Thus, when long-distance trade of Hyllestad quernstones was taken up in the late tenth century, it followed the routes along which these other commodities had been traded for almost two centuries. These routes led to a rather limited area in southern Scandinavia, namely eastern Jylland, Fyn, Sjælland, and Skåne; that is, medieval Denmark. The stone commodities from the north have not been retrieved in noticeable quantities further south, for example in Dorestad or Hamwic. The spread of these commodities to the British Isles, Ireland, and the North Atlantic is, as noted by Baug (this vol.), most likely the result of travellers carrying them as personal possessions. How were such long-lasting patterns of trade and non-trade established, and what were the factors contributing to maintaining them over several hundred years?

Fittingly, Baug adapts Sindbæk's (2005) concept of 'routinised trade' for such patterns, and relates the routines to traditions, alliances, and cultural and political regions. One could add that the same agents who conducted the trade in whetstones and soapstone vessels possibly included the Hyllestad quernstones among their trade goods. It is noteworthy that the Viking-Age trade across Skagerrak was preceded by other forms of contact. Peaceful and hostile movement from western to southern Scandinavia has been frequent since the Stone Age (Østmo 2011). Conversely, based on the very limited finds of Iron Age imports to western Scandinavia from the Baltic, sea travel in that direction appears to have been rather sporadic. Likewise, North Sea crossings do not appear to have commenced until the late eighth century, while crossing the North Atlantic to Iceland began in the late ninth. When long-distance trade from production sites in western Scandinavia across the Skagerrak was taken up around 800, travel patterns established in the eighth century and previously may have directed trade. More recently established routes, such as those to Britain and Ireland, appear not to have been used for trade purposes – or only to a very limited degree (Skre 2011b).

Judging by the imports to western Scandinavia, there is one exception to this pattern of trade routes. Finds from Kaupang indicate that the town was connected to Frisian trade networks in the first half of the ninth century. The Frisians brought in glass vessels, glass beads, amber, raw glass, copper alloy, pottery, and metalwork – some of these as trade goods, others as personal possessions (Skre 2011b). However, the overseas imports do not appear to have been brought in vast quantities into Kaupang's hinterland in Vestfold

16 Dagfinn Skre

and the Uplands. Possibly, the majority of such commodities were consumed at Kaupang by artisans living there, by local agents in the trade networks who delivered overseas goods, and by agents who brought iron and other commodities to Kaupang from woodland and alpine regions in the hinterland.

Production, trade, and consumption: free agents or aristocratic control?

While many scholars have regarded aristocratic demands and initiatives as the prime movers in the post-Roman economic upsurge in Europe (e.g. Hodges 1982; Wickham 2009), studies of production sites, find contexts, and trade goods make increasingly clear that peasant and freeholder agency, individual as well as communal, was significant at various times in post-Roman Europe in production, trade, and consumption alike (Iversen et al. 2007; Skre 2008: 338–41; Theuws 2012).

Except for artisans, production is the lesser known of the three spheres in this respect. The social basis and organisation of large-scale rural commodity production is largely unknown and can be glimpsed only through indirect evidence – for instance, the fact that iron production thrived in areas where most farmers were freeholders (Tveiten and Loftsgarden this vol.) can be taken as an indication of individual or communal agency. As pointed out by Stene and Wangen (this vol.), the exploitation of resources must have been managed on a communal level, potentially supracommunal, particularly in cases where different resources in the same area are exploited contemporaneously. Furthermore, considerable expertise, extensive division of labour, and complex cooperative arrangements will have been necessary for managing the logistics of production. Communal involvement in resource management and conflict solving is inevitable; the question is whether it was the communal institutions or the aristocratic families that initiated and had their people conduct the various types of production. Probably, this varied between regions and types of production; local studies are needed to address this question. Tveiten and Loftsgarden's contribution to this volume, as well as Stene and Wangen's, open fruitful avenues for future research on such issues.

Turning to the social aspect of the trade sphere, the nature of the networks that brought commodities from mountains and woodlands to the coast is discussed in several contributions to this volume. As Baug has crucially observed, the vast majority of soapstone vessel fragments found at Kaupang appear to be derived from the same quarry – regrettably unidentified but probably located in one of the many soapstone outcrops in the neighbouring regions of Østfold, Romerike, or Agder (Baug 2011: 329–31, this vol.). Considering the vast number – over 100 – of premodern quarries in western Scandinavia and southwestern Sweden, the uniform origin cannot be coincidental. Was the supply of soapstone vessels to this ninth- and early tenth-century town the prerogative of an aristocrat who ran a soapstone quarry, perhaps Kaupang's local lord or one of his associates? Was the lack of competition between suppliers unique for the provision of soapstone vessels to the town, or was this a general pattern for

Viking-Age economic transformations 17

trade, including over longer distances? If the latter is the case, can we speak of market trade, or does Polanyi's concept of 'administered trade' provide a better model for the social context of this exchange? One result from the analysis of a single type of material from a lone site cannot decide such issues. Still, Baug's result brings to the fore questions regarding the nature of production and power in the towns and markets as well as in the trade networks that brought commodities from the interior to the coast and beyond.

Apparently, the nature of these networks changed during the second period of urbanisation – that is, from the mid-tenth century onwards. At that time, both silver and weighing equipment began turning up in substantial numbers in hoards and graves in rural western Scandinavia, indicating that modes of payment from urban contexts and long-distance trade had been adopted in rural trade networks. In his analyses of finds of weights and scales in Jämtland, Olof Holm (this vol.) concludes that farmers there operated as traders in that period. The finds demonstrate that silver was among the types of payment accepted and used. How were these traders connected to producers and consumers? Were they free agents who sought a profit from buying cheaply and reselling, or were they bound by aristocrats who controlled their access to producers and possibly also to consumers? Holm (2012) argues convincingly that because farmers in Jämtland were freeholders of fairly equal status and therefore were not bound by landlords, they could operate as independent agents. If Holm is right, it would seem that in the mid-tenth century freeholders in a rather marginal rural region began acting as independent agents of trade.

Holm's findings are supported by the finds from the municipalities Valle and Bygland in Setesdal discussed by Glørstad and Wenn (this vol.). As was Jämtland, Setesdal was dominated by freeholders. The finds indicate that from the mid-tenth century onwards farmers there acted as independent traders. Probably, they would have brought iron from the extensive extraction activity in the mountains some 50 kilometres to the north to coastal sites and possibly to lands overseas. This suggestion is supported by the wealth of imported items in Valle and Bygland graves. One of the coastal sites may have been Fjære, some 90 kilometres to the southeast; grave finds there also contain a high quantity of weighing equipment and imports (Glørstad and Wenn this vol.). The evidence from Jämtland and Setesdal indicates that from the mid-tenth century onwards, independent freeholders in these regions began buying and selling commodities produced by others in neighbouring and more remote regions, possibly also participating in long-distance networks at coastal trading sites.

Besides Jämtland and Setesdal, only the inland region Hedmarken in western Scandinavia has a concentration of tenth- to eleventh-century finds of weighing equipment, all of them in graves (Pedersen 2008: Fig. 6.14), indicating that traders were buried there. Hedmarken borders on several of the iron-producing regions of the Uplands. However, regarding social stratification, the regions with finds of weights and scales were rather diverse. While traders in Jämtland and Setesdal probably were freeholders who took up trade as an additional activity, Hedmarken was a much more stratified region with landlords

18 *Dagfinn Skre*

and tenants. The majority of the weighing equipment finds there have been retrieved from graves on aristocratic farms with richly furnished burials, indicating that aristocratic landlords or their staff were involved in trade. Possibly, the late tenth- to eleventh-century Hedmarken aristocracy continued a tradition of administered trade established in the early Viking Age, as indicated by Baug's analysis of the soapstone vessels at Kaupang.

The contrast in social structure between Hedmark on the one side and Jämtland and Setesdal on the other indicates that the relationship between trade agency and social stratification was complex and is in need of further locally based studies.

The third and final economic sphere for which the social agency is to be considered here – consumption – is probably the best evidenced in the Viking-Age archaeological record. While production sites and transport routes are sometimes difficult to infer, consumption – at least the ultimate – can in many cases be pinpointed to the site where an item is found.

Analyses of finds assemblages in a grave, a cemetery, or a settlement often aim at encircling the person's, family's, or site's social status. Economic analyses of such assemblages are less common – except those that deal with tools of trade (e.g. Holm this vol.). The scope of finds relevant for such analyses could be expanded. Might, for instance, the presence of certain commodities indicate that residents or sites had particular roles in economic networks? Such analyses have been conducted for towns (Skre 2011c) and for seasonal market sites (e.g. Bill and Rødsrud this vol.), but rarely for finds assemblages from other types of sites.

Still, some general points regarding consumption in different social strata can be made on the basis of the traded commodities' nature and distribution. As noted above, exotic items that have been found in rather large numbers at Kaupang, such as vessel glass, exotic beads, and certain types of pottery (Gaut 2011; Pilø 2011; Resi 2011b), are found very sparsely elsewhere in western Scandinavia. Typically, they occur in aristocratic contexts, such as in the chieftain's residence in Borg in Lofoten, northern Norway (Munch et al. 2003). However, it remains uncertain and perhaps unlikely that such items arrived in Borg via Kaupang. Aristocrats at this high level may have had their own networks where such items were available, and the occurrence in Kaupang probably reflects local consumption.

Less uncertain is the identification of intended users for artisanal products from the types of artisans working at Kaupang. Several aristocratic graves, for instance the nearby Gokstad ship burial, contained non-ferrous metalwork that appears to have been produced by artisans with skills displayed in the Kaupang workshop remains. However, the wide and rich distribution in western Scandinavia of Scandinavian-type ornaments made from overseas raw materials, primarily glass, brass, and amber (Skre 2008: 340–1; Resi 2011c; Pedersen this vol.), indicates that the prime group of consumers of artisanal work from Kaupang-type craftsmen were the average freeholder or moderately well-off farmer. A consideration of trade volumes supports this assessment: to uphold a

Viking-Age economic transformations   19

town of Kaupang's size, the prime consumers would need to be drawn from a vast social group – the general populace. The demand for luxury goods from a narrow aristocratic class would not generate a volume of trade and artisanal production sufficient for sustaining the town.

Turning to the consumption of products from raw materials originating in western Scandinavia, the populace is an even more obvious target group for traders. The products in question – whetstones, iron items, quernstones, antler combs, soapstone vessels, and the like – are everyday utensils, not rare luxuries. Of course, aristocratic farms also needed these items, but their general occurrence in the west-Scandinavian archaeological record demonstrates that the general populace formed the prime market. Probably, only poor peasants would have had to suffice with what whetstones and quernstones they could find in the ground, as everybody had done before such products became available in trade in the early and late Viking Age, respectively.

The interplay between the agencies of farmers, aristocrats, and eventually kings in the three economic spheres in Viking-Age Scandinavia remains largely under-investigated; its continued exploration potentially holds the key to a deeper understanding of the period's economic and social transformations.

The use of silver as payment in rural regions and towns

By contrast with finds of tenth- to eleventh-century weighing equipment, contemporary hoards containing coins do not cluster in certain regions, but rather are dispersed (Skaare 1976: 238–43, maps 7–12). It is noteworthy, however, that hoards were deposited either near the coast or along waterways that led up into woodlands and alpine regions. Several of these finds have been made in the most fertile rural regions, such as Ringerike, Jæren, and Trøndelag, possibly indicating that Hedmark was not the only region of aristocratic involvement in trade in the late Viking Age.

The distribution of weighing equipment and coin hoards indicates that trade routes connecting production areas in woodlands and alpine regions with coastal towns, markets, and harbours prospered from the mid-tenth century onwards. These routes are also detectable in the ninth- and early tenth-century distribution of scales and weights (Pedersen 2008: Fig. 6.14), although at that time the use of silver had hardly spread from the coastal sites to the rural interior. In the early Viking Age, minting and the use of silver appear to have been urban phenomena. Minting in Scandinavia began in Ribe in the mid-eighth century, was taken up in Hedeby from the early ninth, and in Sweden and Norway from just before AD 1000. The use of cut silver as a medium of payment began in Kaupang, probably also in Birka, in the early ninth century, and from the mid-tenth century hoards containing cut silver were deposited in most of Scandinavia.

Apparently, the use of silver as payment, whether in the form of coinage or cut-up silver, was in the eighth and ninth centuries mainly connected to trade in towns with agents for overseas trade networks. The occurrence of silver,

20　*Dagfinn Skre*

scales, and weights in rural areas is predominantly a phenomenon of the late tenth and eleventh centuries – the very period when rural commodity production underwent its second and largest expansion. However, it remains an open question as to whether hoarding of silver and coins and the occurrence of weights and scales in rural areas indicate that these means of exchange were actually used there in the tenth and eleventh centuries. They may have been kept and buried in rural areas until the occasion might arise for their use in towns and on long-distance expeditions. Although Holm (this vol.) presents a convincing case for the burial of actual users of silver, weights, and scales in late tenth- and eleventh-century Jämtland, the items need not have been used locally. Moreover, the fact that such concentrations of silver, weights, and scales are found only in two other regions in western Scandinavia (Setesdal and Hedmarken) would caution against regarding them as expressions of common occurrences. The actual use of coins as payment in rural areas is not securely testified in Norway until the late twelfth century when coins in large numbers began to fall through gaps in the wooden floors of rural churches. In addition to trade, the compensation to *thingmen* for their travels and provision (Iversen and Gullbekk this vol.) may have contributed to bringing coinage into rural people's hands and purses.

However, as pointed out above, securely identified Viking-Age seasonal market sites in western Scandinavia can be counted on one hand. Thus, except for Heimdalsjordet, we do not really have rural sites where the use of silver for payment would occur with a frequency sufficient for noticeable quantities to be lost. As long as arenas for the rural use of coins and silver are absent prior to the late twelfth century, the volume of tenth- to twelfth-century rural coin use cannot be assessed. Identifying and dating potential arenas would be worthwhile.

The coast and the interior

The transformations experienced by west-Scandinavian societies also influenced conceptions of the land. In *Ohthere*'s account recorded at the court of King Alfred the Great c. 890, it is said that the populated zone of his homeland was narrow, except in the east, where cultivated land was found far from the coast (Bately and Englert 2007: 46). The same conception of the land is provided in greater detail in *Historia Norwegie* written in the 1150s or 1160s (Ekrem and Boje Mortensen 2003). There, a distinction is made between two parts of Norway: the *Zona Montana* (the Mountainous Land, the Uplands) and the *Zona Maritima* (the Coastal Land).

Indeed, this division points to the striking characteristics of the western parts of the Scandinavian Peninsula. While the majority of settled land in western and central Norway lies less than 10 kilometres (and a maximum of 50 kilometres) from the sea, settlement in eastern Norway stretches more than 250 kilometres northwards from the inner end of the Oslofjord. There, the most populated regions (the Uplands; e.g., Telemark, Ringerike, Hadeland,

Hedemarken, Hallingdal, Valdres, and Gudbrandsdalen) are found in lowlands and valleys more than 50 kilometres inland; Vestfold and Østfold were the only densely populated coastal regions.

Developments in production and trade contributed to changing this conception of the geography. Of the types of production discussed here, whetstone (dark schist) and quernstone quarrying took place in the *Zona Maritima*. Iron extraction, reindeer hunting, and quarrying of Hyllestad whetstones occurred in the woodlands and mountains of the *Zona Montana*. Soapstone quarrying may have happened in both zones. The same goes for artisanal production, although some types appear to have been conducted primarily in the coastal towns (Pedersen this vol.).

Of these types of commodities, iron – production of which had an average annual output of well over 100 tons throughout the period – will have contributed the most significant economic value. Therefore, the increased commodity production in the Viking Age, particularly that intended for overseas trade, contributed to connecting the *Zona Montana* and the *Zona Maritima*. The trade routes from one zone to the other, established in the early Viking Age and significantly expanded from the late tenth to the thirteenth century, contributed to shaping the administrative landscape of the high medieval Norwegian kingdom. The early organisation in the two rather homogeneous topographic, economic, and climatic zones was converted to administrative units that connected coastal towns with inland and mountainous areas where commodities were produced (Iversen this vol.).

Concluding comment

In the seventh and eighth centuries rural commodity production was modest and directed at satisfying local and regional needs. In the decades around AD 800 (whetstones, soapstone vessels, and iron), and again around AD 1000 (quernstones, reindeer antler, and again iron), this small-scale production and distribution was expanded, reorganised, and developed using novel technologies into large-scale commodity production for long-distance trade. Only the production of soapstone vessels was not preceded by local production, but rather was directed towards long-distance trade from the start.

These two waves coincided with two waves of town foundation. In the early wave four Scandinavian towns were established; none of these endured throughout the Viking Age. The much more numerous towns established in the second wave, c. 950–1100, have endured until the present. While the early towns appear to have been mostly 'producer towns', meaning that the majority of the population was engaged in some sort of craft or artisanal production, the later towns were to a higher degree 'consumer towns' as they housed staff that administered royal and ecclesiastical interests in the region. The early towns had few or no such functions.

These and other developments in Viking-Age urbanism indicate that the connection between rural commodity production and urbanisation is not

22 *Dagfinn Skre*

direct and simple, but indirect and complex. Thus, I find the line drawn by Ashby et al. (2015: 18) is too direct in concluding that those 'involved in foraging expeditions in the Scandinavian outlands were . . . engaged in a quintessentially urban activity'. There is much more to the story of rural commodity production than the emergence of towns. Only a limited proportion of the output from that production made its way to towns – for some commodities only the quantities that were consumed by the towns' inhabitants. Seasonal markets, magnate sites, the rise of economic agency among the rural populace, and ancient routes to the lands overseas – all these elements and more need to be included to understand the profound economic transformations of Viking-Age western Scandinavia.

References

Ashby, Steven 2009: Combs, contact and chronology: reconsidering hair combs in early-historic and Viking-Age Atlantic Scotland. *Medieval Archaeology*, 53: 1–33.

Ashby, Steven, Ashley N. Coutu and Søren M. Sindbæk 2015: Urban networks and Arctic Outlands: craft specialists and reindeer antler in Viking towns. *European Journal of Archaeology*, 2015: 1–26.

Askvik, Helge 2008: Whetstones from Kaupang; petrographic description and provenance. In: Resi, Heid Gjøstein and Helge Askvik (eds): *Whetstones and Grindstones in the Settlement Area: the 1956–1974 Excavations. The Kaupang Finds, vol. III C.* Norske Oldfunn, vol. 29: 5–17. Kulturhistorisk museum, Universitetet i Oslo. Oslo.

Bagge, Sverre 2010: *From Viking Stronghold to Christian Kingdom: State Formation in Norway, c. 900–1350.* Museum Tusculanum Press. København.

Barrett, James, Allan Hall, Cluny Johnstone, Harry Kenward, Terry O'Connor and Steve Ashby 2007: Interpreting the plant and animal remains from Viking-Age Kaupang. In: Skre, Dagfinn (ed.): *Kaupang in Skiringssal.* Kaupang Excavation Project. Publication Series, vol. 1. Norske Oldfunn, vol. 22: 283–319. Aarhus University Press. Århus.

Bately, Janet and Anton Englert (eds) 2007: *Ohthere's Voyages: A Late 9th-Century Account of Voyages Along the Coasts of Norway and Denmark and its Cultural Context.* The Viking Ship Museum. Roskilde.

Baug, Irene 2011: Soapstone finds. In: Skre, Dagfinn (ed.): *Things from the Town: Artefacts and Inhabitants in Viking-Age Kaupang.* Kaupang Excavation Project. Publication Series, vol. 3. Norske Oldfunn, vol. 24: 311–37. Aarhus University Press. Århus.

—— 2013: Quarrying in Western Norway: an archaeological study of production and distribution in the Viking period and the Middle Ages. PhD thesis. Department of Archaeology, History, Cultural Studies and Religion. University of Bergen. Bergen.

Buchwald, Vagn Fabritius 2005: *Iron and Steel in Ancient Times.* Historisk-filosofiske Skrifter, vol. 29. Det Kongelige Danske Videnskabernes Selskab. Copenhagen.

Callmer, Johan 1976: Oriental coins and the beginning of the Viking period. *Fornvännen*, 71: 175–85.

—— 1982: Production site and market area. *Meddelanden från Lunds universitets historiska museum*, 1981–2: 135–65.

—— 1991: Platser med anknytning till handel och hantverk i yngre järnålder. Exempel från södra Sverige. In: Mortensen, Peder and Birgit M. Rasmussen (eds): *Høvdingesamfund og kongemagt: Fra stamme til stat i Danmark.* Jysk Arkæologisk Selskabs Skrifter, vol. 22(2): 29–47. Århus.

Viking-Age economic transformations   23

—— 1994: Urbanization in Scandinavia and the Baltic Region c. AD 700–1000: trading places, centres and early urban sites. In: Ambrosiani, Björn and Helen Clarke (eds): *Developments Around the Baltic and the North Sea in the Viking Age: The Twelfth Viking Congress.* Birka Studies, vol. 3: 50–90. Stockholm.

—— 1995: Hantverksproduktion, samhällsförändringar och bebyggelse. Iakttagelser från östra Sydskandinavien ca. 600–1100 e.Kr. In: Resi, Heid Gjøstein (ed.): *Produksjon og samfunn: Om erhverv, spesialisering og bosetning i Norden i 1. årtusen e.Kr.* Varia 30: 39–72. Universitetets Oldsaksamling. Oslo.

—— 2002: North-European trading centres and the early medieval craftsman: craftsmen at Åhus, north-eastern Scania, Sweden ca. AD 750–850+. In: Hårdh, Birgitta and Lars Larsson (eds): *Central Places in the Migration and Merovingian Periods: Papers from 52nd Sachsensymposium, Lund, August 2001.* Uppåkrastudier, vol. 6: 125–57. Lund.

—— 2007: Urbanisation in Northern and Eastern Europe ca. AD 700–1100. In: Henning, Joachim (ed.): *The Heirs of the Roman West: Post-Roman Towns, Trade and Settlement in Europe and Byzantium,* vol. 1: 233–70. de Gruyter. Berlin.

Christensen, Peter Birkedahl and Erik Johansen 1992: En handelsplads fra yngre jernalder og vikingetid ved Sebbersund. *Aarbøger for Nordisk Oldkyndighed og Historie,* 1991: 199–229.

Christophersen, Axel 1980: *Håndverket i forandring: studier i horn- og beinhåndverkets utvikling i Lund c:a 1000–1350.* Vol. 13. Rudolf Habelt. Bonn.

Dalton, George 1975: Karl Polanyi's analysis of long-distance trade and his wider paradigm. In: Sabloff, Jeremy A. and C. C. Lamberg-Karlovsky (eds): *Ancient Civilization and Trade,* pp. 63–132. University of New Mexico Press. Albuquerque.

—— 1977: Aboriginal economies in stateless societies. In: Earle, Timothy K. and Jonathon E. Ericson (eds): *Exchange Systems in Prehistory,* pp. 191–212. Academic Press. New York.

Dobat, Andres S. Minos 2007: The fifth day. Ohthere's route through the Schlei fjord. In: Bately, Janet and Anton Englert (eds): *Ohthere's Voyages: A Late 9th-Century Account of Voyages Along the Coasts of Norway and Denmark and its Cultural Context,* pp. 130–4. The Viking Ship Museum. Roskilde.

Ekrem, Inger and Lars Boje Mortensen 2003: *Historia Norwegie.* Museum Tusculanum Press. København.

Eldorhagen, Marianne 2001: Ovale spenner i Nord-Norge og Trøndelag. Stil og symbolisme i sosial sammenheng. Unpublished thesis. University of Tromsø.

Elster, Jon 2007: *Explaining Social Behavior: More Nuts and Bolts for the Social Sciences.* Cambridge University Press. Cambridge.

Enghof, Inger Bødker 2006: Pattedyr og fugle fra markedspladsen i Ribe, ASR 9 Posthuset. In: Feveile, Claus (ed.): *Det ældste Ribe: Udgravninger på nordsiden af Ribe Å 1984–2000.* Ribe Studier, vol. 1.1: 167–87. Jysk Arkæologisk Selskab. Højbjerg.

Feveile, Claus and Stig Jensen 2006: ASR 9 Posthuset. In: Feveile, Claus (ed.): *Det ældste Ribe. Udgravninger på nordsiden af Ribe Å 1984–2000.* Ribe Studier, vol. 1.2: 119–89. Jysk Arkæologisk Selskab. Højbjerg.

Finley, Moses I. 1973: *The Ancient Economy.* Chatto and Windus. London.

Flodin, Lena 1989: *Kammakeri i Trondheim ca 1000–1600: en kvantitativ analyse av horn- och benmaterialet på Folkebibliotekets tomt, i Trondheim.* Meddelelser. Fortiden i Trondheim bygrunn: Folkebibliotekstomten, vol. 14. Riksantikvaren, Utgravningskontoret for Trondheim. Trondheim.

24 Dagfinn Skre

Færden, Gerd 1990a: Metallgjenstander. In: Schia, Erik and Petter Molaug (eds): *Dagliglivets gjenstander – del 1*. De arkeologiske utgravninger i Gamlebyen, Oslo, vol. 7: 181–292. Universitetsforlaget. Oslo.

—— 1990b: Smijern fra Gamlebyen – en analyse av spikermaterialet. In: Schia, Erik and Petter Molaug (eds): *Dagliglivets gjenstander – del 1*. De arkeologiske utgravninger i Gamlebyen, Oslo, vol. 7: 301–30. Universitetsforlaget. Oslo.

Gaut, Bjarne 2011: Vessel glass and evidence of glassworking. In: Skre, Dagfinn (ed.): *Things From the Town: Artefacts and Inhabitants in Viking-Age Kaupang*. Kaupang Excavation Project. Publication Series, vol. 3. Norske Oldfunn, vol. 24: 169–280. Aarhus University Press. Århus.

Gustin, Ingrid 2004: *Mellan gåva och marknad. Handel, tillit och materiell kultur under vikingatid*. Lund Studies in Medieval Archaeology, vol. 34. Almqvist and Wiksell. Lund.

Hansen, Inge Lyse and Chris Wickham 2000: *The Long Eighth Century: Production, Distribution and Demand*. The Transformation of the Roman World, vol. 11. Brill. Leiden.

Helbæk, Hans 1977: The Fyrkat grain: a geographical and chronological study of rye. In: Olsen, Olaf and Holger Schmidt (eds): *Borgen og bebyggelsen*. Fyrkat. En jysk vikingeborg, vol. 1:1–41. I kommission hos Lynge og Sønn. København.

Hodges, Richard 1982: *Dark Age Economics: The Origins of Towns and Trade AD 600–1000*. Duckworth. London.

Holm, Olof 2012: *Självägarområdenas egenart: Jämtland och andra områden i Skandinavien med småskaligt jordägande 900–1500*. Historiska institutionen, Stockholms universitet. Stockholm

Holstein, Isabella C. C. von, Steven Ashby, Nienke L. van Doorn, Stacie M. Backs, Michael Buckley, Meirav Meiri, Ian Barnes, Anne Brundle and Matthew J. Collins 2014: Searching for Scandinavians in pre-Viking Scotland: molecular fingerprinting of Early Medieval combs. *Journal of Archaeological Science*, 41: 1–6.

Iversen, Tore, John Ragnar Myking and Gertrud Thoma (eds) 2007: *Peasant Relations to Lords and Government: Scandinavia and the Alpine Region 1000–1750*. Tapir Academic Press. Trondheim.

Jansen, Øystein J. 2015: Provenancing soapstone: Experiences from different geochemical methods. In: Indrelid, Svein, Kari Loe Hjelle and Kathrine Stene (eds): *Exploitation of Outfield Resources*. Joint research at the University Museums of Norway, pp. 167–74. University Museum, University of Bergen. Bergen.

Larsen, Jan Henning 2004: Jernvinna på Østlandet i yngre jernalder og middelalder – noen kronologiske problemer. *Viking*, 2004: 139–70.

Lepiksaar, Johannes, Dirk Heinrich and Christian Radtke 1977: *Untersuchungen an Fischresten aus der frühmittelalterlichen Siedlung Haithabu*. Vol. 10. Wachholtz. Neumünster.

Lie, Rolf 1988: Animal bones. In: Schia, Erik (ed.): *'Mindets Tomt'–'Søndre felt': Animal Bones, Moss-, Plant-, Insect- and Parasite Remains*. De arkeologiske utgravninger i Gamlebyen, Oslo, vol. 5: 153–96. Universitetsforlaget. Oslo.

Lønaas, Ole Christian 2001: Brynestein i middelalderen. En analyse av brynematerialet fra Oslogate 6. Unpublished thesis. IAKK. Universitetet i Oslo. Oslo.

Mikkelsen, Egil 1994: *Fangstprodukter i vikingtidens og middelalderens økonomi. Organiseringen av massefangst av villrein i Dovre*. Universitetets Oldsaksamlings Skrifter. Ny rekke, vol. 18. Universitetets Oldsaksamling. Oslo.

Mikkelsen, Per Hambro 2006: Arkæobotaniske undersøgelser af korn fra ASR 926 Ribelund I og ASR 1357 Giørtzvej. In: Feveile, Claus (ed.): *Det ældste Ribe. Udgravninger på nordsiden af Ribe Å 1984–2000*. Ribe Studier, vol. 1.1: 147–54. Jysk Arkæologisk Selskab. Højbjerg.

Mitchell, J. G., Helge Askvik and Heid G. Resi 1984: Potassium-argon Ages of schist honestones from the Viking Age sites at Kaupang (Norway), Aggersborg (Denmark), Hedeby (West Germany) and Wolin (Poland), and their archaeological implications. *Journal of Archaeological Science*, 11: 171–6.

Munch, Gerd Stamsø, Olav Sverre Johansen and Else Roesdahl 2003: *Borg in Lofoten: A Chieftain's Farm in North Norway*. Lofotr – Vikingmuséet på Borg. Bøstad.

Myrvoll, Siri 1992: *Handelstorget i Skien: A Study of Activity on an Early Medieval Site*. NUB, vol. 2. Riksantikvaren. Bergen.

Oka, Rahul and Chapurukha M. Kusimba 2008: The archaeology of trading systems, part 1: Towards a new trade synthesis. *Journal of Archaeological Research*, 16(4): 339–95.

Østmo, Einar 2011: Stadier i de sjøverts forbindelser over Skagerak i oldtiden. In: Appel, Liv and Kjartan Langsted (eds): *Ressourcer og kulturkontakter: Arkæologi rundt om Skagerrak og Kattegat*, pp. 19–30. Gilleleje museum. Helsingør.

Pedersen, Unn 2008: Weights and balances. In: Skre, Dagfinn (ed.): *Means of Exchange: Dealing with Silver in the Viking Age*. Kaupang Excavation Project. Publication Series, vol. 2. Norske Oldfunn, vol. 23: 119–95. Aarhus University Press. Århus.

Pestell, Tim and Katharina Ulmschneider (eds) 2003: *Markets in Early Medieval Europe: Trading and 'Productive' Sites, 650–850*. Windgather. Bollington.

Pilø, Lars 1990: Early soapstone vessels in Norway from the Late Bronze Age to the Early Roman Iron Age. *Acta Archaeologica*, 60: 87–100.

—— 2011: The pottery. In: Skre, Dagfinn (ed.): *Things from the Town: Artefacts and Inhabitants in Viking-Age Kaupang*. Kaupang Excavation Project. Publication Series, vol. 3. Norske Oldfunn, vol. 24: 281–304. Aarhus University Press. Århus.

Polanyi, Karl 1944: *The Great Transformation*. Farrar and Rinehart. New York.

—— 1957: The economy as instituted process. In: Polanyi, Karl, Conrad M. Arensberg and Harry W. Pearson (eds): *Trade and Markets in the Early Empires: Economies in History and Theory*, pp. 243–70. Free Press. New York.

—— 1963: Ports of trade in early societies. *The Journal of Economic History*, 23: 30–45.

—— 1968: *Primitive, Archaic and Modern Economies: Essays of Karl Polanyi*. Beacon Press. Boston.

Resi, Heid Gjøstein 1979: *Die Specksteinfunde aus Haithabu*. Berichte über die Ausgrabungen in Haithabu, vol. 14. Karl Wachholtz Verlag. Neunmünster.

—— 1990: *Die Wetz- und Schleifsteine aus Haithabu*. Berichte über die Ausgrabungen in Haithabu, vol. 28. Karl Wachholtz Verlag. Neunmünster.

—— 2011a: Whetstones, grindstones, touchstones and smoothers. In: Skre, Dagfinn (ed.): *Things from the Town: Artefacts and Inhabitants in Viking-Age Kaupang*. Kaupang Excavation Project. Publication Series, vol. 3. Norske Oldfunn, vol. 24: 373–93. Aarhus University Press. Århus.

—— 2011b: Gemstones: cornelian, rock crystal, amethyst, fluorspar and garnet. In: Skre, Dagfinn (ed.): *Things from the Town: Artefacts and Inhabitants in Viking-Age Kaupang*. Kaupang Excavation Project. Publication Series, vol. 3. Norske Oldfunn, vol. 24: 143–66. Aarhus University Press. Århus.

26 *Dagfinn Skre*

—— 2011c: Amber and jet. In: Skre, Dagfinn (ed.): *Things from the Town: Artefacts and Inhabitants in Viking-Age Kaupang*. Kaupang Excavation Project. Publication Series, vol. 3. Norske Oldfunn, vol. 24: 107–28. Aarhus University Press. Århus.

Robinson, David Earle, Ida Boldsen and Jan Andreas Harild 2006: Arkæobotaniske analyser af prøver fra markedspladsen i Ribe, ASR 9 Posthuset. In: Feveile, Claus (ed.): *Det ældste Ribe. Udgravninger på nordsiden af Ribe Å 1984–2000*. Ribe Studier, vol. 1.1: 107–32. Jysk Arkæologisk Selskab. Højbjerg.

Rundberget, Bernt 2012: Iron production in Østerdalen in medieval times: A consequence of regional technological change? In: Berge, Ragnhild, Marek E. Jasinski and Kalle Sognnes (eds): *N-TAG TEN. Proceedings of the 10th Nordic TAG conference at Stiklestad, Norway 2009*. BAR International Series, vol. 2399. Archaeopress. Oxford.

—— 2013: *Jernets dunkle dimensjon. Jernvinna i sørlige Hedmark. Sentral økonomisk faktor og premiss for samfunnsutvikling c. AD 700–1300*. IAKH, University of Oslo. Oslo.

Sindbæk, Søren M. 2005: *Ruter og rutinisering: Vikingetidens fjernhandel i Nordeuropa*. Multivers Academic. København.

Skaare, Kolbjørn 1976: *Coins and Coinage in Viking-Age Norway: The Establishment of a National Coinage in Norway in the XI Century, with a Survey of the Preceding Currency History*. Universitetsforlaget. Oslo.

Skjølsvold, Arne 1961: *Klebersteinsindustrien i vikingetiden*. Universitetsforlaget. Oslo.

Skre, Dagfinn 2007: Towns and markets, kings and central places in south-western Scandinavia c. AD 800–950. In: Skre, Dagfinn (ed.): *Kaupang in Skiringssal*. Kaupang Excavation Project. Publication Series, vol. 1. Norske Oldfunn, vol. 22: 445–69. Aarhus University Press. Århus.

—— 2008: Post-substantivist towns and trade AD 600–1000, In: Skre, Dagfinn (ed.): *Means of Exchange: Dealing with Silver in the Viking Age*. Kaupang Excavation Project. Publication Series, vol. 2. Norske Oldfunn, vol. 23: 327–41. Aarhus University Press. Århus.

—— 2011a: Commodity money, silver and coinage in Viking-Age Scandinavia. In: Graham-Campbell, James, Søren M. Sindbæk and Gareth Williams (eds): *Silver Economies, Monetisation and Society in Scandinavia, AD 800–1100*, pp. 67–91. Aarhus University Press. Århus.

—— 2011b: The inhabitants: origins and trading connexions. In: Skre, Dagfinn (ed.): *Things from the Town: Artefacts and Inhabitants in Viking-Age Kaupang*. Kaupang Excavation Project. Publication Series, vol. 3. Norske Oldfunn, vol. 24: 417–41. Aarhus University Press. Århus.

—— 2011c: The inhabitants: activities. In: Skre, Dagfinn (ed.): *Things from the Town: Artefacts and Inhabitants in Viking-Age Kaupang*. Kaupang Excavation Project. Publication Series, vol. 3. Norske Oldfunn, vol. 24: 397–415. Århus University Press. Århus.

—— 2015: Post-substantivist production and trade: Specialized sites for trade and craft production in Scandinavia c. 600–1000 AD. In: Barrett, James (ed.): *Maritime Societies of the Viking and Medieval World*. The Society for Medieval Archaeology Monograph, vol. 37: 156–70. Maney Publishing. Leeds.

—— [in prep.]: Monetary practices in early medieval western Scandinavia (fifth–tenth centuries AD).

Stenvik, Lars 2003: Iron production in Scandinavian archaeology. *Norwegian Archaeological Review*, 36: 119–34.

Viking-Age economic transformations 27

Steuer, Heiko 1987: Der Handel der Wikingerzeit zwischen Nord- und Westeuropa aufgrund archäologischer Zeugnisse. In: Düwel, Klaus (ed.): *Der Handel der Karolinger- und Wikingerzeit*. Untersuchungen zu Handel und Verkehr der vor- und frühgeschichtlichen Zeit in Mittel- und Nordeuropa, vol. IV: 113–97. Vandenhoeck and Ruprecht. Göttingen.

Stylegar, Frans-Arne 2007: The Kaupang cemeteries revisited. In: Skre, Dagfinn (ed.): *Kaupang in Skiringssal*. Kaupang Excavation Project. Publication Series, vol. 1. Norske Oldfunn, vol. 22: 65–128. Aarhus University Press. Århus.

Svanberg, Fredrik and Bengt Söderberg 2000: *Porten till Skåne: Löddeköpinge under järnålder och medeltid*. Skrifter, vol. 32. Riksantikvarieämbetet, Avdelningen för arkeologiska undersökningar. Stockholm.

Swedberg, Richard 2014: *The Art of Social Theory*. Princeton University Press. Princeton.

Theuws, Frans 2012: A world of connections and peasant agency. In: Theuws, Frans, Martine van Haperen and Chrystel Brandenburgh (eds): *The Merovingian Cemetery of Bergeijk-Fazantlaan*. Merovingian archaeology in the low countries, vol. 1: 180–6. Habelt-Verlag. Bonn.

Ulbricht, Ingrid 1978: *Die Geweihverarbeitung in Haithabu*. Vol. 7. Wachholtz. Neumünster.

Ulriksen, Jens 1998: *Anløbsplatser: Besejling og bebyggelse i Danmark mellem 200 og 1100 e. Kr. En studie af søfartens pladser på baggrund af undersøgelser i Roskilde Fjord*. Vikingeskibshallen i Roskilde. Roskilde.

Wiberg, Christina 1977: Kammer. In: Schia, Erik (ed.): *Feltet 'Mindets tomt': stratigrafi, topografi, daterende funngrupper*. De arkeologiske utgravninger i Gamlebyen, Oslo, vol. 1: 413–22. Universitetsforlaget. Oslo.

—— 1987: Kammer. In: Schia, Erik (ed.): *'Søndre felt': stratigrafi, bebyggelsesrester og daterende funngrupper*. De arkeologiske utgravninger i Gamlebyen, Oslo, vol. 3: 413–22. Universitetsforlaget. Oslo.

Wickham, Chris 2009: *The Inheritance of Rome: A History of Europe from 400 to 1000*. Allen Lane. London.

Wigh, Bengt 2001: *Animal Husbandry in the Viking Age Town Birka and its Hinterland*. Birka Studies, vol. 7. Stockholm.

Part I
Trade and traders

2 Approaching trade in pre-state and early state societies

Eivind Heldaas Seland

Introduction

Trade, broadly defined by economic anthropologist Karl Polanyi as 'the mutually appropriative movement of goods between hands' (Polanyi et al. 1957: 266), is a basic human activity like production and reproduction (Oka and Kusimba 2008). The role and importance of exchange, here used interchangeably with trade, has varied between places and over time, but the autarchic, self-sufficient economic unit, whether a family, a village, a tribe or a state, if it ever existed, is an anomaly in the human experience. Polanyi's definition, coined almost 60 years ago, remains useful. It underlines three aspects of exchange: mutuality, materiality and right of disposal. Trade is of central interest to archaeologists. The primacy of materiality is a shared trait between the academic discipline and the object of study, and due to the mutual and property-related nature of trade, it is an important mechanism of wealth distribution, economic specialisation and thus also social stratification.

Almost a century ago sociologist Thorstein Veblen realised how effective scarce resources are in creating and upholding hierarchies, by means of conspicuous consumption (Veblen 1957). Trade, in the broad sense of the word employed here, was and remains arguably the most widespread way of getting access to such resources. Societies demonstrating what scholars somewhat arbitrarily consider sufficient levels of specialisation and stratification are often referred to as complex societies, or in everyday terminology by the more convenient 'states'. This means that understanding the relationship between trade and political power is of key importance to any inquiry into the socio-economic organisation of premodern societies.

Trade in the premodern world was certainly not smooth sailing. Travel was uncomfortable, slow and sometimes dangerous. Information rarely moved faster than people. Political authorities walked a fine line between protection and predation, and effective enforcement of contracts and property rights across political borders was complicated at the very least (Bang 2008: 131–201). People travelled and traded nevertheless, but to do so they needed to create an institutional infrastructure that provided a necessary minimum of security and predictability. This chapter aims to give an overview of how

32   Eivind Heldaas Seland

modern scholarship has sought to engage with this process by developing theo-retical approaches to the study of trade in pre-state and early state societies. The argument is made that conceptualising trade in terms of networks offers opportunities for describing as well as explaining the process, using the partly complementary, partly competing analytical perspectives developed by archae-ologists, historians, economic anthropologists and economists.

Constraints of space, combined with the sheer scope of the subject, impose selectivity with regard to the theoretical traditions discussed and the questions raised below. Many issues within the field are, and have been, subject to fierce scholarly debates. While these have obvious relevance, they are only touched on briefly below, and interested readers are referred to the bibliography (Silver 1983, 2009; Manning and Morris 2005; Temin 2006; Bang 2007; Oka and Kusimba 2008; Hann 2011: 50–71). Some historiographical points should nevertheless be made to clarify the problems that need to be tackled.

The great divide

For nearly a century, scholars working with the economy of premodern societies, whether from a historical or an anthropological point of view, were all but forced to take a stand. The issue at stake was nothing less than the nature of premodern economies. In classical studies the debate peaked in the early decades of the twentieth century as well as in the 1970s to 1980s. In economic anthropology the divide was most outspoken around 1960. Did past economies resemble our own? Were they modern in the sense that they can be approached with the same analytical tools as nineteenth/twentieth-century liberal market economies? Proponents of this approach, such as Eduard Meyer (1979), Mikhail Rostovtzeff (1932, 1936) and Scott Cook (1966), were labelled modernists within classical studies and history, or for-malists within archaeology and economic anthropology. Their opponents, among them Karl Bücher (1979a, 1979b), Johannes Hasebroek (1931), Karl Polanyi (Polanyi et al. 1957; Polanyi 1963) and Moses Finley (1973), who held that economic interaction in premodern societies was embedded in political and social contexts, and thus not possible to study separately, were called primitivists or substantivists. In medieval studies the primitivist/substantivist position found resonance with Henri Pirenne's influential although never uncontroversial model of a minimalist and stagnant early medieval economy (Pirenne 1937; Hodges and Whitehouse 1983; McCormick 2001: 2–18).

By the 1980s, the primitivists seemed to have won the day, and were able to proclaim the establishment of a new orthodoxy based on Finley's model of the ancient economy as primarily subsistence-oriented and status-driven (Hopkins 1983: xi–xiv). The insistence on scholarly orthodoxy effectively put the lid on the discourse, which by the 1990s had grown all but stale. The study of the Greek and Roman economy had to a large extent been transformed into a discipline of cultural history, and the insistence on the uniqueness, even exoticism, of the classical world effectively barred economic historians of other

Approaching trade in early state societies 33

periods and regions from taking an interest in classical antiquity, and students of the ancient economy from making their field relevant and interesting to scholars dealing with other empirical and chronological settings. This, again, has changed over the last decades, with scholars on one hand again taking up modernising and quantitative approaches to the ancient economy (Temin 2001, 2006; Silver 2009), and on the other hand bringing in perspectives from a range of social sciences, emphasising explicit methodology and preferably also testability as the way forward (Manning and Morris 2005; Scheidel et al. 2007; Bang 2008).

Anthropologically oriented archaeology was not untouched by this debate, which found its parallel in the formalist/substantivist controversy. Nevertheless, archaeologists continued to rely on modern models in their approach to data, as a lack of textual sources rendered the hermeneutical alternative less feasible. Several important theoretical works were published in the 1970s, asking how models can be operationalised to incorporate artefactual data (Renfrew 1975; Sabloff and Lamberg-Karlovsky 1975; Earle and Ericson 1977; Renfrew 1977). Arguably, the criticism against neo-evolutionist approaches outlined below, along with the general postcolonial and postmodern trend away from diffusionist interpretations and generalising scholarship, nevertheless caused studies of trade to take a back seat in the development of archaeological research and theory in the 1980s and 1990s.

Models and the study of the past

Readers familiar with the field might have noticed and possibly taken issue with the conscious use of terminology borrowed by cultural anthropology, key labels such as 'pre-state' and 'early state' carrying a scholarly heritage from the neo-evolutionist discourse prevalent from the 1960s into the 1980s (Fried 1967; Claessen and Skalnik 1978; Cohen and Service 1978; Claessen 1984), which became increasingly unfashionable in subsequent decades due to implicit teleology and alleged Eurocentrism (Khoury and Kostiner 1990; Yoffee 2005: 4–41). The critique of the neo-evolutionary school was certainly justified in underlining the uniqueness of societies past and present, the great diversity of trajectories of development, and the problematic, arguably Eurocentric and certainly teleological expectation and ideal of development in past societies. Nevertheless, any archaeological argument builds on analogy, and analogy is by nature comparative (Hodder 1982). Modern scholars do not have direct access to the past, but are left with a mostly fragmentary and unrepresentative record of signs that has come down to us from it. These signs must be interpreted, and in doing this we are creating narratives about the past. The neo-evolutionary narrative has been sidelined in scholarship, but along with other narratives of early societies, it developed a range of analytical models that remain useful for comparison between different empirical settings. Some past societies did actually experience increased economic specialisation and social stratification, and it is interesting and useful to discuss the role of trade in that process. Arguably,

34   *Eivind Heldaas Seland*

this can be done without descending into the fruitless discussions on categorisation and definitions that came to characterise parts of the neo-evolutionary discourse.

Although there is no agreement among anthropologists on what a tribe is, and the nature and organisation of what we call tribal societies vary over time and space, 'tribe' remains convenient shorthand for non-centralised political groups based on perceived common descent. Although complex societies in early history were different from modern complex societies and from each other, 'chiefdom' and 'state' are useful terms insofar as they enable comparison, even if only to highlight diversity (Khoury and Kostiner 1990; Tapper 1990). To cite one of the leading figures in the debate on the role of trade in early societies, Sir Moses I. Finley, who was a strong advocate of the conscious and explicit use of models in the study of the past, 'The familiar fear of *a priorism* is misplaced: any hypothesis can be modified, adjusted or discarded when necessary. Without one, however, there can be no explanation' (Finley 1986: 66). Taking the cue from Finley, a number of analytical models are drawn upon below. Some of them are mutually exclusive, others complementary. They all have shortcomings as general descriptions of how trade took place in prehistory and early history; nevertheless, they are all useful in explaining aspects of exchange in past societies when they are perceived as tools of interpretation rather than analytical straightjackets (Meyer 2000).

Models of interaction

Hungarian-born Karl Polanyi (1886–1964), who can be credited with spurring the substantivist-formalist controversy in economic anthropology, also coined some of the more influential analytical models of premodern trade. His 'port-of-trade' model envisaged small, independent or semi-independent polities, typically city states, which were seen as points of interaction between zones of transit – oceans and deserts for instance, and larger territorial polities (Polanyi et al. 1957; Polanyi 1963). Although the model has long since been discredited as a universal description of how trade took place in the premodern world, it retains its relevance to a number of specific, observable cases.

A more generalised approach to places as arenas of interaction in archaeology is represented by the body of theory known as Central-Place Theory, inspired by Walter Christaller's study of settlement hierarchies in southern Germany (Christaller 1933). Christaller, describing a predominantly rural environment still retaining many premodern traits, was able to show that hierarchies of settlements were based on how far people were willing to travel to get access to certain goods or services. This can be expressed as the *gravity* of a central place (Renfrew 1977: 87; Rivers et al. 2013). Markets for agricultural goods, mills and churches are examples of institutions that were needed on a local level. Access to judicial services and specialised tools and equipment was not sought after on an everyday basis, and people were willing to travel further afield to partake. Central-Place Theory made its way into archaeology in the late 1960s,

Approaching trade in early state societies 35

and has been important in explaining settlement hierarchies as well as the distribution of trade goods (Renfrew 1977).

Central places tend to develop not only into economic nodes but also into centres of political power, combining the factor of how far people are willing to travel with the distance over which it is possible to exercise political and economic dominance (Bekker-Nielsen 1989), thus adding the aspect of *centrality* to that of gravity (Rivers et al. 2013). A major weakness of Christaller's model, however, which has complicated its application to archaeological contexts, was that it did not take into account the challenges and costs of movement and transport in the real world. Many central places are situated at strategic locations, which enable them to control a large hinterland, or make them difficult or impossible to bypass. In this way they are turned into gateways, which control transit between different parts of a network (Rivers et al. 2013).

An example of a model focusing on people is Phillip Curtin's 'trade diaspora': merchants settled permanently or semi-permanently on foreign ground, building cultural expertise and establishing social connections, and thus acting as intermediaries between home and host cultures (Curtin 1984). Curtin's model has drawn criticism for presupposing a centre or home culture as the wellspring of the diaspora community. Many known merchant communities were in fact polycentric, or oriented towards a homeland only in a very symbolic sense. Sebouh D. Aslanian suggests instead the polycentric model of the 'circulation society', which seems better adapted to longstanding groups maintaining a common identity but without regular contact to a common geographic centre (Aslanian 2011: 1–22). Nevertheless, Curtin's model retains its relevance in many other cases. Both models, however, presuppose that groups of merchants were able to achieve a necessary sense of 'groupness' by building social cohesion within the community and maintaining boundaries towards other groups (Barth 1969; Brubaker 2002, 2005, 2009). This could be achieved by drawing on institutional ties such as ethnicity, shared origin and religion (Seland 2013). At the same time, however, they also depended on the ability to link up with other communities.

Turning to the mechanisms of economic interaction, Polanyi, firmly believing that most economic relations in premodern economies were embedded in socio-political contexts, also introduced three models explicitly inspired by the anthropological work of Bronislaw Malinowski and probably also that of Marcel Mauss, namely 'reciprocity', 'redistribution' and 'exchange' (Polanyi et al. 1957: 250–2; Malinowski 2002; Mauss 2007). By reciprocity, sometimes also called gift-exchange, he referred to transactions of more or less equal perceived value, made between individuals of similar social status. Redistribution described the collection and subsequent reallocation of resources through a centralised institution, while exchange referred to what we normally describe as trade, goods changing hands, whether as a result of barter or of market transactions, without imposing further social obligations on the participants. Although Polanyi had definite ideas about how premodern economies worked in practice, his models can be used to characterise economic interaction under

36 *Eivind Heldaas Seland*

any economic regime, including a modern liberal market economy or a highly redistributive welfare state.

New institutional economics

Where substantivists and formalists alike failed at adequately describing the economic organisation of early societies, neo-evolutionists were equally unsuccessful in explaining their political development. Meanwhile, however, the discipline of economics had moved forward. While specialists in prehistory and early history were debating whether the people they were studying had acted rationally in economic respects, many economists had long realised that modern people frequently fail to. Scholars developing the field of New Institutional Economics, in part directly inspired by Polanyi's work, started to investigate how institutions shape economic behaviour (North 1977, 1990; North et al. 2009). Douglass C. North, John J. Wallis and Barry Weingast suggest that societies can be studied as consisting of *organisations* and *institutions*. By organisations North et al. (2009: 15) describe 'groups of individuals pursuing a mix of common and individual goals through partially coordinated behaviour'. In early history, such groups would include tribes, chieftaincies, robber bands, empires and other political organisations. Organisations in premodern societies, according to North et al., specialise in containing violence, and engage in generating revenue that is distributed among elite and non-elite members (2009: 14–19). Trade was one important source of such revenue, along with landed property and plunder, for instance.

Although North and his colleagues hold that political organisations were the predominant form in premodern societies, groups of merchants or artisans could also be approached as organisations within this framework. Institutions, on the other hand, are described as the '"rules of the game", the patterns of interaction that govern and constrain the relationships of individuals' (North et al. 2009: 15). The market is certainly one important institution in this respect, but there are also many others, including the reciprocal and redistributive mechanisms emphasised by Polanyi. New Institutional Economics has also brought a number of other useful approaches to the attention of scholars working with early trade: Transaction Cost Theory is able to deal not only with high costs of transportation but also with issues of security, protection, administration and enforcement (Silver 2011). The realisation that rationality is bounded – restricted and shaped by a lack of information, cultural and social constraints, and so forth (Simon 1997) – also helps explain how different economic mechanisms can come into play at the same time. Agency theory, dealing with situations of imperfect information, where economic actors, 'principals', need to rely on representatives, 'agents', with potentially conflicting self-interest, highlights not only the challenges but also the possibilities for creating trust among actors engaging in economic interaction (Eisenhardt 1989).

The great contribution of New Institutional Economics to the study of early trade is that the field enables us to deal with social, political and economic relations within the same framework, thus allowing for the embedded aspects of premodern economic behaviour and the record of data, which is more often than not fragmentary, and biased towards elite sections of society and their self-representation, while at the same time opening the opportunity to bring in economic concepts and tools describing market transactions, which clearly also held an important place in most premodern economies.

Explaining trade as networks

At the heart of archaeology as well as trade is materiality. The main archaeological proxy of trade is the existence of artefacts that can be traced to points of origin or production different from their find-spots. The scholarly expression of this is the distribution map, showing the spatial contexts of archaeological finds. Under many circumstances, exchange is the likely agent of the mobility of objects, but other mechanisms are also possible and well attested, such as migration, travel, taxation or plunder, to name a few.

Colin Renfrew famously characterised trade as 'action at a distance' (Renfrew 1975). This accurately captures the interactive nature of the undertaking. Trade establishes direct and indirect, explicit and unseen connections between people. A recent surge in scholarly interest in network theory has provided possibilities for approaching this aspect of exchange by combining places, people, objects and relations within the same framework (Malkin 2003, 2011; Sindbæk 2007, 2009; Knappett et al. 2008; Brughmans 2010, 2013; Knappett 2011, 2013; Seland 2013). Networks intersect at nodes, which might be individuals, groups, places or even objects. Nodes are connected by ties, often called 'edges' in network terminology, which can, on one hand, include interpersonal relations of friendship, kinship, personal dependence, contract and so forth, or shared characteristics of religion, ethnicity, profession and so on. On the other hand, ties can also be constituted by routes, roads or simply the presence of similar objects in geographically distinct places, presupposing some kind of connection. In the same manner, however, as moving from distribution maps to interaction poses a potential problem, so, too, are network approaches faced with the challenge of moving from description to explanation. This is where the theoretical dimension comes back into play.

Nodes in a network related to trade will often be places such as find-spots, archaeological sites, known locations of harbours, markets, periodical trading fairs, production sites, settlements, elite residences or places of religious significance. Most archaeological modelling of geographical nodes approaches them as central places. Nodes, however, may also be people. Political elites engaged with trade, either directly, by taking part in the procurement and exchange of goods, or indirectly, by offering protection in return for taxation, or by predation. Groups of merchants constituted social networks, for instance in the form of trading diasporas or circulation societies, and linked up with producers, distributors, transporters, purchasers and political authorities in the process (Seland 2013). Most networks based on trade can be described as belonging to

38 Eivind Heldaas Seland

what in network terminology is known as the 'small-world' type. Such networks are characterised by each individual node being directly connected only to relatively few other nodes, but nevertheless being able to access the whole network indirectly by way of these connections (Wasserman and Faust 1994: 53–4; Malkin 2011: 27–30).

Conclusion

It might be argued that most theoretical approaches to premodern economies are better at explaining than describing, while the opposite is the case for many archaeological applications of network approaches. If this is true there should be considerable analytical potential in combining the two. The defining feature and strength of network approaches is the emphasis on relations. Visualising and, in cases where the data allows it, measuring these ties reveals where explanation is needed. Typical relations in social networks include, but are not limited to, individual ties of friendship, kinship, marriage and enmity, and group-level identity markers such as ethnicity, religious affiliation and profession. They may also include individual and group-level action, such as reciprocity, redistribution and exchange, and also taxation, robbery, warfare or protection. Here network theory intersects with other bodies of theory, including the substantivist and formalist traditions of economic anthropology traditions outlined above, which aim at explaining but lack the descriptive capacity of network analysis. To name but one example, New Institutional Economics enables us to explain social networks in terms of organisations, and most of the ties constituting networks can be described as institutions, thus potentially combining description and explanation.

Sociologist Michael Mann argues that four interrelated fields of power constitute society: ideological, economic, military and political. These fields, however, materialise only in the formation of social elite networks – power cannot be distinguished from the people wielding it, and power is always exercised by people and in relation to people (Mann 1986). For the archaeologist who aims to grasp the role of trade in the formation of such power structures in pre-state and early state societies, the challenge remains to move from the static evidence provided by archaeology to the once dynamic but long-finished process of exchange. Above I have argued that this requires the conscious use of analytical models, some of them developed specifically for the study of premodern trade, others from economics, sociology and anthropology, and that these models should be viewed as complementary rather than mutually exclusive. In my view, conceptualising economic interaction in terms of networks is currently our best bid for describing as well as explaining processes of trade, and integrating them with other aspects of the human experience.

References

Aslanian, Sebouh David 2011: *From the Indian Ocean to the Mediterranean: The Global Trade Networks of Armenian Merchants from New Julfa*. The California World History Library, University of California Press. Berkeley, CA.

Approaching trade in early state societies 39

Bang, Peter Fibiger 2007: Trade and empire: in search of organizing concepts for the Roman economy. *Past and Present*, 195: 3–54.

—— 2008: *The Roman Bazaar: A Comparative Study of Trade and Markets in a Tributary Empire*. Cambridge Classical Studies, Cambridge University Press. Cambridge.

Barth, Fredrik 1969: Introduction. In: Barth, Fredrik (ed.): *Ethnic Groups and Boundaries: The Social Organization of Cultural Difference*, pp. 9–38. Universitetsforlaget. Oslo.

Bekker-Nielsen, Tønnes 1989: *The Geography of Power: Studies in the Urbanization of Roman North-West Europe*. B.A.R. Archaeopress. Oxford.

Brubaker, Rogers 2002: Ethnicity without groups. *Archives européennes de sociologie*, 43(2): 163–89.

—— 2005: The 'diaspora' diaspora. *Ethnic and Racial Studies*, 28(1): 1–19.

—— 2009: Ethnicity, race, and nationalism. *Annual Review of Sociology*, 35: 21–42.

Brughmans, Tom 2010: Connecting the dots: towards archaeological network analysis. *Oxford Journal of Archaeology*, 29(3): 277–303.

—— 2013: Thinking through networks: a review of formal network methods in archaeology. *Journal of Archaeological Method and Theory*, 20(4): 623–62.

Bücher, Karl 1979a [1906]: Die Entstehung der Volkswirtschaft. In: Finley, Moses I. (ed.): *The Bücher-Meyer Controversy*. Arno Press. New York.

—— 1979b: Zur Griechischen Wirtschaftsgeschichte. In: Finley, Moses I. (ed.): *The Bücher-Meyer Controversy*. Arno Press. New York.

Christaller, Walter 1933: *Die zentralen Orte in Süddeutschland: eine ökonomisch-geographische Untersuchung über die Gesetzmässigkeit der Verbreitung und Entwicklung der Siedlungen mit städtischen Funktionen*. Verlag von Gustav Fischer. Jena.

Claessen, Henri J.M. 1984: The internal dynamics of the early state. *Current Anthropology*, 25(4): 365–79.

Claessen, Henri J.M. and Peter Skalník (eds) 1978: *The Early State*. New Babylon: Studies in the Social Sciences, vol. 32. Mouton. The Hague.

Cohen, Ronald and Elman R. Service (eds) 1978: *Origins of the State*. Institute for the Study of Human Issues. Philadelphia.

Cook, Scott 1966: The obsolete 'anti-market' mentality: a critique of the substantive approach to economic anthropology. *American Anthropologist, New Series*, 68(2): 323–45.

Curtin, Philip D. 1984: *Cross Cultural Trade in World History*. Cambridge University Press. Cambridge.

Earle, Timothy K. and Jonathon E. Ericson 1977: *Exchange Systems in Prehistory*. Academic Press. New York.

Eisenhardt, Kathleen M. 1989: Agency theory: an assessment and review. *The Academy of Management Review*, 14(1): 57–74.

Finley, Moses I. 1973: *The Ancient Economy*. Chatto and Windus. London.

—— 1986: *Ancient History: Evidence And Models*. Viking. New York.

Fried, Morton H. 1967: *The Evolution of Political Society*. Random House. New York.

Hann, Chris 2011: *Economic Anthropology*. Polity Press. Cambridge.

Hasebroek, Johannes 1931: *Griechische Wirtschafts- und Gesellschaftsgeschichte bis zur Perserzeit*. J.C.B. Mohr (Paul Siebeck). Tübingen.

Hodder, Ian 1982: *The Present Past: An Introduction to Anthropology for Archaeologists*. Batsford. London.

Hodges, Richard and David Whitehouse 1983: *Mohammed, Charlemagne and the Origins of Europe: Archaeology and the Pirenne Thesis*. Duckworth. London.

Hopkins, Keith 1983: Introduction. In: Garnsey, Peter, Keith Hopkins and C.R. Whittaker (eds): *Trade in the Ancient Economy*, pp. ix–xxv. University of California Press. Berkeley, CA.

40 *Eivind Heldaas Seland*

Khoury, Philip Shukry and Joseph Kostiner 1990: Introduction. In: Khoury, Philip Shukry and Joseph Kostiner (eds): *Tribes and State Formation in the Middle East*, pp. 1–22. University of California Press. Berkeley, CA.

Knappett, Carl 2011: *An Archaeology of Interaction: Network Perspectives on Material Culture and Society*. Oxford University Press. Oxford.

—— 2013: *Network Analysis in Archaeology: New Approaches to Regional Interaction*. Oxford University Press. Oxford.

Knappett, Carl, Tim Evans and Ray Rivers 2008: Modelling maritime interaction in the Aegean Bronze Age. *Antiquity*, 82(318): 1009–24.

Malinowski, Bronislaw 2002: *Argonauts of the Western Pacific: An Account of Native Enterprise and Adventure in the Archipelagoes of Melanesian New Guinea*. Routledge. London.

Malkin, Irad 2003: Networks and the emergence of Greek identity. *Mediterranean Historical Review*, 18(2): 56–74.

—— 2011: *A Small Greek World: Networks in the Ancient Mediterranean*. Greeks overseas, Oxford University Press. New York.

Mann, Michael 1986: *The Sources of Social Power*. Cambridge University Press. Cambridge.

Manning, Joseph Gilbert and Ian Morris 2005: *The Ancient Economy: Evidence and Models*. Stanford University Press. Stanford, CA.

Mauss, Marcel 2007: *Essai sur le don: forme et raison de l'échange dans les sociétés archaïques*. Quadrige (Presses universitaires de France). Grands textes Y, Quadrige/PUF. Paris.

McCormick, Michael 2001: *Origins of the European Economy: Communications and Commerce A.D. 300–900*. Cambridge University Press. Cambridge.

Meyer, Eduard 1979: Die Wirtschaftliche Entwicklung des Altertums. In: Finley, Moses I. (ed.): *The Bucher-Meyer Controversy*. Arno Press. New York.

Meyer, Jørgen Christian 2000: Socialantropologi og komarativ metode. In: Iddeng, Jon W. (ed.): *Ad Fontes: Antikkvitenskap, kildebehandling og metode*, pp. 229–44. Norsk Klassisk Forbund. Oslo.

North, Douglass C. 1977: Markets and other allocation systems in history: the challenge of Karl Polanyi. *Journal of European Economic History*, 6(3): 703–16.

—— 1990: *Institutions, Institutional Change and Economic Performance*. Cambridge University Press. Cambridge.

North, Douglass C., John Joseph Wallis and Barry R. Weingast 2009: *Violence and Social Orders: A Conceptual Framework for Interpreting Recorded Human History*. Cambridge University Press. Cambridge.

Oka, Rahul and Chapurukha M. Kusimba 2008: The archaeology of trading systems, part 1: towards a new trade synthesis. *Journal of Archaeological Research*, 16(4): 339–95.

Pirenne, Henri 1937: *Mahomet et Charlemagne*. Félix Alcan. Paris.

Polanyi, Karl 1963: Ports of trade in early societies. *Journal of Economic History*, 23(1): 30–45.

Polanyi, Karl, Conrad M. Arensberg and Harry W. Pearson (eds) 1957: *Trade and Markets in Early Empires*. Free Press. New York.

Renfrew, Colin 1975: Trade as action at a distance: questions of integration and communication. In: Sabloff, Jeremy A. and C.C. Lamberg-Karlovsky (eds): *Ancient Civilization and Trade*, pp. 3–60. University of New Mexico Press. Albuquerque, NM.

—— 1977: Alternative models for exchange and spatial distribution. In: Earle, Timothy K. and Jonathon E. Ericson (eds): *Exchange Systems in Prehistory*, pp. 71–90. Academic Press. New York.

Rivers, Ray, Carl Knappett and Tim Evans 2013: What makes a site important? Centrality, gateways and gravity. In: Knappett, Carl (ed.): *Network Analysis in Archaeology: New Approaches to Regional Interaction*, pp. 125–50. Oxford University Press. Oxford.

Rostovtzeff, Michael I. 1932: Literatur: Hasebroek, Johannes: Griechische Wirtschafts- und Gesellschaftsgeschichte. *Zeitschrift für die gesamte Staatswissenschaft*, 92: 334–41.

—— 1936: The Hellenistic world and its economic development. *American Historical Review*, 41(2): 231–52.

Sabloff, Jeremy A. and C.C. Lamberg-Karlovsky 1975: *Ancient Civilization and Trade*. University of New Mexico Press. Albuquerque, NM.

Scheidel, Walter, Ian Morris and Richard P. Saller (eds) 2007: *The Cambridge Economic History of the Greco-Roman World*. Cambridge University Press. Cambridge.

Seland, Eivind Heldaas 2013: Networks and social cohesion in ancient Indian Ocean trade: geography, ethnicity, religion. *Journal of Global History*, 8(3): 373–90.

Silver, Morris 1983: Karl Polanyi and markets in the Ancient Near East. *Journal of Economic History*, 43(4): 795–829.

—— 2009: Historical otherness, the Roman bazaar, and primitivism: PF Bang on the Roman economy. *Journal of Roman Archaeology*, 22(2): 421–43.

—— 2011: Transaction/administrative costs in Greco-Roman antiquity with special reference to the implications of Atheism/naturalism in classical Athens. *Marburger Beiträge zur Antiken Handels-, Wirtschafts- und Sozialgeschichte*, 29: 49–93.

Simon, Herbert Alexander 1997: *Models of Bounded Rationality: Empirically Grounded Economic Reason*. Vol. 3. MIT Press. Harvard, MA.

Sindbæk, Søren Michael 2007: The small world of the Vikings: networks in early medieval communication and exchange. *Norwegian Archaeological Review*, 40(1): 59–74.

—— 2009: Open access, nodal points, and central places: maritime communication and locational principles for coastal sites in south Scandinavia, c. AD 400–1200/ Avatud ligipaas, solmpunktid ja keskused: veeteed ja Louna-Skandinaavia rannaasulate paiknemisloogika aastail 400–1200 pKr. *Eesti Arheoloogia Ajakiri*, 13(2): 96–109.

Tapper, Richard 1990: Anthropologists, historians and tribespeople on tribe and state formation in the Middle East. In: Khoury, Philip Shukry and Joseph Kostiner (eds): *Tribes and State Formation in the Middle East*, pp. 48–73. University of California Press. Berkeley, CA.

Temin, Peter 2001: A market economy in the Roman Empire. *Journal of Roman Studies*, 91: 169–81.

—— 2006: The economy of the early Roman Empire. *The Journal of Economic Perspectives*, 20(1): 133–51.

Veblen, Thorstein 1957: *The Theory of the Leisure Class*. George Allen and Unwin. London.

Wasserman, Stanley and Katherine Faust 1994: *Social Network Analysis: Methods and Applications*. Structural analysis in the social sciences. Cambridge University Press. Cambridge/New York.

Yoffee, Norman 2005: *Myths of the Archaic State: Evolution of the Earliest Cities, States, and Civilizations*. Cambridge University Press. Cambridge.

3 The use of silver as a medium of exchange in Jämtland, c. 875–1050

Olof Holm

Introduction

At Viking-period emporia such as Kaupang and Birka there is an abundance of archaeological evidence of silver being used as money (Blackburn 2008; Pedersen 2008; Gustin 2011). This is understandable. Silver in various forms – coins or bullion – was a perfect medium of exchange, being durable, valuable, easily cut and weighed into desired quantities, and widely accepted as a means of payment in large parts of the Old World. For people living at these emporia, who had to trade off their produce to buy food and other necessities, and therefore performed transactions frequently, this medium must have been very practical to use, once it had become accessible (Skre 2011: 81–3; Williams 2011: 355). A commonly accepted medium of exchange expands the possibilities for exchange by enabling purchase and sale to be separated in time and space (see, e.g., Melitz 1974: 53–8).

But what about rural areas in Scandinavia? Dagfinn Skre (2011: 69–80) has remarked that for a farmer whose household was more or less self-supporting with regard to necessary goods, essential commodities with a utilitarian value, such as cattle or cloth, might have been preferred as media of payment in transactions, instead of silver. Silver did not have a utilitarian value (except for the silversmith) and could not sustain people in cases of crisis, for, as Skre puts it, 'Who would exchange their cows, butter or grain for metal in times of famine?' If a household member did not have to buy necessities so often, he or she might have had the time to search for trading partners to barter with. Then one commodity could be traded directly for another commodity, without the use of silver or any other medium of exchange.

Still, there might have been rural areas in the Viking period where, for various reasons, the inhabitants were trading more actively than in others, and therefore found it practical to use silver as money, just as in urban settings. However, according to Skre (2011: 85), this is hard to ascertain:

> There is little evidence to indicate when, and to what extent, silver was taken into use in rural trade outside of markets. Hoarding of silver in rural areas increased in the tenth century, as did the proportion of hack-silver

Silver as a medium of exchange in Jämtland 43

in the hoards (Hårdh 1996). But this cannot be taken as secure evidence of silver being used as payment in rural trade; the silver may have been assembled through raiding or through trade in markets and towns and then hoarded for later use there.

This statement begs a question that warrants further research. In this chapter I will focus on a regional case: an area located inland, right in the middle of the Scandinavian Peninsula, nowadays in Sweden but belonging to Norway between the late twelfth and mid-seventeenth century, namely the province of Jämtland (Figure 3.1).[1] One could perhaps presume that in a remote rural region like this (as seen from Viking-period trading centres such as Birka, Hedeby and Kaupang) silver was not used in trading activities to any large extent among the populace. But the archaeological evidence from the middle and late Viking period (c. 875–1050/75) suggests the opposite.

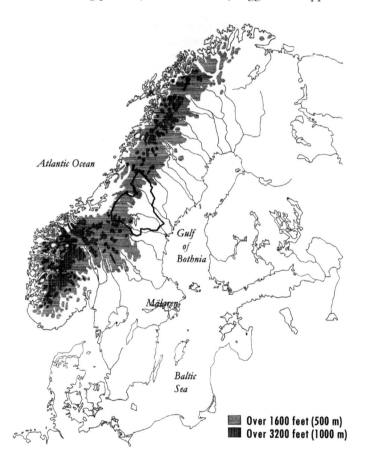

Figure 3.1 The position of Jämtland on the Scandinavian Peninsula.
Source: Map based on Sawyer and Sawyer (1993: Fig. 2.1), with kind permission.

44 Olof Holm

In Jämtland no large-scale metal detector surveys have yet been carried out, and almost no Viking-period settlement sites have hitherto been investigated. It is thus not possible today to study to what extent there are lost coins, hacksilver and small weights lying in the ground on old farms or at possible marketplaces in Jämtland. But a number of graves from the Viking period have been excavated, mainly within agricultural settlement districts close to Storsjön and other larger lakes, but also outside these, in forested and mountainous areas. The latter graves are, in at least some cases, most probably the graves of nomadic or semi-nomadic people. Graves from the middle and late Viking period very often contain weights and/or balances. I will argue that these tools were used for weighing silver in transactions, and that their frequent occurrence in graves implies that trading with silver used as money was widespread in the region.

Weights and balances found in graves in Jämtland

Before I proceed, I would like to make a source-critical remark. It is possible that there was a special meaning behind weights and balances in graves, conditioned by locally rooted religious notions and customs of which we lack knowledge (cf. Gustin 2004: 113, note 6). The bereaved might have considered that the deceased had use for these tools in the afterlife. The weighing equipment may also have been accessories in the funeral rites. However, the weights and balances in question must reasonably have been owned by local people – either by the deceased or by the bereaved who participated in the funerals – before they were deposited in the graves. The balances and almost all weights found in graves in Jämtland belong to types that were, as far as we know, only manufactured at the most important trading places of the middle and late Viking period, such as Birka, Sigtuna and Hedeby (Pedersen 2008: 121, 126–7 and refs. therein; Söderberg 2008: 122–3). Thus, the owners of these items in Jämtland must have made an effort to obtain them from distant places. This makes it reasonable to assume that the local population really needed and used these tools. I will present empirical support for this assumption below.

A huge number (c. 700 or more) of grave mounds, cairns and stone settings have been registered in Jämtland, and we know from experience that a large proportion of them (especially the mounds) contain the cremated or non-cremated remains of men and women buried with grave goods in the middle and late Viking period (cf. Magnusson 1986: Figs 135–6). There are also an unknown number of undetected and practically invisible cremation graves on flat ground in forested and mountainous areas. In addition, innumerable graves have been ploughed out, plundered, excavated by non-professionals or destroyed in other ways. The museums possess an impressive record of stray finds of axes, spearheads, arrowheads, swords, oval brooches and other notable objects from the middle and late Viking period, many of which can be assumed to originate from destroyed graves (Magnusson 1986: Tab. 43). All in all, it can be established that, at least in the more densely populated settlement districts in Jämtland (cf. Figure 3.2), the custom of burying men and women in furnished

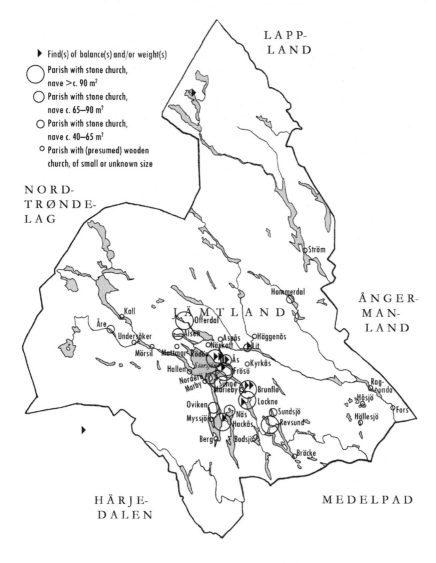

Figure 3.2 Distribution of finds of weights and balances from the middle and late Viking period in Jämtland and sizes of agrarian settlements as expressed by sizes of parish churches built in the twelfth (or in some cases possibly in the thirteenth) century. A find of two weights in a grave at Ljungdalen, in present-day Storsjö parish, Härjedalen (JLM 28050), is marked on the map as well.

Source: The church data are based on Holm (2001, 2012).

Note: Data concerning the parish churches of Berg, Hallen and Oviken are uncertain.

46   *Olof Holm*

graves was widespread during this period. How common this custom was in less populated settlement areas is not so clear.

A small but seemingly representative sample of all graves from the middle and late Viking period in Jämtland has been wholly or partly excavated by professionals. A closer look shows that a remarkably large proportion of the *male* graves from this period (distinguished primarily by weapons and belt buckles) have yielded finds of a more or less fragmented balance and/or one or several weights, despite the fact that the conditions for recovering finds were far from ideal in several cases (Holm 2015b: Catalogues 1 and 2). If we look only at securely dated male graves, eight out of 14 – about one half – contained such weighing equipment. Now, it is of course not always possible to date graves securely before or after c. 875 based on typologies and find combinations, and some graves, where only gender-neutral objects have been recovered, cannot be gendered. But even if we include all such uncertain graves in the calculation, the proportion of male graves containing balances and/or weights is considerable: 8 out of 22 graves, or about one third. Arguably, weights and balances represent the most common category of metal objects found in male graves in Jämtland from the middle and late Viking period, along with knives, firesteels and arrowheads.

Among the expertly investigated graves in Jämtland there are also one or two examples of a *female* grave containing a weight and/or a balance (one of these also contained fragments of oval brooches and an ornamental pendant; the other had a burned cornelian bead and a hook made of copper-alloy wire, probably used for a string of beads). In general, women's graves containing weights and/or balances are unusual in the countryside in Norway and Sweden, while they are much more common in the urban setting of Birka (Kyhlberg 1980: 203; Gräslund 1980: 79–80).[2] There are also finds of weights or balances from two non-expertly excavated graves, and one stray find of a weight. (All finds and their find contexts are described in detail in Holm 2015b: Catalogue 1.) This makes 13 finds in total, mostly from farming settlement districts, but in one case in a grave situated far outside these districts (Figure 3.2).

A few male graves stick out from the rest, being characterised by exclusive and expensive grave goods (see below). These graves might belong to the highest social strata of the population in Jämtland. However, most finds of balances and weights have been made in male graves in farming districts furnished with objects of ordinary standard in Jämtland, such as belt buckles and penannular brooches of copper alloy or iron, axes, spearheads, arrowheads suitable for hunting, knives, combs, fire-making tools and whetstones. Reasonably, these graves represent a middle-class segment of the farming population in Jämtland.

Based on find combinations and typologies, all graves with weighing equipment and with reliable find associations can be dated more or less accurately to the middle and late Viking period (Figure 3.3). The two non-expertly excavated grave finds must belong to this period as well. The single stray find of a weight might originate from a destroyed eleventh-century grave or from an eleventh/twelfth-century settlement context.

Grave	Burial customs	875–900	900–925	925–950	950–975	975–1000	1000–1025	1025–1050	1050–1075
JLM 24336 Prästlägden, Lit	crem.; mound								
JLM 25410 Josvedviken, Rödön	crem.; flat gr.								
JLM 902 Västbyn, Frösö	crem.; mound								
JLM 20774 Prästbordet, Brunflo	crem.; mound								
JLM 26 Sota, Rödön*	crem.; cairn								
JLM 23347 Sanne, Hackås	crem.; mound								
JLM 1001 Rösta, Ås*	inhum.; stone s.						?		
SHM 12426 M IV, Rösta, Ås	inhum.; mound					?			
JLM 29826 Jormön, Frostviken	crem.; flat gr.								
JLM 9036 Höggärde, Lockne	inhum.; mound					?			
SHM 12426 M I, Rösta, Ås	inhum.; mound								
SHM 12426 M III, Rösta, Ås	inhum.; mound								

Figure 3.3 Chronological chart showing approximate datings (based on find combinations and typologies) of graves in Jämtland containing weights and/or balances.

Note: * = Non-expertly excavated; crem. = cremation; gr. = grave; inhum. = inhumation; stone s. = stone setting.

The better-preserved balances were all originally collapsible, with a foldable beam, so that they could be kept securely in a small case of wood or other material (for two examples, see Figures 3.4 and 3.5). In two cremation graves only small fragments of the scale pans were recovered.

Figure 3.4 A balance found in a grave at Höggärde in Lockne parish (JLM 9036, c. AD 975/1000–25). Note how a crack in one of its scale pans (the right one in the picture) has been repaired by making three pairs of extra holes, through which thin threads were inserted. One of these threads is still in position. Diameter of the scale pans: c. 57 mm.

Source: Photo by Bengt Nordqvist, Jamtli.

Note: Two knots, where the suspension threads from each scale pan converged, are not shown in the picture.

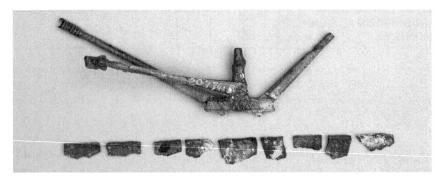

Figure 3.5 A balance found in a grave at Prästbordet in Brunflo parish (JLM 20774, tenth century).

Source: Photo by Bengt Nordqvist, Jamtli.

Figure 3.6 Some of the best-preserved weights found in Jämtland. Upper row from left: 1. Nyland, close to Josvedviken at Lake Storsjön, Rödön parish (JLM 25410). 2. Rösta in Ås parish (JLM 1001); diameter: 26.5 mm. 3. Sanne in Hackås parish (JLM 23347). Lower row: 1–3. Rösta (male grave I; SHM 12426). 4. Jormön in Lake Lill-Jorm, Frostviken parish (JLM 29826). 5. Vamsta in Brunflo parish (belonging to Brunflo *hembygdsförening*). The last is made of copper alloy; all the others are iron weights with a copper-alloy coating.

Source: Photo by Bengt Nordqvist, Jamtli.

All of the metal weights are shaped as oblate spheroids (Figure 3.6), with the sole exception of a small, cubo-octahedral weight in a set of weights in one of the inhumation graves. However, judging from the position of finds in inhumation graves, and from analogies, there are some other objects that probably or possibly have been used as weights as well, such as a knob from an oval brooch (for parallels see Kyhlberg 1980: 224–7 and Jansson 1985: 157), a cube of lead and two small stones.

Equipment for trade?

The use of weights and balances for measuring out the desired amount of silver in payment transactions is well attested in different kinds of sources (Kyhlberg 1980; Steuer 1987, 1997; Sperber 1996; Gustin 2004: 97–107; Kilger 2008, 2011; Brather 2010). But such equipment was also used to weigh non-ferrous metals in connection with casting activities, such as bronze casting (Gustin 2004: 107–8 and refs. therein; Pedersen 2008). Can it be that the weights and balances found in Jämtland have been used for the latter purpose?

The archaeological evidence contradicts this possibility. First, in three out of four inhumation graves in Jämtland, small amounts of hacksilver and silver coins (whole or in pieces) have been found lying together or in close proximity to a balance and one or several weights (Figure 3.7). This makes a

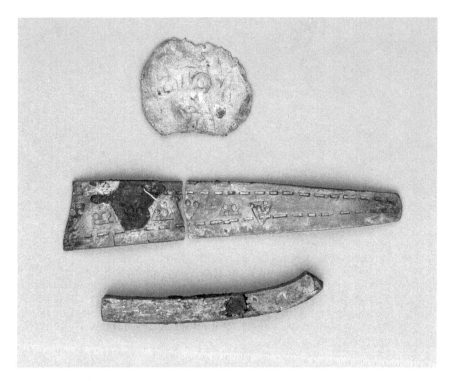

Figure 3.7 Silver found close to the balance (Figure 3.4) and a weight in the Höggärde grave (JLM 9036). Total weight: c. 10 g. Length of rod: 37 mm.

Source: Photo by Bengt Nordqvist, Jamtli.

strong argument that the weights and balances in question actually were used, and maybe also were intended to be used (in the afterlives of the deceased), for weighing silver in payment transactions. Second, in terms of their mass, the oblate spheroid weights found in Jämtland can, in general, be ascribed to the same weight standards that were commonly used in Birka and Sigtuna, for example, in the middle and late Viking period (Schultzén 2014, 2015). Their mass is often calibrated as a certain number of units (usually marked on their polar surfaces) corresponding to multiples of either c. 4.0 g or c. 4.27 g (see Table 3.1).[3] This suggests that the owners of the weights and balances were using the same principles of dealing with silver as people did at these trading centres.

A couple of finds are of special interest. As Figure 3.4 shows, the balance recovered in an inhumation grave at Höggärde, in Lockne parish, had been broken and subsequently repaired. This indicates that the balance was not new and that it had been frequently used by its owner before it ended up in the grave. The weight from a grave at Sanne, in Hackås parish, also bears

Silver as a medium of exchange in Jämtland 51

Table 3.1 A selection of oblate spheroid weights found in Jämtland and Härjedalen divided into two classes: one calibrated to a certain number of units corresponding to multiples of c. 4.0 g, the other calibrated to a certain number of units corresponding to multiples of c. 4.27 g

Units (punch-marks on the poles)	Modules: c. 4.0 g	c. 4.27 g
3 (2+1)	c. 12 g: #3	
6 (3+3)	c. 24 g: #3	c. 25.6 g: #Lj.
8		c. 34.2 g: #Lj.
10 (5+5)	c. 40 g: #3, #6, #12	c. 42.7 g: #8
14		c. 59.8 g: #1?

Note: Figures (#) refer to the finds in Holm 2015b: cat. 1; 'Lj.' refers to weights found in a grave at Ljungdalen, in Storsjö parish in Härjedalen, not far from the present Jämtland border (JLM 28050). The three best-preserved (but now missing) weights from find no. 3 (Man's Grave III at Rösta, Ås parish) are listed here with their weighed masses according to Kjellmark 1905. All others are listed with their reconstructed masses according to Schultzén 2015.

signs of having been used. At the point of manufacture, it must have weighed about 18.3 g, a mass deviating from all possible multiples of the units mentioned. However, on one of its poles, two furrows have been deliberately made, probably with a file (these are now filled with rust from its iron core; see Figure 3.6). The furrows might have been made to adjust the mass of the weight, reducing it to four units of either c. 4.0 g or c. 4.27 g, making the total mass c. 16 g or 17 g, which might have made it more useful (see Steuer 1997: 312–15 for similar cases).

My conclusions, based on analysis of the grave material from Jämtland, can be summarised as follows:

- The balances and weights found in graves have been produced mainly in distant emporia such as Birka and Sigtuna, and were used by people living in Jämtland primarily as tools for trade, namely to weigh silver in payment transactions. (This conclusion does not exclude the idea that the weighing equipment may have carried symbolic meanings when used in the funerary rites.)
- These finds are so common and so widespread among the population in the middle and late Viking period that trading in that period cannot have been restricted to or controlled by a small elite in Jämtland. Instead, many people living there were included in trading networks and participated in buying and selling goods to such an extent that they found it practical to use weighed silver as a medium of exchange.
- The grave finds suggest that mostly – but not exclusively – men were familiar with weights and balances as tools of trade.
- They belonged to households not only in the farming districts of Jämtland but outside the farming districts as well (cf. Figure 3.2).

52   *Olof Holm*

Supporting evidence

These conclusions based on the grave material gain support from other sources. A small silver hoard was found in the early eighteenth century at a farmstead on Frösön formerly called Kråksta (Zachrisson 1991; Wiséhn 1992: Cat. no. 14). It is not preserved but was reported as mainly consisting of Arabic (Islamic) coins cut into pieces. The fact that many coins had been fragmentised is to be expected in an area where silver was used as a means of payment according to weight. This observation also matches the cut coins found in the inhumation graves mentioned above. The Oriental origin of the coins suggests that the hoard was deposited in the middle Viking period.[4]

The runic inscription on the iron ring from Forsa in Hälsingland (Liestøl 1979) is also elucidatory. It has been dated to the tenth century on linguistic and runological grounds (Källström 2010) and tells us that a fine for a certain offence was, according to what was called 'the law of the people' (*liuðrēttr*), one ox and two *aura*. If the offence was repeated, the fine was to be doubled each time. The word *aura* is the plural accusative of *øyrir* (Sw. *öre*; Norw. *øre*), denoting a certain amount of silver (Källström 2010: 229; Jonsson 2011: 254). This piece of evidence shows that the value of such a weight unit of silver at that time was commonly known in Hälsingland, just as was the value of an ox. Reasonably, this implies that oxen as well as weighed silver were used as universal means of payment in this province – which lies not far south-east of Jämtland (cf. Figure 3.2)

A somewhat younger but still very early written source is a legal prescription from the now-lost older Frostathing Law, probably dating from the late eleventh or early twelfth century (*Frostatingslova*: xi; Ljungqvist 2014: 370–1). The prescription has been inserted and preserved in a paragraph (VII: 27) in the extant thirteenth-century version of the same law (*Norges gamle Love indtil 1387* I: 204). The Frostathing Law was the law valid in Trøndelag in Norway, bordering Jämtland in the east. The paragraph states that if the Norwegian king had proclaimed a ban on leaving the country (*farbann*), people were still allowed to travel abroad with the king's permission 'to Frösö or other fairs' (*til Frœseyiar eða i aðrar caupstemnur*) to carry on trading (*caupum caupa*) – even with the king's enemies, if they had gone there too. An institutionalised fair in central Jämtland, attracting visitors from far away, is just what can be expected at that point in time with regard to the widespread use of silver as a medium of exchange here since the tenth century. Fairs are important as interregional trade opportunities for the populace, and the visibility of marketplace transactions is necessary to deter fraud (Lie 1992: 513).

Concluding remarks

The Jämtland case demonstrates that even in a rural area far from the large trading centres of the Viking period, there might have been many people who were active in buying and selling goods, performing transactions with many partners and using silver as a medium of exchange – not dissimilar to what urban people did. To help them in this they had weights and balances, which in Jämtland are very commonly found in male graves from the middle and late Viking period.

But how do we explain why so many people in Jämtland were actively trading? An explanation that immediately suggests itself is that the conditions for grain production in this region were risky, due to the harsh climate. There are many historical parallels of marginal areas where farmers try to increase the margin of security against want by seeking out the possibilities of market-oriented production and extensive trade (see, e.g. Martens 1992; Maarbjerg 2001; Loveluck 2013: 361). With access to exchange products or capital, households had better chances to barter or buy things which they really needed but which were sometimes missing, such as seed after crop failures. Reasonably, this must have been an incentive not only for a few but for numerous farming households in Jämtland to get involved in trading activities and produce goods for exchange (Holm 2011: 213).

However, this explanation alone is not sufficient. Northern Norway, for example, was likewise a marginal area for farming, but it seems that silver did not circulate as a medium of exchange to any large extent there. Hoards found there usually consist of whole silver objects and scarcely any hacksilver (Hårdh 1996: 120, 172–3). A complementary explanation might be that Jämtland was a region characterised by comparatively low local stratification, which enabled popular participation in trade, while exchange in northern Norway may to a larger extent have been in the hands of chieftains (as outlined by Hansen 1990; this explanation is developed in Holm 2015b).

The evidence I have put forward suggests that Jämtland was not stratified in the middle and late Viking period to the degree that a small, dominant elite group was in control of trade. But there were still differences in wealth and power between households and individuals. For example, the wealth necessary to acquire and deposit the valuable horse equipment in male grave III at Rösta, in Ås parish (SHM 12426), including silver-coated bridle mounts (Kjellmark 1905: Fig. 11), appears different from the more modest wealth needed for depositing the simple horse equipment in the contemporary or somewhat older grave at Höggärde, in Lockne parish (i.e. the grave with the repaired balance, JLM 9036). The state-of-the-art sword of Petersen's type S with silver inlay on the pommel and guards (Holm 2015b: Fig. 10), deposited in the grave at Jormön in Frostviken parish (JLM 29826), displays greater affluence than, for example, the simpler type-M sword (though with a decorated antler grip) deposited in another, probably somewhat older grave in a mountainous area of Jämtland (Holm 2015a).

Popular involvement in trade in Jämtland must also have been facilitated by the fact that winter, not summer, was the best season for transport in this part of Scandinavia (cf. Friberg 1951: 78–9, 88, 104, 119, 276–81). Members of the farmers' households were in wintertime not occupied with agricultural activities and thus more free to travel with their horses on trading journeys, using sledges for transporting goods. Other factors might have been important

54   *Olof Holm*

as well, such as the peculiar geographical position of Jämtland, between eastern and western Scandinavia, in an area where the mountain range was comparatively low (Figure 3.1), and economic complementarity between farmers and other groups of people living in the region.

The evidence put forward in this chapter originates from the middle and late Viking period. In the early Viking period (late eighth century – c. 875), people in Jämtland might have been involved in trading networks as well, using media of exchange other than silver, or to a large extent trading one commodity directly for another. This is impossible to know, due to the lack of sources. However, it seems very likely that silver facilitated exchange, once it became more accessible in the middle Viking period and once principles of dealing with it were accepted. It is thus possible that the use of silver as a medium of exchange stimulated the economy as a whole in the region of Jämtland – a region which saw a considerable population growth throughout the Viking period (Holm 2011: 222).

A final reflection might be appropriate. The Viking-period expansion of trade in Jämtland and the acceptance of principles of dealing with silver as a medium of exchange came about even though Jämtland was not incorporated into a medieval kingdom. In *Historia Norwegie* (c. 1150/75) Jämtland is still described as belonging neither to Norway nor to *Svethiudh* (the core of the Swedish realm; Holm 2003: 183). This reminds us of the relevance of a remark made by Dagfinn Skre (2008: 340), namely that 'production and trade grow out of natural conditions, social relationships, cultural norms and an economic agency all of which lay well beyond the range of control of the earliest kings' (cf. Sindbæk 2005: 25–7, 266–7; Roslund 2009: 219, 237–8; Loveluck 2013: 367).

Acknowledgements

The research presented in this chapter was funded by Landsprosten Erik Anderssons Minnesfond and by a postdoctoral scholarship from the Department of History, Stockholm University. My thanks especially to Joakim Schultzén (Archaeological Research Laboratory, Stockholm University) for analysing the mass of several weights and to Bengt Nordqvist and Anders Edvinsson (JLM) for help with accessing finds.

Abbreviations

JLM: Jamtli (Jämtlands läns museum), Östersund, Sweden (number denotes inventory number)

SHM: Historiska museet, Stockholm (number denotes inventory number)

Notes

1 For two other recently published regional case studies, see Gullbekk (2014) on Vestfold and Ingvardson (2014) on Bornholm.

Silver as a medium of exchange in Jämtland   55

2 Anne Stalsberg (1991: 78–9) asserts that '17%' of 47 gendered graves in Norway containing balances are female graves. That figure, often cited in the literature (e.g. Sørheim 2014: 114), is not reliable, since she has included a number of non-expertly recovered and obviously mixed or uncertain grave finds in her calculation (see Christensen 1996: 6–8). Erik Jondell (1974: 34), analysing the same material, could not observe any definite female graves containing balances.

3 The best-preserved weights from Jämtland have been analysed by Joakim Schultzén at the Archaeological Research Laboratory, Stockholm University, using CAD methodology to digitally reconstruct their original volumes and masses (for the method, see Schultzén 2011).

4 Another lost hoard consisting of Islamic coins has been reported from Hällesjö in eastern Jämtland (Hasselberg 1976: 11–12). A couple of stray finds of Viking-period coins and hacksilver have been recorded as well (Wiséhn 1992: Cat. no. 22; JLM 996).

References

Blackburn, Mark 2008: The Coin Finds. In: Skre, Dagfinn (ed.): *Means of Exchange: Dealing with Silver in the Viking Age*. Kaupang Excavation Project Publication Series, vol. 2. Norske Oldfunn, vol. 23: 29–74. Aarhus University Press. Århus.

Brather, Sebastian 2010: Silver, Weights and Scales around the Baltic, 8th to 11th Centuries. In: Ludowici, Babette, Hauke Jöns, Sunhild Kleingärtner, Jonathan Scheschkewitz and Matthias Hardt (eds): *Trade and Communication Networks of the First Millennium AD in the Northern Part of Central Europe*. Neue Studien zur Sachsenforschung, vol. 1: 143–64. Theiss. Stuttgart.

Christensen, Johan 1996: *Kvinnor, män och vågar*. Unpublished seminar paper in archaeology, Stockholm University.

Friberg, Nils 1951: *Vägarna i Västernorrlands län: Typiska drag i deras naturgeografiska struktur och äldre utveckling jämte utblickar över det svenska vägväsendet i övrigt, speciellt i Norrland*, vol. 1. Meddelande från Geografiska institutet vid Stockholms högskola, vol. 80. A. Åströms. Härnösand.

Frostatingslova. Hagland, Jan Ragnar and Jørn Sandnes (trans.) 1994: Norrøne bokverk. Det Norske Samlaget. Oslo.

Gräslund, Anne-Sofie 1980: *Birka*, vol. IV. *The Burial Customs*. Kungl. Vitterhets Historie och Antikvitets Akademien. Stockholm.

Gullbekk, Svein Harald 2014: Vestfold: A Monetary Perspective on the Viking Age. In: Naismith, Rory, Martin Allen and Elina Screen (eds): *Early Medieval Monetary History: Studies in Memory of Mark Blackburn*, pp. 331–47. Ashgate. Aldershot.

Gustin, Ingrid 2004: *Mellan gåva och marknad: Handel, tillit och materiell kultur under vikingatid*. Lund Studies in Medieval Archaeology, vol. 34. Almqvist and Wiksell. Stockholm.

—— 2011: Coin Stock and Coin Circulation in Birka. In: Graham-Campbell, James, Søren Sindbæk and Gareth Williams (eds.): *Silver Economies, Monetisation and Society in Scandinavia, AD 800–1100*, pp. 227–44. Aarhus University Press. Århus.

Hansen, Lars Ivar 1990: *Samisk fangstsamfunn og norsk høvdingøkonomi*. Novus. Oslo.

Hasselberg, Bertil 1976: Hällesjö sockens äldre historia. In: Hasselberg, Bertil, Harald Eriksson and Gustav Lund: *Bidrag till Hällesjö sockens historia*, vol. 1: 11–127.

Historia Norwegie. Inger Ekrem and Lars Boje Mortensen (eds), Peter Fisher (trans.) 2003. Museum Tusculanum. København.

Holm, Olof 2001: Jämtarnas kyrkobyggande under medeltiden. *Jämten*, 95: 86–106.

56   Olof Holm

—— 2003: Den norsk-svenska riksgränsens ålder och hävd: En studie av rikssamlingsprocesser och gränsbildning i mellersta Skandinavien. *Collegium medievale*, 16: 135–237.

—— 2011: Jämtlands karaktärsdrag 1000–1645: Försök till en syntes och förslag till vidare forskning. In: Holm, Olof (ed.): *Jämtland och den jämtländska världen 1000–1645.* Konferenser, vol. 75: 206–41. Kungl. Vitterhets Historie och Antikvitets Akademien. Stockholm.

—— 2012: *Självägarområdenas egenart: Jämtland och andra områden i Skandinavien med småskaligt jordägande 900–1500.* PhD thesis in history, Stockholm University.

—— 2015a: A Viking Period Sword from Skäckerfjällen with a Decorated Antler Grip. *Fornvännen*, 110: 289–90.

—— 2015b: Trading in Viking-Period Scandinavia: A Business Only for a Few? The Jämtland Case. *Viking and Medieval Scandinavia*, 11: 79–126.

Hårdh, Birgitta 1996: *Silver in the Viking Age: A Regional-Economic Study.* Studia archaeologica Lundensia. Series in 8°, vol. 25. Almqvist and Wiksell. Stockholm.

Ingvardson, Gitte Tarnow 2014: Trade and Power: Bornholm in the Late Viking Age. In: Gulløv, Hans Christian (ed.): *Northern Worlds: Landscapes, Interactions and Dynamics. Research at the National Museum of Denmark.* Publications from the National Museum. Studies in Archaeology and History, vol. 22: 325–37. Copenhagen.

Jansson, Ingmar 1985: *Ovala spännbucklor: En studie av vikingatida standardsmycken med utgångspunkt från Björkö-fynden.* Aun, vol. 7. Uppsala University Institute of North European Archaeology. Uppsala.

Jondell, Erik 1974: Vikingatidens balansvågar i Norge. Unpublished seminar paper in archaeology, Uppsala University.

Jonsson, Kenneth 2011: Sweden in the Tenth Century: a Monetary Economy? In: Graham-Campbell, James, Søren Sindbæk and Gareth Williams (eds): *Silver Economies, Monetisation and Society in Scandinavia, AD 800–1100*, pp. 245–57. Aarhus University Press. Århus.

Kilger, Christoph 2008: Wholeness and Holiness: Counting, Weighing and Valuing Silver in the Early Viking Period. In: Skre, Dagfinn (ed.): *Means of Exchange: Dealing with Silver in the Viking Age.* Kaupang Excavation Project Publication Series, vol. 2. Norske Oldfunn, vol. 23: 253–325. Aarhus University Press. Århus.

—— 2011: Hack-Silver, Weights and Coinage: The Anglo-Scandinavian Bullion Coinages and their Use in Late Viking-Age Society. In: Graham-Campbell, James, Søren Sindbæk and Gareth Williams (eds): *Silver Economies, Monetisation and Society in Scandinavia, AD 800–1100*, pp. 259–81. Aarhus University Press. Århus.

Kjellmark, Knut 1905: Ett graffält från den yngre järnåldern i Ås i Jämtland. *Ymer*, 25: 351–71.

Kyhlberg, Ola 1980: *Vikt och värde: Arkeologiska studier i värdemätning, betalningsmedel och metrologi under yngre järnålder. I Helgö. II Birka.* Acta Universitatis Stockholmiensis. Stockholm Studies in Archaeology, vol. 1. Stockholm.

Källström, Magnus 2010: Forsaringen tillhör 900-talet. *Fornvännen*, 105: 228–32.

Lie, John 1992: The Concept of Mode of Exchange. *American Sociological Review*, 57: 508–23.

Liestøl, Aslak 1979: Runeringen i Forsa: Kva er han, og når vart han smidd? *Saga och sed*, 1979: 12–27.

Ljungqvist, Fredrik Charpentier 2014: *Kungamakten och lagen: En jämförelse mellan Danmark, Norge och Sverige under högmedeltiden.* PhD thesis, Stockholm University.

Loveluck, Christopher 2013: *Northwest Europe in the Early Middle Ages, c. AD 600–1150: A Comparative Archaeology.* Cambridge University Press. Cambridge.

Maarbjerg, John P. 2001: The Peasant, His Land and Money: Land Transactions in Late Sixteenth-Century East Bothnia. *Scandinavian Journal of History*, 26: 53–68.

Magnusson, Gert 1986: *Lågteknisk järnhantering i Jämtlands län.* Jernkontorets bergshistoriska skriftserie, vol. 22. Jernkontoret. Stockholm.

Martens, Irmelin 1992: Some Aspects of Marginal Settlement in Norway during the Viking Age and the Middle Ages. In: Morris, Christopher D. and D. James Rackham (eds): *Norse and Later Settlement and Subsistence in the North Atlantic.* Occasional Paper Series, vol. 1: 1–7. Department of Archaeology, University of Glasgow. Glasgow.

Melitz, Jacques 1974: *Primitive and Modern Money: An Interdisciplinary Approach.* Addison-Wesley. Reading, MA.

Norges gamle Love indtil 1387. Rudolf Keyser and P.A. Munch (eds) 1846–95, vols I–V. Chr. Gröndahl. Christiania.

Pedersen, Unn 2008: Weights and Balances. In: Skre, Dagfinn (ed.): *Means of Exchange: Dealing with Silver in the Viking Age.* Kaupang Excavation Project Publication Series, vol. 2. Norske Oldfunn, vol. 23: 119–95. Aarhus University Press. Århus.

Roslund, Mats 2009: Varuutbyte och social identitet. Alsengemmer som emblematisk stil. In: Mogren, Mats, *Mats* Roslund, Barbro Sundner and Jes Wienberg (eds): *Triangulering: Historisk arkeologi vidgar fälten.* Lund Studies in Historical Archaeology, vol. 11: 216–42. Department of Archaeology and Ancient History, Lund University. Lund.

Sawyer, Birgit, and Peter Sawyer 1993: *Medieval Scandinavia: From Conversion to Reformation, circa 800–1500.* The Nordic Series, vol. 17. University of Minnesota Press. Minneapolis, MN.

Schultzén, Joakim M. 2011: Remodelling the Past: Archaeometrological Analysis Applied on Birka Weight Material Using a 3D Scanner and Computer-Aided Design. *Journal of Archaeological Science*, 38: 2378–86.

—— 2014: On the Metrology of Birka and Early Sigtuna: Tools of Trade in the Viking Age Lake Mälaren Valley. *Archäologisches Korrespondenzblatt*, 44(1): 127–35.

—— 2015: Archaeometrological Study of Bi-Polar Spheroid Weights from Jämtland and Härjedalen, Sweden. Unpublished report, Archaeological Research Laboratory, Stockholm University.

Sindbæk, Søren M. 2005: *Ruter og rutinisering: Vikingetidens fjernhandel i Nordeuropa.* Multivers. København.

Skre, Dagfinn 2008: Post-Substantivist Towns and Trade AD 600–1000. In: Skre, Dagfinn (ed.): *Means of Exchange: Dealing with Silver in the Viking Age.* Kaupang Excavation Project Publication Series, vol. 2. Norske Oldfunn, vol. 23: 327–41. Aarhus University Press. Århus.

—— 2011: Commodity Money, Silver and Coinage in Viking-Age Scandinavia. In: Graham-Campbell, James, Søren Sindbæk and Gareth Williams (eds): *Silver Economies, Monetisation and Society in Scandinavia, AD 800–1100*, pp. 67–91. Aarhus University Press. Århus.

Söderberg, Anders 2008: Metall- och glashantverk. In: Wikström, Anders (ed.): *På väg mot paradiset: Arkeologisk undersökning i kvarteret Humlegården 3 i Sigtuna 2006.* Meddelanden och rapporter från Sigtuna museer, vol. 33: 97–130. Sigtuna.

Sørheim, Helge 2014: Female Traders and Sorceresses. In: Coleman, Nancy L. and Nanna Løkka (eds): *Kvinner i vikingtid*, pp. 107–19. Scandinavian Academic Press. Oslo.

58 *Olof Holm*

Sperber, Erik 1996: *Balances, Weights and Weighing in Ancient and Early Medieval Sweden.* Theses and Papers in Scientific Archaeology 2. Stockholm University. Stockholm.

Stalsberg, Anne 1991: Women as Actors in North European Viking Age Trade. In: Samson, Ross (ed.): *Social Approaches to Viking Studies*, pp. 75–83. Cruithne Press. Glasgow.

Steuer, Heiko 1987: Gewichtsgeldwirtschaften im frühgeschichtlichen Europa. In: Düwel, Klaus, Herbert Jankuhn, Harald Siems and Dieter Timpe (eds): *Untersuchungen zu Handel und Verkehr der vor- und frühgeschichtlichen Zeit in Mittel- und Nordeuropa*, vol. 4. *Der Handel der Karolinger- und Wikingerzeit*. Abhandlungen der Akademie der Wissenschaften in Göttingen. Phil.-Hist. Klasse. 3. F., vol. 156: 405–527. Vandenhoeck and Ruprecht. Göttingen.

—— 1997: *Waagen und Gewichte aus dem mittelalterlichen Schleswig. Funde des 11. bis 13. Jahrhunderts aus Europa als Quellen zur Handels- und Währungsgeschichte.* Zeitschrift für Archäologie des Mittelalters. Beiheft 10. Rheinland-Vlg/Habelt. Köln/Bonn.

Williams, Gareth 2011: Silver Economies, Monetisation and Society: An Overview. In: Graham-Campbell, James, Søren Sindbæk and Gareth Williams (eds): *Silver Economies, Monetisation and Society in Scandinavia, AD 800–1100*, pp. 337–72. Aarhus University Press. Århus.

Wiséhn, Eva 1992: *Sveriges mynthistoria: Landskapsinventeringen*, vol. 7. *Myntfynd från Härjedalen, Jämtland och Medelpad.* Kungl. Myntkabinettet. Stockholm.

Zachrisson, Inger 1991: En vikingatida myntskatt från Jämtland. *Svensk numismatisk tidskrift*, 1991(4–5): 96–9.

4 Domestic and exotic materials in early medieval Norwegian towns

An archaeological perspective on production, procurement and consumption

Gitte Hansen

Introduction

A new generation of towns emerged in Norway in the late tenth to early eleventh centuries. During the Middle Ages the towns became local, regional or even superregional and international centres of administration, religion and trade. What types of production took place in these towns; what was consumed? From where and how did raw materials and produce end up there? In research on towns of the Viking Age these are almost classical questions that have received much attention (e.g. Callmer 1994; Sindbæk 2005, 2007). In contrast to this situation, broad comparative studies of medieval urban production, procurement and consumption of domestic and exotic materials are rare; most often towns, crafts, objects or raw material groups are treated individually (e.g. Christophersen and Walaker Nordeide 1994; Hansen 2005; Baug 2013; and papers in Gläser et al. 1999; Gläser et al. 2006; Gläser et al. 2008; Engberg et al. 2009). In a Scandinavian context Broberg and Hasselmo's (1982) study of seven Swedish towns is still a rare example of a broader synthesising approach.

The present chapter is a first attempt to give a broadly based overview of early medieval Norwegian urban production, procurement and consumption of domestic and exotic materials. The chapter is mainly based on archaeological sources. It is broad in the sense that it involves several types of production, raw materials and goods and applies a comparative perspective where most of the known early medieval Norwegian urban sites are included. It is narrow, however, in its time perspective, focusing in detail on the early phases of the towns' history, from their beginnings in the tenth or early eleventh century to the middle of the twelfth century. The survey includes major productive activities carried out in the early medieval Norwegian towns and the raw materials included in the production. The most frequent domestic and exotic products consumed in the towns are also included. Procurement networks that supplied the urban consumers with raw materials and goods are addressed on a general level with a view to the resource areas that delivered the raw materials

60   *Gitte Hansen*

and products. The social aspects of the networks will not be addressed at any length, since this is a subject that cannot be given justice within the limits of the chapter. The aims are thus to give a first overview and a discussion of immediate patterns, and to uncover potential for further studies.

Data and methodology

In documentary records, fourteen places are mentioned in urban terms in relation to the period before 1200 in medieval Norway (Helle and Nedkvitne 1977: 206). With the exception of Steinkjer in Nord-Trøndelag County, where no relevant data is found for the period in focus here (Helle et al. 2006: 53), all of these places are included. To avoid the classic discussion of *if* and *when* these places were towns, I cut the Gordian knot and call them *towns* from their earliest non-rural phases onwards. Dates for the first relevant activities differ. In Trondheim, Veøy, Borgund, Kaupanger and Skien, non-rural activities based on various criteria and levels of certainty date from different parts of the tenth century (Myrvoll 1992: 167; Christophersen and Walaker Nordeide 1994: 266–74, Fig. 23; Knagenhjelm 2008; Larsen 2008; Solli 2008: 122; Brendalsmo and Molaug 2014). Meanwhile, in Vågan, Bergen, Stavanger, Tønsberg, Oslo, Hamar, Borg (Sarpsborg) and Kungahälla (the latter located in present-day Sweden), the first non-rural activities are tentatively dated to parts of the eleventh century (Lindh 1992; Hansen 2005; Helle et al. 2006: 41–62; Carlsson 2008: 229; Molaug 2008: 76; Ulriksen 2008: 96–7). Figure 4.1 shows the location of the places in today's counties and the approximate dates of their oldest non-rural phases. The survey addresses production and consumption in the first 150 to 200 years of the towns' history, here called *the early medieval period*, from their beginnings to the mid-twelfth century (c. 1150–70). As a finely meshed chronology for the early medieval period is not available for most places, the period is treated as a whole.

To establish analytical categories, the towns are classified as large, medium or small based on the approximate number of monuments erected or initiated during the early Middle Ages (see survey of monumental building activities below; for a similar approach, see Andrén 1985). Furthermore, a distinction is made between the western and eastern Norwegian towns.

- Small – one or two monuments: Veøy, Kaupanger, Stavanger, Hamar and Borg.
- Medium – three to five monuments: Borgund, Skien, Tønsberg and Kungahälla.
- Large – six or more monuments: Trondheim, Bergen and Oslo.

The grouping is rough, and knowing in retrospect that places like Hamar and Stavanger became important ecclesiastical centres, and that Borgund in the late fourteenth century was characterised as a small trading place (koupstad) in a law of 1384 (NgL: 222), it might be argued that the number of early medieval

Figure 4.1 Counties in today's Norway and thirteen early medieval towns in medieval Norway, with approximate dates for the oldest non-agrarian activities. The size of the dots reflect the size of the town: L = large, M = medium, S = small.

Source: Map by Gitte Hansen.

monuments is not a valid measure of size or 'importance'. In the present survey, however, the early medieval period is in focus and a perspective from this period is considered relevant.

62   *Gitte Hansen*

For Scandinavia, written sources that concern urban production, consumption and procurement of materials and goods are rare and deal almost exclusively with periods after the early Middle Ages. For our purpose the archaeological data thus constitutes the main source. Information from the urban places varies greatly, for example from the written records' brief mention of the foundation of a church or of small-scale archaeological data from the early days of medieval archaeology, to detailed datasets retrieved in recent decades from large-scale excavations. In Trondheim, Bergen, Tønsberg and Oslo large-scale excavations have been carried out and much data has been investigated and made accessible (e.g. Oslo 1977–91; Bergen 1985–2013; Trondheim 1985–94; Tønsberg 1989; Christophersen and Walaker Nordeide 1994; NIKU 1996–2016; papers in Andersson et al. 2008). For these places it seems likely that the published and otherwise accessible data is fairly representative for production and consumption in these towns' early medieval phases. Objects dating before 1100 are, for methodological reasons, limited in Bergen, but from c. 1100 the dataset is considered fairly representative for activities here (Hansen 2005). The sources for Skien and Kungahälla also seem quite satisfactory; here a few, rather large sites excavated by modern methods provide relevant finely meshed information (e.g. Myrvoll 1992; Andersson et al. 2001). While it is hard to judge whether the material from these two towns is representative in the true meaning of the word, here it is assumed that the finds reflect some general trends for the towns. From Veøy and Kaupanger, old, relatively small-scale excavation data, supplemented with more recent pinpoint investigations, gives valuable insight albeit not so finely meshed as regards dating (Solli 1996, 2008; Knagenhjelm 2004, 2008). From Borgund a large dataset exists, but only a few artefact categories have been studied, and generally the data is not published in any detail (e.g. Larsen 2008). Regarding Stavanger, data is sparse, mostly retrieved during the early days of medieval archaeology (e.g. Lillehammer 1972), and is not extensively published. From Vågan (Bertelsen 2008) and Hamar archaeological sources are not informative for the period under research.

If the available sources from the individual sites were representative of the production and consumption occurring during the early medieval period, one might conclude based on both the presence of materials and *ex silentio*. However, with the actual variation in the level of detail and amount of data from town to town, the main approach in this survey has been to emphasise the presence rather than absence of information, and thematically include the individual towns in so far as relevant data was available. Archaeological and historical studies of individual towns, crafts, object groups and raw materials, syntheses of large excavation projects and to some extent original documentation in museum archives have been surveyed.

In a comprehensive study of activities in early medieval Bergen, sixteen productive activities were identified archaeologically (Table 4.1) (Hansen 2005: Tab. 58). The Bergen list gives an empirically well-founded example of the rather narrow scope of archaeologically recognised crafts encountered in a newly established early medieval Norwegian town. In several of the contemporary towns many of the same activities are found. Here an overview is attempted for the most common and most raw material/resource-demanding

Table 4.1 Production documented from c. 1020/30–c. 1170 in Bergen

Date	Combmaking	Antler, bone, horn and whale/walrus bone working	Shoemaking	Leatherworking	Metalworking	Large-scale stoneworking	Small-scale stoneworking	Large-scale woodworking	Small-scale woodworking	Skin dressing	Textile production	Fishing	Hunting/war/game	Basic cooking	Food processing	Beverage processing
1020/30– c. 1070						?										?
c. 1070– c. 1100			?	?		X		X				?		?		?
c. 1100– c. 1120s		X			X	X	X	X	X	X			X		X	X
c. 1120s– c. 1170	X	X			X	X	X	X	X	X	X	X	X	X	X	X

Source: After Hansen (2005: Tab. 58).

productive activities. Also, the most commonly recognised domestic and exotic objects are included in the survey and the presence of early medieval monumental structures mentioned in written records is incorporated.

The raw materials and objects in focus originated from Norway (domestic) and from areas outside medieval Norway (exotic) and were brought to the towns through procurement networks. As already mentioned, the social dimensions of networks are not addressed at any length here. The distances between the towns and source areas define procurement networks with three levels of geographical reach: (1) Networks with a *regional* reach that supplied the towns with resources and products derived from the town's hinterland. The hinterland is defined broadly as the modern-day county where the respective towns are located (cf. Figure 4.1); (2) Networks with an *interregional* reach that supplied the towns with materials from domestic regions beyond the county; (3) Networks with an *international* reach that supplied the towns with exotic resources and objects. The presentation follows this three-levelled scale: First, large-scale production requiring domestic raw materials; second, small-scale crafts production involving domestic and exotic materials and portable objects made of domestic stone materials; and third, imported pottery.

Production, procurement and consumption

Constructing the towns: consumption of stone and timber

The large-scale production carried out in the early medieval towns involved construction of the towns' buildings and infrastructure. From archaeological

64   *Gitte Hansen*

and written sources we know that churches, royal seats, bishops' seats and monasteries were planned and erected in this period. Often the exact number of monuments is difficult to establish and it is hard to decide how to count successive generations of buildings. A tentative overview shows the following: in Vågan one church was founded and in Trondheim the number adds up to about nine (Helle et al. 2006: 50–4), at Veøy two or three (Solli 1996), at Borgund three or four (Larsen 2008: 42), at Kaupanger one (Knagenhjelm 2008), in Bergen fifteen monuments were initiated before 1170 (Hansen 2005), in Stavanger at least one (Helle et al. 2006: 48) and in Skien one church and two monasteries (Myrvoll 1992: 17), altogether making three monumental building complexes, in Tønsberg perhaps four or five (Ulriksen 2008), in Oslo about six (Molaug 2008: 76–85), at Hamar at least one, two at Borg (Helle et al. 2006: 58) and finally three or perhaps four in Kungahälla (Carlsson 2008: 229–30). Most of the monuments were, if not initially, then eventually built in *stone* and altogether more than fifty stone-built monumental structures were initiated in the towns' early medieval period. Some may have been quite small so an assessment of stone resource demands should be balanced according to the place in focus. Still, from the end of the eleventh/beginning of the twelfth century, stone seems to be the preferred material, and then only roof constructions and details in the building were made of wood (Ekroll et al. 2000: 11, 19).

Wood was the main resource used in the towns' non-monumental secular settlement and the towns' infrastructures – roads, passages, wells, harbour structures, etc. – were almost exclusively built in timber. Figure 4.2 shows the reconstruction of central areas of the largest towns in the eleventh to twelfth centuries: Trondheim, Bergen and Oslo. We get the impression of rather sparsely built settlement areas. The eleventh to twelfth-century Norwegian towns were not very large by any measures. Still, some towns, notably Bergen and Oslo, were repeatedly ravaged by large fires and the need for fresh timber was significant, even though wood was reused (Hansen 2015a). An estimate based on archaeological data suggests that 10,000 *mål* (1 mål = 1000 m^2) of woodland was required to meet the demand for buildings in Oslo about AD 1300 (Fett 1989: 85–8). The estimate is not directly transferrable to the early medieval phases of the towns, but nevertheless gives an idea of the demand for timber to satisfy the needs of a medieval urban community in Norway.

It's obvious that we are dealing with large amounts of stone and wood, which had to be procured and transported to the new towns. Building stones that have been identified in early medieval monuments in different parts of the country include granite in the Østfold and Vestfold counties, limestone in the Mjøsregion, marble in Trøndelag and Northern Norway and chlorite schist and soapstone in West and Central Norway (Ekroll et al. 2000: 22). The type of stone that was used thus varies from one part of the country to another, and suggests a regional provenance of raw materials. Geological and archaeological cross-disciplinary determination of the provenance of chlorite schist building stone in the Stavanger cathedral, chlorite schist and soapstone used in the Nidaros Cathedral in Trondheim and soapstone in the twelfth-century Bergen

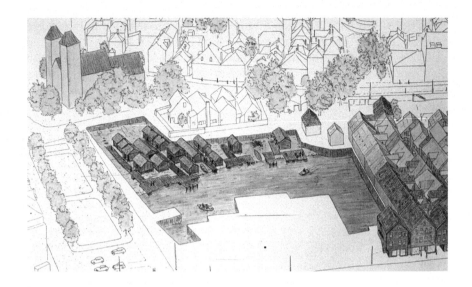

a

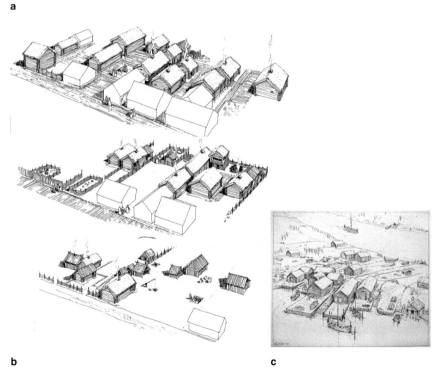

b   c

Figure 4.2 Reconstruction of central settlement areas in early medieval Bergen (a), Oslo (b) and Trondheim (c).

Source: Trondheim: from Christophersen and Nordeide (1994: Fig. 222), drawing by Kari Støren Binns; Oslo: from Molaug 2008, drawing by Marianne Brochmann; Bergen: drawing by Egill Reimers and Per Bækken ©University Museum of Bergen.

66   *Gitte Hansen*

churches confirms that both ashlars and ornamental stones came from regional quarries (Ekroll et al. 2000: 22; Storemyr and Heldal 2002; Jansen 2005; Jansen et al. 2009; Storemyr et al. 2010; Storemyr 2015: 173–236). For wood, growth ring patterns in Norwegian conifer dendro-chronologies show that consumers in Trondheim, Bergen and Oslo received their construction timber from regional forests (Thun 2002: 218–27).

To sum up, large-scale investments in building the towns' infrastructure were carried out. The production required large quantities of stone and wood, obtained from regional quarries and forests.

Small-scale crafts: consumption involving domestic and exotic raw materials

Articles for everyday use and personal accessories were produced and consumed in the towns. Here crafts production and consumption related to iron working, non-ferrous metalworking, comb production and shoemaking are treated. Some of these productive activities potentially involved raw materials of both domestic and exotic origin (see Table 4.2).

Iron may have been supplied to the towns as a raw material that was further processed in town or as finished objects. In the archaeological literature, *iron working* in the towns is mainly identified through finds of slag and scrap iron (Hansen 2005: 165 with references). In central areas of Trondheim deposits of small amounts of slag dating from c. 1000 and throughout the early medieval period are interpreted as the remains of iron working (Bergquist 1989: 108–21). From c. 1150 and on, large-scale iron production was established in the outskirts of the town (Christophersen 2015). At Veøy smithies were

Table 4.2 Summary of the small-scale urban production involving domestic and exotic raw materials in early medieval Norway. 10th: Tenth century, E11th: Early eleventh century (c. 1000–1030), M11th: Middle eleventh century (c. 1030–70), L11th: Late eleventh century (c. 1070–1100), E12th: Early twelfth century (c. 1100–30), M12th: Middle twelfth century (c. 1130–70)

			Metalworking/iron					
	Size	*Site name*	*10th*	*E11th*	*M11th*	*L11th*	*E12th*	*M12th*
West	L	Trondheim 900s–						
	S	Veøy 900s–						
	S	Kaupanger 900s/1000–s						
	L	Bergen 1020/30–						
East	M	Tønsberg 1000s–						
	L	Oslo c. 1000–						
	M	Kungahälla c. 1100–						

	Size	Site name	Metalworking/non-ferrous					
			10th	E11th	M11th	L11th	E12th	M12th
West	L	Trondheim 900s–						
West	L	Bergen 1020/30–						
East	M	Skien 900s–						
East	M	Tønsberg 1000s–						
East	L	Oslo c. 1000–						
East	M	Kungahälla c. 1100–						

	Size	Site name	Combmaking					
			10th	E11th	M11th	L11th	E12th	M12th
West	L	Trondheim 900s–						
West	L	Bergen 1020/30–						
West	S	Stavanger 1100s–						
East	M	Skien 900s–						
East	M	Tønsberg 1000s–						
East	L	Oslo c. 1000–						
East	M	Kungahälla c. 1100–						

	Size	Site name	Shoemaking						E = embroidery, S = silk yarn
			10th	E11th	M11th	L11th	E12th	M12th	
West	L	Trondheim 900s–							E/S
West	M	Borgund 900/1000s–?							E
West	L	Bergen 1020/30–							E/S
East	M	Skien 900s–							E
East	M	Tønsberg 1000s–							
East	L	Oslo c. 1000–							E/S
East	M	Kungahälla c. 1100–							

Note: Merged cells = broad dating evidence. Only towns with available data are included.

68   *Gitte Hansen*

established in the course of the twelfth century, and iron working intensified in the subsequent periods (Solli 1996: 176). At Kaupanger iron working dates back to the period under research and is intensified in the subsequent periods (Knagenhjelm 2008: 64 and Christoffer Knagenhjelm pers. comm. 2016). In Bergen, iron working is documented through small amounts of slag from the 1120s and, according to written sources, some blacksmiths were probably sedentary from the mid-twelfth century (Hansen 2005: 165–8). In Tønsberg iron working is documented from c. 1150 onwards (Jakobsen 1991). In Oslo slag associated with iron working is found from the late eleventh century (Molaug 2002: 62, Petter Molaug pers. comm. 2016). In Kungahälla, iron working is documented through small amounts of slag from c. 1140 (Rytter 2001: 78, 104).

As seen in Table 4.2, iron working has been documented in seven of the towns. In Trondheim, Bergen, Tønsberg, Oslo and Kungahälla the documented iron working seems modest, with only small amounts of slag found. In the smaller west Norwegian towns of Veøy and Kaupanger, data is too sparse to make any speculations on the size of production in the early Middle Ages, but iron working seems to become important here, as in Trondheim, in the periods to come. The craft was probably carried out by both sedentary and itinerant smiths (Hansen 2005, 2015b). Iron working is documented to have taken place in central parts of the towns where ordinary people lived. Additional iron working may, being a fire hazardous activity, perhaps also have been carried out in the outskirts of the towns, as mandated in Magnus Lagabøter's late thirteenth-century town law (Helle 1982: 432 with references). In Bergen no traces of major iron working have been found in the outskirts of the early medieval town even though large areas have been investigated, so for this town the impression of modest early medieval production is still valid. Iron may well also have been worked in connection with the development of monumental buildings, but this cannot be substantiated from the archaeological sources at hand. The impression from the survey is thus that iron working in large and medium towns both in the west and east of Norway was rather modest in the early medieval period. The size of production in small western towns awaits further research.

Urban consumption of iron has to date not been studied in detail, and information on iron finds from the above-mentioned towns is scarce. In a pilot study the variety of objects used, and the amount of iron needed in medieval Scandinavian towns, was addressed with Bergen as one of the cases. A compilation of iron object categories found in mid-twelfth–century Bergen showed that, even if the repertoire of objects was not particularly wide, iron was used in many spheres of life, for example in connection with buildings e.g. door hinges and door locks, and as portable objects e.g. tools and keys (Andersson et al. 2015). It is possible that this applies to all towns. In Skien, iron objects are thus found from the earliest phases and onwards (Myrvoll 1992: Appendix), and the same applies to Oslo (G. Færden 1990: Tab. p. 183).

The urban consumption of iron is worth more consideration. When the amount of iron consumed in a fifty-year period in mid-twelfth-century Bergen was estimated, quite surprising results came up: Based on the weight of

Materials in early medieval Norwegian towns   69

archaeological objects of iron retrieved per excavated m², and the size of Bergen in the mid-twelfth century, a calculation showed that iron objects amounting to only c. 82 kg would have been lost or discarded by the townspeople during this time, and thus would have gone out of circulation. Even if the weight is multiplied several times to consider, for instance, taphonomic factors, the amount of iron that went out of use was much smaller than expected (for further details see Andersson et al. 2015: 223–5). So, in spite of the fact that the calculation does not directly reflect the amount of iron in circulation in Bergen, one is still left with the impression that Bergen was not a large consumer of iron during the twelfth century. In contrast, medieval iron objects in Oslo retrieved archaeologically are characterised as 'numerous' (G. Færden 1990: 184); Petter Molaug (pers. comm. 2016) has kindly informed me that at the Mindets Tomt site iron finds make up c. 9 per cent of the total find assemblage from the eleventh century to the early twelfth century. In Bergen, iron finds from the mid-twelfth century make up 1.9 per cent of the total finds from the town area (Andersson et al. 2015: 223). If we take these numbers at face value, the consumption in Bergen is relatively modest compared to Oslo. The seemingly modest consumption in Bergen could be explained by the town's location some distance away from the most significant iron production districts; most iron production took place in the eastern parts of Norway, as well as in the Trøndelag region, beyond Bergen's hinterlands in the period under study (e.g. Stenvik 1997; Larsen 2009; Christophersen 2015: 100).

In conclusion, one may assume that since some urban iron working has been documented, some objects must have been produced by smiths in town. Trace element analysis showed that iron objects from Oslo dated to the period before c. 1275 must have come from four main resource areas; after 1275, the number of sources diminishes and includes only one source area after 1500 (A. Færden 1990: 328). The resource areas are not localised. The analysed material is limited, but if we accept this data, it may imply a development over time from many to fewer suppliers involved in providing urban consumers with iron objects/raw material (cf. Schia 1989: 151). Still, whether the early medieval Norwegian towns were self-suppliers of objects of iron, or if some were brought into town, cannot be substantiated through the available datasets. Several large-scale iron production sites were located in valleys and mountain areas in mid- and eastern Norway. With this in mind, iron was most likely a domestic product. Since the extraction areas were some distance from the towns, it is assumed here that iron was brought to the towns through networks with an interregional reach.

Non-ferrous metalworking is documented in the towns through crucibles, moulds, metal waste and specialised tools. Identification of metals through geochemical analysis has only been carried out in a few of the places. In Trondheim remnants of non-ferrous metalworking are found from the end of the 900s and throughout the early Middle Ages. Copper with zinc and/or lead were the most important metals. Silver was also used for personal accessories and from 1050–1100 minting was possibly carried out

70   *Gitte Hansen*

(Christophersen and Walaker Nordeide 1994: 217–22 with references; Christophersen 2015). At Veøy and Kaupanger non-ferrous metalworking is documented, but whether the activities date back to the period under study is uncertain (Solli 1996: 176; Knagenhjelm 2008: 64). In Bergen non-ferrous metalworking is documented from c. 1100 (Hansen 2005: 165–8, 191–4). In Skien metalworking involving copper alloys is recognised from the second half of the 900s onwards (Myrvoll 1992: 240–4: Figs 90–1). In Tønsberg the presence of non-ferrous metalworking is considered to be likely from c. 1150 (Jakobsen 1991: 152). In Oslo non-ferrous metalworking is demonstrated from the eleventh century, using copper alloys, silver and lead (G. Færden 1990: 186–95; Wikstrøm 2006: 68–70). Finally non-ferrous metalworking is documented in Kungahälla from c. 1140 (Rytter 2001: 102–5). It is likely, but not empirically confirmed, that, like in Viking-Age Kaupang (Pedersen 2015), crucibles used by the early medieval urban crafts people were made of kaolin clay. This kind of clay has been sourced in Southwest Scandinavia and Western Europe (Pedersen 2010: 306–9 with references). Copper alloys must also originate from places outside Norway. Aachen in Southwest Germany has been suggested as a likely candidate for Viking-Age copper alloys (Pedersen 2010: 233–8 with references).

The inventory of non-ferrous objects consumed in the towns is not yet widely studied (but see Molaug 1998; Viken 2009), and the consumption of non-ferrous objects in the urban setting cannot be securely assessed. Also, the products from urban non-ferrous metalworkers are not well covered in archaeological research. Still, in Trondheim moulds show that objects with a Christian symbolic content were in the repertoire (Christophersen and Walaker Nordeide 1994: 217–22 with references; Christophersen 2015). In Bergen, it is documented that some non-ferrous metalworkers were also combmakers who made rivets and decorative plates for the combs that were produced and consumed in the town (Hansen 2015b: 44–6), and the same can be seen in Kungahälla (Rytter 2001: 102–5). In all the documented cases the amounts of production waste and detritus are sparse and spread over several properties (for a discussion of relative amounts of production waste and detritus, see Hansen 2005: 180–4).

As seen in Table 4.2, the survey shows that non-ferrous metalworking was carried out in at least six of the towns during the period under study. These were large towns in western Norway and large and medium-size towns in eastern Norway. Regarding the small towns, data is uncertain for the early medieval period. Overall production is relatively small. I have argued elsewhere that it was for intra-urban consumption and carried out by itinerant craftspeople (Hansen 2005: 203, 2015b). The procurement of raw materials needed for non-ferrous metalworking involving copper alloy and crucibles – possibly of kaolin clay – must thus in all likelihood have come to the towns via networks with an international reach.

For *combmaking*, reindeer antler and copper alloy rivets and decorative details were the preferred raw materials in early medieval Norway (Wiberg 1977;

Materials in early medieval Norwegian towns 71

Flodin 1989; Rytter 1997; Hansen 2005). Combmaking is mainly identified through reindeer antler production waste and specialised tools. In Trondheim, combmaking occurs in the earliest phases, in the mid-900s – and through the entire period investigated here (Flodin 1989). In Bergen reindeer antler detritus, along with melted drops of copper alloy, is documented from c. 1100 until c. 1170 (Hansen 2005, 2015b: 45). In Stavanger the craft is also documented in the period under study (Lillehammer 1972; Reed 2005; dates for the material pers. comm. Reed 2010). In Skien combmaking is documented from the second half of the 900s onwards (Myrvoll 1992: Figs 90–1). In Tønsberg antler production waste is found in the late twelfth century (Ulriksen 1996: Fig. 27). In Oslo, reindeer antler have been found from the last half of the eleventh century onwards (Wikstrøm 2006: 62 with references), and finally in Kungahälla combmaking is documented from c. 1140 (Rytter 2001: 75–110). In all the places where combmaking is documented, detritus occurs in relatively small amounts and is spread over several properties (for a discussion on relative amounts, see Hansen 2005: 180–4).

Detritus from combmaking has been documented in six of the towns (cf. Table 4.2). These include two large and one small town in the west and one large and two medium towns in the east. When encountered, production is small scale, and most likely carried out by itinerant craftspeople for intra-urban consumption (see discussion in Hansen 2005: 203, 2015b). The reindeer antler is derived from Norwegian mountain regions that hosted wild populations of reindeer in the Middle Ages. We await the results from ongoing ancient DNA analyses of production waste from Trondheim, Bergen and Skien to see which mountain areas supplied craftspeople with antler (Røed and Hansen 2015). Antler must have ended up in the towns via networks with an interregional reach. The combmakers also needed copper alloys for the manufacture of comb rivets and decorative plates for the combs. The occurrence of melted drops of copper alloy in production waste testify to the fact that combmakers handled non-ferrous metal needed in combmaking (Hansen 2015b). They would thus also need crucibles, probably made of kaolin clay. Copper alloys and clay for crucibles, as already mentioned, must have come to Norway via networks with an international reach (cf. Pedersen 2010: 233–8 with references). Raw materials needed for combmaking accordingly arrived in towns via both interregional and international networks.

Shoemaking is identified through leather waste and specialised tools such as lasts. In Trondheim the craft is documented from the 900s and throughout the period studied here (Christophersen and Walaker Nordeide 1994: 231–4). At Borgund shoes were made in phases tentatively given a broad dating 'from the tenth/eleventh centuries until sometime before 1100' (compare dates in Larsen 1970, 2008). In Bergen the craft is documented from c. 1100 (Hansen 2005: 162–5, 186–9). In Skien shoemaking is documented from the second half of the tenth century (Myrvoll 1992: Figs 90–1). In Tønsberg leather crafts have been broadly dated to the eleventh and twelfth century (Ulriksen 2008: 102).

72   Gitte Hansen

In Oslo shoemaking is carried out from c. 1000 (Tørhaug 1999; Wikstrøm 2006 with references), and in Kungahälla remnants of shoemaking are found, but are later than the period under study (see Rytter 2001: 78). With the exception of Borgund, where data regarding the quantity of the waste materials is not available, detritus generally occurs in relatively small amounts (for a discussion on relative amounts, see Hansen 2005: 180–4). Embroidery yarn of silk has been demonstrated on early medieval shoes from Bergen, Trondheim and Oslo (Hansen 2015c). In the archaeological collections from Borgund shoes with embroidery have been observed (Larsen 1970). Typologically they date to the early Middle Ages. According to Myrvoll's observations (1992: Fig. 40), a shoe found in twelfth-century Skien has incised décor. Based on my experience with twelfth-century shoe material, I find that this shoe is almost certainly an embroidered shoe where thread is not preserved. Embroideries on shoes were surprisingly common in the period studied here. Thus one-third of all shoes retrieved from the twelfth century in Trondheim, Bergen and Oslo were embroidered with decorative seams. Studies of Bergen shoes show that embroidery yarn of silk was most common. A rough calculation of the amount of silk embroidery yarn consumed in Bergen during the middle of the twelfth century shows that at least 5 kg of yarn would have been used over a fifty-year period (Hansen 2015c).

As seen in Table 4.2, shoemaking was documented in six of the towns: these comprise two large and one medium-sized town in the west as well as one large and two medium-sized towns in the east. Shoes with traces of embroideries were found in five of the surveyed towns. In three of these towns (all large) silk yarn has been observed. We do not know precisely when silk embroidery yarn was introduced during the early Middle Ages. Where shoemaking has been studied in some detail, it was found to be a small-scale enterprise, suggesting that shoes were produced primarily by itinerant craftspeople for intra-urban consumption (see discussion and further references in Hansen 2005: 203, 2015b).

Shoemaking required supplies of tanned leather, sewing thread, and for some shoes embroidery yarn for decoration of the shoe. Tannery sites have not been identified in any of the towns prior to the late twelfth century so it is possible that leather was brought to the towns ready-tanned. This, as well as assessing the types of leather used, awaits further research. However, in twelfth-century material from Bergen I have observed that goat leather was commonly used, but the issue has not been dealt with in any detail. Also in Bergen thread of animal hair/wool from goat has been used to stitch the shoe together (Pedersen 1982). Leather and sewing thread may have domestic origins through networks with regional or interregional reach, although this has not yet been examined. However, the silk yarn in all probability came from the Mediterranean area, distributed to Norwegian towns via networks with an international reach (Hansen 2015c). Thus raw materials needed for shoemaking must have come to the towns via both networks with a regional/interregional reach and networks with international reach.

Table 4.3 Summary of the urban consumption of domestic stone products in early medieval Norway. 10th: Tenth century, E11th: Early eleventh century (c. 1000–1030), M11th: Middle eleventh century (c. 1030–70), L11th: Late eleventh century (c. 1070–1100), E12th: Early twelfth century (c. 1100–30), M12th: Middle twelfth century (c. 1130–70)

			Quern stones: H = Hyllestad, O = Unspecified					
	Size	*Site name*	*10th*	*E11th*	*M11th*	*L11th*	*E12th*	*M12th*
West	L	Bergen 1020/30–						H
East	L	Oslo c. 1000–			o/O		o/O	o/O

			Hones: E = Possible Eidsborg, C = Possible Caledonian, O = Other					
	Size	*Site name*	*10th*	*E11th*	*M11th*	*L11th*	*E12th*	*M12th*
West	L	Trondheim 900s–	E, c/C, o/O					
West	L	Bergen 1020/30–					E, c/C, o/O	
East	M	Skien 900s–	e					
East	M	Tønsberg 1000s–					E, C, o	
East	L	Oslo c. 1000–	E, C, o/O					
East	M	Kungahälla c. 1100–					E, C, o	

			Bakestones: Øl = Ølve, S = Soapstone, O = Unspecified					
	Size	*Site name*	*10th*	*E11th*	*M11th*	*L11th*	*E12th*	*M12th*
West	L	Trondheim 900s–			o			
West	L	Bergen 1020/30–					øl, s/S	
East	M	Skien 900s–						
East	M	Tønsberg 1000s–						
East	L	Oslo c. 1000–				ØL	ØL, s/S	
East	M	Kungahälla c. 1100–						s

			Soapstone vessels: A, B, C = Myrvoll's types, O = Other/unspecified					
	Size	*Site name*	*10th*	*E11th*	*M11th*	*L11th*	*E12th*	*M12th*
West	M	Borgund 900/1000s–?	a/A, b/B					
West	L	Bergen 1020/30–					a/A, b/B, C	

(continued)

74   *Gitte Hansen*

Table 4.3 (continued)

			Soapstone vessels: A, B, C = Myrvoll's types, O = Other/unspecified					
	Size	Site name	10th	E11th	M11th	L11th	E12th	M12th
East	M	Skien 900s–					c/C	
	M	Tønsberg 1000s–					c/C	
	L	Oslo c. 1000–					A, b/B, c/C	
	M	Kungahälla c. 1100–						o/O

Note: Small letters = regional supply, capital letters = interregional supply, merged cells = broad dating evidence. Only towns with available data are included.

To sum up (Table 4.2), production in the form of iron working took place in large, medium and small towns in the west and east. Production of accessories that involved both domestic and exotic raw materials was found in both large and medium-sized towns in the west and in the east. Data regarding these crafts is generally scarce for the small towns. However, combmaking was documented in the small town of Stavanger. There seems to be no significant difference in the variety of small-scale crafts present in the large and medium-sized towns of the west and the east.

Consumption of domestic stone products

The most common portable objects made from domestic stone resources include quern stones, baking slabs, hones and soapstone vessels (Table 4.3).

Quern stones are seldom found in the published material on the towns treated here. We thus await results from the Mill stone project on this subject, but see Baug (2002, 2013). However, some published information has been retrieved: in early medieval Bergen, one fragment and one complete quern stone have been found from before 1170. Both are provenanced to the quarries in Hyllestad in the Sogn og Fjordane County in southwestern Norway (Hansen 2005: Tab. 57, classification pers. comm. Irene Baug, Tom Heldal and Øystein J. Jansen 2010; Baug 2013: 219). Furthermore, according to an Oslo study (Wikstrøm 2006: 31), one quern stone fragment was found to date between 1025 and 1075, none have been found that date to the period between 1050 and 1100, and only a few have been found that date to later periods. This gives the impression of few quern stones in the early medieval period in Oslo. Quarries that delivered quern stones are not located in Oslo's or Bergen's regions, thus quern stones must have been distributed through networks with an interregional reach.

Hones/whetstones are frequently found in archaeological contexts, and their provenances are especially interesting. During the early Middle Ages two large suppliers of quartz-muscovite schist hones are known. Eidsborg quarries in the Telemark County in South Norway delivered hones of light-grey,

Materials in early medieval Norwegian towns 75

fine-grained schist. The second source is of an unknown location which produced dark-grey, very fine-grained schist hones. The latter hones are of stone dated to the Caledonian era – and are commonly called Caledonian hones – which place the quarries in a geological area in western Norway (Mitchell et al. 1984). In addition to these two types, a variety of whetstones of other stone sorts are often found. Their provenance is unknown but the hones are often thought to have a local or regional origin. In the present examination, hones are divided into three categories: *Eidsborg* (i.e. *possible* Eidsborg), *Caledonian* (i.e. *possible* Caledonian) and *other*. The identification method used in the published data is ocular, not geochemical; however, in most cases geologists or archaeologists with a special competence in stone have been involved in the identification, and general trends in the spatial distribution patterns should be reliable. Finely meshed chronological studies of early medieval urban hone consumption have not yet been given detailed attention in archaeological research; however, see Myrvoll (1986: Fig. 10). The present survey is thus rather sparse.

In Trondheim, hones (N = ?, precise numbers are not given) are found from the tenth century onwards, with Eidsborg hones constituting the largest share in the period studied here. A 'violet' hone type has also been found from the mid-tenth century onwards. Additionally, hones of ten other stone types occur until the mid-twelfth century (see Christophersen and Walaker Nordeide 1994: Fig. 213, with references to Siri Myrvoll). By the description of the 'violet' hones, I suggest we may be dealing with Caledonian hones – this is based on observations of the variety of colours of hones classified as Caledonian in the Bergen material in connection with my research (see below). The Eidsborg hones must have arrived in Trondheim through networks with interregional reach. Regarding the remaining hones, precise provenances are not known and they may have arrived through both regional and interregional networks.

In Bergen 124 hones are found in layers dating to between 1100 and 1170. The hones have been identified by the author with the help of geologist Helge Askvik; 59 per cent are identified as Eidsborg type, 19 per cent are of Caledonian type and the rest – 22 per cent – are of unknown origin. Of the twenty-three Caledonian hones 30 per cent are unused blanks, compared to 7 per cent of the seventy-four Eidsborg hones and 10 per cent of the twenty-nine unknown types (Hansen 2005: 205–18 and author's research data). The high percentage of Caledonian stone blanks could perhaps indicate that they were brought to Bergen and intended for transit. The Eidsborg hones must have arrived in Bergen through networks with an interregional reach. The remaining hones may have arrived through both regional and interregional networks (i.e. their provenance is unknown).

In Skien, hones in large numbers (N = ?, precise numbers are not given) geologically matching Eidsborg stone are found from the late 900s and onwards, where unused blanks are the most common (Myrvoll 1986, 1992). Skien is located in Telemark County, some 100 km directly from the Eidsborg quarries. Skien is connected to the quarry area by *Telemarkvassdraget*, a river system which may well have suited as a regional transport vein. Siri Myrvoll has suggested

76 *Gitte Hansen*

that the blanks found in Skien were to be re-distributed from there, which may indicate that Skien functioned as a transit port (Myrvoll 1986, 1992). The Eidsborg hones must have come to Skien via regional networks. In Tønsberg, Eidsborg hones have been found from the 1100s (Myrvoll 1986: Fig. 10). It is not established whether other stone types have been found here. Eidsborg hones must have come to Tønsberg via interregional networks.

Hones in Oslo were studied in a Master's thesis that dealt with a 670 m^2 large site (Lønaas 2001). We may assume that the results are quite representative of the consumption trends in this town. Here it was found that the pre-urban phase, from the 900s to c. 1050, yielded one Eidsborg hone. From c. 1050 and through the Middle Ages (precise dates and numbers are not given), Eidsborg is responsible for 83 per cent of the hones and 85 per cent of the hone blanks found at the site (Lønaas 2001: 14–16; see also Myrvoll 1986). Other stone types are also present in the early medieval phases at the site, both a 'violet' stone type and hones in stone types that may have regional provenance (Lønaas 2001: 14–16). By the description of the 'violet' type, I suggest that Caledonian hones were also present in Oslo during the early Middle Ages. Oslo was thus most likely supplied with hones via networks with both regional and interregional reaches.

In Kungahälla, hones (N = ?, precise numbers are not given) dating to the mid-twelfth century are described as 'a light and a dark kind', and are believed to include Eidsborg, Caledonian and regional hones, the latter from the local 'Marstrand formation' (Kindgren 1991). Kungahälla was accordingly supplied with hones through networks with both regional and interregional reaches.

Altogether, hones were identified in six of the surveyed towns (Table 4.3). Possible Eidsborg hones are found in large and medium-sized towns in the west and east. Possible Caledonian hones are also found in large and medium-sized towns in the east, but not in Skien. The lack of Caledonian hones in this medium-sized town may perhaps have methodological explanations, but with Skien's proximity to the Eidsborg quarries in mind, one might rather suggest that consumers in Skien found no reason to procure hones from other places. It appears that the early medieval Norwegian towns received hones through networks with interregional reach. Additionally they have also likely received hones from regional – as yet unknown – quarries.

Bakestones are circular or oval stone slabs of chlorite-rich talc-amphibole schist (clorite schist) or soapstone, incised with grooves and used for baking and heating foodstuffs over fire. In Norway three quarry areas are known for the production of chlorite schist slabs: Øye in the Trøndelag County, Ølve/Hatlestrand in the Hordaland County and Rennesøy in the Rogaland County (Weber 1989; Baug 2015). The location of quarries for soapstone baking slabs is not known.

Bakestones are found in small numbers at the Library site in Trondheim from c. 1050–1100; the stones did not become more frequent until after c. 1150. The provenance is believed to be regional, but is unknown. Slabs that may come from Ølve/Hatlestrand in Hordaland are dated from the last quarter of the twelfth century onwards (Weber 1989: Fig. 3; Christophersen and Walaker

Materials in early medieval Norwegian towns 77

Nordeide 1994: 249). At Veøy two fragments of bakestones were retrieved; their precise dates are unclear (Solli 1996: 174) and their provenance is unknown.

In Bergen, 379 bakestones are dated to between 1100 and c. 1170 (Hansen 2005: Tab. 57). In a study of raw material for bakestones from a tenement in the central parts of the town area, a good half of the stone slabs from the twelfth century were identified as probable Ølve/Hatlestrand slabs. The remainder were of soapstone. In the group of soapstone slabs, great variety in the visual appearance of the stone was observed (Tengesdal 2010: 20–1, 35, Fig. 5.3). Such variation is, however, characteristic of soapstone sources/quarries (Hansen et al. 2017). Thus, visual variety alone cannot indicate whether the soapstone slabs came from few or many quarries. The Ølve/Hatlestrand quarries are located in Bergen's regional area. Sigrun S. Tengesdal points out that 59 per cent of the bakestones do not have traces of use (soot traces), suggesting that Bergen may have been a transit port for stone slabs for cooking. Information provided in Tengedal's (2010) appendix showed that 56 per cent of the bakestones dated to between 1120 and 1170 have no traces of soot, of which 59 per cent are of soapstone slabs and 41 per cent of chlorite schist slabs. Thus in the period before 1170, the share of slabs without visible traces of use is high for both stone types. If we accept lack of soot as a tentative criterion for unused slabs, the high share of unused soapstone slabs might indicate that Bergen functioned as a transit port for bakestones, not only from Ølve/Hatlestrand, as suggested in earlier research (Tengesdal 2010; Baug 2013: 317), but also from as yet unknown soapstone quarries where bakestones were produced. Given that soapstone quarries in Hordaland County (where Bergen is located) delivered the majority of soapstone vessels to Bergen in the period under study (see below) (Hansen et al. 2017), it is highly likely that many bakestones of soapstone found in Bergen were also produced in the region. Chlorite schist bakestones from Ølve/ Hatlestrand came to Bergen via networks with a regional reach; it is suggested that the same applies to slabs of soapstone. Additionally, bakestones may have been supplied through networks with an interregional reach.

In Skien, bakestones have not been found at the excavation at Handelstorget, where the youngest phase is dated from the middle of the 1100s to late 1100s/ early 1200s (Myrvoll 1992: 167, 246). In Tønsberg bakestones are found in small numbers from the end of the twelfth century, but so far not in the early medieval phases (Ulriksen 1996: 92). In Oslo bakestones seem to be few before c. 1100, thus at Mindets Tomt and Søndre felt sites only two slabs are found that date to between 1050 and 1100, and they may originate from Ølve. The share of Ølve stones is, according to Birthe Weber (1989: 18), 'small' until c. 1300. In addition to chlorite schists slabs, soapstone baking slabs are also found in medieval Oslo (Wikstrøm 2006: Tab. 1), but more precise find data is not provided in the archaeological literature used here. In Kungahälla, bakestones of soapstone have been dated to the 1100s (Kindgren 1991: Tab. 9). Four slabs have been analysed by a geologist applying ocular methods and a provenance to regional quarries is suggested (Kindgren 1991: 69).

78   *Gitte Hansen*

As summarised in Table 4.3, bakestones have been identified in at least four towns in the early medieval period; these comprise two large towns in western Norway as well as one large and one medium town in the eastern part of the country. Baking slabs seem to be found less frequently and later in the east compared to the west. In Oslo bakestones were probably supplied through networks with interregional reach, possibly from Ølve/Hatlestrand. It is assumed that Bergen received soapstone bakestones through networks with a regional reach. Thus, urban consumers received bakestones via networks of both regional and interregional reaches.

Medieval *soapstone vessels* are only rarely given attention in archaeological reports or synthesising studies; however, a short summary of the situation may be attempted. Soapstone vessels of the medieval type A and type B (typology according to Lossius 1977) were most likely produced in western Norway (Lossius 1977). It is not known whether differences in type have functional or chronological significance, or if both types were produced in the same quarry or region. One may thus expect to find both types A and B within an assemblage of vessels quarried in early medieval west Norway. Type A and B vessels in western Norwegian towns may have been supplied by both regional and interregional networks. Vessel type C is held to be of east Norwegian origin (Lossius 1977: 63–7), but the locations of quarry sites are as yet unknown. If such vessels are found in eastern Norwegian towns, they may thus have been supplied through either regional or interregional networks.

At Borgund a comprehensive study of soapstone vessels is at our disposal where vessel types A and B are represented (Lossius 1977). Soapstone vessels are found in phases broadly dated to 'from the tenth/eleventh centuries until sometime before 1100' (compare context information in Lossius 1977 and new dating evidence in Larsen 2008). The presence of both type A and B vessels indicates several suppliers. The vessels may have been distributed through networks with regional and interregional reaches.

In Bergen, ninety-four vessels are dated to before 1170. Through transdisciplinary analyses of geochemical and archaeological datasets, provenance studies found that about two-thirds of the vessels (both types A and B) originated from several different regional quarries, while one-third probably stems from quarries located outside the Hordaland region. The non-regional vessels were mostly of type A, but type B and C were also represented in small numbers. Bergen was thus supplied with soapstone vessels through networks with a regional and interregional reach (Hansen et al. 2017).

In Skien a vessel of type C was found at the Handelstorget site, dating to the early medieval period (Myrvoll 1992: Appendix, p. 297). In Tønsberg, a vessel of type C dating to the twelfth century has been found (Lossius 1977: 51). In her thesis on material from the Nordre bydel (Northern part) of Tønsberg, Eli Ulriksen (1996: 45) mentions soapstone vessels dated to the twelfth century, but does not quantify or describe the vessels. In a Skien and Tønsberg context type C vessels may be of a regional or non-regional provenance.

Materials in early medieval Norwegian towns 79

In Oslo soapstone vessels of type A, B and C have been found. It seems that type C vessels are the most common, whereas A and B vessels are few in the period under study (Lossius 1977: 51, 1979: 70). The variety of types shows that several sources supplied the town with vessels, certainly through interregional reaches, but perhaps also from regional networks.

In Kungahälla vessels of a 'round bottom type' are dated to the 1100s. Four vessels have been analysed by geologists applying ocular methods, and the aluminium and magnesium contents of one of the shards have been assessed. Based on this a provenance to two different local soapstone deposits is suggested (Kindgren 1991: 71–2). Recent research has shown that provenancing soapstone is complicated due to the inhomogeneous character of the rock (e.g. Hansen et al. 2017 with references). This calls for caution regarding the provenance of the Kungahälla shards, and for now, it feels safe to treat the shards as unprovenanced. They may accordingly have come to the town through networks with a regional or interregional reach.

Thus, soapstone vessels have been identified in six towns (Table 4.3): one large and one medium-sized town in the west and one large and three medium-sized towns in the east. In Bergen and Oslo vessels were supplied through both regional and interregional networks. We do not know the reach of networks that supplied Borgund, Skien, Tønsberg and Kungahälla; they may be either regional or interregional.

To sum up, the consumption of domestic stone products is not well studied in the materials from the small towns, so they are hardly present in the survey. Regarding other towns, stone products have been consumed in both large and medium towns in west and east Norway. There are some interesting differences in the procurement and consumption patterns when looking at the western versus the eastern towns, and looking at Bergen versus other western towns. These themes are addressed further in the discussion.

Exotic products: ceramics

In early medieval Norway no domestic pottery traditions existed, thus all ceramics found here are imported from European pottery districts through networks with an international reach. Ceramics are found in many of the towns in the survey, both in well-dated contexts and without detailed contextual information. In the latter cases ware types produced before c. 1150 are included if present at the sites. The pottery has almost exclusively been visually provenanced, generally by archaeologists with special expertise. The number of ware types from each pottery district is summarised for each town. Some ware names may cover several pottery producers whereas a few ware names may have different conventions for the same ware. For our purposes, this is unproblematic. Unprovenanced pottery is not included here, except for the category 'Black ware cooking pot', which is frequently encountered in western Norway. This category might contain wares of Baltic type.

80 *Gitte Hansen*

Table 4.4 Summary of the urban consumption of pottery in early medieval Norway

	Size	Site name	Great Britain	France	Mediterranean 'Byzans?'	SW Germany	Belgium	Southern Scandinavia	Baltic sea area	Black ware cooking pot	Total
West	L	Trondheim	4–5		1	2	1				8–9
	M	Borgund	3			2	1			1	7
	S	Kaupanger				1	1			1	3
	L	Bergen	7	3		2	1			1	14
	S	Stavanger				2	1				3
East	M	Skien				1			1		2
	M	Tønsberg	1			2	1				4
	L	Oslo	1			2	1	1	1		6
	M	Kungahälla				1	1		1		3

In early medieval Norway, nine ware types from the British Isles are mentioned in the archaeological literature: East Midlands, Grimston, Hedon, Lincoln-type, London, Scarborough, Shelly, Stamford and Torksey wares. From the Belgian pottery district Andenne ware is represented. From southwest Germany (SW-Germany) Paffrath and Pingsdorf wares are represented. From south Scandinavia one ware type – 'coarse ware cooking pots' – is identified. From the Mediterranean area one type is found in the archaeological literature, termed 'Byzans?'. Three wares are found from the French pottery district: 'Normandy gritty', 'French type' and 'Northern France'. From the Baltic Sea area pottery districts the 'Slavonic/Baltic'-type wares are identified. These wares have not been further subdivided into types in the literature used here, but detailed studies have shown that the 'Slavonic/Baltic'-type wares may have been produced in various places around the Baltic Sea both in Slavic areas and in southeastern Scandinavia (Roslund 2001). Both cooking wares and table wares are represented in the ceramic types found. Table 4.4 summarises the urban consumption of pottery.

In Trondheim, pottery types identified before c. 1150 comprise four or five wares from the British Isles, two wares from SW-Germany and one from Belgium. Additionally, the Mediterranean district is represented by one shard from the early eleventh century (Reed 1990: Fig. 23, appendix 1–2).

At Borgund eleventh to twelfth-century pottery in undated contexts includes: three wares from the British Isles, two from SW-Germany and one from Belgium. In addition, 'Black ware cooking pots' are identified (A. Rory Dunlop in Manuscript by Arne J. Larsen, TopArk). At Kaupanger eleventh to twelfth-century pottery found in poorly dated contexts comprises one SW-German ware, one Belgian and Black ware cooking pots (Knagenhjelm 2004: 60, 98). In Bergen seven wares from the British Isles are represented before c. 1170. In addition, two SW-German, three French,

Materials in early medieval Norwegian towns 81

one Belgian and Black ware cooking pots are found (Hansen 2005: 205–18, notes 81–4). In Stavanger relevant pottery found in undated contexts comprises two SW-German and one Belgian type (Lillehammer 1972: 65–6). In Skien, ceramics dating to before the late twelfth century comprise Baltic wares and one type from SW-Germany (Myrvoll 1992: Fig. 64, p. 162). From the twelfth century in Tønsberg, two wares from the SW-German area are identified, possibly also one from the Belgian area and possibly one from the British Isles (compare Molaug 1987; Eriksson 1990: 84). In Oslo only a few unprovenanced shards have been dated to the eleventh century. From the twelfth century, two SW-German, one Belgian and one south Scandinavian ware are found in addition to Baltic-type wares. One type of ware from the British Isles is introduced after 1125 in small amounts representing less than 5 per cent of the pottery (Molaug 1977: 110, 1987: 314, Fig. 49, dates: Fig. 8, 1999: 541). In Kungahälla, Baltic wares prevail in the late eleventh and first half of the twelfth centuries. Additionally one SW-German and one Belgian ware are represented (Carlsson 2001: 71).

As seen in Table 4.4, imported pottery was found in nine of the surveyed towns. Pottery was consumed in large, medium and small-sized towns in both the west and east. There are some distinct differences in the consumption patterns between the western and eastern towns and to some extent between the towns of various size. This is treated in more detail below.

General patterns discerned and comments for further studies

From the observations made theme by theme, some general patterns in the production, procurement and consumption transcend the various sized towns in the west and east. Differences are also observed among towns.

Urban production

In all urban sites treated here, large quantities of domestic stone and wooden materials were needed to establish the towns' monumental architecture and secular settlements. The amount of raw materials of course depended on the number of monuments and the size of the built-up areas. In addition to large-scale building enterprises, small-scale iron production took place in both large and medium-sized towns in the west and east. The extent of this production in the small towns is a question for future research. In Trondheim, iron production increases after c. 1150. As small towns are generally underrepresented in the datasets regarding other production, the patterns discerned here have some uncertainties. Small-scale production of accessories that involved both domestic and exotic raw materials, i.e. non-ferrous accessories, shoes with silk embroidery and combs with copper alloy details, was found in both large and medium-sized towns in the west and east. Furthermore, combmaking took place in the small town of Stavanger in the west. There seem to be no significant differences in the variety of small-scale crafts present in the large and medium-sized towns of the

82   *Gitte Hansen*

Table 4.5 Procurement of raw materials and products through networks of various reach

Raw material/product	Made in the town	Regional	Interregional	International
Building stone		X		
Timber		X		
Iron raw material			X	
Iron objects	X			
Non-ferrous metal				X
Clay for crucibles				X
Non-ferrous accessories	X			
Reindeer antler			X	
Combs	X			
Tanned leather		X?		
Sewing thread (goat-wool?)		X?		
Embroidery yarn of silk				X
Shoes	X			
Quern stones			X	
Hones		X	X	
Bakestones		X	X	
Soapstone vessels		X	X	
Pottery				X

west and east. Altogether, one may point out that crafts production in the early medieval towns was modest and thus in all likelihood for intra-urban consumption. That is, production was primarily aimed at the townspeople's needs, even if visitors could probably buy things as well (see e.g. Christophersen and Walaker Nordeide 1994: 236–8; Rytter 2001: 107; Hansen 2005: 157–205; Andersson et al. 2008). Consumption of urban products in the rural hinterlands of towns should be addressed in future research, to further elucidate the character and scope of early medieval urban production. However, based on the current data, one may assert that in contrast to their Viking-Age counterparts, early medieval Norwegian towns were primarily consumers, not producers.

Procurement and consumption

From a procurement perspective, raw materials and products ended up in towns through networks with varying reach (Table 4.5). The towns were, however, not only consumers and an end station for the materials consumed; they also served as nodes in international, interregional or regional networks of exchange.

Domestic materials and objects

The survey of iron consumption in Oslo showed that several resource areas/ rural producers supplied Oslo with iron in the early Middle Ages. Similarly, when looking at the use of domestic stone products, the towns generally received similar utensils from several suppliers. An exception to this rule is Skien where Eidsborg hones were apparently preferred to other kinds of whetstones. There are accordingly many producers on the market, as opposed to a monopoly situation. It would be interesting to follow up the survey over a longer time period to examine whether the trend observed for the distribution of iron to Oslo – from many suppliers to fewer in the later Middle Ages – is a general trend that has bearing for other resources and domestic products. From a rural producer perspective, one can furthermore make the point that producers of domestic household utensils generally supplied many towns and many engaged in both regional and interregional distribution networks.

The survey has accumulated some useful details on concrete physical nodes in procurement networks: Skien has in earlier research been suggested as an important port of export for Eidsborg hones (Myrvoll 1986, 1992), Oslo has been suggested as an intermediate station for this product (Lønaas 2001) and Bergen has been proposed as a transit port in a trading route for chlorite schist bakestones from Ølve/Hatlestrand (Tengesdal 2010; Baug 2013). Here Bergen is suggested as a transit harbour for Caledonian hones, and possibly for bakestones of soapstone as well.

To further elaborate on domestic stone objects as commodities, both newcomers and old timers in the long-distance trade market are represented; Eidsborg and Caledonian hones, quern stones from Hyllestad and soapstone vessels were traded internationally during the Viking Age (Resi 1979, 1987; Mitchell et al. 1984; Myrvoll 1986; Baug 2013: 231, this volume). In contrast, bakestones are a new phenomenon in early medieval Norway. Against this backdrop it is interesting to assess the behaviour involved in the use of old and new products in the domestic distribution networks of the early Middle Ages. Are there differences across the Norwegian towns of different sizes, and between towns of the west and east?

In large and medium-sized early medieval towns, both in the west and east, the Eidsborg and Caledonian hones are the stone commodities encountered earliest and most frequently, with the exception of Skien where only Eidsborg stones were found. One may ask if the producers and distributors of Eidsborg and Caledonian hones managed to have such a wide distribution because they leaned on old traditions for long-distance international exchange, and thus had well-organised and established network relations as a foundation for trade with the new urban communities.

Regarding soapstone vessels, successful international trade appears to dwindle by the early Middle Ages (Risbøl 1994; Sindbæk 2005: 137; Baug this volume). However, in early medieval Norwegian towns soapstone vessels are still encountered, both in large and medium-sized towns in the west and east,

84   *Gitte Hansen*

and generally speaking they are distributed through networks of both regional and interregional reach. However, despite this interregional exchange, the survey revealed that west Norwegian towns mainly consume west Norwegian products (types A and B) and east Norwegian towns mainly consume vessels of east Norwegian origin (type C). The early medieval soapstone procurement networks apparently have a relatively limited radius. Did the operators of the networks not have the social contacts needed for strong recurrent relations between eastern and western parts of the country? Did fundamental changes in the organisation of soapstone vessel production and procurement take place during the transition to the early medieval period, so that even though old traditions for long-distance trade had existed, these were not sustained into the early medieval period?

Bakestones are found in both large and medium-sized towns in the west and east; however, and again when examining details, there are some differences in where and when the bakestones appear in the large town of Bergen and the towns in the west and east. With the premise that the surveyed literature from Trondheim and Oslo gives a fairly representative picture of the early medieval consumption of bakestones in these towns, it seems that this new domestic product was not a part of the earliest phases of Trondheim's and Oslo's history. In the eastern Norwegian towns of Skien and Tønsberg, bakestones are also late phenomena; here no slabs have been dated to the period under research. In Bergen, however, the slabs are *numerous* from c. 1100. Recall that portable finds are, for methodological reasons, scarce in Bergen before 1100, so we do not know exactly how far back the use of bakestones dates in this town. In recent research it has been suggested that bakestones were introduced to Norway from the British Isles, and that the associated food traditions spread by way of the sailing routes along the coast. These suggestions are based on early dates of bakestones in Atlantic Scotland and the spatial distribution of bakestones found in (broadly dated) rural and urban contexts along the coast of Norway (Øye 2009; Baug 2015 with references). With the present survey's relatively high temporal resolution, the contours of the spread of bakestone usage may be discerned in more detail: if the patterns recognised here are valid, they indicate that bakestones were introduced first in the west – perhaps in the Bergen area or perhaps through Bergen – and were gradually introduced and consumed in other parts of Norway during the latter part of the early Middle Ages, with towns in eastern Norway as latecomers.

Early medieval domestic procurement has great research potential that has not attracted deserved attention; debates of exchange organisation, between producers and consumers in the towns, as well as the scale and reach of domestic interregional exchange networks, are worthwhile. In the survey of the different domestic raw materials and products some insights from previous studies have been accumulated and new details added. A comparative approach to the domestic materials provides new insights and new questions arise. One insight is – with the fear of stating the obvious – that domestic resources and products must have circulated in a variety of perhaps competing networks

Materials in early medieval Norwegian towns 85

which operated within different geographical and perhaps social orbits. Future research might usefully apply an actor perspective on the sources and address who were the consumers of raw materials and objects, and who owned quarries, forests and the bogs with iron ore. Through such an approach one may develop a deeper understanding of the social dimension of the domestic procurement networks; how, by whom and for whom networks were operated and controlled on different social levels.

Exotics

Distinct differences are discerned in the consumption of pottery, along the east–west axis and among the various sized towns. A general observation is that the large towns have a greater variety of wares, as seen in Table 4.4. Bergen has fourteen wares, Trondheim eight to nine and Oslo six, whereas the smaller and medium towns, except Borgund (with seven wares), have between two and four wares. Furthermore, the west Norwegian towns have more ware types than the east Norwegian towns. A bias that influences the east–west imbalance may be that there is a research tradition for dividing British and French wares into many subgroups, whereas this is not the case for the Baltic and south Scandinavian wares (compare Reed 1990 and Molaug 1987), thus more suppliers might 'hide' in the latter groups. If so, this would raise the number of wares encountered in the large and medium-sized towns in eastern Norway, where Baltic and south Scandinavian wares prevail. It seems valid that the large towns received more wares than those of lesser size. This may be interesting for our understanding of the procurement of goods in a domestic network perspective; cf. studies of Viking-Age networks and towns (e.g. Sindbæk 2005, 2007).

Going into more detail on the pottery, we observe that in all towns where data is available, pottery from the Belgian and/or SW-German districts is found. In contrast, other pottery types are not consumed so uniformly between the west and east. In the west Norwegian towns pottery from the British district is represented in great variety. In the large town of Bergen, French types are also present; wares procured from western Europe/the North Sea area thus dominate in the west Norwegian towns. In Bergen, and perhaps Borgund and Kaupanger, there is possibly an association eastwards, indicated by the black ware cooking pot category, which may perhaps 'hide' some Baltic wares. A rarity in the west is a single shard of a Mediterranean 'Byzans?' ware found in Trondheim. In contrast to this, British wares are scarce in eastern Norwegian towns and they are introduced late in the period under research. Furthermore, in eastern Norwegian towns, wares from the Baltic and south Scandinavian districts prevail.

The many pottery types from the British Isles in western towns testify to strong repeating connections across the North Sea. Judging by the amount of pottery shards found in these towns, ceramics was a commodity and not brought to the towns as personal belongings by visitors. Trade across the North

86 *Gitte Hansen*

Sea in the early Middle Ages is also reflected in written records, for example for twelfth-century Bergen (Orkn 1913–16: 141; Holtsmark 1970: 93–4). The relatively early consumption of bakestones in the west fits well with this picture. The early medieval connections may have roots back into the Viking Age, when connections across the North Sea were practised on many levels (e.g. papers in Hines et al. 2004; Barrett 2015; Sindbæk 2015). They may thus reflect a continuation – or knowledge – of long traditions for interaction across the North Sea from western Norway.

Baltic and south Scandinavian pottery frequently found in eastern Norwegian towns may in the same fashion reflect an eastern and southern orientation towards the Baltic Sea, south Scandinavia and resource areas there. A similar trend for Swedish towns was observed by Broberg and Hasselmo (1982) in their survey of slightly younger phases of Swedish towns, where especially the details from Lödöse, located south of Kungahälla, are of relevance here. The eastern orientation of the early medieval Norwegian towns thus seems to be a tendency that finds support in other datasets. A continuation of older traditions or knowledge of such contacts may also be reflected here (e.g. Christophersen 1991; Callmer 1994; Sindbæk 2005).

Pottery from the Belgian and SW-German districts are, like the Eidsborg and Caledonian hones, widely found both in western and eastern Norwegian towns. The same goes for copper alloys (and possibly kaolin clay for crucibles), used in connection with the non-ferrous metalworking and antler crafts. As stated above, Aachen in SW-Germany, close to the Belgian border, has been suggested as a resource area for ingredients in copper alloys of the Viking Age (Pedersen 2010: 233–8). The Belgian ware Andenne as well as the SW-German wares Pingsdorf and Paffrath are all from the same general resource area (the area is today located in different countries). Badorf-type pottery, also from SW-Germany, as well as copper alloys, are found in the Viking-Age town Kaupang in Vestfold County in eastern Norway (Pedersen 2010; Pilø 2011: 286–91). Again it may be suggested that old trading routes or knowledge of such were applied. One might suggest that the routes went by way of Haithabu where Eidsborg and Caledonian hones as well as Norwegian soapstone vessels were consumed during the Viking Age (see Resi 1979). One may also suggest that well-maintained social or economic networks were leaned on and made it possible to distribute the products from this part of northern Europe so widely into the new urban landscape in Norway.

Like copper alloys (and possibly kaolin clay), silk yarn used for embroidery on leather shoes is another exotic commodity found both in the western and eastern Norwegian towns. There are indications that this exotic material was procured by way of western/North Sea connections; shoes similar to the Norwegian specimens are known from several British towns and the shoes here display embroidery patterns that are similar to those found on the Norwegian shoes (Hansen 2015c). With the silk yarn probably being a Mediterranean commodity, it is tempting to ask how the Mediterranean pottery in Trondheim may possibly fit into the picture. Having said this, shoes with silk embroideries in the same style as in Norway are also found in contemporary Sweden and Denmark (Hansen 2015c), so no conclusions should be drawn without more research on this issue.

Details concerning the distributive networks of exotic commodities such as silk embroidery yarn, non-ferrous metals and possibly kaolin clay and how they entered Norway are thus still unresolved. And we do not know whether the raw materials were introduced through one or several towns or harbours. It is thought-provoking that the exotic raw materials were worked by craftspeople that visited the newly established Norwegian towns for a short time and made affordable accessories for townspeople. Søren Sindbæk has demonstrated that a hierarchy existed within the eighth to ninth-century towns in northern Europe; here crafts that required exotic raw materials in addition to domestic were only found in the largest centres of trade, the nodal points that had direct access to international trade. At smaller centres that served a local market these crafts were not found since artisans could not procure the exotic raw materials here (Sindbæk 2007). If a similar model situation is relevant for the early medieval period (some 200 years later), it would implicate a direct import of exotics in all the towns where combmakers, shoemakers and non-ferrous metalworkers carried out their crafts. A question is, however, whether the craftspeople acquired their raw materials upon arrival in the towns, as implied in Sindbæk's model for the earlier period. Or perhaps, as an alternative scenario, one might suggest, they were 'vehicles' in the domestic distribution of the exotic materials, i.e. procuring the exotics at one port, and then transporting them from place to place as part of a raw material stock?

As with the domestic materials, the exotic objects and raw materials were certainly distributed through intersecting and perhaps competing networks that worked within different geographical and social orbits. Again, one may usefully ask who were the producers and consumers and through an actor perspective get better insight into the ways of procurement networks.

Final comments

Urban production, procurement and consumption in early medieval Norway have not previously been surveyed, and much less studied within a narrow chronological framework, neither on a broad basis nor in a comparative perspective with archaeological sources as a foundation. Medieval archaeology has traditionally dealt with single towns, single crafts, single raw material groups and single object groups. With the present study a first overview is given of the most common urban production and the domestic and exotic raw materials involved, as well as significant groups of domestic and exotic objects consumed in thirteen of medieval Norway's fourteen known towns. Much interesting information lies in the details, thus some new and basic insights have been obtained, and patterns have

88   *Gitte Hansen*

been discussed. However, with new insights more questions usually arise. Medieval archaeology as a discipline has rapidly developing research fields where, for instance, focus on objects and raw materials with a provenance attracts increasing attention. With cross-disciplinary studies involving archaeology and diverse natural sciences, new research data and insights are made available, enabling large research potentials to be realised.

Acknowledgements

I am grateful to Axel Christophersen, A. Rory Dunlop, Christoffer Knagen-hjelm, Petter Molaug, Eli Ulriksen and Brit Solli for comments on the chapter. Errors that may still lie in the empirical data are of course my responsibility, as are the interpretations. Also Steven P. Ashby is thanked for valuable and constructive feedback, and the editors of this volume deserve thanks for their patience and efforts.

References

Andersson, Hans, Kristina Carlsson and Maria Vretemark (eds) 2001: *Kunghälla. Problem och forskning kring stadens äldsta historia.* Lund Studies in Medieval Archaeology, vol. 28. Bohusläns museums förlag. Stockholm-Uddevalla.

Andersson, Hans, Gitte Hansen and Sonia Jeffery 2015: Järn och städer. Tankar kring det arkeologiska materialet i Bergen och Gamla Lödöse. In: Berglund, Bengt (ed.): *Järnet och Sveriges medeltida modernisering*, pp. 215–58. Jernkontoret. Halmstad.

Andersson, Hans, Gitte Hansen and Ingvild Øye 2008: *De første 200 årene – nytt blikk på 27 skandinaviske middelalderbyer.* UBAS Universitetet i Bergen Arkeologiske Skrifter. Nordisk, vol. 5. Institutt for arkeologi, historie, kulturvitenskap og religion, Universitetet i Bergen. Bergen.

Andrén, Anders 1985: *Den urbana scenen. Städer och samhälle i det medeltida Danmark.* Acta Archaeologia Lundensia, vol. 13. CWK Gleerup. Malmö.

Barrett, James 2015: Maritime societies and the transformation of the Viking Age and Medieval world. In: Barrett, James H. and Sarah Jane Gibbon (eds): *Maritime Societies of the Viking and Medieval World.* Society for Medieval Archaeology Monograph 37, pp. 1–13. Maney. Oxford, Oakville.

Baug, Irene 2002: *Kvernsteinsbrota i Hyllestad. Arkeologiske punktundersøkingar i steinbrotområdet i Hyllestad i Sogn og Fjordane.* Norsk Bergverksmuseums skriftserie, vol. 22. Norsk Bergverksmuseum. Kongsberg.

—— 2013: Quarrying in Western Norway: An archaeological study of production and distribution in the Viking period and the Middle Ages. Unpublished PhD thesis. University of Bergen. Bergen.

—— 2015: Stones for bread. Regional differences and changes in Scandinavian food traditions related to the use of quernstones, bakestones and soapstone vessels c. AD 800–1500. In: Baug, Irene, Janicke Larsen and Sigrid Samset Mygland (eds): *Nordic Middle Ages – Artefacts, Landscapes and Society.* UBAS Universitetet i Bergen Arkeologiske Skrifter, vol. 8: 33–47. Institutt for arkeologi, historie, kulturvitenskap og religion, Universitetet i Bergen. Bergen.

Bergen 1985–: *The Bryggen Papers Main Series Vols. 1–8 and Bryggen Papers Supplementary Series vols. 1–9.* Norwegian University Press and Fagbokforlaget. Bergen.

Bergquist, Ulla 1989: *Gjutning och smide.* Meddelelser. Fortiden i Trondheim bygrunn, vol. 16. Riksantikvaren. Trondheim.

Bertelsen, Reidar 2008: Vagar i de første to hundreårene. In: Andersson, Hans, Gitte Hansen and Ingvild Øye (eds): *De første 200 årene – nytt blikk på 27 skandinaviske middelalderbyer.* UBAS Universitetet i Bergen Arkeologiske Skrifter. Nordisk, vol. 5: 125–34. Institutt for arkeologi, historie, kulturvitenskap og religion, Universitetet i Bergen. Bergen.

Brendalsmo, Jan and Petter Molaug 2014: To norske byer i middelalderen – Oslo og Tønsberg før ca. 1300. *Collegium Medievale*, 27: 136–202.

Broberg, Birgitta and Margareta Hasselmo 1982: Keramik, kammar och skor – variationer i fyndmaterialet i olika regioner. *Bebyggelseshistorisk tidsskrift*, 3: 89–103.

Callmer, Johan 1994: Urbanisation in Scandinavia and the Baltic region c. AD 700–1100: Trading places, centres and early urban sites. In: Ambrosiani, Bjørn and Helen Clarke (eds): *Developments Around the Baltic and the North Sea in the Viking Age.* Birka Studies, vol. 3: 50–90. Riksantikvarieämbetet and Statens Historiska Museer. Stockholm.

Carlsson, Kristina 2001: Keramiken i Kungahälla – kronologi, handel och funktion. In: Andersson, Hans, Kristina Carlsson and Maria Vretemark (eds): *Kunghälla. Problem och forskning kring stadens äldste historia.* Studies in Medieval Archaeology, pp. 57–74. Bohusläns museums förlag. Stockholm.

—— 2008: Kungahälla, Lödöse och Skara – om urbanisering i ett tidligmedeltida gränsland. In: Andersson, Hans, Gitte Hansen and Ingvild Øye (eds): *De første 200 årene – nytt blikk på 27 skandinaviske middelalderbyer.* UBAS Universitetet i Bergen Arkeologiske Skrifter. Nordisk, vol. 5: 227–43. Institutt for arkeologi, historie, kulturvitenskap og religion, Universitetet i Bergen. Bergen.

Christophersen, Axel 1991: Ports and trade in Norway during the transition to historical time. In: Crumlin-Pedersen, Ole (ed.): *Aspects of Maritime Scandinavia AD 200–1200. Proceedings of the Nordic Seminar on Maritime Aspects of Archaeology, Roskilde 13th–15th March, 1989*, pp. 159–70. The Viking Ship Museum, Roskilde. Roskilde.

—— 2015: The hinterland connection: metalworking as social practice. In: Baug, Irene, Janicke Larsen and Sigrid Samset Mygland (eds): *Nordic Middle Ages – Artefacts, Landscapes and Society.* UBAS Universitetet i Bergen Arkeologiske Skrifter, vol. 8: 93–103. Institutt for arkeologi, historie, kulturvitenskap og religion. Universitetet i Bergen. Bergen.

Christophersen, Axel and Sæbjørg Walaker Nordeide 1994: *Kaupangen ved Nidelva.* Riksantikvarens skrifter, vol. 7. Trondheim.

Ekroll, Øystein, Morten Stige and Jiri Havran 2000: *Kirker i Norge. Middelalder i stein*, vol. 1. Arfo. Oslo.

Engberg, Nils, Anne Nørgaard Jørgensen, Jakob Kieffer-Olsen, Per Kristian Madsen and Christian Radtke (eds) 2009: *Archaeology of Medieval Towns in the Baltic and North Sea Area.* Publications of the National Museum PNM/Studies in Archaeology and History, vol. 17. Copenhagen.

Eriksson, Jan E.G. (ed.) 1990: *De arkeologiske undersøkelsene i Storgaten 47, Tønsberg 1971.* Arkeologisk rapporter fra Tønsberg, vol. 5. Riksantikvaren, Utgravningskontoret for Tønsberg. Tønsberg.

Fett, Trygve 1989: Bygninger og bygningsdetaljer. In: Schia, Erik (ed.): *Hus og gjerder.* De arkeologiske utgravninger i Gamlebyen, Oslo, vol. 6: 15–92. Alvheim og Eide Akademisk Forlag. Øvre Ervik.

Flodin, Lena 1989: *Kammakeriet i Trondheim ca. 1000–1600.* Meddelelser, vol. 14. Riksantikvaren. Trondheim.

90   *Gitte Hansen*

Færden, Arne 1990: Dagliglivets gjenstander – Del 1. Smijern fra Gamlebyen – En analyse av spikermaterialet. In: Molaug, Petter and Erik Schia (eds): *Dagliglivets gjenstander del I.* De arkeologiske utgravninger i Gamlebyen, Oslo, vol. 7: 301–30. Alvheim og Eide Akademisk Forlag. Øvre Ervik.

Færden, Gerd 1990: Dagliglivets gjenstander – Del 1. Metallgjenstander. In: Molaug, Petter and Erik Schia (eds): *Dagliglivets gjenstander del I.* De arkeologiske utgravninger i Gamlebyen, Oslo, vol. 7: 181–292. Alvheim og Eide Akademisk Forlag. Øvre Ervik.

Gläser, Manfred, Regina Dunckel, Ulrike Oltmanns and Lübeck Bereich Archäologie der Hansestadt 1999: *Lübecker Kolloquium zur Stadtarchäologie im Hanseraum II: der Handel.* Verlag Schmidt-Römhild. Lübeck.

Gläser, Manfred, Ilka Hillenstedt, Claudia Kimminus-Schneider, Doris Mührenberg and Manfred Schneider (eds) 2006: *Lübecker Kolloquium zur Stadtarchäologie im Hanseraum: das Handtwerk,* vol. 5. Schmidt-Römhild. Bereich Archäologie der Hansestadt. Lübeck.

Gläser, Manfred, Claudia Kimminus-Schneider and Lübeck Bereich Archäologie und Denkmalpflege der Hansestadt 2008: *Lübecker Kolloquium zur Stadtarchäologie im Hanseraum VI: Luxus und Lifestyle.* Schmidt-Römhild. Lübeck.

Hansen, Gitte 2005: *Bergen c 800–c 1170, the Emergence of a Town.* Bryggen Papers Main Series, vol. 6. Fagbokforlaget. Bergen.

―― 2015a: After the town burned! Use and reuse of iron and building timber in a medieval town. In: Baug, Irene, Janicke Larsen and Sigrid Samset Mygland (eds): *Nordic Middle Ages – Artefacts, Landscapes and Society.* UBAS Universitetet i Bergen Arkeologiske Skrifter, vol. 8: 159–74. Institutt for arkeologi, historie, kulturvitenskap og religion, Universitetet i Bergen. Bergen.

―― 2015b: Itinerant Craftspeople in 12th Century Bergen, Norway – Aspects of Their Social Identities. In: Hansen, Gitte, Steven P. Ashby and Irene Baug (eds): *Everyday Products in the Middle Ages: Crafts, Consumption and the Individual in Northern Europe c. AD 800–1600,* pp. 28–50. Oxbow Books. Oxford and Philadelphia.

―― 2015c: Luxury for everyone? Embroideries on leather shoes and the consumption of silk yarn in 11th–13th century northern Europe. In: Ling Huang, Angela and Carsten Jahnke (eds): *Textiles and the Medieval Economy: Production, Trade, and Consumption of Textiles, 8th–16th Centuries.* Ancient Textiles Series, pp. 86–103. Oxbow Books. Oxford.

Hansen, Gitte, Øystein J. Jansen and Tom Heldal 2017: Soapstone vessels from town and countryside in Viking Age and early medieval western Norway. A study of provenance. In: Hansen, Gitte and Per Storemyr (eds): *Soapstone in the North – Quarries, Products and Organisation. 7000 BC–AD 1700* UBAS Universitetet i Bergen Arkeologiske Skrifter, vol. 9. Bergen.

Helle, Knut 1982: *Kongssete og Kjøpstad. Fra opphavet til 1536.* Bergen bys historie, vol. 1. Universitetsforlaget. Bergen.

Helle, Knut, Finn-Einar Eliassen, Jan Eivind Myhre and Ola Svein Stugu (eds) 2006: *Norsk byhistorie. Urbanisering gjennom 1300 år.* Pax Forlag. Oslo.

Helle, Knut and Arnved Nedkvitne 1977: Norge. In: Autén Blom, Grethe (ed.): *Urbaniseringsprocessen i Norden. Middelaldersteder,* vol. 1: 189–272. Universitetsforlaget. Oslo.

Hines, John, Alan Lane and Mark Redknap (eds) 2004: *Land, sea and home. Settlement in the Viking period.* Society for Medieval Archaeology Monograph, vol. 20. Maney. Leeds.

Materials in early medieval Norwegian towns 91

Holtsmark, Anne 1970: *Orkenøyingenes saga*. H. Aschehaug og Co. Oslo. Forskning i Felleskap: http://norark.no/utmarka. read 25.05.16.

Jakobsen, Sigmund 1991: *Hersker og smed*. *Smedarbeider i Tønsberg i tiden 1150–1350*. Arkeologiske rapporter fra Tønsberg, vol. 8. Riksantikvaren, Utgravningskontoret for Tønsberg. Tønsberg.

Jansen, Øystein J. 2005: Kleberbruddet ved gården Urda i Bømlo – storleverandør av kirkestein i middelalderen. *Sunnhordland Årbok*, 86: 42–59.

Jansen, Øystein, Tom Heldal, Rolf Birger Pedersen, Y. Ronen and Sigrid Hillern H. Kaland 2009: Provenance of soapstone used in medieval buildings in the Bergen region, Western Norway. In: Maniatis, Yannis (ed.): *Asmosia VII, Proceedings of the 7th International Conference of Association for the Study of Marble and Other Stones in Antiquity. Thassos 15–20 September 2003*. Bulletin de Correspondance Hellénique, pp. 581–95. École Francaise d'Athénes. Athens.

Kindgren, Hans 1991: Täljsten, skiffer, bärnsten. In: Carlsson, Kristina (ed.): *Kungahällaarkeologi 1989*. Kulturhistoriska rapport, vol. 22: 67–76. Länsstyrelsen i Göteborgs och Bohus län. Göteborg.

Knagenhjelm, Christoffer 2004: Kaupanger. En analyse av kuapangens lokalisering og funksjon. Unpublished Master's thesis in archaeology. Universitetet i Bergen. Bergen.

—— 2008: Kaupanger i Sogn – etablering, vekst og bydannelse. In: Andersson, Hans, Gitte Hansen and Ingvild Øye (eds): *De første 200 årene – nytt blikk på 27 skandinaviske middelalderbyer*. UBAS Universitetet i Bergen Arkeologiske Skrifter. Nordisk, vol. 5: 57–71. Instutut for arkeologi, historie, kulturvitenskap og religion, Universitetet i Bergen. Bergen.

Larsen, Arne J. 1970: *Skomaterialet fra utgravningene i Borgund på Sunnmøre 1954–1962*. Årbok for Universitetet i Bergen. Humanistisk serie, vol. 1. Norwegian Universities Press. Bergen.

—— 2008: Borgund på Sunnmøre – de eldste konstruksjonene. In: Andersson, Hans, Gitte Hansen and Ingvild Øye (eds): *De første 200 årene – nytt blikk på 27 skandinaviske middelalderbyer*. UBAS Universitetet i Bergen Arkeologiske Skrifter. Nordisk, vol. 5: 41–56. Instutut for arkeologi, historie, kulturvitenskap og religion, Universitetet i Bergen. Bergen.

Larsen, Jan Henning 2009: *Jernvinneundersøkelser. Faglig program, bind 2*. Varia 78. Kulturhistorisk museum. Oslo.

Lillehammer, Arnvid 1972: Arkeologisk bidrag til Stavangers mellomalderhistorie. *Stavanger museums årbok*, 1971: 51–90.

Lindh, Jan (ed.) 1992: *Arkeologi i Tønsberg I – Søndre bydel*. Riksantikvarens rapporter, vol. 20. Riksantikvaren. Oslo.

Lønaas, Ole Christian 2001: Brynestein i middelalderen. En analyse av brynemateriale fra Oslogate 6. Unpublished Master's thesis. IAKK, Det historisk filosofiske fakultet, Universitetet i Oslo. Oslo.

Lossius, Siri Myrvoll 1977: *Klebermaterialet fra Borgund*. Arkeologiske avhandlinger fra Historisk museum, vol. 1. Historisk museum, Universitetet i Bergen. Bergen.

—— 1979: Klebermaterialet. In: Schia, Erik (ed.): *De arkeologiske utgravninger i Gamlebyen, Oslo. "Oslogate 3 og 7" Bebyggelsesrester og funngrupper*. De arkeologiske utgravninger i Gamlebyen, Oslo, vol. 2: 64–71. Alvheim og Eide Akademisk Forlag. Øvre Ervik.

Mitchell, John G., Helge Askvik and Heid Gjøstein Resi 1984: Potassium-argon ages of schist honestones from Viking Age sites at Kaupang (Norway), Aggersborg

92   Gitte Hansen

(Denmark), Hedeby (West Germany) and Wolin (Poland), and their archaeological implications. *Journal of Archaeological Science*, 11: 171–6.

Molaug, Petter 1977: Leirkarmaterialet fra 'Mindets Tomt'. In: Høeg, Helge Irgens, Hans-Emil Lidén, Aslak Liestøl, Petter Molaug, Erik Schia and Christina Wiberg (eds): *Feltet Mindets Tomt. Stratigrafi – Topografi – Daterende funngrupper.* De arkeologisk utgravninger i Gamlebyen, Oslo, vol. 1: 72–120. Universitetsforlaget. Oslo.

—— 1987: Leirkarmaterialet. In: Schia, Erik (ed.): *Søndre Felt. Stratigrafi, bebyggelsesrester og daterende funngrupper.* De arkeologiske utgravninger i Gamlebyen, Oslo, vol. 3: 229–328. Alvheim og Eide Akademisk Forlag. Øvre Ervik.

—— 1999: Archaeological evidence for trade in Oslo from the 12th to the 17th centuries. In: Dunckel, Regina, Manfred Gläser and Ulrike Oltmanns (eds): *Lübecker Kollquium zur Stadarchaeologie im Hanseraum II: Der Handel,* pp. 533–46. Lübeck.

—— 2002: Oslo: Husenes, bygårdenes og bydelenes funksjon. In: Molaug, Petter (ed.): *Strategisk instituttprogram 1996–2001. Norske middelalderbyer. Norsk Institutt for kulturminneforskning,* pp. 54–66. NIKU publikasjoner vol. 117. Oslo.

—— 2008: Oslo blir by – fra 1000 til 1200. In: Andersson, Hans, Gitte Hansen and Ingvild Øye (eds): *De første 200 årene – nytt blikk på 27 skandinaviske middelalderbyer.* UBAS Universitetet i Bergen Arkeologiske Skrifter. Nordisk, vol. 5: 73–92. Institutt for arkeologi, historie, kulturvitenskap og religion, Universitetet i Bergen. Bergen.

Molaug, Sonja 1998: Smykker og draktutstyr fra middelalderens Bergen. Unpublished Master's thesis in archaeology. University of Bergen. Bergen.

Myrvoll, Siri 1986: Skien og Telemark – naturressurser, produkter og kontakter i sen vikingtid og tidlig middelalder. *Viking,* XLIX 1985/6: 161–80,

—— 1992: *Handelstorget i Skien – A Study of Activity on an Early Medieval Site.* NUB Nytt fra Utgravningskontoret i Bergen, vol. 2. Riksantikvaren, Utgravningakontoret for Bergen. Bergen.

NgL = Norges gamle love. Række 2: 1388–1604: Grethe Authén Blom (ed.) 1966–81. Norsk historisk kjeldeskrift-institutt. Oslo.

NIKU 1996–2016: Several-publication series from Norsk institutt for kulturminneforskning: from 1996–2001: *Fagrapport, Oppdragsmelding, Temahefte* and from 2001: *NIKU Publikasjoner.* NIKU. Oslo. http://www.niku.no/no/publikasjoner/om_publikasjoner/read 25.05.16.

Orkn = *Orkneyinga saga:* Sigurður Nordal (ed.) 1913–16: *Orkneyinga saga,* vol. XL. Samfund til Udgivelse af gammel nordisk Litteratur. København.

Oslo 1977–91: *De Arkeologiske utgravninger i Gamlebyen, Oslo vols 1–10.* Universitetsforlaget/Alvheim and Eide akademisk forlag. Oslo/Øvre Ervik.

Øye, Ingvild 2009: Food and technology – Cooking utensils and food processing in medieval Norway. In: Klápste, Jan and Peter Sommer (eds): *Processing, Storage, Distribution of Food. Food in the Medieval Rural Environment.* Ruralia, vol. VIII: 225–34. Turnhout. Spain.

Pedersen, Inger Raknes 1982: Tekniske analyser og undersøkelser av prydsømmene på skomaterialet fra Bryggen (BRM 0). Konserveringsbygget. Historisk Museum, Universitetet i Bergen. Bergen.

Pedersen, Unn 2010: I smeltediglen. Finsmedene i vikingtidsbyen Kaupang. Unpublished PhD thesis. Institutt for arkeologi, konservering og historie, Universitetet i Oslo. Oslo.

—— 2015: Urban craftspeople at Viking-Age Kaupang. In: Hansen, Gitte, Steven P. Ashby and Irene Baug (eds): *Everyday Products in the Middle Ages: Crafts, Consumption and the Individual in Northern Europe c. AD 800–1600,* pp. 51–68. Oxbow Books. Oxford and Philadelphia.

Materials in early medieval Norwegian towns 93

Pilø, Lars 2011: The pottery. In Skre, Dagfinn (ed.): *Things from the Town. Artefacts and Inhabitants in Viking-Age Kaupang*. Kaupang Excavation Project Publication Series, Volume 3, Norske Oldfunn XXIV, Aarhus University Press and Kaupang Excavation Project, University of Oslo. Aarhus and Oslo.

Reed, Ian 1990: *1000 Years of Pottery. An Analysis of Pottery, Trade and Use.* Meddelelser, vol. 25. Riksantikvaren. Trondheim.

Reed, Stan 2005: Stavanger Torg, Topographical archive, Project no. S12198. Arkeologisk museum Stavanger, Universitetet i Stavanger.

Resi, Heid Gjøstein 1979: Die Specksteinfunde aus Haithabu. In: Schietzel, Kurt (ed.): *Berichte über die Ausgrabungen in Haithabu*, vol. 14: 9–167. Karl Wachholtz Verlag. Neumünster.

——— 1987: Reflections on Viking Age local trade in stone products. In: Knirk, James (ed.): *Proceedings of the Tenth Viking Congress. Larkollen, Norway, 1985.* Universitets Oldsaksamlings Skrifter. Ny rekke nr. 9: 95–102. Oslo.

Risbøl, Ole 1994: Sosialøkonomiske aspekter ved vikingetidens klæberstenshandel i Sydskandinavien. *LAG*, 5: 115–61.

Roslund, Mats 2001: *Gäster i huset. Kulturell overföring mellan slaver och skandinaver 900–1300.* Vetenskapssocieteten i Lund. Lund.

Rytter, Jens 1997: Gevirhåndverket i Konghelle ca 1140–1300. Unpublished Master's thesis. IAKN, Det Historisk-filosofiske Fakultet. Universitetet i Oslo. Oslo.

——— 2001: Håndverk i middelalderens Konghelle. In: Andersson, Hans, Kristina Carlsson and Maria Vretemark (eds): *Kunghälla. Problem och forskning kring stadens äldste historia.* Studies in Medieval Archaeology, pp. 75–110. Bohusläns museums förlag. Stockholm.

Røed, H. Knut and Gitte Hansen 2015: DNA from ancient reindeer antler as marker for transport routes and movement of craftspeople, raw material and products in medieval Scandinavia. In: Indrelid, Svein, Kari Loe Hjelle, Kathrine Stene, Birgitta Berglund, Martin Callanan, Sigrid Hillern H. Kaland and Lars Stenvik (eds): *Exploitation of Outfield Resources: Joint Research at the University Museums of Norway.* Universitetsmuseet i Bergen skrifter, University Museum of Bergen. Bergen.

Schia, Erik 1989: Varetilførsel fra landsbygda til Oslo i middelalder. Med bakgrunn i arkeologiske utgravninger i Gamlebyen. *Universitetets Oldsaksamling. Årbok*, 1986–8: 143–60.

Sindbæk, Søren Michael 2005: *Ruter og rutinisering: vikingetidens fjernhandel i Nordeuropa.* Multivers Academic. København.

——— 2007: Networks and nodal points: the emergence of towns in early Viking Age Scandinavia. *Antiquity*, 81(311): 119–32.

——— 2015: Steatite vessels and the Viking diaspora: migrants, travellers and cultural change in early medieval Britain and Ireland. In: Barrett, James H. and Sarah Jane Gibbon (eds): *Maritime Societies of the Viking and Medieval World.* Society for Medieval Archaeology Monograph 37, pp. 198–218. Maney. Oxford, Oakville.

Solli, Brit 1996: *Narratives of Veøy. An Investigation into the Poetics and Scientifics of Archaeology.* Universitetets Oldsaksamlings Skrifter, vol. 19. Universitetet i Oslo. Oslo.

——— 2008: Kjøpstedet på Veøya i Romsdal. In: Andersson, Hans, Gitte Hansen and Ingvild Øye (eds): *De første 200 årene – nytt blikk på 27 skandinaviske middelalderbyer.* UBAS Universitetet i Bergen Arkeologiske Skrifter. Nordisk, vol. 5: 109–24. Institutt for arkeologi, historie, kulturvitenskap og religion, Universitetet i Bergen. Bergen.

Stenvik, Lars F. 1997: Iron production in Mid-Norway, an answer to local demand? In: Hässeler, H.J. (ed.): *Studien zur Sachenforschung*, vol. 10: 253–63.

Storemyr, Per 2015: *Nidarosdomens grunnfjell. I steinbrytenes fotspor fra Det gamle Egypt til Europas nordligste katedral.* Nidaros Domkirkes Restaureringsarbeiders forlag. Trondheim.

94 *Gitte Hansen*

Storemyr, Per and Tom Heldal 2002: Soapstone production through Norwegian history: geology, properties, quarrying, and use. In: Herrmann Jr., John J., Norman Herz and Richard Newman (eds): *Asmosia V, Interdisciplinary Studies on Ancient Stone. Proceedings of the Fifth International Conference of the Association for the Study of Marble and Other Stones in Antiquity, Museum of Fine Arts, Boston 1998*, pp. 359–69. Archetype Publications Ltd. London.

Storemyr, Per, Nina Lundberg, Bodil Østerås and Tom Heldal 2010: Arkeologien til Nidarosdomens middelaldersteinbrudd. In: Bjørlykke, Kristin, Øystein Ekroll and Birgitta Syrstad Gran (eds): *Nidarosdomen – ny forskning på gammel kirke*, pp. 238–67. Nidaros Domkirkes Restaureringsarbeiders forlag. Trondheim.

Tengesdal, Sigrun Solbakken 2010: Å steike! En kontekstuell materialeanalyse av steikeheller funnet i et bygårdskompleks i middelalderens Bergen. Unpublished Master's thesis. Instututt for arkeologi, historie, kulturvitenskap og religion, Universitetet i Bergen. Bergen.

Thun, Terje 2002: *Dendrochronological Constructions of Norwegian Conifer Chronologies Providing Dating of Historical Material*. PhD thesis. Faculty of Natural Sciences and Technology, Department of Biology, Norwegian University of Science and Technology, NTNU. Trondheim.

Tønsberg 1989–92: *Arkeologiske rapporter fra Tønsberg*, vol. 1–9. Riksantikvaren Utgravningskontoret for Tønsberg, Riksantikvaren. Tønsberg.

TopArk = Topografisk Arkiv, Borgund BRM 1, Sunnmøre, The Medieval Collections, University Museum of Bergen, University of Bergen. Bergen.

Tørhaug, Vanja 1999: Skomakerhåndverket i Oslo i middelalderen. *Primitive tider*, 2: 20 37.

Trondheim 1985–90: *Prosjektet Fortiden i Trondheim, bygrunn: Folkebibliotekstomten*, vol. 1–25. Riksantikvaren, Utgravningskontoret for Trondheim. Trondheim.

Ulriksen, Eli 1996: *Utkantens håndverkere og arbeidere. En aktivitetsanalyse av "Nordre bydel" i middelalderens Tønsberg*. NIKU Temahefte. Tønsberg.

—— 2008: Tønsberg – bebyggelse og beboere fra 1000–tall til 1200–tall. In: Andersson, Hans, Gitte Hansen and Ingvild Øye (eds): *De første 200 årene – nytt blikk på 27 skandinaviske middelalderbyer*. UBAS Universitetet i Bergen Arkeologiske Skrifter. Nordisk, vol. 5: 93–108. Institutt for arkeologi, historie, kulturvitenskap og religion, Universitetet i Bergen. Bergen.

Viken, Synnøve 2009: Å smykke seg. Drakttilbehør og sosiale strategier belyst ved arkeologisk materiale fra middelalderens Trondheim. Unpublished Master's thesis in archaeology. Vitenskapsmuseet/NTNU. Trondheim.

Weber, Birthe 1989: *Baksteheller – en handelsvare*. Meddelelser: Fortiden i Trondheims bygrunn, vol. 15. Riksantikvaren, Utgravningskontoret for Trondheim. Trondheim.

Wiberg, Christina 1977: Horn og benmaterialet fra 'Mindets Tomt'. In: Høeg, Helge, Hans-Emil Lidén, Aslak Liestøl, Petter Molaug, Erik Schia and Christina Wiberg (eds): *De arkeologisk utgravninger i Gamlebyen, Oslo. Feltet Mindets Tomt. Stratigrafi – Topografi– Daterende funngrupper*, vol. 1: 202–13. Universitetsforlaget. Oslo.

Wikstrøm, Tone 2006: Utviklingen av hushold og håndverk i Oslos tidlige middelalder. Urbaniseringsprosessen belyst ved aktivitetsanalyser fra Søndre felt og Mindets tomt. Unpublished Master's thesis. IAKH, Det humanistiske fakultet, Universitetet i Oslo. Oslo.

5 The price of justice and administration of coinage

Frode Iversen and Svein H. Gullbekk

The *thing* is the oldest known communal organization in Northern Europe. The term *þing* or *thing* existed in all Germanic languages. It is derived from the Gothic term for time, *þeihs*, and another word meaning 'to congregate'. The meaning of *thing* is therefore 'to meet at a certain place at a certain time' (Iversen 2013), and the *thing* participants had to travel to these meetings.

In its early phase, the *thing* was the highest authority in all areas of society. The highest judicial power sat at shire level. During the Viking Age, *lawthings* were established for even bigger judicial areas in Norway, such as the Gulathing, Frostathing, Eidsivathing, Borgarthing and Hålogaland (Iversen 2014, 2015a, 2015b). These were representative *things*, which attracted delegates from vast areas.

Expenses and travel routes

This chapter will investigate the cost of arranging *lawthings* in the thirteenth century. The calculations are based on the so-called *tingfareøret* (economic compensation for attending the *thing*) in the Rural Law of Magnus the Lawmender from 1274 (L I, 2). The guiding principle of the compensation scheme was simple: the longer the distance, the higher the compensation. The Faroe Islands can be used to illustrate how the travel compensation was calculated. According to Faroese law, the island group was divided into no fewer than 21 tariff zones (NgL IV: 666). Representatives living closest to the assembly site, from Kollafjørður, Ragtangi and Nólsoy, received five ells of woollen cloth (*vaðmál*), while those furthest away, from the southern part of Suðuroy, received as much as 20 ells of cloth (Taranger 1915: 8). Norway differed significantly from the Faroe Islands both administratively and geographically. As an extension of the *thing* compensation scheme (*tingfareøret*), it will also be investigated how the king and the state used the *thing* to administrate the monetary system, namely to exchange old coins for new ones – so-called recoinage or *renovatio monetae*. A recoinage meant that all old coins were replaced with new ones issued by the king. This was a widespread European phenomenon, described in detail for the first time in Carolingian sources: in the Edict of Pitres from AD 864. In Norway, this phenomenon can be traced from the reign of Olav Kyrre (1067–93) to the middle of the fourteenth century.

96 *Frode Iversen and Svein H. Gullbekk*

What kinds of sums or values were in circulation at the Norwegian *lawthings*? According to the sections attributed to King Olav in the Gulathing Law, each *thingman* was entitled to half a month's worth of food as travel compensation, unless he had even further to travel. In addition, he should also receive a *sold* of malt and an *øre* in silver. This custom existed in the eleventh century but it may be even older. In the slightly later text of King Magnus the travel compensation was specified according to region (G 3).

According to Christian IV's Norwegian Law of 1604, *thingmen* were to receive four Danish shillings for every *mil* (c. 11.3 kilometres) as travel compensation (C IV, 2). By this time, the system had been changed, as both the Gulathing Law Code and the Rural Law of Magnus the Lawmender calculated the compensation on the basis of provinces and *thing* districts. In addition, from 1604 there was no longer a set number of representatives. The royal ombudsman or bailiff (*fogd*) appointed as many *thingmen* as he saw fit. The Rural Law of Magnus the Lawmender, on the other hand, specified both the number of representatives and the travel compensation paid out to the different districts. These regulations form the basis of our calculations. The additional expenditure for priests and high-ranking royal officials (*lendmaðr* and *sysselmaðr*) has not been included in this study.

The Rural Law of Magnus the Lawmender mentions 31 areas in total, spread over three law-districts, namely the Gulathing, Frostathing and Eidsvathing, and it is clear which areas belonged to the different *lawthings*. In accordance with customary law, the *thingmen* of the Borgarthing district were also to be compensated, but unfortunately these areas are not specified in the law. There is, however, a law from the fifteenth century which provides information on this for the law-district of Skien (NgL IV: 478). This means we have information regarding travel compensation for four *lawthings* in medieval Norway. The available sources contain information on how much *bóndafé* (payment from farmers) was required for holding the *lawthings* in 1274, while the information for the Skien *lawthing* is somewhat later. The funds were collected under the auspices of the lawman, who, according to the Rural Law of Magnus the Lawmender, should later present his accounts to the *thing* (L III, 1, 6; KLNM II, 83).

The overwhelming majority of the tariffs for travel compensations in the Rural Law of Magnus the Lawmender are based on silver, namely on the following units: 1 mark silver = 8 *øre* = 216 grams of silver. On two occasions (for Namdalen and Nordmøre) it is clear that the law refers to weighed silver. This particular measurement often formed the basis for the payments set out in the laws. Tariffs based on coins were more unstable and more difficult to use, since they varied with the royal minting strategy. Weighed silver was also closer to a burnt mark, the most common unit of value in the time of the Rural Law of Magnus the Lawmender. Indeed, silver marks constituted the most common measurement for official purposes in Norway in the High Middle Ages. For the mountainous areas of the Gulathing law-district, on the other hand, the tariffs were calculated in monthly allowances of butter.

Justice and the administration of coinage 97

This was a traditional measurement used in areas where the economy was largely based on animal husbandry. In 1274, nine units of butter (*mmb*) were equal to one burnt mark silver. The tariff zones of the Gulathing Law are defined in more exact terms than the areas from which the representatives were to be selected. For example, 30 *thingmen* were to be appointed in Rogaland, an area divided into two tariff zones with an estimated 15 representatives per zone. Corresponding regulations applied to the whole Gulathing district, with the exception of Agder, Sogn and the mountainous areas.

Tariffs are provided for six geographical areas of the Frostathing district: Namdalen, Nordmøre, Inntrøndelag, Uttrøndelag, Oppdal and Romsdalen (Table 5.2; Figure 5.2). The tariffs varied from 6 øre silver for each representative from the most outlying areas (Namdalen and Romsdalen) to 2 øre silver for the representatives closest to the *thing* site (Inntrøndelag and Uttrøndelag). Representatives from the areas at an intermediate distance were compensated with 4 øre silver (Oppdal and Nordmøre). The total sum for the 485 *thingmen* of the Frostathing district was 1208 øre silver, which amounted to 32.6 kilograms of silver.

The coastal area of the Gulathing law-district was divided into ten different tariff zones (Table 5.1; Figure 5.1). There were also four valleys in the interior to which the same tariff was applied: Valdres, Hallingdal, Setedal and Otredal

Tables 5.1–5.4 Travel compensation and geographical zones stipulated in the Rural Law of Magnus the Lawmender (1274), and the regulations for the Skien *lawthing* (fifteenth century)

The Gulathing	Representatives	Tariff	Sum
Agder	12	10	120
Ryfylke, South	15	8	120
Ryfylke, North	15	7	105
Sunnhordland	20	5	100
Nordhordland	20	3	60
Sogn	20	5	100
Firda, South	10	6	60
Firda, North	10	7	70
Sunnmøre, South	6	8	48
Sunnmøre, North	6	10	60
Sum	**134**		**843**
Silver (kilogram)			**22,761**
Valdres	4	5	20
Hallingdal	4	5	20
Setesdal	2	5	10
Otredal	4	5	20
Mmb butter	14	20	70
Silver (kilogram)			**5,04**
In total, silver (kilogram)			**27,81**

(continued)

98   *Frode Iversen and Svein H. Gullbekk*

Tables 5.1–5.4 (continued)

The Frostathing	Representatives	Tariff	Sum
Namdalen	18	6	108
Nordmøre	48	4	192
Inntrøndelag	160	2	320
Uttrøndelag	240	2	480
Oppdal	3	4	12
Romsdalen	16	6	96
Sum	**485**		**1208**
Silver (kilogram)			**32,616**

The Eidsivathing	Representatives	Tariff	Sum
Gudbrandsdalen, North	4	6	24
Gudbrandsdalen, South	8	4	32
Hedmark	24	3	72
Romerike	24	2	48
Hadeland	24	3	72
Østerdalen, South	4	4	16
Østerdalen, North	2	6	12
Sum	**90**		**276**
Silver (kilogram)			**7,452**

The Skien lawthing	Representatives	Tariff	Sum
Hovin (Gjerpen)	2	6	12
Grenland	4	6	24
Bamble	2	6	12
Numedal	2	6	12
Sum	**10**		**60**
Silver (kilogram)			**162**
Skattlandet			
Hjartdal	2	6	12
Tinn	2	6	12
Vinje	2	6	12
Lårdal	2	6	12
Seljord	2	6	12
Fyresdal	2	6	12
Kviteseid	2	6	12
Tørdal	2	6	12
Sum	**16**		**96**
Silver (kilogram)			**2,592**

(5 *mmb* butter). The tariffs applied to the coastal zones varied from 3 *øre* in Nordhordland to 10 *øre* in Agder and Sunnmøre, which lay furthest from the assembly site. The total compensation for the 134 *thingmen* from the coastal

Justice and the administration of coinage 99

area was 843 *øre* silver (22.8 kilograms of silver), and from the four mountain districts 70 monthly rations of butter (5 kilograms of silver) were to be paid out. In total this amounted to 27.8 kilograms silver, which is slightly less than for the *lawthing* at Frosta.

The Eidsvathing district was divided into seven tariff zones: Gudbrandsdalen north of Rosten, Gudbrandsdalen south of Rosten to Humlen, Hedmark, Romerike, Hadeland and Østerdalen south of Åmot and Østerdalen north of Åmot (Table 5.3). Here, too, the principle of 'the longer the journey, the higher the compensation' was applied. Furthest away were northern Gudbrandsdalen and northern Østerdalen (6 *øre*). The tariff for Romerike, where the assembly site was situated, was only two *øre* per *thingman*. The total for the 90 representatives was 276 *øre* or 7.5 kilograms of silver.

According to the fifteenth-century law for the area of Skien, two men were to ride from Hovin (Gjerpen) to the Skien *lawthing* (Table 5.4). There were also to be four *thingmen* from Grenland (Lindheim and Ulefoss) and two from Bamble (NgL IV: 478; Taranger 1915: 7f.). Finally, there were to be two representatives from Numedal. In addition, there were two representatives from every parish in *Skattlandet*, considered to be synonymous with upper Telemark County. The tariff for these areas was set at 6 *øre* silver. In 1647 there were eight parishes in upper Telemark: Hjartdal, Tinn, Vinje, Lårdal, Seljord, Fyresdal, Kvitseid and Tørdal. If only these 18 *thingmen* were compensated, the total sum would have come to 96 *øre* silver; that is, 2.6 kilograms of silver. If all the *thingmen* were paid compensation, this would have meant an extra 1.6 kilograms of silver.

In total, the cost of full attendance of the Frostathing was 32.6 kilograms of silver. The equivalent for the Gulathing was 27.8 kilograms. The Eidsvathing had fewer representatives, most of whom had a shorter journey, and the cost of holding this assembly therefore came to about 7.5 kilograms of silver. Some uncertainty surrounds the Skien *lawthing*, but the likely cost for *Skattlandet* alone was 2.6 kilograms of silver. There is no information for the law-areas of Hålogaland and Jämtland or for the Borgarthing district. It is also uncertain whether Voss, Hardanger, Mandal and Nedenes were included in the tariffs for the Gulathing district (Iversen 2015a). These areas were home to just over 30 per cent of the population of Norway, Bohuslän and Jämtland in 1769.[1]

An overview of the compensation scheme

The holding of the *thing* meetings for the four known *lawthings* came to a total of 70.5 kilograms of silver in *bóndafé*. To this must be added the cost for the areas for which the compensation rates are unknown. An estimate suggests that holding the *lawthings* in the late thirteenth century cost approximately 100 kilograms of silver a year. This sum, if converted to coins, corresponded to about 500,000 bracteates (0.2 grams), which were minted in large quantities during Magnus the Lawmender's reign until the 1270s, when a major

100 *Frode Iversen and Svein H. Gullbekk*

coin reform took place. At this time the bracteates were replaced by the more solid *penninger* (1.2 grams). About 80,000 of these would have covered the cost of travel to the *things* at the end of the reign of Magnus the Lawmender (Gullbekk 2005).

It is reasonable to assume that the costs of holding the *thing* meetings were much lower in the High Middle Ages than before. The number of *thingmen* in the Law of the Gulathing had been severely reduced from the eleventh century onwards. According to the text attributed to king Olav the Saint (1015–28, 1030), there were to be 375 *thingmen* in Firda, Sogn, Hordaland, Rogaland and Agder. The circumstances stipulated here for the year 1274 applied to 122 representatives in this area and to 148 for the whole Gulathing district, which by this time had been expanded in geographical terms. In total, this is still only close to 40 per cent of the number of representatives in the eleventh century. A similar development is plausible for the other law-districts, and – assuming that the level of compensation in the eleventh century was similar to that of the thirteenth century – the costs would have been correspondingly higher.

The economic system of the thing site

When it comes to the question of the economic reality faced by the *thingmen* and the organizers of the *thing* system in thirteenth-century Norway, it seems clear that the compensation mirrors the willingness and ability to use economic tools to sustain the social order. In this context, it is interesting to examine what types of economic values and money were used at Norwegian *thing* sites.

The provincial laws contain many references to economic value and money, the majority referring to marks and *øre*. It can be hard to determine whether these terms refer to mark silver, in terms of monetary value, or to the mark as a common denominator for other values. The laws had to be generally applicable, and it is therefore likely that they refer to the latter form of mark and *øre*, in which case it would have been up to the parties involved to agree on an acceptable payment. One article in the Law of the Gulathing provides an insight into valid commodities used for payments of wergild (*mannebøter*). This concerns the fine for manslaughter, regulated according to social status (G 223).

The provincial laws are preserved in documents dating from the second half of the twelfth and the beginning of the thirteenth century. There is an abundance of scholarly works dealing with the provincial laws: cf. Sandvik 1997.

> Now payments can be made in grain, bulls, and cows of calf-bearing age, fines and *baugar*. The *wergeld* shall be paid in gold or burned silver, if these are available. Pay in horses, but not mares; stallions, but not geldings; and no horse that has a protruding rectum or a whitish sheath or weak urinary organs or is wall-eyed or suffers from some other defect. Sheep may be given in payment, but not goats; *odal* land may be given in payment, but not land acquired by purchase. A ship may be given in payment, but not one that has been rebuilt or is so old that the original rowlocks have rotted

Justice and the administration of coinage 101

away; nor shall one give a ship with a broken prow or one that is patched with boards, unless they were laid when the ship was raised on supports (was built). Nothing that is worth less than an *øre* shall be given in payment, unless someone has a fine of smaller amount coming to him; then he shall take the payment [in things of less value]; but the one who pays may increase the fine to one *øre* . . .

Weapons may be given in payment, if they have been tested by use [and are] whole and hard and without defect; those that the man was slain with shall not be offered. Let no one pay *wergild* with a sword, except it be fretted with gold or silver. *Wadmal* or linen cloth may be offered in payment, [if it is] entirely new, or any other cloth that is new and uncut, or even cut cloth, if it is new and the payee is willing to accept it. One may pay with cloth; for men, but not for women; new cloth, and not old. Black sheep pelts may be given in payment, [if they are] new and not worn, and finer cloth, [if it is] new and uncut. Slaves may be given in payment, if they have all been brought up at home and are not younger than 15 winters, unless the payee is willing to take them younger. Bondwomen shall not be given to pay the *wergeld*. Now the [classes of] property that may be used to pay the *wergeld* have been enumerated (G 233).

(Larson 1935)

These are the most detailed regulations concerning valid forms of payment that have been preserved from medieval Norway. The guidelines are so detailed that they seem to be based on a long tradition of actual experiences in old Norwegian society, in which various forms of payment were defined in detail. These regulations refer to high-quality goods. A horse was not accepted as payment unless it was in perfect health. Similarly, a ship that had been repaired and patched with new strakes was not considered adequate payment. Slaves are mentioned along the same lines as other forms of payment. This does not mean that ships and slaves were common payment types. Slavery was abolished in Norway in the thirteenth century, and Viking ships or other ships are not mentioned as payment in contracts for land transactions from the end of the thirteenth or the fourteenth century, a time when prices and the means of payments used are often described in detail. The regulations quoted above provide an intriguing insight into the system of payments in kind in a particular context, but cannot be applied as a basis for ascertaining what types of money were accepted or commonly used in medieval Norway as a whole.

The lack of regulations regarding minting in the provincial laws is in stark contrast to our current knowledge of minting and the organized monetary system of Norway in the second half of the eleventh century, the last quarter of the twelfth century and the thirteenth century. One possible explanation could be that it was not the issuer of coins – the king – who formulated the laws. The older sections of the provincial laws were discussed and agreed on by the *things*, partly as agreements between the farmers and partly as agreements between the farmers and the official powers, i.e. the king and the Church. The earliest examples of regulations for the whole kingdom date from the 1150s and 1160s, but these still had to be accepted by the *lawthings* to become valid law. This is despite the fact that the role of the *things* in the issuing of law had been reduced. It was not the royal coinage, but the types of money used by the farming community that was the most important to the men who issued law at the *lawthings*.

Money and its use at the thing

In the economic system of the Middle Ages the use of goods as a form of payment was based on tradition, while the monetary system was organized by the kings. To organize this for the kingdom as a whole, it seems likely that the Crown made use of the *lawthings*. Here, changes could be announced and practical measures introduced to the most important men within each law-district. These men then returned home and announced the royal decrees at the *things* at shire and local levels. The distances separating the central power and the Norwegian farmers could be measured by the organization of the *thing* system. In this context it is reasonable to assume that the kings used the *thing* meetings on various occasions when coinage was on the political agenda, for instance in the implementation of monetary measures, such as *renovatio monetae*, or recoinage.

Recoinages can be identified on the basis of numismatic, archaeological and written sources, and were carried out especially after the accession of new kings. New rulers asserted themselves through the monetary system; this was one of their time-honoured royal regalia. A supply of silver was essential for this custom, and since Norway did not have any substantial natural silver resources in the Middle Ages, it was through recoinages that the new kings obtained silver for their new coins. This was also an opportunity for the king to rid the monetary system of foreign coins. Medieval Norwegian recoinages seem to have been carried out with great efficiency, as the great majority of coin hoards dating from about 1070 to 1320 only contain coins issued by one king or of a singular type, rather than many different ones (Gullbekk 2009: 33).

During such recoinages the *thingmen* would bring their own coins as well as those of others, and exchange them for new coins in accordance with the royal decree. At the same time, royal representatives would have had an opportunity to travel to the *thing* meetings where new coins were to be introduced. There are no written sources stating that such procedures took place at the assemblies, but from what we know of the *thing* site as a venue for trade and exchange it is difficult to imagine that processes of national character, such as recoinages, took place without the use of the *thing* as a well-established forum of society. In this way, the use of coins quickly became part of the economics of the *thing* site.

The text of the laws suggests that the *thingmen* brought coins to the assemblies. That coins were part of the world of the lawmakers is reflected in the Law of the Gulathing, where it is stated that all *thingmen* should pay their fines

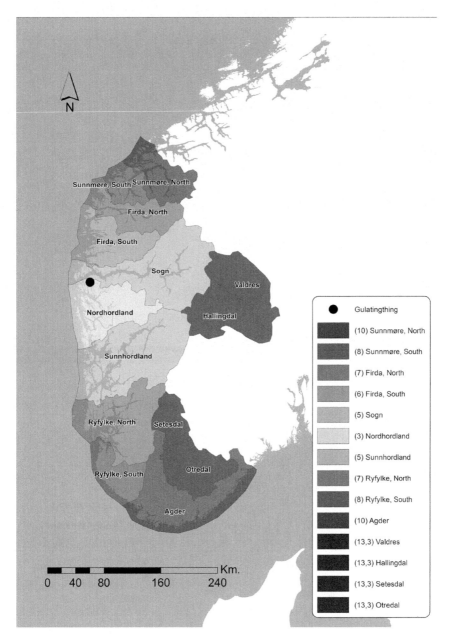

Figures 5.1–5.2 (continued)

(continued)

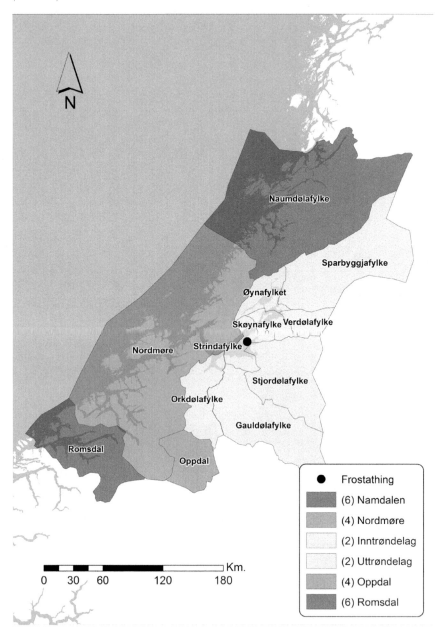

Figures 5.1–5.2 Travel compensation and geographical zones in the Gulathing and Frostathing law-areas stipulated in the Rural Law of Magnus the Lawmender (1274) © Frode Iversen/Svein Gullbekk.

Justice and the administration of coinage 105

at the assembly (G 3: 22), irrespective of whether the guilty party or his relatives intended to pay. If he did not accept his obligation to pay the fine, the king or barons (*lendmaðr*) should pay and then claim twice the amount from the guilty party after his return home (G 3: 23).

> Until he shall offer atonement at the *thing* or in the presence of assembled men and have the money there to pay over. (G 34: 4) . . . [T]hen he shall proceed to the *thing* and shall show by witness what their agreement was; then he shall offer [redemption] money. But if the other man has authorised no one to receive the money, let the suitor have it and keep it until the other man comes to get it.
>
> (G 286: 6–7)

It is difficult to imagine how the *thingmen* could have brought other forms of payment than silver and coins to meet the demands of compensation at the *thing*. Unfortunately, there are no extant accounts of how fines were paid at the *lawthings* in the High Middle Ages (Gullbekk 1998; Lunden 1999). For such descriptions we need to look to the Faroe Islands and Iceland. The Faroe Islanders' Saga describes how Thorir paid his compensation for manslaughter:

> Finn shouted to him to bring out the money. Thorir told him to go ashore and then he would bring it. Then Finn and his men went ashore and Thorir came to him and paid out silver. Out of one bag he produced ten marks by weight, and then took out a number of purses. Some held a mark by weight, others half a mark or perhaps several öre.
>
> (Faroe Islanders' Saga 1975: ch. 45)

There is no doubt that Thorir paid his fine in silver. Several accounts in the Icelandic sagas confirm that silver and coins were used at the assemblies (Gullbekk 2011), among them Egil's Saga, where we are told that the old Egil planned to scatter English silver coins from the law rock to create chaos among the *thingmen*. Egil was, however, persuaded to stay at home with his chests full of English silver, which had been given to him by King Aethelstan after the Battle at Brunanburh in 937 (Egs: 85).

The Norwegian provincial laws contain numerous references to silver and coins. One such regulation, which illustrates the economics of the *thing*, is found in the Law of the Frostathing (F I: 2), 'Concerning the holy bands that the royal steward (*ármaðr*) set up', which states that:

> All men who are appointed to the law court shall sit in it as long as men wish the thing to remain [in session], except that one may leave for private needs. But if a man leaves the law court and goes elsewhere outside the enclosure, he shall be fined a mark in current coin (*tald mark*).
>
> (F I: 2)

The term *tald mark* means marks by the tale and refers to Norwegian coins or royal coins that had been minted in one of the king's workshops and were valid currency. Foreign coins were, on the whole, not seen as valid unless they contained burnt silver. In Norway it was above all English sterling that was in wide circulation. As everywhere, counterfeiting coins was considered a severe offence. The Rural Law of Magnus the Lawmender explicitly stated that 'If someone counterfeits the coins of our king, he shall be punished by permanent outlawry (*ubotamål*)' (L IV: 4.2).

As mentioned above, the assembly regulations stated that the representatives of Namdalen and Romsdalen were entitled to 6 øre silver in travel compensation, while the representatives from Nordmøre and Oppdal were entitled to 4 øre and those from the interior to 2 øre. The money was to be paid to the 'farmers' fund' of Nidaros, a joint fund for the levy fleet (*leiðang*) and the *lawthing* managed by the lawman, who was a royal henchman as well as a trusted farmer (Taranger 1929: 17).

A similar 'levy-fleet fund' is mentioned in Bergen, too (Helle 1995: 542). If a levy-fleet man travelled home without access to food, he was allowed to slaughter two sheep equivalent in value to that of one cow without incurring a fine, as long as he left the hide and head along with 2 øre silver in current coin. Everyone in the Gulathing district should pay half a weighed øre in lawman's toll (NgL III, no. 60). Those responsible for these law texts must have been living in a time when it was common for those on levy-fleet missions to carry coins. This most likely meant that others who travelled in Norway likewise brought money, thus forming part of the economic sphere of the *thing* and the *thingmen*.

Ecclesiastical law and money

In terms of the Church and church law, the monetary fine system was already established in the earliest ecclesiastical laws (Kolsrud 1937–9: 472). In 1162 Archbishop Øystein made a deal with the farmers in the bishopric that fines should be paid in weight rather than coins by tale, i.e. twice the value of the royal fines, which would be paid in coins of burnt silver, but with reduced weight (Hkr., Magnus Erlingssons saga: chs 16, 21). This led to a dispute between Erling Skakke and the archbishop. Erling argued that such an increase in the ecclesiastical fines contradicted the laws of king Olav the Saint. The archbishop responded that there was nothing in Olav's laws prohibiting an increase of God's share (Kolsrud 1937–9: 474–5). This continued to be a source of conflict during the reign of Sverre Sigurdsson, who again brought it up for discussion. A letter of privilege issued by Pope Celestine III for the Norwegian Church on 15 June 1194 reads:

> No king or chieftain should be allowed to change the accepted regulations and laws of the kingdom without the consent of the bishops and wise men, nor the monetary fines for clerics and lay people, contradicting old custom, to the detriment of the Church or the clerics.

As sagas mention this dispute on several occasions, in addition to which it is confirmed by a papal letter, it seems reasonable to assume that the Church had established a functioning monetary fine system already in the middle of the twelfth century or perhaps even earlier.

Conclusions

The *lawthing* served as a hub for spreading news, decisions and proclamations, which delegates brought back to the *things* at shire and local levels across the kingdom. With regard to recoinages, the exchange of coins was announced at the *thing*, and it is argued that gatherings at various levels of society were used as venues for the exchange of old coins for new ones. The economy of the *thing* was, just as other parts of the economy, multi-faceted. As coins gained a wider distribution in society during the High Middle Ages, the royal money became more and more important for the *thing* economy.

The size of the compensation for the *thingmen* who met at assemblies during the course of a year added up to 100 kilograms of silver or 467 marks of burnt silver, which would have been the equivalent of several hundred thousand bracteates in the middle of the thirteenth century, or close to a hundred thousand *penninger* around 1300. Despite the fact that the economic system of medieval Norway was to a large extent dependent on goods and money, it seems that silver and coins were practical forms of payment at the *thing*. People travelled great distances, and it was expected that settlements would be reached during the *thing* meetings. The coins constituted the royal means of payment and were easy to bring on journeys. In this sense they were well suited as payment for the *thingmen* across the realm. Compared to the tax collected by the king at around 1300 – estimated at 3,500 marks of burnt silver annually – the compensation paid for the *thingmen*'s travel in the time of Magnus the Lawmender constituted about 15 per cent. In reality, the costs of implementing the *thing* system were significantly higher, and were to a large extent covered by Norwegian farmers.

Note

1 This constituted 217,000 out of 691,000 (31.4 per cent). The Norwegian figures are taken from the census of 1769. There were then 90,000 inhabitants in the areas corresponding to Borgarthing district (apart from Grenland, which is included in the Skien law-district) in the Middle Ages (an estimated 22,000 for Bohuslän). Altogether, there were c. 60,000 inhabitants in Hålogaland and Finnmark (c. 6,000), and c. 52,000 in Nedenes, Voss and Hardanger. The estimate for Jämtland is c. 15,000.

References

Bjørkvik, Halvard 1980: Landskyld. *Kulturhistorisk Leksikon for Nordisk Middelalder*, vol. X: 281.
Faroe Islanders' Saga: George Johnston (ed.) 1975: *Faroe Islanders' Saga*. Oberon. Canada.

108 *Frode Iversen and Svein H. Gullbekk*

Gullbekk, Svein H. 1998: Medieval law and money in Norway. *Numismatic Chronicle*, vol. 158: 173–84.

—— 2005: Lite eller mye mynt i Norge i middelalderen. *Historisk Tidsskrift*, vol. 84: 552–72.

—— 2009: *Pengevesenets fremvekst og fall i Norge i middelalderen.* Museum Tusculanum Forlag. København.

—— 2011: Money and its use in the saga society: silver, coins, and commodity money. In: Sigmundsson, Svavar (ed.): *Viking Settlements and Viking Society. Papers from the Proceedings of the Sixteenth Viking Congress, Reykjavík and Reykholt, 16–23 August 2009,* pp. 176–89. University of Iceland Press. Reykjavík.

Helle, Knut 1995: *Bergen bys historie. Kongssete og kjøpstad. Fra opphav til 1536.* Bind 1. Alma Mater Forlag. Bergen.

Iversen, Frode 2013: Concilium and Pagus – revisiting the early Germanic thing-system of northern Europe. *Journal of the North Atlantic,* 5: 5–17.

—— 2014: Om aritmetikk og rettferdighet. Tinget i randen av Europa i jernalderen. In: Gullbekk, Svein (ed.): *Ja, vil elsker frihet – En antologi,* pp. 246–56. Dreyer. Oslo.

—— 2015a: Community and society – the thing at the edge of Europe. *Journal of the North Atlantic,* 8: 1–17.

—— 2015b: Hålogaland blir en rettskrets. *Heimen,* 2: 103–25.

Kolsrud, Olaf 1937–9: Kong Magnus Erlingssons kronings-eid 1163. Nye document til norsk historie millom1152 og 1194. *Historisk Tidsskrift,* vol. XXXI: 453–88.

Larson, Lawrence M 1935: *The Earliest Norwegian Laws: Being the Gulathing law and the Frostathing Law.* Translated from the Old Norwegian by Lawrence M. Larson. Records of Civilisation 20. New York. Columbia University Press.

Lunden, Kåre 1978: *Korn og Kaup. Studiar over prisar og jordbruk på Vestlandet i mellomalderen.* Universitetsforlaget. Oslo-Bergen-Tromsø.

—— 1999: Money economy in medieval Norway. *Scandinavian Journal of History,* vol. 24: 245–65.

Sandvik, Gudmund 1997: Dei norske landskapslovene frå mellomalderen. Nokre aktuelle problemstillingar og forskningsoppgåver. In: Dybdahl, Audun and Jørn Sandnes (eds): *Nordiske middelalderlover – tekst og kontekst.* Skrifter, vol. 5: 33–8. Senter for Middelalderstudier. Trondheim.

Taranger, Absalon (ed.) 1915: *Magnus Lagabøtes landslov,* translated by Absalon Taranger 1915. Cammermeyers boghandel, Kristiania.

Taranger, Absalon 1929: *Trondheims forfatningshistorie.* Det Kongelige Norske Videnskabers Selskabs skrifter 5. Trondheim.

Part II

Production and resources

6 The extensive iron production in Norway in the tenth to thirteenth century

A regional perspective

Ole Tveiten and Kjetil Loftsgarden

Introduction

Iron production from bog ore, often referred to as 'bloomery' or 'primitive' iron production, is known in Scandinavia from the Early Iron Age up to the end of the Middle Ages. In this chapter we will discuss the intensification of iron production from the late tenth century AD onwards. An important question in this regard is: what factors made it possible – what were the preconditions for this increase during the later Viking Age, and for subsequent large-scale production during the eleventh to thirteenth century? This chapter aims to examine these questions by discussing aspects of the structure and technology of iron production, as well as the actors involved. Our main focus areas are the valleys and mountainous areas of South Norway. A closer look at the general development in this area is presented through a case study of Gravdalen in Valdres, Oppland, South-East Norway (see Skre this vol., Figure 1.1), which illustrates the comprehensive changes in iron technology and intensity of production. However, we argue that the themes explored will be applicable and have relevance beyond South Norway.

Today over 3,500 iron production sites (*jernvinneanlegg*) are listed in the Norwegian database for cultural heritage, Askeladden; similarly, the number of such sites (*blästbrukslämning*) in the Swedish database for cultural heritage, Fornsök, is well over 5,000 (Figure 6.1). These sites represent iron production over a period of at least two millennia, from the last centuries BC to the late eighteenth century AD. Based on the chronology of the iron production sites, it is possible to sort the material, thus revealing certain patterns concerning use of the landscape. In general, it is clear that during the sixth century AD production was gradually moving away from the arable land and central settlements, into more marginal areas.

The earliest iron production in Norway, currently known from a few sites dated to the Pre-Roman Iron Age (500–1 BC), occurs in connection with central farming settlements (Larsen 2009: 53–4; Larsen and Rundberget 2014). Similar finds from Sweden indicate that the earliest iron production started in central bronze-casting milieus in the later part of the Bronze Age (Hjärthner-Holdar 1993: 38). In Denmark, iron production is known from approximately

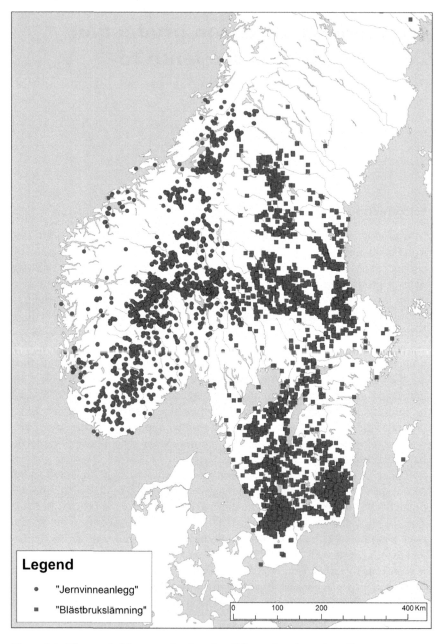

Figure 6.1 All recorded iron production sites (Norw. *jernvinneanlegg*; Sw. *blästbrukslämning*) ranging from the fourth century BC to the nineteenth century AD in Norway and Sweden. As of September 2015 this includes 3,609 *jernvinneanlegg* and 5,466 *blästbrukslämning*.

Source: Data from the Norwegian database for cultural heritage, Askeladden, and the Swedish database for cultural heritage, Fornsök.

400–200 BC (Jouttijärvi and Voss 2013: 83). During the last centuries BC, the activity increased, and several excavations have recorded extensive iron production during the Roman Iron Age (AD 1–400) and most of the Migration Period (AD 400–550). Shaft furnaces with a slag pit are the preferred technology of the period, as in most of the Germanic areas (Pleiner 2000: 45). In Norway, furnaces of this type are generally found at elevations approximately between 150 and 1,000 m a.s.l. In some areas, the iron production is concentrated at historical shielings, frequently in outfield areas. Excavations and pollen analyses have in some cases documented a correlation between these, indicating that the iron production preceded the agricultural use of the land, perhaps even as a means of clearing the land (Tveiten and Pettersson 2013: 52).

The sixth and seventh centuries AD witnessed major changes in material culture, language and social structure (Gräslund and Price 2012). These societal changes are also reflected in the iron technology. During the seventh and eighth centuries AD, the furnaces with slag pits were gradually replaced by smaller furnaces with slag-tapping. The changes in Norwegian and Swedish iron production in this period seem to be paralleled by similar changes in other parts of North-Western Europe, where iron production moved away from settlements into areas offering easier access to raw materials, wood and iron ore (Nørbach 1999: 245; Larsen 2009: 95). In Norway, iron production moved higher up in the woodland and low mountain areas than before, and spread over larger areas.

From about 900 AD, the activity was further intensified, and by the end of the twelfth century iron production using the slag-tapping furnace reached its largest extent in Norway, with sites found up to the upper tree limit, about 1,200 m a.s.l. (Bloch-Nakkerud and Lindblom 1994: 41–2; Larsen and Rundberget 2009: 48). The intensity of iron production is apparent from the thousands of production sites recorded. It has been estimated that in South-East Norway alone as much as 130,000 tonnes of iron was produced in this time period (Rundberget 2013: 253–4). While the earlier furnaces used wood as fuel, separate pits used for charcoal production were introduced together with the new type of slag-tapping furnace. These structures, easily recognisable as 1–5-m-deep circular or square pits dug into the ground, are frequently found in the areas of iron production, and today well over 20,000 such pits are recorded (Loftsgarden 2015).

Figure 6.1 shows the general distribution of iron production sites in Sweden and Norway from the Early Iron Age (c. 200 BC) to the late eighteenth century AD. The largest numbers of sites consist either of slag pit furnaces or slag-tapping furnaces, but a general lack of comprehensive descriptions makes a detailed division difficult. A way of highlighting the distribution of slag-tapping furnaces is by analysing the distribution of charcoal pits. In Norway, as in Sweden, these are closely related to iron production in the Viking Age and Middle Ages (c. AD 800–1450), and are most often found in clusters of between 3 and 15 within a kilometre of the nearest iron production site. This material gives an indication of the core areas of iron production during the Viking Age

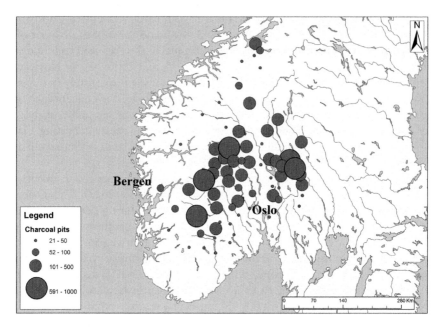

Figure 6.2 Distribution of charcoal pits (20,462 pits), indicating iron production sites in the Viking Age and Middle Ages, tenth to fourteenth century, in Norway.

Source: Data from the Norwegian database for cultural heritage, Askeladden.

and Middle Ages; in Norway these correspond mainly to the upper parts of the valleys of South-East Norway (Figure 6.2).

On the other hand, remains from iron production in Denmark during the Viking Age and Middle Ages are few and far between. Whether this indicates large-scale iron import from Swedish and Norwegian areas, as suggested by Jørgen Elsøe Jensen (2010), or whether it may partly be attributed to the fact that the Danish slag-tapping furnace seems to leave almost no trace in an intensively cultivated landscape (Lyngstrøm 2013: 131) is an interesting question, but one that is beyond the scope of this chapter.

Figure 6.2 shows that the slag-tapping furnaces, to a larger degree than the earlier sites, are concentrated in the upper parts of the main valleys in eastern Norway, namely Setesdal, Telemark, Hallingdal and Valdres, and the middle part of Østerdalen, towards the Swedish border (see Figure 6.1 for an overview). Equally interesting is the lack of iron production sites in the central and more populated areas closer to the coast of South Norway or in Trøndelag, which had at least some earlier iron production (Larsen 2009: 94–5). Regional specialisation must have occurred, where areas that were marginal from an agricultural perspective took on the role of iron producers, while other areas may have specialised in other products (Narmo 2003; Tveiten 2012). Stable networks with a functional market economy, trade routes and hubs must obviously have been an important factor in making this specialisation possible (Loftsgarden 2011).

Technological changes in iron production

For a long time, since the age of Thomsen and Montelius, evolutionism has exerted a significant influence throughout the discipline of archaeology, and this has been a central factor in explaining the variation in furnaces found during excavations in Scandinavia, especially in the period before the radiocarbon method of dating was available. Since archaeologists were dependent on dateable objects to estimate the age of iron production, and since such finds were generally rare at iron production sites, the process of estimating the age of the furnaces was rather difficult. Still, a general agreement has existed that an evolutionary approach should be adopted to understand the development, with the assumption that it moved from primitive to more complex technology. The furnaces were expected to have developed from small pits dug into the ground to large furnaces built with stones during the sixteenth and seventeenth centuries (Hauge 1946: 134). All changes in the archaeological record could be interpreted as improvements in the efficacy of the technology, which in turn caused changes in society.

However, a paradox of pre-industrial iron production in Norway and Scandinavia is that the technological changes seem to move in the opposite direction, from large and complex sites to smaller and simpler sites. Some of the largest sites documented in Norway are found in Trøndelag, dating mainly to the period 200 BC–AD 500. On these sites between four and eight furnaces occur, lined up on a ridge, usually close to a river or lake. As much as 100 tonnes of slag is documented at some of these sites, making them by far the largest in Norway (Farbregd et al. 1985; Stenvik 1997). Large-scale iron production sites from approximately 1–700 AD are also found at several other places in South Norway (Johansen 1973; Indrelid 1988; Larsen 1991, 2003; Larsen and Rundberget 2009). Compared with these production sites, those of the Viking Age and Middle Ages are small. The largest sites, usually with two furnaces and between 20 and 45 tonnes of slag, occur in Østerdalen (Narmo 1997; Rundberget 2007, 2013). Further west, most sites are substantially smaller, rarely with more than two to five tonnes of slag (Larsen 2004: 152). Why do these changes from large and complex to smaller and simpler sites occur?

Two aspects of the new technology are of interest here: the charcoal pits and the new furnaces. Both elements were introduced during the latter part of the Iron Age, prior to the massive rise in iron production in the Viking Age and particularly the first part of the Middle Ages. While the earlier iron production was based on pine, generally thought to have been charred in the furnaces prior to smelting, the new charcoal pits facilitated the use of all sorts of wood, pushing iron production further upwards to the tree limit, 1,100–1,200 m a.s.l. Also, the charred wood could be stored in the pits for a long time after the charring process (Narmo 1996: 53–4). Since the furnace was no longer used for the process of charring wood, its size could be reduced, from a diameter of about 1.0 m to less than 0.5 m. The method of slag-tapping also changed, from a pit dug under the furnace shaft in the earlier periods to horizontal tapping of the slag from the shaft in the Viking Age and medieval furnaces (Larsen 2004: 140–2).

One of the most important consequences of these technological changes is that it made iron production more mobile. Instead of investing a lot of resources on one site for a long time, possibly several generations, smaller and simpler sites were used for a few seasons, before production was moved to a new site, close to the resources – charcoal and ore. The technology itself was probably not more effective than the earlier one, but the mobility made it less rigid, and thus more robust and adaptable to political and economic changes.

Another important consequence is that iron production could more easily be adjusted to varying patterns of supply and demand. Inhabitants of the relatively marginal inner valleys and mountain regions of Norway would not risk spending time and resources in producing large quantities of iron from bog ore if they were not confident that they could exchange iron for goods they needed or wanted. The smaller and thus more flexible furnaces from the Viking Age and Middle Ages enabled iron production to become one of several outfield resources to be exploited, depending on economic factors such as demand, or the existence of stable social and economic networks, along with marketplaces enabling trade.

The example of Gravfjellet

To provide an example of the technological changes outlined, and to illustrate the massive iron production occurring particularly in the eleventh to thirteenth century, we will present a recent survey of iron production sites in a local context. Gravfjellet is an area in the valley district of Valdres, a region with considerable remains of iron production. At Gravfjellet, Oppland County Council has conducted extensive surveys, combined with testing of new methods and technologies such as LIDAR (Light Detection And Ranging). This technology is used to create detailed three-dimensional maps of the landscape, making it possible to identify cultural heritage sites, particularly charcoal-burning and hunting pits (Pilø et al. 2012, 2013; Pilø 2013).

Gravfjellet is located 0.5 to 7 km from the nearest Iron Age and medieval settlements, and between 600 and 1,100 m a.s.l. The area is dominated by bog and forest (spruce, birch and pine), with shielings scattered across the landscape. Iron production was known to have taken place in the area, making it suitable as a test area for LIDAR technology. In 2011 the area was scanned, and preliminary surveys were conducted. During the summer and autumn of 2012 more extensive surveys were conducted, covering about 10 km² of Gravfjellet. After these surveys, some 100 iron production sites and 450 charcoal pits were documented in the area. However, the distribution of iron production sites is

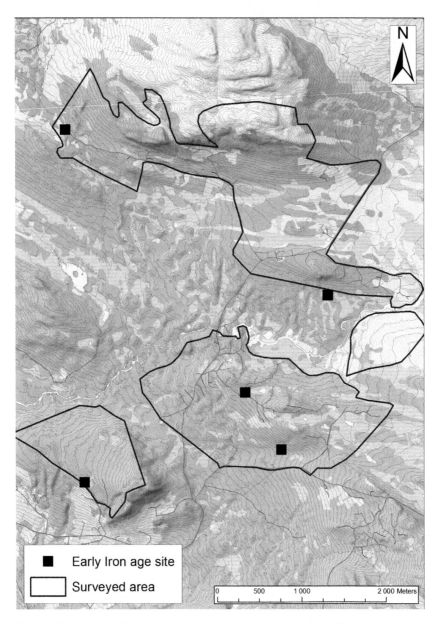

Figure 6.3 Recorded Early Iron Age sites in the Gravfjellet area. The map also shows the surveyed areas.

much wider than this area. Based on the LIDAR scanning, it is estimated that the municipality of Øystre Slidre, where Gravfjellet is located, has some 700 iron production sites and 4,000 charcoal pits (Pilø et al. 2012; Tveiten and

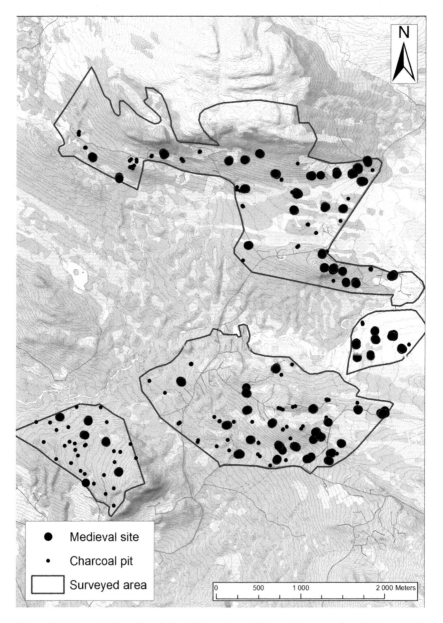

Figure 6.4 Recorded medieval sites (eleventh to thirteenth century) and charcoal pits in the same area.

Pettersson 2013). The survey at Gravfjellet demonstrates the magnitude of iron production during the late Viking Age and Middle Ages, and indicates that it must have constituted a vital economic factor during this period.

In the surveyed area, five of the approximately 100 iron production sites were found to be shaft furnaces with slag pits. The rest of the sites were shaft furnaces with slag-tapping. Radiocarbon dating of some of the sites in Gravfjellet, as well as nearby excavated sites, indicates that the main period of iron production was the early eleventh to mid-thirteenth century, with a rapid decline in the latter half of the thirteenth century (Narmo 1996: 186; Mjærum 2007: 185; Tveiten and Pettersson 2013: 40). The area thus also illustrates the major differences between the two main phases of iron production in Norway. While the earlier sites (slag pit furnaces) are represented by a few relatively large sites, the later type (slag-tapping furnaces) is represented by smaller sites, found in vast numbers across the outfield landscape (see Figures 6.3 and 6.4).

Actors in the iron production

The number of sites and overall size and complexity of the iron production are substantial, and must have involved a large number of actors with the right skills and resources. In the early modern period, from the early sixteenth century onwards, the Scandinavian kings were heavily involved in the growing industry of iron production (Christophersen 1974: 33–5). The earlier period, particularly from the eleventh to the fourteenth centuries, may be seen as a period where the relatively newly established Norwegian kingdom gradually gained power over larger areas of the country, and where laws and regulations increasingly were affecting everyday life. The sources regarding these processes are few, with the regional laws from the twelfth and early thirteenth century (*Gulatingslovi* and *Frostatingslova*) and the national law (*Magnus Lagabøters Landslov*) replacing the prior in the year 1274, constituting the main sources. None of these laws give much information concerning iron production or other outfield activities, other than stating that the conditions should be as they traditionally have been. In *Frostatingslova* and *Magnus Lagabøters Landslov*, forges in the outfield are mentioned – probably meaning iron production sites – but only in connection with compensation for damages. Even if regional and national laws hardly mention iron production, diplomas mainly from the late thirteenth and fourteenth centuries – which often are more specific than the general laws – indicate some tendencies of the king's as well as the Church's view on iron production (see Table 6.1). The main point to take from this limited material is that the Church as well as the king did not initiate or control the iron production. Instead, there seems to have been a gradual process towards a regulated market for iron, mainly in the cities.

One of the main incomes of the Church in the Middle Ages was the tithe, where the farmers had to offer a tenth of their harvest to the Church. From the late fourteenth century, this tax also included outfield products, but for iron only half a tithe – one in twenty – had to be paid in tax to the Church. Even with this low tithe, the Church's income in the form of iron must have been substantial, but it seems that the different units of the clergy had unequal incomes of iron. In the western part of the country, medieval iron production

120 *Ole Tveiten and Kjetil Loftsgarden*

Table 6.1 Documents from the thirteenth and fourteenth centuries concerning iron

Year	Text	Reference
1263	Iron producers must pay tithe to the Church.	RN 1: 1009
1277	One out of 20 pounds of iron must be paid as tithe to the Church.	RN 2: 181
1308	Properties given to the bishop in Stavanger may be paid out either in iron or butter.	DN IV no. 77
1282	Price regulations on iron in Bergen.	NgL III no. 2
1293	Guilds among smiths in Bergen are banned.	NgL III no. 6
1338–40	The Bishop of Bergen is in need of iron and asks the Bishop of Stavanger and Trondheim for help.	DN VIII no. 102; DN IX no. 118; DN VII no. 173
1358	The people of Østerdalen are given the right to make iron in the outfield areas and sell it at any market.	DN VI no. 238
1377	Price regulations on forging in Trondheim.	NgL III no. 110
1384	Price regulations on forging in Bergen.	NgL III no. 120

Note: RN = Regesta Norvegica, DN = Diplomatarium Norvegicum, NgL = Norges Gamle Love.

appears to have been minimal, and the written sources indicate that the Bishop of Bergen, in particular, seems to have lacked a steady supply of iron.

The king and Church could, of course, have owned farms or parts of farms in the areas of great iron production, gaining access to the outfield resources in this way. However, this does not seem to have been the case. When comparing the areas of large-scale medieval iron production with the structure of ownership, we find that most of the iron production occurred in areas dominated by private ownership, undertaken either by the farmer himself or by other farmers in the area (Bjørkvik and Holmsen 1972: 71; Helle 1974: 158).

The role of iron in these inner valleys and mountain regions of South Norway can be glimpsed through diplomas from the thirteenth and fourteenth centuries; Valdres is especially prominent in this regard. In all, five different smiths are mentioned here; iron is also mentioned in the sale of farms, being used as payment on three separate occasions (Blom 1991: 82–3). The smiths are often found as members of the jury in local trials, indicating that they were prominent members of the community. Iron was used as payment together with grain, cattle and butter, all of these being locally available commodities.

Conclusion

The massive increase in iron production in Norway and Sweden from the ninth century onwards follows certain general trends, including a rise in population, agrarian expansion and the establishment of towns. However, in this chapter we have taken a regional viewpoint and from this perspective have tried to point out some of the most important aspects and preconditions enabling the increase in iron production.

The technology changed prior to the rise in iron production, from a few large sites with large furnaces, to many smaller and more flexible sites. By reducing the size of the furnaces and the investment in each site, and introducing a more flexible and mobile technology instead, bog ore and wood could be exploited in areas hitherto left undisturbed. We further argue that the most plausible interpretation of the many small iron production sites found in the valleys and mountainous regions of South Norway is that iron production was organised by specialised farmers. Iron production could be carried out in parallel with animal husbandry, and the small iron production sites enabled flexibility in response to trends and forces in the demand for iron or in society as a whole. Consequently, stable social and economic networks, with smithies or seasonal marketplaces as hubs, where the iron-producing farmers could exchange the iron they had produced were a necessary precondition for the massive rise in iron production on a regional as well as national level.

References

Bjørkvik, Halvard and Andreas Holmsen 1972: *Kven åtte jorda i den gamle leiglendingstida?: fordelinga av jordeigedomen i Noreg i 1661*. Tapir. Trondheim.

Bloch-Nakkerud, Tom and Inge Lindblom 1994: *Far etter folk i Hallingdal: På leiting etter den eldste historia*. Buskmål AS. Gol.

Blom, Grethe Authen 1991: Jern og kobber i eldre skriftlige kilder. In: Stenvik, Lars F. (ed.): *Arkeo-metallurgi: Kurs ved Universitetet i Trondheim 11.–15. januar 1988*. Rapport. Arkeologisk Serie 1991: vol. 1: 79–99. Vitenskapsmuseet, Universitetet i Trondheim. Trondheim.

Christophersen, Halfdan Olaus 1974: *Hammerslag på hammerslag: Fra jernverkenes historie i Norge*. Grøndahl and Søn. Oslo.

DN: *Diplomatarium Norvegicum I–XXIII*. 1847–1998. Riksarkivet. Christiania/Oslo.

Elsøe Jensen, Jørgen 2010: *Gensidig afhængighed: en arv fra fortiden. Danmarks middelalderbyer – et vidnesbyrd om spredningen af vestlig civilisation*. Syddansk universitetsforlag. Odense.

Farbregd, Oddmund, Lil Gustafson and Lars F. Stenvik 1985: Tidlig jernproduksjon i Trøndelag. Undersøkelsene på Heglesvollen. *Viking XLVIII*: 103–29.

Frostatingslova: Hagland, Jan Ragnar and Jørn Sandnes (eds) 1994: *Frostatingslova*. Norrøne bokverk. Det norske samlaget. Oslo.

Gräslund, Bo and Neil Price 2012: Twilight of the gods? : The 'dust veil event' of AD 536 in critical perspective. *Antiquity*, 86(33): 428–43.

Gulatingslovi: Robberstad, Knut (ed.) 1937: *Gulatingslova*. Norrøne bokverk 33. Det norske samlaget. Oslo.

Hauge, T. Dannevig 1946: *Blesterbruk og myrjern. Studier i den gamle jernvinna i det østenfjeldske Norge*. Universitetets Oldsaksamlings skrifter, vol. III. Oslo.

Helle, Knut 1974: *Norge blir en stat: 1130–1319*. Universitetsforlaget. Bergen.

Hjärthner-Holdar, Eva 1993: *Järnets och järnmetallurgins introduktion i Sverige*. Aun 16. Uppsala.

Indrelid, Svein 1988: Jernalderfunn i Flåmsfjella: Arkeologiske data og kulturhistorisk tolking. In: Indrelid, Svein, Sigrid Kaland and Bergljot Solberg (eds): *Festskrift til Anders Hagen*, pp. 106–19. Arkeologiske skrifter, vol. 4. Historisk museum, University of Bergen. Bergen.

122 Ole Tveiten and Kjetil Loftsgarden

Johansen, Arne B. 1973: Iron production as a factor in the settlement history of the mountain valleys surrounding Hardangervidda. *Norwegian Archaeological Review*, 6(2): 84–101.

Jouttijärvi, Arne and Olfert Voss 2013: Drengsted/Scharmbeck slaggegrube ovnen i Danmark og i Skandinavien. In: Rundberget, Bernt, Jan Henning Larsen and Tom H. Borse Haraldsen (eds): *Ovnstypologi og ovnskronologi i den nordiske jernvinna: Jernvinna i Oppland: symposium på Kittilbu. 16.–18. juni 2009*, pp. 83–93. Portal. Oslo.

Larsen, Jan Henning 1991: *Jernvinna ved Dokkfløyvatn: De arkeologiske undersøkelsene 1986–1989*. Varia 23. Universitetets Oldsaksamling. Oslo.

—— 2003: Lokalt initiativ og jernvinneforskning i Snertingdal, Gjøvik kommune i Oppland: bidrag til forståelsen av jernutvinningen i eldre jernalder på Østlandet. *Viking LXVI*: 79–104.

—— 2004: Jernvinna på Østlandet i yngre jernalder og middelalder: noen kronologiske problemer. *Viking LXVII*: 139–70.

—— 2009: *Jernvinneundersøkelser: Faglig program. Bind 2*. Varia 78. Kulturhistorisk museum. Oslo.

Larsen, Jan Henning and Bernt Rundberget 2009: Raw materials, iron extraction and settlement in South-East Norway 200 BC–AD 1150. In: Brattli, Terje (ed.): *The 58th International Sachensymposium 1–5 September 2007*. Vitark 7: 38–50. Acta Archaeologica Nidarosiensia. Tapir Akademisk Forlag. Trondheim.

—— 2014: Iron bloomery in South and Central Norway, 300 BC–500 AD. In: Cech, Brigitte and Thilo Rehren (eds): *Early Iron in Europe*, pp. 231–49. Monographies instrumentum, vol. 50. Editions Monique Mergoil. Montagnac.

Loftsgarden, Kjetil 2011: Jernonna i Vest-Telemark: Jern som utmarksressurs og bytemiddel for ein lokal gardsbusetnad i vikingtid og mellomalder. *Primitive tider*, 13: 61–73.

—— 2015: Kolgroper: gull eller gråstein? In: Inger Marie Berg-Hansen (ed.): *Arkeologiske undersøkelser 2005–2006*, pp. 142–54. Portal. Kulturhistorisk Museum. Oslo.

Lyngstrøm, Henriette 2013: Slaggeaftapningsovne i Danmark, udgravninger og forsøg. In: Rundberget, Bernt, Jan Henning Larsen and Tom H. Borse Haraldsen (eds): *Ovnstypologi og ovnskronologi i den nordiske jernvinna: Jernvinna i Oppland: symposium på Kittilbu. 16.–18. juni 2009*, pp. 119–34. Portal. Oslo.

Magnus Lagabøters Landslov: Taranger, Absalon (ed.) 1915: *Magnus Lagabøters Landslov* Universitetsforlaget. Oslo.

Martens, Irmelin 1988: *Jernvinna på Møsstrond i Telemark: En studie i teknikk, bosetning og økonomi*. Norske oldfunn XIII. Universitetets Oldsaksamling. Oslo.

Mjærum, Axel 2007: Jord og jern. Jernvinna på Beitostølen i middelalderen. *Årbok for Valdres 2007*: 176–88.

Narmo, Lars Erik 1996: *Jernvinna i Valdres og Gausdal: et fragment av middelalderens økonomi*. Varia 38. Universitetets Oldsaksamling. Oslo.

—— 1997: *Jernvinne, smie og kullproduksjon i Østerdalen: Arkeologiske undersøkelser på Rødsmoen i Åmot 1994–1996*. Varia 43. Universitetets Oldsaksamling. Oslo.

—— 2003: Relations between settlement pattern, social structure and medieval iron production: A case study from Gausdal, Southern Norway. In: Nørbach, Lars Christian (ed.): *Prehistoric and Medieval Direct Iron Smelting in Scandinavia and Europe: Aspects of Technology and Society. Proceedings of the Sandbjerg Conference 16th to 20th September 1999*. Acta Jutlandica LXXXVI(2): 27–32. Humanities series 75. Århus.

Nørbach, Lars Christian 1999: Organising iron production and settlement in north-western Europe during the Iron Age. In: Farbech, Charlotte and Jytte Ringtved (eds): *Settlement and Landscape: Proceedings of a Conference in Århus, Denmark, May 4–7 1998*, pp. 237–47. Jutland Archaeological Society. Højbjerg.

Pilø, Lars 2013: FoU *delprosjekt: Utredning av egnethet av HD-lidarkartlegging som arbeidsverktøy i kulturminneforvaltningen*. Kulturhistoriske skrifter 2013/1. Oppland County Concil.

Pilø, Lars, Anne Engesveen and Susanne Pettersson 2012: *Opplandsprosjekt på tidlig avklaring av kulturminner med ny teknologi. Rapport frå forprosjektet*. Kulturhistorisk serie 2012/1. Oppland County Concil.

Pilø, Lars, Anne Engesveen, Susanne Pettersson and Ole Tveiten 2013: *OPPtakt. Årsrapport 2012*. Kulturhistorisk serie 2013/1. Oppland County Concil.

Pleiner, Radomir 2000: *Iron in Archaeology: The European Bloomery Smelters*. Archeologický ústav AV ČR. Prague.

RN: *Regesta Norvegica*. 1989–. Riksarkivet. Oslo.

Rundberget, Bernt 2007: *Jernvinna i Gråfjellområdet: Gråfjellprosjektet. Bind I*. Varia 63. Kulturhistorisk museum. Oslo.

—— 2013: *Jernets dunkle dimensjon: Jernvinna i sørlige Hedmark – sentral økonomisk faktor og premiss for samfunnsuvikling c. AD 700–1300*. PhD thesis in archaeology. University of Oslo.

Stenvik, Lars F. 1997: Iron production in Mid-Norway, an answer to local demand? *Studien zur Sachsenforschung*, 10: 253–63.

Tveiten, Ole 2012: *Mellom aust og vest: Ein arkeologisk analyse av jarnvinna kring Langfjella i yngre jarnalder og mellomalder*. PhD thesis in archaeology. University of Bergen.

—— 2013: Bondejarn? Produksjon og distribusjon av jarn til Vestlandet. In: Diinhoff, Søren, Morten Ramstad and Tore Slinning (eds): *Jordbruksbosetningens utvikling på Vestlandet: Seminar om dagens kunnskapsstatus, presentasjon av nye resultater og fremtidige problemstillinger*. UBAS 7: 205–16. University of Bergen.

Tveiten, Ole and Susanne Pettersson 2013: *Kulturminne i Gravfjellet: Kulturhistoriske registreringer i Gravfjellområdet, Øystre Slidre i Oppland*. Kulturhistoriske rapporter 2013/2. Oppland County Council.

7 Viking-period non-ferrous metalworking and urban commodity production

Unn Pedersen

Introduction

The production of metal jewellery flourished in Scandinavia in the early Viking period, concurrent with the emergence of new centres for trade and craft (Callmer 1995; Sindbæk 2007; Pedersen 2010, 2016a). In this chapter I shall discuss the relationship between the production and the exchange of metal dress accessories on the basis of the archaeological finds from the Viking-period town of Kaupang in Vestfold (Skre 2007a) – the place in Norway that currently offers the best picture of non-ferrous metalworking. Based on previous research, I will discuss more closely the variety and scope of non-ferrous metalworking identified at Kaupang. I argue that the production, distribution and use of jewellery and other items are closely related, and much more complex than hitherto acknowledged. The manufacture of these products cannot be seen in isolation from the social context of use and disposal, and the craftspeople must have navigated through various types of exchange modes and social spheres.

Urban commodity production?

A lead mould for wax models and 25 different lead models (Figure 7.1) show that serial production of dress accessories was a characteristic feature of the non-ferrous metalworking at Kaupang (Pedersen 2016a: 38–78). These tools were used to make clay moulds, and they are both suited to the production of a large number of virtually identical moulds which were subsequently used to manufacture extended series of more or less indistinguishable products. Stylistic datings and the context of the lead models reveal that this serial production continued from the foundation of Kaupang, around the year 800, right through the ninth century and into the tenth, possibly right up until the cessation of urban activity around the year 930 (Pedersen 2016a: 190).

Serial production has long been recognized as a typical feature of metal-casting in the Viking-period towns (Brinch Madsen 1984: 93) and is also reflected in the burial finds through an evident standardization of dress accessories (Callmer 1984, 1995). According to Callmer (1995: 66), serial production began during the eighth century and flourished in the ninth and tenth

Figure 7.1 A lead mould for wax models (upper row, centre) and lead models for making equal-armed brooches and strap-ends.
Source: © Museum of Cultural History, University of Oslo. Photo by Eirik Irgens Johnsen.

centuries. It differed from a preceding style of production to order, under which individualistic items were more prominent, and Callmer (1995: 66) claims that the serial production was directed at customers with whom the producers had, at most, limited contact.

The largest group of lead models from Kaupang is for making equal-armed brooches (Pedersen 2016a: 40–9), while amongst the few clay moulds in which the impression can be identified there are several for oval brooches (Pedersen 2016a: 100–1). In both cases, the graves show that these were dress accessories of copper alloy which were worn by large numbers of women and were popular over large areas of Scandinavia (Jansson 1985; Callmer 1999). These two types of brooch have also been highlighted by archaeologists who have discussed serial production (Brinch Madsen 1984; Callmer 1984, 1995). The lead models of equal-armed brooches from Kaupang are for different types, and stylistic datings indicate that several types of brooch were manufactured at the same time (Pedersen 2016a: Fig. 4.28). In the same way, Claus Feveile (2002: 24–5) has shown that various types of oval brooch and other items of jewellery were being produced within a single workshop in Ribe. The evidence from the two Viking-period towns thus indicates that, at any one time, residents and visitors could choose between different types and variants of copper-alloy brooches.

The sequence of production suggests that the equal-armed brooches were made in advance. The clay moulds could only be used once, and it takes time

126   *Unn Pedersen*

to manufacture a series of equal-armed brooches using a single lead model. This is slow serial production, as each mould is shaped around the model when the clay is wet, and the lead model has to remain in the clay mould until the latter has dried, which can require 24 hours for each of the two halves that make up the mould (Hedegaard 2005: 11). It would, therefore, take at least 100 days to produce 50 equal-armed brooches using just one lead model. It is, therefore, reasonable to suppose that the craftspeople cast greater or smaller stocks of brooches with a view to eventually trading them. They may alternatively have prepared stocks of moulds for eventual use (Dunér and Vinberg 2006: 21).

At Kaupang, more regular mass production of items that were extremely similar has also been demonstrated, along with serial production (Pedersen 2016a: 82–3). A mould of volcanic tuff provides an insight into the manufacture of simple cast pendants (Figure 7.2). A large number of pieces could in this case be cast in the re-usable mould within a very short space of time, and six lead pendants are local products from this style of mass production (Figure 7.3). Similar and contemporary items of lead and tin jewellery are known from Frankish and Frisian regions, where they are interpreted as affordable jewellery (Wamers 1994: 197–8), and large quantities of lead from Kaupang also show that this metal was considered cheap (Pedersen 2016a: 192). Once again, it is reasonable to suppose that the extensive production was directed at customers with whom the craftspeople had limited contact, and that the producers were able to sell the products of their craft.

The Viking-period towns brought large numbers of people together and had relatively large populations – in the case of Kaupang up to 800 inhabitants (Stylegar 2007: 87). The preconditions were thus laid for the craftspeople to be able to produce series of equal-armed or oval brooches in the hope of subsequently disposing of them. The finds from the towns emphasize that these were places of buying and selling, with a system of exchange which made it easy to dispose of trade goods. The weights and hacksilver from Kaupang indicate that even products of minor value were bought and sold (Hårdh 2008; Pedersen 2008). Thus, the towns were fora in which the artisans could sell pre-manufactured dress accessories, including pieces of limited economic value. They received a recognized currency in return. The hacksilver could be used as a means of payment for the purchase of raw materials or other necessary items, and also itself served as a raw material in non-ferrous metalworking. The latter point is illustrated by the half-melted contents of a crucible found at Kaupang (Blackburn 2008: Fig. 3.1). In this case the process of melting down coins, a fragment of an armring and other hacksilver was interrupted.

I have earlier suggested (Pedersen 2015a) that the manufacture of pendants as well as equal-armed and oval brooches therefore seems to offer a direct connection with the concept of 'urban commodity production', the objective of which was commercial disposal in the market (Christophersen 1982). The past has been described as a foreign place (Lowenthal 1985), but the production of large numbers of Type P37 oval brooches (Petersen 1928: Fig. 37) of consistent and reliable quality does not appear so peculiar in an age in which we make

Figure 7.2 Mould for lead pendants.
Source: © Museum of Cultural History, University of Oslo. Photo by Eirik Irgens Johnsen.

pilgrimages to IKEA to furnish our homes with bookcases called *Billy*. We are likewise not unfamiliar with the concept of a new design first being copied by skilled copyists and then becoming the object of less careful mass production, just as Signe Horn Fuglesang (1987) has demonstrated in the case of the oval brooches. Does the non-ferrous metalworking actually provide us with an insight into a field in which there were striking similarities to our own time?

Figure 7.3 Lead pendant.
Source: © Museum of Cultural History, University of Oslo. Photo by Eirik Irgens Johnsen.

128   *Unn Pedersen*

Serial production to order

Starting from Callmer's position, serial production has been treated as identical to production for an anonymous market, and as fundamentally different from the production of individual ('bespoke') pieces to order (Skre 2007a: 450). Callmer himself (1995: 65–9) insisted that the relations were more complex, a point reinforced by the evidence found at Kaupang. The lead models show that very different artefacts were produced serially. One of these implements was used to produce cruciform pendants of gold or silver foil which were decorated with filigree (Figure 7.4). An item of gold jewellery of this kind is known from the hoard of Lackalänga in Skåne (Strömberg 1961: 62), and the Hiddensee find on Rügen indicates that a number of items of pressed-foil jewellery could be collected together in a valuable necklace (Paulsen 1936). The lead model was thus used for the production of jewellery that is less likely to have been made in the general hope that a purchaser would just turn up. The valuable metal and the considerable investment of time in every single pendant suggests that this was made to order, as was generally the case with later medieval goldsmiths' work in Norway (Kielland 1927: 35). As noted, bespoke production of this kind has also been proposed as a characteristic of both earlier and contemporary political centres (Callmer 1995: 64–5).

Detailed investigations of the archaeological record suggest that urban production to order may have been of some size. Melted globules are the product of metal having splashed or run down onto the ground during casting, and such waste is often used to determine which metals the craftspeople were working. From the fieldwork at Kaupang of 1998–2003 one minute drop of gold was collected, very limited quantities of silver, and large quantities of globules of both lead and copper alloy (Pedersen 2013: Fig. 3). At first it thus appeared as if the artisans had been working almost entirely in alloys of lead and copper. Archaeometallurgical analyses of the crucibles revealed that this was not the case, however. They showed that silver had been melted as often as copper alloys, and gold much more frequently than the one tiny drop would imply (Jouttijärvi 2006; Pedersen 2016a: 121–5). The casting waste reflects how the craftspeople treated different metals. Every tiny fragment of valuable gold was taken care of, while lead was handled very liberally.

This observation also illustrates the limitations of the evidence retrieved from Kaupang – and from other sites of non-ferrous metalworking. Production may have been much more diverse than we can see. Against this background, it is possible that the gold pendants referred to may provide a hint of an area of production that cannot be traced in the archaeological evidence. Without this one lead model, the serial production of pressed-foil jewellery would have been unknown. From the Viking period we know of some pressed-foil objects which must have been made in much lower numbers, such as the gold spur from Værne in Østfold, Norway (Rygh 1885: Fig. 583). Individualistic items of silver and gold were also made with the aid of wax models that were destroyed in the process, and in moulds that cannot easily be identified. It is difficult to determine if unique metal artefacts were or were not made at

Kaupang, but the demonstrable use of the materials shows that this was possible, and this might suggest that serial production to order formed part of an even more complex picture.

The lead mould for wax models referred to above (Figure 7.1) shows that the craftspeople at Kaupang produced objects for the elite of Vestfold. This piece of equipment was used to manufacture small mounts. A very similar gilt copper-alloy mount has been found in the Gokstad ship-grave (Hougen 1934: Fig. 2), and comparable mounts in the Borre ship-grave (Brøgger 1916: Figs 1 and 14) and other graves belonging to the uppermost strata of society (e.g. Rydh 1936: Figs 302–3). The Borre find reveals that a series of 44 mounts adorned a horse's head-piece, and this may explain why a lead mould was used. A large number of equivalent mounts which were to be placed close together had to be cast, and therefore it was probably desirable that they should be as similar as possible, which the lead mould would help to ensure. It is also reasonable to imagine that the craftspeople wanted to make all of the mounts in a short period of time – which, again, the lead mould allows, unlike a lead model (Pedersen 2016a: 190). In a lead mould, wax models can be cast quickly, and each wax model can then immediately be baked inside a clay mould. When the moulds are dry, all the wax models can be melted out at the same time, and a large number of mounts can be cast, one immediately after the other. Once more, the substantial investment in each individual set implies production to order.

Serial production at Kaupang thus appears to have been complex. It was carried out in various ways, was targeted at different social classes and resulted in products of various values. The objective would appear to have been to produce a large number of equivalent items, irrespective of how they subsequently changed hands. As a result, there appears to be no reason to equate serial production with production for an anonymous market. Areas of serial production were most probably directed towards (relatively) unknown consumers; but in addition to this, sets of objects as well as individual items were

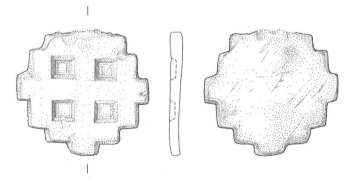

Figure 7.4 Lead model for making cruciform pendants.

Source: © Museum of Cultural History, University of Oslo. Drawing by Bjørn-Håkon Eketuft Rygh.

130 Unn Pedersen

serially produced to order. Serial production was first and foremost a technical option adopted by the craftworkers. The artisans at Kaupang had a number of techniques they could choose from when they intended to produce a series of items, and one group of craftspeople could choose between various forms of serial production (Pedersen 2016a: 189–93, Fig. 4.31). The choice of technique seems to have been governed by several different factors, such as which material was best suited for presenting a particular motif, the extent to which the jewellers were copying an existing artefact, the time available and whether there was any likelihood of recommencing production at a later date.

More than trade goods

In any case, Viking-period jewellery represented more than just goods for trade. Pieces of jewellery could be status symbols, requisites for rituals, gifts to seal alliances, markers of identity and/or religious emblems (e.g. Glørstad 2010, 2012; Røstad 2012; Kershaw 2013). Two lead models show that armrings were serially produced at Kaupang (Pedersen 2016a: 58–9), and armrings from graves and hoards indicate that the models may have been used to manufacture items of very different economic value. One of the lead models has close parallels amongst armrings of copper alloy as well as gold, and there are similar examples in silver (Petersen 1928: 153–8; Hårdh 1996: Fig. 29). Neither the lead models nor their context provides information about which metals were used in the making of armrings; by contrast, the archaeometallurgical analyses of the crucibles referred to might provide some guidelines in that they show that silver was frequently melted at Kaupang, as, to a certain extent, was gold (Jouttijärvi 2006; Pedersen 2013: Fig. 3). It is therefore possible that armrings of gold and silver were also cast at Kaupang, and such craft products were undoubtedly of high economic value and strongly linked to the Viking-period elite (Schramm 1955: 538–43). Urban production could, if this was the case, have included significant political symbols with religious connotations, presented as gifts to establish hierarchies. Two lead models for the making of penannular brooches may reinforce this view. Zanette Glørstad (2010, 2012) has argued that such brooches were powerful political symbols, and that a cloak with a cloak brooch of this kind formed a set given as alliance-forming gifts to men in the circle of King Harald Finehair.

The complexity of Viking-period serial production is further underlined by the four lead models just referred to, and it is immediately difficult to imagine that the craftspeople were producing heavily value-laden artefacts for disposal in an open market. It is more logical to consider items of jewellery such as these as the result of bespoke production whereby items of jewellery were made to order, or by command. An order need not be incompatible with buying and selling, but Viking-period economy was complex (e.g. Samson 1991; Hedeager 1993; Skre 2013), and other forms of exchange appear more relevant to bespoke products of this sort of significance. It is conceivable, for instance, that those in power at Kaupang demanded specific products from

Viking-period non-ferrous metalworking   131

the craftspeople who wished to operate at the site, and they may in such cases themselves have provided the raw material for craft production. The output may have been reckoned a form of toll, in the same way as the merchants and craftworkers in towns in the Frankish area had to pay in coin or in products (Gaut 2015: 150 and refs. therein). Some of the artisans may have belonged to the retinue of the local ruler, like the craftsmen in the retinue of the King Alfred of Wessex at the end of the ninth century (Maddicott 1989: 4). The craftspeople at Kaupang may have made presents of some brooch or another to create social ties, but there is little to indicate that they themselves were the donors of a significant number of alliance-forming items of jewellery having considerable metal value.

The variation observed in the output of the non-ferrous metalworking reflects the fact that Kaupang was much more than just a market site (Pedersen 2000: 14). The town was part of the central-place complex of Skiringssal, where there was also a major burial ground, an aristocratic hall, a *thing* site and possibly a sacred lake, too (Blindheim 1982; Brink 2007; Skre 2007b). The Viking-period town represents something new in Scandinavian society, while the Skiringssal complex has much in common with both earlier and contemporary political centres, like Tissø. Modes of exchange such as gift-exchange, redistribution and the payment of fines, tolls and tribute were thus closely associated with Kaupang. The specific context of production provides limited information on the subsequent exchange of the finished items. The lead models for making penannular brooches were found in the modern plough-layer, and their original context has been lost; however, the spatial distribution indicates that they were made in an area of the town where oval and equal-armed brooches were also manufactured (Pedersen 2016a: Fig. 4.26). One of the lead models for making armrings was found in a layer of waste together with a miscast lead pendant; in this case, then, it is possible that armrings and cheap lead jewellery were produced in close proximity, possibly even in the same workshop. Weights and silver have been identified in the same area (Pedersen 2008: Fig. 6.29), so it might be assumed that these objects were made for buying and selling, although this is no reason to exclude other possible forms of exchange, or the use of other means of payment. Several of the forms of exchange referred to are much less easy to demonstrate in the archaeological evidence than trade using silver as a currency.

The first non-ferrous metalworking at Kaupang took place around the year 800, immediately after a substantial area had been divided into plots and the newly founded site brought into use. The single lead model from the first phase shows that there was serial production of objects from the very start. The fact that this is a lead model for making armrings might indicate that everything began in the mode of bespoke production, and it is not inconceivable that the first craftspeople were invited to the site, or in some cases brought to the site, by whoever was responsible for its foundation. However, stylistic datings of other models indicate that the production of simple equal-armed brooches of copper alloy began around the same time, and it is just as likely

132   Unn Pedersen

that a mixed production of items to order and for sale may have been a feature of this production from the very beginning.

Same, but different

Glørstad (2010, 2012) emphasizes the difference between imported penannular brooches and locally produced types, but does not otherwise distinguish between penannular brooches of different materials and/or quality of workmanship. The size of the model for making penannular brooches implies that its ultimate products at Kaupang would have been of copper alloy, like the oval and equal-armed brooches. Noting that armrings of copper alloy and precious metal have often been interpreted quite differently in social terms (e.g. Petersen 1928; Schramm 1955), one may question whether all penannular brooches were gifts to establish hierarchical relationships. It is conceivable that it was primarily the larger silver brooches known in hoards that functioned as gifts, while the serially produced copper-alloy examples from Kaupang were trade goods, like the oval and equal-armed brooches. It is, however, at least equally plausible that the thorough analysis of the social role of the penannular brooches has identified something that is relevant to other classes of brooch, too. The traditional view, which attaches especial importance to costume, may be too restricted in the case of the equal-armed and oval brooches as well. These types are characterized by their variety and Signe Horn Fuglesang (1987) has argued that oval brooches can be divided into three quality groups, namely 'outstanding', 'good' and 'poor' (see also Fuglesang 2013). This makes it possible that items of copper-alloy jewellery were also produced for different reasons, and may also have been exchanged in different ways by the craftspeople, even within a Viking-period town. Future research, considering the various find contexts of the finished items of jewellery, the active use of material culture in social strategies, craft quality and the nature of the raw material, will be able to contribute more subtle interpretations.

The Viking-period graves in the same area illustrate that the craftspeople produced very similar copper-alloy artefacts of different value. The exceptionally rich ship-grave at Borre contained a gilt harness mount cast in copper alloy (Rygh 1885: Fig. 595), while in local terms a more typically furnished Viking-period grave at Gulli, less than 10 km away, contained a very similar harness mount cast in copper alloy but coated in the cheaper metal tin (Gjerpe 2005: Fig. 20). The finishing treatment very clearly demonstrates their different social context and setting, and it is difficult to believe that the variation in quality went unnoticed at the time. At Gulli, the burial context provides further thought-provoking information, as textile fragments and a cord indicate that the harness mount was carefully packed in textile (Gjerpe 2005: 38). It thus appears that the 'cheaper' of the two mounts was treated as an object of especial value, possibly indeed as a gift. This observation reminds us that a gift becomes a gift when it is given, irrespective of the materiality of the object (Mauss 1966). The Borre find was not the result of a properly conducted excavation, so how the harness mount there was treated is not known. It is, nevertheless, reasonable to sketch out various possible scenarios for these two mounts, which are similar yet also different. Both could be traded items, purchased by different people with different economic capacities; both could have been ordered and given as gifts by an individual who established or maintained a hierarchy in which each of the two deceased was assigned their place; and indeed both could have been bought or ordered by the man buried in the Borre grave, who subsequently gave one as a gift that was adapted to demonstrate his superior position.

Altogether, this indicates that we should not equate the type of object directly with the aim of production. Establishing a direct association that links the modern market-oriented concepts of buying and selling to urban commodity production is unfortunate, because it assumes that the objects were *produced* as trade goods. This was not necessarily so. The complex economy of the Viking period and the modular serial production imply that the relationships were more complicated. We have very little opportunity to show how the artisans exchanged their craft products, and we face major problems in assessing whether the items of jewellery became trade goods during their production, before this point or when they eventually came to be disposed of. That the craftworkers produced items that first became trade goods when they were sold is a likely scenario, and commodity production is therefore an ill-fitting term.

The significance of standardization

Various types of dress accessory and other costume-related objects such as keys were also produced at Kaupang (Pedersen 2016a: Fig. 4.28). The craftspeople could relatively easily have adjusted their moulds and wax models to make items of jewellery which differed rather more from one another, but they did not do so. The finishing work which must have been carried out on the great majority of the objects equally appears not to have created any greater variation within each type or variant – apart from the metal coating noted. Viewed in the light of a single workshop producing a range of variants and types, it would, therefore, seem as if many of the women and men of the Viking period wanted to possess the same piece of jewellery as their neighbours, and as people over large areas of Scandinavia. In Viking-period towns such as Kaupang, and at a range of sites with market activity (Pedersen 2016b), these wishes could be met. The majority of the products were worn very visibly, and it is probable that they were used to produce, emphasize and promote social position, economic standing and political allegiance. In these circumstances, standardized products are very effective: they can be directly compared, and deliver a message that a very large number of people understand.

This standardization may, in part, have been initiated by the elite, as in the case of the penannular brooches, and it may also in some respects have had considerable chronological depth, as the armrings suggest (Werner 1980; Hedeager 1992: 204); it may also partly have been driven by 'most people's' wish to be like others, as the large numbers of equal-armed and oval brooches may show; it must also have been attractive for the craftspeople to produce many objects more easily and quickly, and therefore more cheaply. The simple cast copper-alloy examples of armrings and penannular brooches may have been the bottom rung of a hierarchical scale of gifts, but their production could also have been initiated or encouraged by the fact that 'most people' desired to copy the elite and so bought copies of the status symbols of the rich and powerful. This may indeed be precisely what is manifested through the copying of oval brooches, on which the details of the decoration could often be neglected while the brooch as a whole still looks roughly the same (Fuglesang 1987). For the craftspeople at Kaupang, adaptation for the market could have been a very simple matter: they could use an existing model and a cheaper material. It is difficult to see that such initiatives faced any opposition from the elite, who thus saw the impact of symbol-laden gifts reinforced. If the significance of the object was already established, as in the case of the penannular brooches, the elite may well have had nothing against someone paying for their own more expensive penannular brooch and so for the ostensibly obligation-forming gift which unambiguously signalled whom one had accepted as a lord. It is, then, also conceivable that the craftspeople might have used one and the same model for gifts made to order and trade goods for the market.

Conclusion: navigation in a new landscape

The buying and selling of dress accessories does, on the whole, appear to have been a phenomenon that can be associated with the Viking-period towns, and market forces did influence the output of non-ferrous metalworking. Despite the fact that the craft products could be trade goods, it has proved less easy to link market-oriented buying and selling to particular forms of production or specific types of artefact. Considering the complex economy of the Viking period, it is reasonable to conclude that the craftspeople at Kaupang could dispose of a newly made piece of jewellery in a range of different ways besides selling it to consumers with whom they had little or limited contact. It is conceivable that a finished item may have been exchanged for some raw material, one of life's necessities or some other attractive item. The craftworkers may also have paid toll, plot- or house-rent in finished items of jewellery. They probably took some bigger and smaller orders from people with whom they had different degrees of contact, and it is also conceivable that those in power at Kaupang demanded products that the artisans were obliged to provide to start or continue their work. In the case of the production of gold and silver jewellery, the person ordering may have provided the raw material him- or herself, and the jeweller may have kept a proportion of the metal as payment.

These are manifest differences from IKEA's Billy, which is much easier to identify as a trade item produced for sale at a fixed price. Our contemporary economy is also complex, and we would hardly have to search far and wide for stories of Billy bookcases having been given as gifts. Such a bookcase is every bit as much a result of commodity production, and was manufactured as

Viking-period non-ferrous metalworking 135

a trade item meant to be sold. This was not necessarily the case with Viking-period oval brooches of Type P37 or other non-ferrous metal products. The production waste at Kaupang indicates that the craftspeople were responsible for a modular and variable style of production comprising both trade goods and non-commodities. The discussion shows that there is no reason to equate forms of production with modes of exchange, or the types of jewellery with the reasons why they were made. Several types of jewellery could be trade goods that were disposed of through buying and selling, but they were not necessarily produced to be such trade goods. Commodity production appears to be a poorly suited concept, and the artisans were obliged, like everyone in Viking society, to navigate carefully within an economic system with complicated social rules of play, in a period when it was not only their metal that might feel the heat of the fire.

The economic rationality was under negotiation, and the craftspeople themselves contributed to the moulding of a new economic landscape. Consequently, there was more than the power of the market guiding the output of non-ferrous metalworking, even in a Viking-period town. It seems highly likely that this was the case in the more populous Viking-period towns, too, considering the close connection between Birka and the royal manor of Adelsö (Clarke and Ambrosiani 1995: 75–6) and the production of precious metal jewellery in Hedeby (Armbruster 2004). The studies of the production waste and equipment from non-ferrous metalworking reveal a degree of complexity in the relationship between production and exchange, the depth of which we have not hitherto grasped.

Translated by John Hines

References

Armbruster, Barbara 2004: Goldsmiths' Tools at Hedeby. In: Hines, John, Alan Lane and Mark Redknap (eds): *Land, Sea and Home*. The Society for Medieval Archaeology Monograph, vol. 20: 109–23. Maney. Leeds.

Blackburn, Mark 2008: The Coin-finds. In: Skre, Dagfinn (ed.): *Means of Exchange: Dealing with Silver in the Viking Age*. Kaupang Excavation Project. Publication Series, vol. 2. Norske Oldfunn, vol. 23: 29–74. Aarhus University Press. Århus.

Blindheim, Charlotte 1982: Commerce and Trade in Viking Age Norway. Exchange of Products or Organized Transactions? *Norwegian Archaeological Review*, 15: 8–18.

Brinch Madsen, Helge 1984: *Metal-casting: Techniques, Production and Workshops*. Ribe Excavations 1970–6, vol. 2. Sydjysk Universitetsforlag. Esbjerg.

Brink, Stefan 2007: Skiringssal, Kaupang, Tjølling: The Toponymic Evidence. In: Skre, Dagfinn (ed.): *Kaupang in Skiringssal*. Kaupang Excavation Project. Publication Series, vol. 1. Norske Oldfunn, vol. 22: 53–64. Aarhus University Press. Århus.

Brøgger, A.W. 1916: *Borrefundet og Vestfoldkongernes graver*. Videnskapsselskapets skrifter II. Hist.-filos. klasse, vol. 1. Jacob Dybwad. Kristiania.

Callmer, Johan 1984: Aspects on Production and Style: An Essay with Reference to the Merovingian and Early Viking Period Material of Scandinavia. In: Høgestøl, Mari, Jan Henning Larsen, Eldrid Straume and Birthe Weber (eds): *Festskrift til*

136 *Unn Pedersen*

Thorleif Sjøvold på 70-årsdagen. Universitetets Oldsaksamlings Skrifter. Ny rekke, nr. 5: 57–85. Universitetets Oldsaksamling. Oslo.

—— 1995: Hantverksproduktion, samhällsförändringar och bebyggelse: Iakttagelser från östra Sydskandinavien ca. 600–1100 e.Kr. In: Heid Gjøstein Resi (ed.): *Produksjon og samfunn. Om erverv, spesialisering og bosetning i Norden i 1. årtusen e.Kr.* Varia 30: 39–72. Universitetets Oldsaksamling. Oslo.

—— 1999: Vikingatidens likearmade spännen. In: Birgitta Hårdh (ed.): *Fynden i centrum: Keramik, glas och metall från Uppåkra.* Uppåkrastudier 2. Acta Archaeologica Lundensia. Series in 8°, no. 30: 201–20. Almqvist and Wiksell. Lund.

Christophersen, Axel 1982: Den urbane varuproduktionens oppkomst og betydning for den tidligmiddelalderske byutviklingen. *Den medeltida staden. Bebyggelseshistorisk Tidsskrift,* 3: 104–22.

Clarke, Helen and Björn Ambrosiani 1995: *Towns in the Viking Age.* Leicester University Press. London and New York.

Dunér, Jan and Ann Vinberg 2006: *Barva: 2000 år vid Mälarens södra strand.* UV mitt rapport 2006: 20. Arkeologiska förundersökningar och undersökningar. http://samla.raa. se/xmlui/bitstream/handle/raa/4170/rm2006_20_text.pdf?sequence=1, read 03.03.16.

Feveile, Claus 2002: Støbning af ovale skålspænder i Ribe: type- og teknikvariation. In: Henriksen, Mogens Bo (ed.): *Metalhåndværk og håndværkspladser fra yngre germansk jernalder, vikingetid og tidlig middelalder.* Skrifter fra Odense Bys Museer, vol. 9: 17–26. Odense.

Fuglesang, Signe Horn 1987: 'The Personal Touch'. On the Identification of Workshops. In: Knirk, James E. (ed.): *Proceedings of the Tenth Viking Congress. Larkollen, Norway, 1985.* Universitetets Oldsaksamlings skrifter. Ny rekke, nr. 9: 219–30. Universitetets Oldsaksamling. Oslo.

—— 2013: Copying and Creativity in Early Viking Ornament. In: Reynolds, Andrew and Leslie Webster (eds): *Early Medieval Art and Archaeology in the Northern World,* pp. 825–41. Brill. Leiden.

Gaut, Bjarne 2015: Manors and Markets: Continental Perspectives on Viking-Age Trade and Exchange. In: Eriksen, Marianne Hem, Unn Pedersen, Bernt Rundberget, Irmelin Axelsen and Heidi Lund Berg (eds): *Viking Worlds: Things, Spaces and Movement,* pp. 144–59. Oxbow. Oxford.

Gjerpe, Lars Erik 2005: Gravene: en kort gjennomgang. In: Gjerpe, Lars Erik (ed.): *Gravfeltet på Gulli.* E18-prosjektet Vestfold. Bind I. Varia 60: 24–104. Kulturhistorisk museum, Fornminneseksjonen, Universitetet i Oslo. Oslo.

Glørstad, Ann Zanette Tsigaridas 2010: *Ringspennen og kappen: Kulturelle møter, politiske symboler og sentraliseringsprosesser i Norge ca. 800–950.* PhD dissertation. Department of Archaeology, Conservation and History. University of Oslo.

—— 2012: Sign of the Times? The Transfer and Transformation of Penannular Brooches in Viking-Age Norway. *Norwegian Archaeological Review,* 45(1): 30–51.

Hårdh, Birgitta 1996: *Silver in the Viking Age: A Regional-Economic Study.* Acta Archaeologica Lundensia. Series in 8°, no. 25. Almquist and Wiksell. Stockholm.

—— 2008: Hacksilver and Ingots. In: Skre, Dagfinn (ed.): *Means of Exchange: Dealing with Silver in the Viking Age.* Kaupang Excavation Project. Publication Series, vol. 2. Norske Oldfunn, vol. 23: 95–118. Aarhus University Press. Århus.

Hedeager, Lotte 1992: *Danmarks jernalder: Mellem stamme og stat.* Aarhus Universitetsforlag. Århus.

—— 1993: Krigerøkonomi og handelsøkonomi i vikingtiden. In: Lund, Niels (ed.): *Norden og Europa i vikingetid og tidlig middelalder,* pp. 44–68. Museum Tusculanums forlag. København.

Viking-period non-ferrous metalworking 137

Hedegaard, Ken Ravn 2005: Casting Trefoil Brooches. *Viking Heritage Magazine*, 2005(1): 8–13.

Hougen, Bjørn 1934: Studier i Gokstadfunnet. *Universitetets Oldsaksamling Årbok*, 1931–2: 74–112.

Jansson, Ingmar 1985: Ovala spännbucklor: En studie av vikingatida standardsmycken med utgångspunkt från Björkö-fynden. Aun, vol. 7. Uppsala universitet. Uppsala.

Jouttijärvi, Arne 2006: Analyser af digler fra Kaupang. Heimdal-archaeometry. Unpublished report. Museum of Cultural History archive.

Kershaw, Jane F. 2013: *Viking Identities: Scandinavian Jewellery in England*. Medieval History and Archaeology. Oxford University Press. Oxford.

Kielland, Thor 1927: *Norsk guldsmedkunst i middelalderen*. Steenske forlag. Oslo.

Lowenthal, David 1985: *The Past is a Foreign Country*. Cambridge University Press. Cambridge.

Maddicott, J.R. 1989: Trade, Industry and the Wealth of King Alfred. *Past and Present*, 123: 3–51.

Mauss, Marcel 1966: *The Gift: Forms and Functions of Exchange in Archaic Societies*. Cohen. London.

Paulsen, Peter 1936: *Der Goldschatz von Hiddensee*. Führer zur Urgesch, vol. 13. Leipzig.

Pedersen, Unn 2000: Vektlodd: sikre vitnesbyrd om handelsvirksomhet? Vektloddenes funksjoner i vikingtid. En analyse av vektloddsmaterialet fra Kaupang og sørøst-Norge. Hovedfagsoppgave. Department of Archaeology, Conservation and History, the Faculty of Humanities, University of Oslo.

—— 2008: Weights and Balances. In: Skre, Dagfinn (ed.): *Means of Exchange: Dealing with Silver in the Viking Age*. Kaupang Excavation Project. Publication Series, vol. 2. Norske Oldfunn, vol. 23: 119–95. Aarhus University Press. Århus.

—— 2010: *I smeltedigelen. Finsmedene i vikingtidsbyen Kaupang*. PhD dissertation. Department of Archaeology, Conservation and History, University of Oslo.

—— 2013: Det store i det små – vikingtidens finsmeder under lupen. *Primitive tider*, 15: 71–83.

—— 2015a: Noe for enhver smak. Smykkeproduksjon i vikingtidsbyene. In: Risvaag, Jon Anders, Terje Brattli and Ragnhild Berge (eds): *Inn i fortida – ut i verden – i museet!* Acta Archaeologica Nidarosiensia. Vitark, vol. 9: 52–60. Museumsforlaget. Trondheim.

—— 2015b: Urban Craftspeople at Viking-Age Kaupang. In: Ashby, Steven, Irene Baug and Gitte Hansen (eds): *Everyday Products in the Middle Ages: Crafts, Consumption and the Individual in Northern Europe c. AD 1000–1600*, pp. 51–68. Oxbow. Oxford.

—— 2016a: *Into the Melting Pot: Non-Ferrous Metalworkers in Viking-Period Kaupang*. Kaupang Excavation Project. Publication Series, vol. 4. Aarhus University Press. Norske Oldfunn, vol. 25. Aarhus University Press. Aarhus.

—— 2016b: Non-ferrous Metalworking in Viking-Age Scandinavia: A question of Mobility. In: Turner, Val E., Olwyn A. Owen and Doreen J. Waugh (eds): *Shetland and the Viking World: Papers from the Seventeenth Viking Congress*: 263–9. Shetland Heritage Publications. Lerwick.

Petersen, Jan 1928: *Vikingetidens smykker*. Stavanger Museum. Stavanger.

Rydh, Hanna 1936: Förhistoriska undersökningar på Adelsö. Kungl. vitterhets historie och antikvitets akademien. Stockholm.

Rygh, Oluf 1885: *Norske Oldsager*. Alb. Cammermeyer. Christiania.

Røstad, Ingunn 2012: En fremmed fugl: Danske smykker og forbindelser på Østlandet i overgangen mellom vikingtid og middelalder. *Viking*, 75: 181–210.

Samson, Ross 1991: *Social Approaches to Viking Studies*. Cruithne Press. Glasgow.

138   *Unn Pedersen*

Schramm, P.E. 1955: *Herrschaftszeichen und Staatssymbolik: Beiträge zu ihrer Geschichte vom dritten bis zum sechzehnten Jahrhundert.* Band II. Anton Hiersemann. Stuttgart.

Sindbæk, Søren 2007: Networks and Nodal Points: The Emergence of Towns in Early Viking Age Scandinavia. *Antiquity,* 81(311): 119–32.

Skre, Dagfinn 2007a: Towns and Markets, Kings and Central Places in South-western Scandinavia c. AD 800–950. In: Skre, Dagfinn (ed.): *Kaupang in Skiringssal.* Kaupang Excavation Project. Publication Series, vol. 1. Norske Oldfunn, vol. 22: 445–69. Aarhus University Press. Århus.

—— 2007b: Introduction. In: Skre, Dagfinn (ed.): *Kaupang in Skiringssal.* Kaupang Excavation Project. Publication Series, vol. 1. Norske Oldfunn, vol. 22: 13–24. Aarhus University Press. Århus.

—— 2013: Money and Trade in Viking-Age Scandinavia. In: Mateusz Bogucki and Marian Rębkowski (eds): *Economies, Monetization and Society in the West Slavic Lands 800–1200 AD.* Wydawnictwo IAE PAN. Szczecin.

Strömberg, Märta 1961: *Untersuchungen zur jüngeren Eisenzeit in Schonen. Völkervandrungszeit – Wikingerzeit* I. Textband. Acta Archaeologica Lundensia. Series in 4°, no. 4. CWK Gleerups förlag. Lund.

Stylegar, Frans-Arne 2007: The Kaupang Cemeteries Revisited. In: Skre, Dagfinn (ed.): *Kaupang in Skiringssal.* Kaupang Excavation Project. Publication Series, vol. 1. Norske Oldfunn, vol. 22: 65–128. Aarhus University Press. Århus.

Wamers, Egon 1994: *Die Frühmittelalterlichen lesefunde aus der Löhrstrasse (Baustelle Hilton II) in Mainz.* Mainzer Archäologishe Schriften, vol. 1. Archäologische Denmalpflege. Mainz.

Werner, Joachim 1980: *Der goldene* Armring des Frankenkönigs Childerich und die germanischen Handgelenkringe der jüngeren Kaiserzeit. *Frühmittelalterliche Studien,* 14: 1–49.

8 Soapstone vessels and quernstones as commodities in the Viking Age and Middle Ages

Irene Baug

Introduction

From the early Viking Age until the late Middle Ages, a period spanning roughly the ninth to fourteenth century, the use of different resources in out-lying areas of Norway evidently became more intensive, and a change from small-scale to large-scale exploitation can be seen. Various resources offered possibilities of creating surpluses for larger markets, and special mineral out-crops, for instance, were exploited on a near-industrial scale during this period. The widespread use of various stone objects can be traced: these include vessels of soapstone, also referred to as steatite, and quernstones made of other rock types. The aim of this study is to look into the distribution of these products and possible trade in them. They were everyday products and important tools in the household, produced for ordinary people. Their dispersal suggests that they were widely available; still, there are unresolved questions relating to the way they were distributed and acquired.

Thus, a central question is whether the soapstone vessels and quernstones represent traded commodities, or whether their distribution is the result of other modes of transfer, such as migration of people. For a fuller understand-ing of the circulation of steatite vessels and quernstones, along with possible trade in these objects, investigation of the spatial and chronological distribution of the products is necessary. In the first part of this chapter I will thus give a brief presentation of the distribution patterns in Northern Europe of soapstone vessels and quernstones from Norway. The distribution of these products and transactions involving them seem to have been integrated into major economic systems, involving large parts of Northern Europe. In the second part of the paper the empirical data will be analysed and discussed in relation to shifting societal conditions during the Viking Age and the Middle Ages.

Soapstone vessels in time and space

In north-west mainland Europe, soapstone outcrops are only found in certain parts of Scandinavia: mainly in Norway, but also in south-western Sweden (Risbøl 1994: 121). A variety of soapstone objects were produced, such as ves-sels, spindle whorls, loom-weights, sinkers, moulds and tuyères. In this chapter,

140   *Irene Baug*

I focus mainly on the vessels, as the other artefact types to a large degree represent secondary products made from broken vessels (cf. Resi 1979: 58, 72–3, 84–5; Forster 2004: 48, 162; Baug 2011: 334). At the transition to the Viking Age, about AD 800, large-scale production of soapstone vessels started. Production continued throughout the Viking Age and into the Middle Ages. Approximately 200 soapstone quarries have been identified in Norway, and about half of them seem to have been production sites for soapstone vessels (Figure 8.1) (Baug 2011: 331).

In Norway, soapstone vessels were preferred to pottery in both the Viking Age and the Middle Ages, and dominate as cooking and storage vessels. A reason for this may be that vessels of soapstone were more durable than pottery. The use of vessels is documented in both rural and urban contexts, and the large-scale production and use seem to have increased in the Middle Ages (cf. Randers 1982; Kaland 1987; Risbøl 1994: 133; Øye 2011: 231). The vessel design changed from the Viking Age to the Middle Ages, but the vessels in each period exhibit shared characteristics, with similarities in shape and size, and with more or less standardised vessels types (Resi 1979; Vangstad 2003: 26–7; Baug 2011: 313–15). Standardisation may possibly point towards the use of somewhat standard units of measurement of liquids and solids, but may also indicate serial production, often directed towards a market where the producer does not necessarily know the customer (Skre 2007: 450).

From the beginning of the ninth century, soapstone vessels were distributed southwards to Denmark and westwards to the North Atlantic islands – Iceland, Shetland and the Faroe Islands (Sindbæk 2005: 137, 149–50; Forster 2009: 58, 65). In Denmark, soapstone vessels seem to be found in most settlement areas (Jensen 1990: 126; Risbøl 1994: 122; Sindbæk 2005: 137–42). Yet the distribution shows a regional tendency, where the quantity of soapstone vessels diminishes towards southern Denmark, and where the majority of these vessels are found in northern and south-western parts of Jutland (Jensen 1990; Risbøl 1994: 127; Sindbæk 2005: 139, 161). The Viking-Age town of Hedeby marks the southern limit of the distribution of soapstone products. The distribution of soapstone objects in Denmark ends during the eleventh to twelfth century (Risbøl 1994: 123; Sindbæk 2007: 137).

Compared to Denmark, soapstone vessels have far less commonly been identified in Sweden. Here, the vessels are mainly found in the south-western parts of the country. It has been suggested that the lack of soapstone vessels in large parts of Sweden may have to do with the smaller number of settlement excavations that have taken place compared to Denmark; however, the lack of soapstone vessels in burials seems to confirm the general picture derived from their overall distribution in settlement contexts (Risbøl 1994: 126, 130).

Quernstones in time and space

For more than 1,100 years, from the early Viking Age and into the Modern period in Norway, approximately from the ninth to the twentieth century,

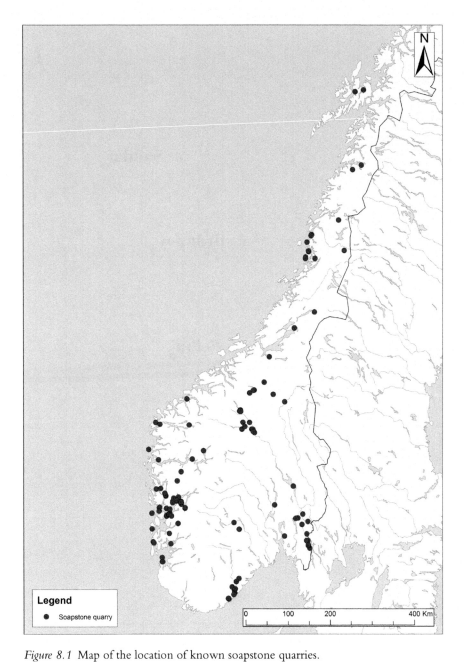

Figure 8.1 Map of the location of known soapstone quarries.

Source: Data from the Geological Survey of Norway mineral resource database, www.prospecting.no. Map by Kjetil Loftsgarden.

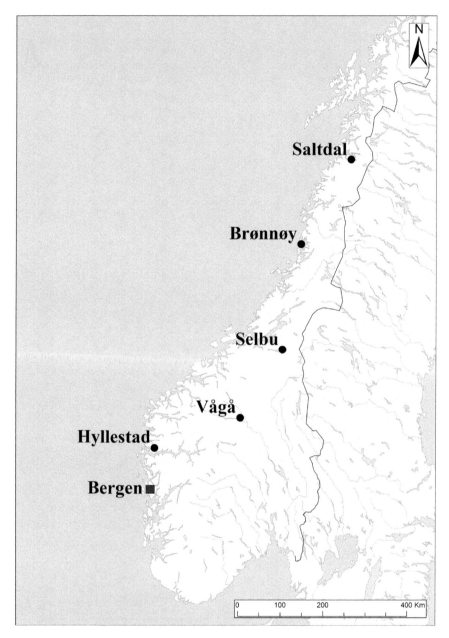

Figure 8.2 Map showing the largest quernstone quarries in Norway.
Source: Baug (2015a: Fig. 1.3). Map by Kjetil Loftsgarden.

quernstones were largely produced of garnet mica schist. Several quarries of this type are known in the country (Figure 8.2).

The oldest and one of the largest production sites for quernstones is located at Hyllestad by the fjord Åfjorden in Sogn og Fjordane County. Production at Hyllestad may go back to the early ninth century, but large-scale production and distribution is documented from the latter half of the tenth century, with this activity continuing and increasing into the Middle Ages. Archaeological investigations in the quarries indicate a peak in production from the eleventh to the thirteenth century (Baug 2002, 2015a: 33–71). The distribution of quernstones from Hyllestad dates back to the late Viking Age, beginning approximately in the latter half of the tenth century, even though a couple of stones in Denmark may date from the late ninth and early tenth century (Carelli and Kresten 1997: 120–2; Baug 2015a: 110–13). An increase in the distribution of quernstones can be documented from the twelfth century. Quernstones from Hyllestad were mainly distributed within Norway, the eastern parts of medieval Denmark, north-eastern Jutland and the islands, including Scania and Bornholm. In some areas, such as Århus in Denmark and Lund in Sweden, stones from Hyllestad seem to have dominated the market, both in the Viking Age and the Middle

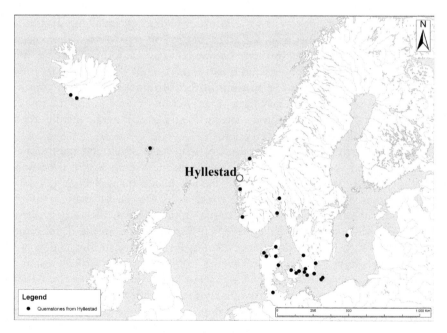

Figure 8.3 Distribution of quernstones from Hyllestad. In Norway, only finds from the medieval towns are indicated.

Source: Baug (2015a: Fig. 7.8). Map by Kjetil Loftsgarden.

144 *Irene Baug*

Ages. In the same way as for the soapstone vessels, Hedeby seems to mark the southern limit of the distribution of Norwegian quernstones (Carelli and Kresten 1997; Baug 2015a: 111–14).

Quernstones from Hyllestad were also distributed to Iceland and the Faroe Islands (Figure 8.3), although far less than to southern Scandinavia. Only a few stones date from the Viking Age, and the majority of the material is from the Middle Ages (Baug 2015a: 114–15).

Another important Norwegian quarry site dating from the Viking Age and the Middle Ages is located in Saltdal in Nordland County. These quarries have been dated to approximately the tenth to thirteenth century (Helberg 2010: 114, 2010/2011: 9). The activity seems to have started in the late Viking Age, but became increasingly important during the Middle Ages. In Norway, quernstones from Saltdal in Nordland are present both in medieval towns and on rural sites, and in the medieval town of Oslo, for instance, they outnumber the stones from Hyllestad (Baug 2015a: 108–9). However, outside of Norway, quernstones from Hyllestad seem to have dominated the market, with stones from the other Norwegian quarries occurring rarely.

Viking-Age trade?

It is, of course, difficult to assess the forms of transaction involving soapstone products and quernstones from the archaeological material alone. The objects found at different sites in Northern Europe reflect some form of contact, but the spread of soapstone objects and quernstones cannot always be understood in terms of trade. Various explanations of the distribution should be considered. Forms of distribution may have varied in time and space, and the spread of the objects therefore needs to be analysed and discussed with regard to their spatial, chronological and societal context.

Judging by the relatively few finds of soapstone vessels and quernstones from Hyllestad in the North Atlantic region in the Viking Age, it is possible that the objects were brought there by the inhabitants themselves, rather than being exported as commodities on a larger scale. Objects of soapstone were an important part of Norwegian material culture, and in the earliest phase the Norse settlers seem to have played an important role in the distribution of the vessels to the North Atlantic islands. For instance in Shetland, soapstone vessels from Norway are recovered from early Norse settlements, and imported Norwegian soapstone vessels seem largely to belong to the settlement phase corresponding approximately to the ninth to the tenth century. From the tenth to the twelfth century, imported soapstone gave way to locally produced vessels, and the use of Shetland steatite dominated in this period (Forster 2009: 61, 65, 67). One should also bear in mind that, even though migration of people seems to have been an important factor for the distribution of Norwegian soapstone vessels to the North Atlantic region, some imported Norwegian vessels may, of course, have been transmitted, perhaps

Soapstone vessels and quernstones 145

in the form of exchange, where the products went from hand to hand through networks of personal contacts.

Norwegian quernstones have a more limited distribution on the North Atlantic islands, and are, as stated above, only found in Iceland and the Faroe Islands. It is, however, striking that, except for BergÞórsvoll, none of the *landnám* farms in Iceland seem to have quernstones from Hyllestad (see, e.g. Gestsson 1959: 71–2; Magnússon 1971: 68, 72–4). The numbers of vessels and quernstones give no indication of organised and purely commercial trade in these commodities within this area in the early period, and only a sporadic distribution to the North Atlantic islands seems to have taken place.

The scale and range of distribution of quernstones from Hyllestad and soapstone vessels to nodes in southern Scandinavia reveals a somewhat different picture. Already from the ninth century, eastern parts of medieval Denmark appear as important areas for goods from Norway. The fact that the vessels and quernstones are found at marketplaces and in towns in fairly large quantities makes it likely that they represent traded commodities. The vessels occur within the same areas of Scandinavia as the quernstones, but are not contemporaneous. The vessels appear in southern Scandinavia shortly after AD 800 but disappear during the eleventh to twelfth century (Sindbæk 2007: 137). The absence of soapstone in medieval Danish households has been explained in terms of the introduction of a new pottery technology in the twelfth to thirteenth century. Monks immigrating to Denmark introduced the potter's wheel and pottery kilns, which made pottery production more efficient (Risbøl 1994: 123), and during the early Middle Ages the soapstone vessels seem to have been completely replaced by pottery. The export of soapstone to Denmark ends approximately at the same time as the beginning of the large-scale export of quernstones from Hyllestad, which has been dated to the late Viking Age, about AD 950–1000 (Carelli and Kresten 1997: 121; Birkedahl 2000: 36; Birkedahl and Johansen 2000: 29; Baug 2015a: 147). The use of quernstones from Hyllestad in southern Scandinavia continues throughout the Viking Age and the Middle Ages.

Both merchants and merchandise needed to be protected, and an organisation to secure and protect goods and trading routes as well as markets was important. Such protection could be guaranteed by an institutionalised political authority based on a strong military force, but this alone would probably not suffice. Trade between strangers required commercial transactions embedded in social and legal norms shared by people over a larger area than the law region or the social networks. This could be achieved at central places like trading sites (Gustin 2004: 243, 248, 264; Sindbæk 2005: 272–3; Skre 2007: 451). Power to secure trade and protect the trading routes and markets was thus important. At the same time, large-scale production and distribution demanded contact networks and access to a larger number of customers, which would have been easier if distribution was via marketplaces and towns.

146   *Irene Baug*

Kaupang: a redistribution centre for soapstone goods?

In the Viking-Age town of Kaupang in Vestfold County, no quernstones from Hyllestad or any other known quernstone quarries have been found. The activity at Kaupang ended approximately AD 960–80 (Pilø 2007: 178); that is, before the large-scale distribution of quernstones from Hyllestad started. On the other hand, Kaupang has been seen as a redistribution centre for soapstone products from Norway (Skjølsvold 1961: 117, 130; Christophersen 1991: 166). Identifying the quarries from which the soapstone came may provide information about probable trade routes and contact zones. As there are no soapstone outcrops in Vestfold, the soapstone objects must have been imported from other regions. Geochemical analyses, using the technique of inductively coupled plasma mass spectrometry (ICP-MS), have been undertaken on soapstone objects from Kaupang. According to the analyses, a single production site, still unidentified, seems to have manufactured vessels for the town, while some of the other artefact types of soapstone probably came from a range of different production sites. It is possible that there was stricter control of the production and distribution of vessels than of many of the other soapstone objects – where the latter may, to a large degree, represent personal possessions brought to Kaupang by travellers, not necessarily as commodities. However, to suggest possible production sites and assess the associated transport routes, the results from the ICP-MS analyses will have to be scrutinised in the light of an expanded chemical database of Norwegian soapstone (Baug 2011: 329–31, 334)

Many of the soapstone artefacts recovered at Kaupang bear clear signs of having been used (Baug 2011). The need for various soapstone objects, both for household use and in certain craft activities, most likely explains the occurrence of much of the material recovered in the town. Neither is there any clear evidence in the assemblage that soapstone constituted an important export article from Kaupang, even though this cannot be excluded (Baug 2011: 334–5). Kaupang had significant links with long-distance trade systems in the Viking period (Skre 2007: 453), and soapstone artefacts appear in southern Scandinavia shortly after AD 800, which corresponds closely with the establishment of Kaupang. There also seems to be a predominance of soapstone in northern Jutland (Risbøl 1994: 127; Sindbæk 2005: 161), an area having close contact with Kaupang, which is reflected in pottery finds (Hougen 1969: 98; Pilø 2011: 296–300). However, the pottery assemblage at Kaupang also reflects close contacts with the Rhineland (Hougen 1969: 98; Pilø 2011: 286–92, 295), where only a few soapstone artefacts have been identified (Kars and Wevers 1983: 169).

This makes it difficult to evaluate Kaupang's role in the trading of soapstone goods, but most evidence suggests that Kaupang played a modest role in the long-distance distribution of these artefacts (Baug 2011: 327). Outside of Norway, it was pottery that provided cooking utensils, and different traditions in the preparation of food may have been decisive for the distribution of soapstone vessels – they were never able to compete with the pottery vessels in

Soapstone vessels and quernstones   147

a foreign market. There is also much to suggest that other Viking-Age towns, such as Hedeby and Ribe, should be seen as recipients rather than centres of redistribution for soapstone products. The distribution map of soapstone in Denmark and northern Germany shows that the area around the Limfjord and the coast of the Kattegat were the main areas receiving soapstone in southern Scandinavia, while the areas surrounding Hedeby and Ribe have far fewer finds. The soapstone artefacts around the Kattegat could have been brought there as personal possessions or distributed by travelling people, and somewhat sporadic exchange between farmers and fishermen instead of organised trade is possible (Sindbæk 2005: 141–2, 160). However, the fact that soapstone objects largely occur at marketplaces and in towns during the Viking Age makes it perhaps more likely that the objects represent commodities within a more organised and regular trade.

Different trade networks?

In the eleventh to twelfth century, when the trade in soapstone vessels starts to decrease, quernstones are introduced as a new type of commodity from Norway. Geological and contextual analyses of quernstones and millstones from Danish sites show that nearly all quernstones of garnet mica schist originate from Hyllestad, even though a few quernstones from other quarries are found. In some areas of north-eastern Denmark, Hyllestad seems to have been a major supplier of quernstones for several hundred years (Baug 2015a: 111–13), and I would argue that this, too, is in all likelihood the result of organised, commercially based trade.

Some regional trends with regard to the types of quernstone used in southern Scandinavia have earlier been pointed out by Carelli and Kresten (1997: 124–6). Thus, quernstones originate from four different areas: (1) garnet mica schist from Hyllestad, (2) Mayen basalt from Rhineland in Germany, (3) schistose sandstone from Malung in Sweden and (4) gneiss from Lugnås in Sweden (Carelli and Kresten 1997: 124) (Figure 8.4). In the north-eastern parts of Denmark and south-western parts of Sweden, Hyllestad stones were preferred to others, while there are few stones of garnet mica schist in the western parts of Denmark. Here, the distribution area of Hyllestad stones meets an area dominated by basalt from the Rhine area, the western limit following a line through Jutland from the outlet of the Limfjord in the west, along the eastern coast of Jutland to Hedeby. To the east, the distribution of Hyllestad stones borders an area dominated by schistose sandstone produced at Malung in Sweden (Carelli and Kresten 1997: 123–5; Sindbæk 2005: 148–50).

This distribution map does not, however, give a completely accurate representation. A few stones of garnet mica schist are recorded in addition to the Hyllestad stones, and more quarries than the two mentioned are known in Sweden, for instance at Sala in Västmanland (Zachrisson 2014; Baug 2015a: 149). Even so, the map indicates some regional trends. The different distribution patterns most likely testify to different contact and trading networks, which

148 *Irene Baug*

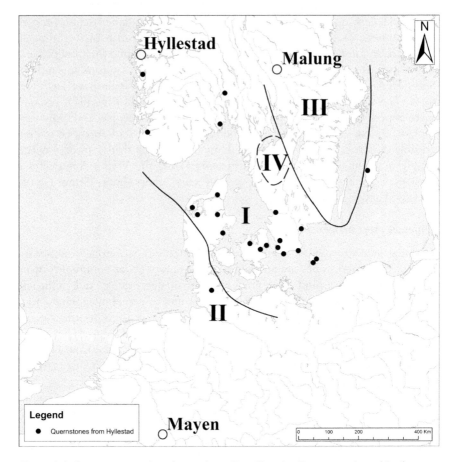

Figure 8.4 Quernstone regions in southern Scandinavia. (I) garnet mica schist from Hyllestad, (II) Mayen basalt from Rhineland in Germany, (III) schistose sandstone from Malung in Sweden and (IV) gneiss from Lugnås in Sweden.

Source: Carelli and Kresten (1997: Fig. 18). Map by Kjetil Loftsgarden.

gave differential access to diverse types of quernstones. However, it should also be mentioned that the four quernstone regions are not entirely contemporaneous. Quernstones of basalt were exported to Denmark from the eighth century onwards, which is about 200 years before Hyllestad quernstones appear. Thus, the northern limit of the distribution of basalt was not limited by competing export areas in the early Viking Age, but rather represents a boundary between the presence and absence of organised trade in quernstones (Sindbæk 2005: 149). Organised and regular trade in quernstones in the northern and eastern parts of medieval Denmark first appeared in the latter part of the Viking Age with the import of quernstones from Hyllestad. The fairly limited production of good-quality quernstones in Scandinavia may have opened up the possibility for actors at Hyllestad to become important suppliers within certain areas. The eastern parts of medieval Denmark had no large-scale, organised production of quernstones of their own, and Hyllestad stones more or less supplanted locally produced quernstones. The distribution pattern of the stones was largely sustained throughout the Viking Age and the Middle Ages.

As noted above, the area where stones from Hyllestad are found also represents the main area for soapstone vessels from Norway in southern Scandinavia. In northern and eastern parts of Denmark there seems to have been strong contact and possibly trade with Norway from the ninth century onwards, whereas this area largely turned its back on trade with the Rhine area (Sindbæk 2007: 149–50). Thus, it is an area that had relatively close contacts with Norway for centuries, and the contact zones and knowledge of Norwegian resources preceded the distribution of quernstones.

The eastern limit of the distribution of Hyllestad stones largely coincides with the border between the Danish and Swedish kingdoms in the Middle Ages. Perhaps these two kingdoms also represented separate trading regions within separate contact networks, as has been suggested by Carelli and Kresten (1997: 126). This could possibly explain the absence of quernstones from Hyllestad and the marginal export of soapstone vessels to large parts of Sweden. The distribution of soapstone vessels and quernstones indicates an organised and regular trade with long-lasting trade networks. There are no signs that the limits of the spread southwards and eastwards were caused by any difficulties or obstacles to further distribution, and the limits were not established because of lack of contact between the different regions. Traditions, alliances and conscious choices have, most likely, been of importance for distribution and trade, and the networks within which soapstone and quernstones circulated seem to have coincided with cultural and political regions. Several elements represented along the south-western coast of Denmark, such as burial practice, pottery types and building construction, indicate influence from the Frisian and Frankish areas. The same influence is not evident in eastern Denmark (Sindbæk 2008: 70–1), indicating different contact networks and alliances. Thus, the distribution of quernstones and soapstone does not appear accidental, and it seems the geographical pattern identified indicates export within specific networks.

Commodity export from Norway to southern Scandinavia is also evident from finds of whetstones dating from the eighth century and into the Middle Ages (cf. Resi 1990, 2011; Myrvoll 1991; Sindbæk 2005: 142–5), and raw materials such as iron and antler. However, not all commodity types from Norway are limited to north-eastern Denmark, in the way that the quernstones are, and to a certain degree the soapstone vessels as well. It is suggested that reception of imported goods may have been dependent on cultural identities and social ties (Sindbæk 2005: 161). Perhaps this was of special importance when it came to household artefacts like quernstones and soapstone vessels, which are both connected with the preparing of food. Both food and the

150 *Irene Baug*

utensils used in food processing symbolise social and cultural affiliation; and food as well as food processing constitute some of the most conservative aspects of culture (Øye 2002: 405, 2008: 225; Baug 2015b). The making of food and the utensils used may, thus, to a larger degree have been dependent on traditions, social ties and habitual practices, compared to other spheres of society, which may explain the somewhat limited distribution of the quernstones and soapstone vessels.

The nodes at the Carolingian-German border, Hedeby as well as Dorestad, generally seem to mark the southern limit for traded commodities from the Nordic countries, such as soapstone, quernstones, whetstones, iron and antler (Steuer 1987: 187). At Hedeby, more than 3,000 vessel sherds have been identified (Resi 1979: 17). Provenance studies of the finds indicate that the vessels were produced in Halden in Norway, or Halland or Bohuslän in Sweden (Alfsen and Christie 1979: 182). Hedeby also represents the southernmost findspot of Hyllestad stones, and a site where quernstones of both Mayen basalt and garnet mica schist from Hyllestad occur. However, while large amounts of soapstone have been recovered in the town, only a small number of Hyllestad stones found their way here. Only 1 per cent of the total number of quernstone fragments (48 out of 5,875 pieces) are identified as coming from Hyllestad, while one fragment may originate from Saltdal (Baug 2015a: 113). In medieval Schleswig, 11 per cent (12 out of 88 pieces) are from Hyllestad (Schön 1995: 12, 22; Baug 2015a: 113–14). Most quernstones in Hedeby are of basalt. The relatively small number of quernstones from Hyllestad in Hedeby and later in medieval Schleswig does not indicate large-scale trade. It appears that Hyllestad stones were only exceptionally distributed to this area.

During the Viking Age, distribution took place in a mainly rural and protourban society, although the process of urbanisation started already in the Viking Age in southern parts of Scandinavia. Little is known about the complex networks of nodes, towns and individuals that made the distribution and trade in the objects possible, and various ways of organising the trade may have existed. The distribution demonstrates a shared artefact type but not necessarily a connection between the sites where they have been found. In the pre-urban Viking Age in Norway, ships may have sailed more or less directly from the quarries or areas nearby to markets in the North Atlantic region and southern Scandinavia. Three knots is normally estimated as an average speed for rowing, which means that a rowing ship would travel 36 nautical miles per day. Under sail, a ship would be able to reach 72 nautical miles per day (Morcken 1964: 22, 38). At this speed, then, it would be possible to sail between the quarries at Hyllestad and Hedeby within eleven days at a minimum, depending on the weather conditions. Somewhat similar travel time should also be expected for several of the soapstone quarries in Norway.

It has been suggested that Viking-Age trade was organised within networks and routes between different nodes, where large cargoes could be loaded or unloaded for further distribution (Sindbæk 2007). A similar distribution system should also be considered for soapstone vessels and quernstones. Several

Soapstone vessels and quernstones 151

actors may have been involved at different levels, and regional marketplaces and nodes may have been situated near the quarry sites (cf. Schou 2007, 2015). Peripheral parts of the country may in this way have been connected to inter-regional trading networks via local or regional middlemen, implying that there was not necessarily direct contact between the quarries and all the centres or marketplaces where the quernstones and steatite products are found.

For instance, Sebbersund on the Limfjord and Århus in eastern Jutland seem to have been marketplaces which received commodities from Norway that were reloaded for further export (Skov 1999: 603, 606; Birkedahl and Johansen 2000: 29). These centres may have served as gateways for various kinds of products from Norway. The contact between Hyllestad and some of the marketplaces where the Hyllestad quernstones are found may there-fore have been indirect, based on transhipment and redistribution. Similarly organised distribution should probably be expected in the case of soapstone objects.

It is also possible that the distribution of both soapstone goods and quern-stones is the result of the stone products being transported as ballast. To stabilise the ship and prevent capsize, ballast was needed, normally in the form of stones or sand. Various stone products, such as quernstones, soapstone vessels and whetstones, may have functioned as an economic form of ballast, or commodity ballast that could be sold (Forster 2004: 344, 351, 360, 366, 2009: 61; Nymoen 2011: 67; Baug 2015a: 155). A similar situation has been suggested regarding the distribution of building stones (cf. Buckland and Sadler 1990).

Trade in the Middle Ages

The distribution of products and transactions involving them were integrated parts of larger economic systems, but of a different character, before the emer-gence of towns in Scandinavia during the early and High Middle Ages. The medieval trade in various products was largely channelled via the Norwegian towns, which acted as redistribution centres; among these, Bergen, in particu-lar, became a centre for further export. From the middle of the twelfth century onwards, Bergen was known as the largest commercial centre in the country (Helle 1982: 167, 2006: 83–6). The Urban Code of Bergen, from 1276, states that quern- and millstones should be sold in a designated area of the town, at Stranden on the western side of the Vågen Bay (Bl VI: 8). Quernstones from rural areas in the counties of Hordaland and Sogn og Fjordane show a high degree of concurrence with the types of quernstones found in Bergen (Baug 2015a: 109–10), indicating the town's role in local and regional trade.

Soapstone vessels may also have been traded in Bergen; however, most of the vessels found bear clear signs of use (Vangstad 2003: 76), indicating import based on the needs of the town itself. Nevertheless, as Bergen represented the most important medieval trading centre in Norway, it is likely that the town also played a role in local and regional soapstone trade in the Middle Ages. Long-distance distribution of the artefacts did, however, most likely not take

152   *Irene Baug*

place, as soapstone disappears from Denmark during the eleventh and twelfth centuries (Sindbæk 2007: 137).

Quernstones from Hyllestad did not play an unrivalled role in medieval Norway. Based on finds from urban contexts, the towns functioned as important markets for two of the large production areas, Hyllestad and Saltdal. The numbers of quernstones from Hyllestad and Saltdal indicate organised distribution to Bergen in the Middle Ages, and the two quarry areas were most likely competing in some of the same markets. The sailing distance by boat from Hyllestad to Bergen is quite short: 62 nautical miles, normally with a travel time of one day. From the quarries in Saltdal the distance is 560 nautical miles, taking about eight days, depending on the wind and sailing conditions. Consequently, bringing products from Saltdal would have needed more investment in transportation. It was more time-consuming and perhaps also involved greater costs and risks (Baug 2015a: 150–1). Nevertheless, in medieval Norway, the Saltdal quarries seem to have played an important role as suppliers of quernstones. That quernstones from Saltdal were widely distributed is indicated, for instance, by the archaeological material from Oslo and Tønsberg.

The spread of quernstones from Saltdal should perhaps be seen in connection with the growing stockfish trade in the Middle Ages. Most likely, stockfish and quernstones were transported southwards on the same ships, which opened up larger markets for the Saltdal stones. A plausible situation is that the quernstones functioned as commodity ballast aboard the ships transporting stockfish. One of the main areas involved in the stockfish trade, Lofoten, is located about 140 km north–west of Saltdal. According to written sources, commercial fishing of spawning cod was established here in the eleventh century, and developed further in the twelfth century. The fishing village of Vågan (Norse: Vágar) in Lofoten is mentioned in written sources in the early twelfth century, and the site developed into a marketplace from the thirteenth century onwards. Vågan received stockfish from both Hålogaland and Finnmark, and according to a document from 1384, merchants from Bergen were directed to travel to Vågan to buy stockfish (Nielssen 2014: 195–7). The relatively short distance between Vågan and Saltdal may have made it convenient to use the quernstones as temporary ballast before selling them together with the stockfish in towns such as Trondheim and Bergen, which were of special importance for stockfish export. From there, they may have been distributed further south, but mainly within Norway.

In the medieval town of Oslo there are far more quernstones from Saltdal compared to Hyllestad. Oslo does not seem, however, to have functioned as a redistribution centre for quernstones in the same way as Bergen. Most of the quernstones found in Oslo have traces of use, whereas in Bergen several of the stones seem to be unused. Quernstones from the large quarry areas are only exceptionally represented within the rural districts of eastern Norway, indicating local small-scale production meant for local use (Baug 2015a: 108–10, 118–19).

Hyllestad clearly dominated at the largest commercial centre in Norway, Bergen, and the stones also continued to dominate abroad, where the

Soapstone vessels and quernstones 153

pre-established contact networks and markets for the Hyllestad stones seem to have been strong (Baug 2015a: 118–19). Hyllestad was the only Norwegian quarry site to gain a foothold within a foreign market. Quernstones of garnet mica schist from other Norwegian quarries are so far only exceptionally found outside of Norway. The Saltdal quarries were further from the markets of southern Scandinavia compared to Hyllestad, making it more complicated and resource-demanding to establish the routes, networks and alliances necessary for effective distribution. However, it is more likely that limited distribution in the Viking Age was the result of the small scale of production, surpluses being insufficient for interregional trade in this early period. In the Middle Ages, well-established tradition and knowledge of how to organise transport and exchange may have given Hyllestad an advantage over other quarry sites. Long-lasting trade contacts were important for maintaining trust and security (Gustin 2004: 176, 249, 264). Trade routes and networks were, thus, based not merely on topography and distance but also on social structures; a route is not only a geographical construct but a repetitive praxis, a routine (Sindbæk 2005: 30–3). This means that tradition and routines may have been important aspects in the export of quernstones. Hyllestad operated within well-established trade routes and markets, perhaps also networks, and the trading routes and foreign markets established during the Viking Age were largely sustained, giving an advantage to the Hyllestad quarries compared to others (Baug 2015a: 152–3).

The character of the distribution to the North Atlantic islands may have changed during the Middle Ages, as the islands became more integrated into medieval trade, perhaps because of their close contact with Bergen. People from the North Atlantic islands had close political-administrative and economic connections to Norway (see, e.g., Arge 1989; Crawford 2002; Øye 2008). From the thirteenth century, Bergen was a cultural, economic and legal centre for the North Atlantic islands, which were subject to the *fehird*[1] in Bergen from the beginning of the fourteenth century, meaning that taxes were paid to the Norwegian crown (Helle 1982: 173–4, 331). Medieval Bergen was also the most important town and trading centre in Norway. From the twelfth century onwards, people from the North Atlantic region travelled to Bergen to buy and sell goods. In Bergen, a variety of objects were acquired and brought back to the North Atlantic islands – most likely also soapstone vessels and quernstones. Most trade was, however, conducted by Norwegian traders and ecclesiastical institutions in Bergen, several ships being sent westwards every year with Norwegian commodities (Helle 1982: 165, 360–4). Most likely, quernstones and soapstone vessels, too, were brought westwards on these ships, along with other commodities.

Actors in trade

People involved in producing and trading objects are difficult to identify in the material record, and little is known about them. The manufacture of both soapstone vessels and quernstones bears witness to large-scale production of a

154   *Irene Baug*

nearly industrial character, where the aim was trade and exchange. It has been suggested that male burials of the Viking Age containing soapstone vessels should be seen in connection with the distribution and exchange of the goods. The vessels represent household utensils used by ordinary people, and there is nothing to indicate that there was status connected with owning a soapstone vessel. The use of the vessels in food processing was most likely carried out by women. Yet, most vessels found in burials occur in male burials − and the majority are from rich burials (Risbøl 1994: 133–4). Most likely, then, the status connected with the vessels did not relate to owning the vessels but more probably to the production of the artefacts and/or trade in them. It is, of course, possible that status attached to soapstone vessels may also be connected with the contents of the vessels, but as the vessels seem to represent an everyday product relating to the household, this is perhaps less likely.

Male burials containing vessels are found in areas that seem to have been involved in trade, and many of these burials also contained weights and balances. This makes it more likely that people buried in rich graves containing vessels can somehow be linked to the production and exchange of such goods (Risbøl 1994: 133–4, 136–40; Schou 2007, 2015). If this is the case, then those who organised and administered the production and exchange of the vessels may have been of high status. Vestfold is one of the regions in Norway with the highest frequency of soapstone vessels from graves, and there is a predominance of graves containing vessels in the burials around Kaupang (Skjølsvold 1961: 117; Risbøl 1994: 136–8). It is likely that the quantity recovered is in some way connected with the trading of soapstone. Kaupang may have acted as a local or regional distribution centre for soapstone vessels, but involvement in long-distance trade in these products cannot be excluded either.

In the case of Hyllestad, both the character of production and the scale of distribution of the products indicate an intensive and well-organised activity. I have earlier suggested that the landowners at Hyllestad, magnates and freeholders in the Viking Age and ecclesiastical institutions in the Middle Ages, controlled the production (Baug 2002, 2015a). The landowners need not have been central agents in the trade, but they would most likely have ensured that their surplus production was taken to market (Skre 2008: 353). During the Middle Ages, it seems to have been common for landowners belonging to the societal elite, both ecclesiastical and secular, to be involved in distributing and trading goods received as land rent. The landowners had their land rent products brought into the towns, where they were sold further on (Helle 1982: 330–7, 346, 354).

Both magnates and ecclesiastical institutions were to a certain degree directly involved in foreign trade with their own ships and commodities (Helle 1982: 398, 402). It is also possible that tenants and others working in the quarries were involved in the trade. Cooperation in the frame of a *félag* to provide a ship and organise transportation may have made it easier for the workers to transport their products to marketplaces and towns. Quite often, the ship, its crew and independent traders were hired (Helle 1982: 370, 372; Sigurðsson 1999: 165). Consequently, various ways of organising the trade in soapstone vessels and quernstones may have existed, and different actors – both individuals and institutions – from different levels of society may have taken part in the trade.

Conclusions

The distribution of steatite goods and quernstones and exchange in these products took place in several different social contexts, which varied in time and space, from a more random distribution and exchange in the North Atlantic region, to a larger and more commercially based trade in the southern parts of Scandinavia. Itinerant people may have been important regarding the dispersal to the North Atlantic region. Immigrants to the islands may have been a decisive factor for the spread of soapstone, in particular in the Viking Age, even though some kind of exchange may also have taken place. The export to southern Scandinavia, on the other hand, most likely demanded a wider network and regular practices of sailing long distances. Certainly, the presence of the goods in urban settings and marketplaces in southern Scandinavia indicates a more organised and commercially based trade at trading centres such as Kaupang, Sebbersund on the Limfjord and the early town of Århus, and to a certain degree also Hedeby and Ribe. The distribution of stone products from Norway seems, therefore, to have been organised within defined contact zones from the beginning of the Viking Age and was maintained throughout the Middle Ages.

The current evidence indicates that that a dynamic trade in soapstone vessels and quernstones took place during the Viking Age and the Middle Ages, exhibiting both change and stability. The trading activities were part of political, social and economic systems that created both possibilities and restrictions. The actors involved in trade changed over time, and so did the nodes and central places along the trading routes. After the establishment of medieval towns in Norway in the eleventh and twelfth centuries, export was largely channelled through these, which led to changes in sailing routes and redistribution centres compared to the preceding period. Still, within southern Scandinavia and the North Atlantic region, the same areas as before stand out as recipients of the Norwegian goods. However, while the distribution indicates long-lasting and stable contact zones and trading networks, a change in the type of commodity over the centuries – from soapstone vessels to quernstones – becomes evident. The networks and contact zones established in the early Viking Age seem largely to have been sustained throughout the Middle Ages. Established routines and traditions were most likely important for distribution and trade. Despite changing societal relations, new actors and urbanisation, as well as new types of commodities, the trading networks seem to have been stable and predictable through the centuries.

156 *Irene Baug*

Note

1 In the Middle Ages the king's income was paid in commodities and money to a regional *fehird*. In the fourteenth century the *fehirdsle* in Bergen was the largest one in the country – and also included the islands in the North Atlantic region (Helle 1982: 331).

References

Alfsen, Bjørg Elisabeth and Olav H.J. Christie 1979: Massenspektrometrische Analysen von Specksteinfunden aus Haithabu und wikingerzeitlichen Specksteinbrüche in Skandinavien. In: Resi, Heid Gjøstein: *Berichte über die Ausgrabungen in Haithabu*, Bericht 14. Karl Wachholtz Verlag. Neumünster.

Arge, Símun V. 1989: Om landnåmet på Færøerne. *Hikuin*, 15: 103–28.

Baug, Irene 2002: *Kvernsteinsbrota i Hyllestad. Arkeologiske punktundersøkingar i steinbrotsområdet i Hyllestad i Sogn og Fjordane*. Bergverksmuseet, Skrift 22. Prinfo Vanberg. Kongsberg.

—— 2011: Soapstone Finds. In: Skre, Dagfinn (ed.): *Things from the Town: Artefacts and Inhabitants in Viking-Age Kaupang*. Kaupang Excavation Project. Publication Series, vol. 3. Norske Oldfunn, vol. 24: 311–37. Aarhus University Press. Aarhus.

—— 2015a: *Quarrying in Western Norway: An Archaeological Study of Production and Distribution in the Viking Period and Middle Ages*. Archaeopress Archaeology. Oxford.

—— 2015b: Stones for bread: Regional differences and changes in Scandinavian food traditions related to the use of quernstones, bakestones and soapstone vessels c. AD 800–1500. In: Baug, Irene, Janicke Larsen and Sigrid Samset Mygland (eds): *Nordic Middle Ages: Artefacts, Landscapes and Society. Essays in Honour of Ingvild Øye on her 70th Birthday*, UBAS 8: 33–47. University of Bergen. Bergen.

Birkedahl, Petter 2000: Sebbersund – en handelsplads med trækirke ved Limfjorden – forbindelser til Norge. In: Karmøy kommune (ed.): *Havn og Handel i 1000 år. Karmøyseminaret 1997*, pp. 31–9. Dreyer bok. Stavanger.

Birkedahl, Petter and Erik Johansen 2000: The eastern Limfjord in the Germanic Iron Age and the Viking Period. *Acta archaeologica*, 71: 25–32.

Bl = *Magnus Lagabøters bylov*. Translated by Knut Robberstad, 1923. Kristiania.

Buckland, P.C. and Jon Sadler 1990: Ballast and building stone: A discussion. In: Parson, David (ed.): *Stone: Quarrying and Building in England AD 43–1525*, pp. 114–25. Phillimore and Co Ltd. Sussex.

Carelli, Peter and Peter Kresten 1997: Give us this day our daily bread: A study of late Viking Age and medieval quernstones in South Scandinavia. *Acta Archaeologica*, 68: 109–37.

Christophersen, Axel 1991: Ports and trade in Norway during the transition to historical time. In: Pedersen, O. Crumlin (ed.): *Aspects of Maritime Scandinavia AD 200–1200*, pp. 159–70. The Viking Ship Museum. Roskilde.

Crawford, Barbara E. 2002: *Papa Stour and 1299: Commemorating the 700th Anniversary of Shetland's First Document*. Shetland Times Ltd. Lerwick.

Forster, Amanda K. 2004: Shetland and the trade of steatite goods in the North Atlantic region during the Viking and early medieval period. Unpublished PhD thesis. Department of Archaeological Sciences, University of Bradford.

—— 2009: Viking and Norse steatite use in Shetland. In: Forster, Amanda K. and E. Val Turner (eds): *Kleber: Shetland's Oldest Industry. Shetland Soapstone Since Prehistory*, pp. 58–69. Shetland Amenity Trust. Lerwick.

Soapstone vessels and quernstones 157

Gestsson, Gísli 1959: Gröf í Öræfum. In: Eldjárn, Kristján (ed.): *Árbók hins íslenzka fornleifafélags*, pp. 5–87. Isa Foldarprentsmidju. Reykjavik.

Gustin, Ingrid 2004: *Mellan gåva och marknad: Handel, tillit og materiell kultur under vikingatid*. Lund Studies in Medieval Archaeology, vol. 34. Almqvist and Wiksell International. Malmö.

Helberg, Bjørn Hebba 2010: Kvernsteinsindustri i vikingtid og tidlig middelalder i Saltdal kommune, Nordland fylke. *Viking*, 2010: 103–20.

—— 2010/11: Rapport vedrørende overvåking av inngrep i skogsvei (Sypranvegen) ved kvernsteinsbruddet i Hestgarden, Saksenvik i Saltdal kommune, Nordland. Unpublished report. Topografisk arkiv, Tromsø Museum, Universitetet i Tromsø.

Helle, Knut 1982: *Bergen bys historie. Bind I. Kongssete og kjøpstad. Fra opphavet til 1536*. Universitetsforlaget. Bergen.

—— 2006: DEL I. Frå opphavet til omkring 1500. In: Helle, Knut, Finn-Einar Eliassen, Jan Eivind Myhre and Ola Svein Stugu (eds.): *Norsk byhistorie. Urbanisering gjennom 1300 år*, pp. 23–142. Pax Forlag A/S, Oslo.

Hougen, Ellen Karine 1969: Leirkarmaterialet fra Kaupang. *Viking*, 33: 97–118.

Jensen, Stig 1990: Handel med dagligvarer i vikingetiden. *Hikuin*, 16: 119–38.

Kaland, Sigrid 1987: Viking/medieval settlement in the heathland area of Nordhordland. In: Knirk, James (ed.): *Proceedings of the Tenth Viking Congress*. Universitetets Oldsaksamlings skrifter. Nye rekke, nr. 9: 171–90. Universitetets Oldsaksamling. Oslo.

Kars, Henk and J.M.A.R. Wevers 1983: Early medieval Dorestad, an archaeo-petrological study. Part III: A trachyte mortar, the soapstone finds and the tuýeres. *Berichte ROB*, 32: 169–82.

Magnússon, Þor 1971: Sögualdarbyggð í Hvítárholti. In: Eldjárn, Kristján (ed.): *Árbók hins íslenzka fornleifafélags*, pp. 5–80. Isa Foldarprentsmidju. Reykjavik.

Morcken, Roald 1964: *Den nautiske mil gjennom tusen år*. Bergen Sjøfartsmuseums Årshefte. Bergen.

Myrvoll, Siri 1991: The hones. In: Bencard, Mogens, Lise Bender Jørgensen and Helge Brinch Madsen (eds): *Ribe Excavations 1970–76*, vol. 3: 115–42. Sydjysk Universitetsforlag. Esbjerg.

Nielssen, Alf Ragnar 2014: 8. Kysten – overgangen fra vikingtid til middelalder. In: Kolle, Nils and Alf Ragnar Nielssen (eds): *Fangstmenn, fiskerbønder og værfolk. Fram til 1720*, pp. 187–207. Fagbokforlaget. Bergen.

Nymoen, Pål 2011: Kun for den smarte skippers regning? Skipsvrak med omsettelig ballast: på sporet av kvernstein, kleber og brynehandelen fra Norge ca 800–1800. *Nicolay*, 114: 65–75.

Øye, Ingvild 2002: Landbruk under press 800–1350. *Jorda blir levevei: 4000 f.Kr.–1350 e.Kr. Norges Landbrukshistorie I*, pp. 215–414. Samlaget. Oslo.

—— 2008: Kontakten mellom Bergen og Færøyene i middelalderen i arkeologisk og historisk lys. In: *Paulsen, Caroline and Helgi Dahl Michelsen (eds): Símunarbók. Heiðursrit til Símun V. Arge á 60 ára degnum. 5 September 2008*, pp. 243–52. Faroe University Press. Tórshavn.

—— 2011: Food and technology: Cooking utensils and food processing in medieval Norway. In: Klapste, Jan and Petr Sommer (eds): *Processing, Storage, Distribution of Food: Food in the Medieval Rural Environment*. Ruralia VIII. 7–12 September 2009, 225–334. Brepols Publishers. Lorca.

Pilø, Lars 2007: The settlement: Extent and dating. In: Skre, Dagfinn (ed.): *Kaupang in Skiringssal*. Kaupang Excavation Project. Publication Series, vol. 1. Norske Oldfunn, vol. 22: 161–78. Aarhus University Press. Aarhus.

158   *Irene Baug*

—— 2011: The pottery. In: Skre, Dagfinn (ed.): *Things from the Town: Artefacts and Inhabitants in Viking-Age Kaupang*. Kaupang Excavation Project. Publication Series, vol. 3. Norske Oldfunn, vol. 24: 281–304. Aarhus University Press. Aarhus.

Randers, Kjersti 1982: Høybøen: en ødegård på Sotra. En undersøkelse av bruksperioder og erverv basert på bosetningsspor fra eldre jernalder og middelalder. Unpublished Master's thesis in archaeology. University of Bergen.

Resi, Heid Gjøstein 1979: *Die Specksteinfunde aus Haithabu*. Berichte über die Ausgrabungen in Haithabu, Bericht 14. Karl Wachholtz Verlag. Neumünster.

—— 1990: *Die Wetz- und Schleifsteine aus Haithabu*. Berichte über die Ausgrabungen in Haithabu, Bericht 28. Karl Wachholtz Verlag. Neumünster.

—— 2011: Whetstones, grindstones, touchstones and smoothers. In: Skre, Dagfinn (ed.): *Things from the Town: Artefacts and Inhabitants in Viking-Age Kaupang*. Kaupang Excavation Project. Publication Series, vol. 3. Norske Oldfunn, vol. 24: 373–93. Aarhus University Press. Aarhus.

Risbøl, Ole 1994: Sosialøkonomiske aspekter ved vikingetidens klæberstenshandel i Sydskandinavien. *Lag*, 5: 115–61.

Schou, Torbjørn Preus 2007: Handel, produksjon og kommunikasjon: en undersøkelse av klebersteinsvirksomheten i Aust-Agders vikingtid med fokus på Fjære og Landvik. Unpublished Master's thesis in archaeology. University of Bergen.

—— 2015: The soapstone vessel production and trade of Agder and its actors. In: Hansen, Gitte, Steven Asbhy and Irene Baug (eds): *Everyday Products in the Middle Ages: Crafts, Consumption and the Individual in Northern Europe c. AD 800–1600*, pp. 204–28. Oxbow Books. Oxford.

Schön, Volkmar 1995: *Die Mühlsteine von Haithabu und Schleswig: Ein Beitrag zur Entwicklungsgeschichte des mittelalterlichen Mühlenwesens in Nordwesteuropa*. Wachholtz. Neumünster.

Sigurðsson, Jon Viðar 1999: *Norsk historie 800–1300: Frå høvdingmakt til konge- og kyrkjemakt*. Samlaget. Oslo.

Sindbæk, Søren M. 2005: *Ruter og rutinisering: Vikingetidens fjernhandel i Nordeuropa*. Multivers Academic. København.

—— 2007: The small world of the Vikings: Networks in early medieval communication and exchange. *Norwegian Archaeological Review*, 40(1): 59–74.

—— 2008: Kulturelle forskelle, sociale netværk og regionalitet i vikingetidens arkæologi. *Hikuin*, 35: 63–84.

Skjølsvold, Arne 1961: *Klebersteinsindustrien i vikingetiden*. Universitetsforlaget. Oslo.

Skov, Hans 1999: Archaeological evidence of trade in Århus, Denmark, from the 10th to the 17th centuries. In: Dunckel, Regina, Manfred Gläser and Ulrike Oltmanns (eds): *Lübecker Kolloquium zur Stadtharchäologie im Hansaraum II. Der Handel*, pp. 603–11. Schmidt-Römhild. Lübeck.

Skre, Dagfinn 2007: Towns and markets, kings and central places in south-western Scandinavia c. AD 800–950. In: Skre, Dagfinn (ed.): *Kaupang in Skiringssal*. Kaupang Excavations Project. Publication Series, vol. 1. Norske Oldfunn, vol. 22: 445–69. Aarhus University Press. Aarhus.

—— 2008: Dealing with silver: Economic agency in south-western Scandinavia AD 600–1000. In: Skre, Dagfinn (ed.): *Means of Exchange*. Kaupang Excavation Project. Publication Series, vol. 2. Norske Oldfunn, vol. 23: 343–55. Aarhus University Press. Aarhus.

Steuer, Heiko 1987: Der Handel der Wikingerzeit zwischen Nord- und Westeuropa aurgrund archäelogischer Zeugnisse. In: Düwel, Klaus (ed.): *Untersuchungen zu Handel*

Soapstone vessels and quernstones 159

und Verkehr der vor- und frühgeschichtlichen Zeit in Mittel- und Nordeuropa, pp. 113–97. Vandenhoeck and Ruprecht. Göttingen.

Vangstad, Hilde 2003: Kleberkarene fra Bryggen i Bergen: En arkeologisk analyse av kleberkarene funnet på Bryggen i Bergen fra middelalder og etterreformatorisk tid. Unpublished Master's thesis in archaeology. University of Bergen.

Zachrisson, Torun 2014: Rotary querns and bread: A social history of Iron Age Sweden. In: Selsing, Lotte (ed.): *Seen Through a Millstone*. AmS-Skrifter vol. 24: 181–91. Museum of Archaeology, University of Stavanger.

9 The Uplands
The deepest of forests and the highest of mountains – resource exploitation and landscape management in the Viking Age and early Middle Ages in southern Norway

Kathrine Stene and Vivian Wangen

Introduction

The emergence of trading sites (marketplaces and towns) and the increasing economic specialisation of trade and craft production have a central position in explanations for the social and political changes in European societies in the period c. AD 800–1200. In this chapter, however, we will highlight the extensive resource exploitation in the wooded and mountainous areas of southern Norway and discuss what we believe may have been the prerequisites for these changes. In these landscapes, a significant surplus production of raw materials and products has been taking place in various times and spaces, which is important for illuminating social, political and economic developments. Although an increasing number of local studies have drawn attention to rural districts and spheres of production, they have received strikingly little attention in socio-economic analyses of the period (e.g. Brink and Price 2008; Bagge 2010; Sindbæk and Poulsen 2011). In the scientific literature, these production areas are generally described as 'outfield' or 'the mountain land'. One can therefore get the erroneous impression of such areas as homogenous and uniform, as opposed to the more 'central' places and regions along the coast. This type of simple dichotomisation has been debated, pointing out the biased perspective that comes from taking the farm and the agricultural economy as a granted point of departure in explaining how the use of the outfield resources has taken place and what social context these can be related to (Holm et al. 2009). We wish to argue in favour of more complex and varied resource exploitation, with an importance going far beyond the rural production areas, where the local inhabitants and their communities played an active part in the transformation of the general contemporary society.

A central question is how organised surplus production can be established and operated in a landscape that has been used in various ways since the early part of the Mesolithic (c. 9000–8000 BC). An increasingly more intensive exploitation of resources in an area must have resulted in new forms of

The Uplands: exploitation and management 161

collaboration, labour differentiation and specialisation through time. In addition, the establishment of surplus production and possibilities for economic gain may have led to conflicts of interests between different actors' desire to use the same resources in the same landscape, and between divergent wishes for intensive utilisation of some resources over others. Would it, for example, have been possible to operate large-scale trapping in areas with intensive iron production or livestock grazing? In this connection it is therefore essential to discuss what social and political arrangements were established to carry out surplus production, and how the systems of operation and the regulation of land use may have taken place. Resource exploitation in wooded and mountainous regions must therefore be viewed in connection with both the local settlements and the greater societal contexts.

The study takes three different landscape types in the interior of South Norway as a starting point (Figure 9.1). These are areas that in many respects appear furthest away from the central trading sites that emerged along the coast of South Norway during the Viking Age (AD 800–1050) and early Middle Ages (AD 1050–1150). In the first part of the chapter the three areas will be briefly presented, outlining their geographical, environmental and archaeological features, and describing recorded economic activities and resource exploitation. Thereafter, the areas will be compared and evaluated to identify similarities and differences in landscape use over time. To make this possible it is necessary to emphasise a wider time span than only the periods of main interest.[1] Factors that will be accentuated are changes in land use, the degree of intensity of resource exploitation and variations in operational systems and technology. In the second part of the chapter issues concerning who were the prime movers and who organised surplus production will be discussed by focusing on local settlements and social institutions. Through this we aim at presenting new, locally based perspectives on how wooded and mountainous landscapes have been managed and exploited in the Viking Age and early Middle Ages in southern Norway.

The Uplands

The three study areas lie in the inland region, which is usually referred to as 'the Uplands' (Norw. *Opplandene*) in historical sources, including *Historia Norwegie* (*Zona mediterranea* or *Zona montana*, translated as 'the inland area', 'the mountain region' or 'the Uplands' in Ekrem and Boje Mortensen 2003: 52–9, 176–82. See also Salvesen 1969: 19–21; Ekrem 1998). In written medieval sources 'Upland' is usually a common name for the inland region of eastern Norway (Bagge 2008: 151). Today, the three study areas lie in the counties of Hedmark and Oppland, relating to the two main valleys, Østerdalen and Gudbrandsdalen (Figure 9.1). The regional name *Oppland* (translated as 'Upland') is thereby still in use, referring to one administrative county of southern Norway, which is considerably smaller than the medieval *Opplandene*, the Uplands.

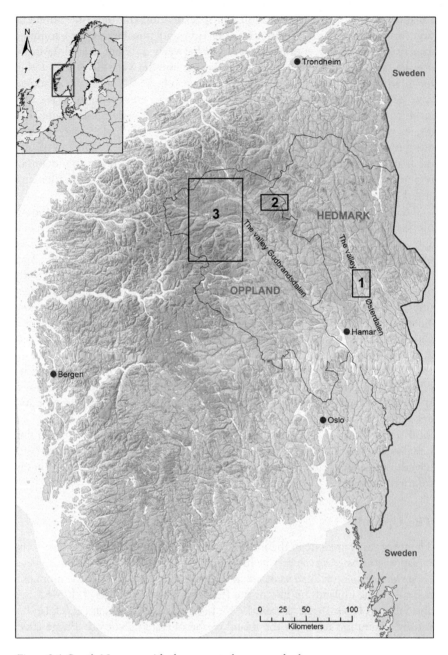

Figure 9.1 South Norway with the presented areas marked.

Source: Magne Samdal and Vivian Wangen, Museum of Cultural History, University of Oslo (approval number NE12000-150408SAS, The Norwegian Mapping Authority).

The Uplands: exploitation and management 163

Extensive archaeological excavations and surveys have been carried out in all three areas in recent years: in the wooded areas of Gråfjell and Rødsmoen (area 1),[2] in the mountain valley Grimsdalen (area 2)[3] and on melting snow patches in the high mountains of North Gudbrandsdal (area 3)[4] (Figures 9.2–9.4, respectively; see colour plate section). Although the background and scale of the investigations are different, the results illustrate what source material and source potential exists here. The areas represent three dissimilar resource bases, whose total potential of resource exploitation seems to have been used in different ways and with varying intensity through time.

Area 1: woodlands

The two adjacent wooded areas, the Gråfjell area and Rødsmoen, are situated near the Swedish border in Østerdalen, about 220–1000 m above sea level. This landscape is part of the vast boreal zone (taiga) starting about 35 km south of Gråfjell/Rødsmoen and stretching across North Scandinavia and Russia. Today, agricultural land and good pasture for livestock are spread out in this landscape, and the large rivers are teeming with fish. Most archaeological finds, ancient sites and remains in the two wooded areas can be associated with hunting and trapping of elk (*Alces alces*), extraction of iron and summer farming (Figure 9.5). Archaeological and palynological investigations show that an agrarian style of life was established around the beginning of the Christian era (Høeg 1996; Solem 2004; Stene 2014a). There are relatively few archaeological sites and remains from the latter part of the Early Iron Age (cf. note 1), but trapping of elk has taken place in pitfall trap systems that were established in the Bronze Age, and some small-scale iron production (shaft furnaces with a slag pit) also occur in the Early Iron Age. During the Late Iron Age, a marked change in the use of the wooded areas can be traced. The scale of livestock grazing increased, and new pitfall trap systems were built. In the Early and High Middle Ages large-scale iron production took place (slag-tapping furnaces), and in the late Middle Ages a farm and the summer farming system (shielings) was established (Bergstøl 1997, 2008; Narmo 1997, 2000; Risbøl 2005; Amundsen 2007; Rundberget 2007; Stene 2014a).

Area 2: mountain valley

Grimsdalen is a mountain valley that lies between Dovrefjell in the north and Rondane to the south, about 860–1170 m above sea level. The vegetation in the upper part of Grimsdalen is characterised by Scandinavian montane birch forest, which reaches up to about 1100 m above sea level. In the bottom of the valley, on the large river plains, there is lush grass vegetation. The reindeer migrated across the valley before the twentieth century, from winter pastures in Rondane to summer pastures on Dovrefjell.[5] The landscape of Grimsdalen is today marked by centuries of summer farming. The majority of surveyed

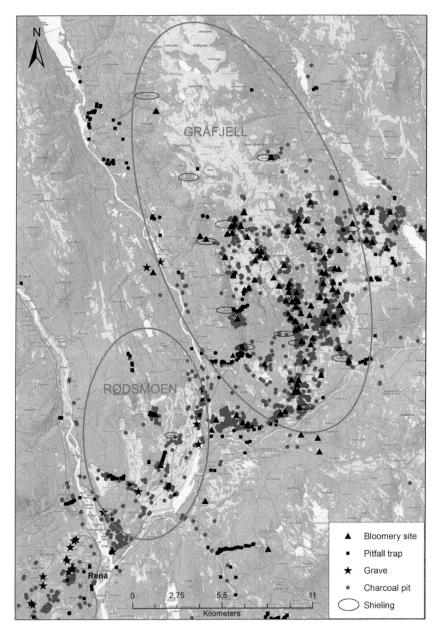

Figure 9.5 Sites and monuments surveyed in the Gråfjell area and Rødsmoen (area 1). The distribution of archaeological sites is based on information from the Norwegian Cultural Heritage Database, Askeladden (the Norwegian Directorate for Cultural Heritage).

Source: Magne Samdal, Kathrine Stene and Vivian Wangen, Museum of Cultural History, University of Oslo (approval number NE12000-150408SAS, The Norwegian Mapping Authority).

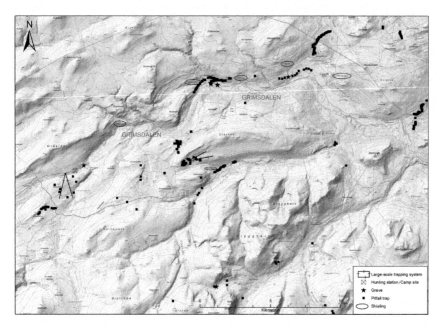

Figure 9.6 Sites and monuments surveyed in Grimsdalen (area 2). The distribution of archaeological sites is based on information from the Norwegian Cultural Heritage Database, Askeladden (the Norwegian Directorate for Cultural Heritage).

Source: Magne Samdal, Kathrine Stene and Vivian Wangen, Museum of Cultural History, University of Oslo (approval number NE12000-150408SAS, The Norwegian Mapping Authority).

sites and remains relate to hunting and trapping of wild reindeer (Figure 9.6). Through time there have been changes in the way hunting and trapping were performed and organised, and also in scale; for instance, a pitfall trap system was established at the transition to the Late Bronze Age (c. 1000 BC) and was in use into the Roman Iron Age (up to c. AD 200), while large-scale trapping in extensive and complex structures mainly took place in the Early and High Middle Ages. Stray finds of iron arrowheads indicate hunting with bow and arrow from around AD 400 and into the Middle Ages. Radiocarbon dates of single pitfall traps and small pitfall trap systems suggest that these were used c. AD 1300–1650. Pollen analysis shows traces of livestock grazing in the pre-Roman Iron Age (500 BC–AD), and these traces become distinct from the beginning of the Christian era. Several graves suggest that permanent settlement may have been established in this mountain valley in the Viking Age. During the fifteenth century the summer farming system (shielings) was established here (Mikkelsen 1994; Barth 1996; Wangen 2006; Risbøl et al. 2011; Stene 2014b; Stene et al. 2015).

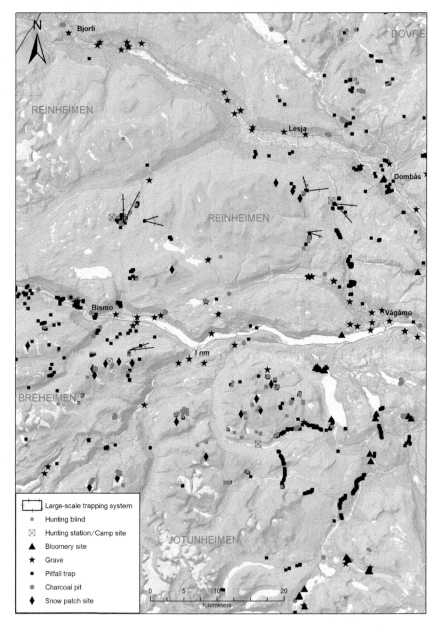

Figure 9.7 Sites and monuments surveyed in the south-western part of North Gudbrandsdal (area 3). The distribution of archaeological sites is based on information from the Norwegian Cultural Heritage Database, Askeladden (the Norwegian Directorate for Cultural Heritage), Finstad and Pilø 2010, Jordhøy et al. 2011.

Source: Magne Samdal and Vivian Wangen, Museum of Cultural History, University of Oslo (approval number NE12000-150408SAS, The Norwegian Mapping Authority).

Area 3: high mountain areas

The high mountain areas in the south-western part of North Gudbrandsdal (Jotunheimen, Breheimen and Reinheimen) represent by far the highest massifs in South Norway, with several peaks more than 2000 m above sea level. This high alpine landscape is characterised by a harsh mountain climate with forest-free, low-growing and poorly productive vegetation dominated by heather, moss and lichen (Moen et al. 1998: 64, 94). Above the tree line (c. 1100 m above sea level) and at the transition to the low alpine vegetation zone there are good pastures for livestock and possibilities for haymaking and summer farming, but the majority of archaeological finds and ancient sites and monuments are linked to hunting and trapping, particularly for wild reindeer (Figure 9.7). Several stray finds of arrowheads, hunting blinds of stone, hunting sites on snow patches, several hundred pitfall traps, funnel-shaped mass trapping systems, hunting huts and campsites show that the hunters have used the entire landscape and exploited the possibilities that were available (Hofseth 1980; Mølmen 1988; Fossum 1996; Einbu 2005; Jordhøy et al. 2005; Jordhøy 2007; Finstad and Vedeler 2008; Finstad and Pilø 2010, 2011; Jordhøy et al. 2011; Solli and Wangen 2011; Nesje et al. 2012).

Continuity and variation in resource exploitation

Variation both in the diversity and types of resources that have been exploited in the three selected landscape zones is, of course, a result of natural conditions. In general it is possible to maintain that the higher above sea level, the fewer forms of exploitation have taken place. Resource utilisation in the high mountain areas of Gudbrandsdalen (area 3) is dominated by hunting and trapping of wild reindeer, while in the woodlands in Østerdalen (area 1) several types of activities have taken place, such as hunting and trapping of elk, iron production, livestock grazing and summer farming. In the intervening landscape zone, the mountain valley Grimsdalen (area 2), hunting and trapping of wild reindeer, livestock grazing and summer farming have been prominent. The nature and quantity of resources combined with the possibilities of access determine the potential and limitations of exploitation. In all the three landscape zones there are resources that enable large yields, but this potential has not been used continually (Figure 9.8).

At Rødsmoen, the use of pitfall trap systems seems to have occurred simultaneously with small-scale livestock grazing and some cultivation in the latter part of the Early Iron Age. Here, use of the pitfall trap systems ceased c. AD 600, at the transition to the Late Iron Age, while such systems, on the other hand, were constructed in the neighbouring Gråfjell area at this time (Høeg 1996; Bergstøl 1997, 2008; Solem 2004; Amundsen 2007; Stene 2014a). It is interesting that the pitfall trap systems in the Gråfjell area went out of use when the production of iron started, c. AD 1000. Some of the pits lying close to iron production sites were reused for charcoal production. This indicates

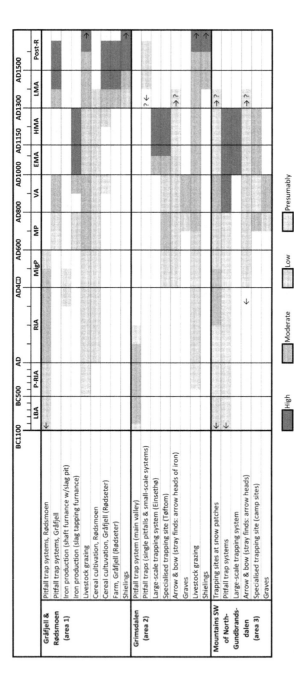

Figure 9.8 Timetable presenting an overview of the different types of resource exploitation in the three areas of investigation. In a long-term perspective it is possible to distinguish both differences in the degree of utilisation (shown by different shades of grey) and variation in operational systems and technology.

Note: The periods are defined according to current Norwegian archaeology (Solberg 2000; Myhre and Øye 2002; Østmo and Hedeager 2005),[6] and are marked with abbreviations as follows: Early Bronze Age (1750–1100 BC); LBA = Late Bronze Age (1100–500 BC); P-RIA = Pre-Roman Iron Age (500–1 BC); RIA = Roman Iron Age (AD 1–400); MigP = Migration Period (AD 400–570); MP = Merovingian Period (AD 570–800); VA = Viking Age (AD 800–1030); EMA = Early Middle Ages (AD 1030/1050–1150); HMA = High Middle Ages (AD 1150–1350); LMA = Late Middle Ages (AD 1350–1537, Reformation); Post-R. = Post-Reformation; Early Iron Age = Pre-Roman Iron Age–Migration Period; Late Iron Age = Merovingian Period and Viking Age.

The Uplands: exploitation and management 169

that these wooded areas could no longer be used for elk trapping when the extraction of iron started. Iron production was at its most intensive in the second half of the twelfth and the first half of the thirteenth century; then it decreased rapidly and came to an end c. AD 1300 (Rundberget 2007: 309–11, 21; 2012: 303). Calculated estimates indicate a total production of about 950–1750 tonnes of iron, pointing to considerable surplus production, where the product – iron – must have been intended for and distributed to external markets. The organisation and scale of the operation show that several actors must have been involved in production. When iron production ceased, at the end of the thirteenth century, the pitfall systems were reused and extended in the Gråfjell area.

Trapping was at its most intensive in the late Middle Ages, from c. AD 1400, and ended c. AD 1650. If the majority of all the six known pitfall trap systems were in use simultaneously, then trapping must have resulted in the obtainment of products far exceeding local demand. This implies that trapping was most likely organised through collaboration between several farms (Stene 2014a: 66). Intensive trapping of elk and extensive iron production therefore seem to be mutually exclusive in this area. The change in resource exploitation c. AD 1000 may be the result of a deliberate choice made by the local inhabitants, considering what types of resources they wanted to exploit from these woods, or the change may have been requested or imposed by one or several external actors or central members of the community (Stene 2014a: 137). If, in fact, the actual work of producing iron – chopping of wood, digging of pits and burning charcoal, digging and roasting bog ore, and extraction (Figure 9.9, see colour plate section) – was performed by the local population, it may have effected a collective change in their daily work, since iron production before the transition to the Middle Ages had been on a very modest scale.

Concurrent with the re-establishment of the pitfall trap systems in the late thirteenth/early fourteenth century, an intensification of agrarian activities took place; a farm at Rødseter in the Gråfjell area was probably built c. AD 1300, and shielings were established during the fourteenth century (Stene 2014a: 145–9). The simultaneous occurrence of these events suggests that the same group of people were behind the different forms of occupation. A combination of large-scale trapping of elk as well as animal husbandry and grain cultivation may well have been possible to carry out, as the activities took place at different times of the year. The farm settlement and grain cultivation at Rødseter were most extensive in the period AD 1400–1650. This subsequently ceased in the middle of the seventeenth century, at the same time as elk trapping in the pitfall trap system close to the farm went out of use. This suggests that the farm economy largely depended on a stable yield from other resources in the wooded area, and that agriculture did not provide a sufficient basis for running a farm of this type. Farming was no longer viable when trapping could not be sustained. The farm has therefore been interpreted as a type with a mixed economy – 'mixed farming' (Martens 1992), where the agricultural activities and elk trapping were integrated parts in the operation of the farm (Stene 2014a: 104).

170   *Kathrine Stene and Vivian Wangen*

In Grimsdalen, as at Rødsmoen, a pitfall trap system (for wild reindeer) was established on the bottom of the valley during the Bronze Age, and the system was in use into the third century AD, when trapping ended (Stene and Gustafson 2011: 68–9, 196). As mentioned above, pollen analysis shows distinct traces of livestock grazing from the beginning of the Christian era (Høeg 2011). Radiocarbon dates also show intentional filling-in of pitfall traps in the latter part of the Early Iron Age, something that might indicate the rise of livestock grazing, as it prevented domestic animals from falling into the pits. This suggests an altered use of the landscape, where an agricultural activity now prevailed. Nonetheless, the many stray finds of arrowheads show that hunting with bow and arrow was still important for the local population.

An assemblage of five burial mounds, most likely from the Late Iron Age, and two, possibly three, grave finds from the Viking Age in the same part of the valley (Hougen 1947; Mikkelsen 1994; Stene 2014b), may reveal a settlement that was founded on a mixed economy involving animal husbandry and hunting. Both the assemblage of graves and burials of men, women and children may suggest a relatively sedentary family settlement. The numerous arrowheads in the graves indicate that hunting played an important part in the economy of the people who buried their deceased at these sites. The graves and an intensification of livestock grazing towards the end of the Viking Age may therefore indicate mountain farms, as previously suggested by Hougen (1947) and Mikkelsen (1994), or a relatively sedentary settlement that would not necessarily have been permanent.

It is interesting that this relatively sedentary settlement, which can be related to both animal husbandry and hunting, was probably established at the same time as the mass trapping of wild reindeer started at Einsethø, in the higher western part of the river valley (c. 1100–1230 m above sea level, cf. Figure 9.6). This large-scale trapping system was an extensive and complex funnel-shaped structure consisting of several-kilometres-long entrapping fences, a collecting pen and a smaller enclosure where the animals were killed (Mikkelsen 1994; Barth 1996; Jordhøy et al. 2005). Based on available radiocarbon dates, the system was used during the period c. AD 1000–1280. Close to the collecting pen, at a place called Tøftom, the remains of a hunting station with several buildings have been found. Radiocarbon and typological-chronological dates show that the site has been in use from the fifth century AD, but that the first buildings were established during the Merovingian Period (AD 600–800). The most intensive phase at the site was around AD 1000–1300, simultaneous with the use of the mass trapping system (Mikkelsen 1994: 55–61). The total data indicates that trapping ceased abruptly a few decades before AD 1300.

The presence of a settlement based on livestock husbandry and hunting together with mass trapping of reindeer at the end of the Late Iron Age and in the early Middle Ages may suggest that there was, to some extent, more room for various kinds of intensive resource exploitation in Grimsdalen (than in Gråfjell/Rødsmoen). The conditions for a joint operation like this would be that the mass trapping system and the animal husbandry were localised in

The Uplands: exploitation and management 171

different parts of the valley; one in high mountain areas with sparse vegetation and the other down on the more lushly overgrown valley bottom (Figures 9.3 and 9.10; see colour plate section). Another prerequisite must have been that the animal husbandry was either modest in scale or organised in such a way as not to disturb the migration of the reindeer through the area. This suggests that 'regulations' existed concerning where in the landscape the different types of activity could take place and what the scale could be.

The various forms of hunting and trapping in the high alpine areas have somewhat different times of operation. Both stray finds of arrowheads and stone-built hunting blinds can be related to the archery tradition in the area in general, from the Early Stone Age to the post-medieval period. The recent discovery of several hunting sites at ice patches in Oppland County reveals some new insights into the exploitation of the highest mountain massifs, mostly because the finds are of organic material, excellent for radiocarbon dating (cf. Callanan 2010; Finstad and Pilø 2010). Even though this work is connected with an ongoing project (cf. note 2), some of the preliminary results have been published (Finstad and Pilø 2010, 2011; Nesje et al. 2012). Hunting/trapping on snow patches was seasonal, as the reindeer migrate to the snow patches to avoid troublesome insects (warble and nose bot flies) on hot summer days. Although the snow patches have revealed stray finds of arrowheads dating back to the Late Stone Age and Early Bronze Age, the most intensive hunting on the snow patches seems to have begun at the turn of the fifth century AD, ending at the transition to the Middle Ages (Figure 9.8). Strategically placed hunting blinds and rows of 'scaring-sticks' functioned as proper trapping systems, and this organised hunting/trapping operated over long time spans. Only a few ^{14}C-dates exist from the surveyed pitfall traps and mass trapping systems in the region (cf. Figure 9.10; see colour plate section), but they are concurrent with knowledge of other mountain areas around North Gudbrandsdal, where the majority of the existing dates make it possible to claim that the activity was at its highest in the period from the Late Iron Age to the middle part of the Middle Ages, c. AD 1250 (Weber et al. 2007: 53–4, 58–60; Stene et al. 2015: 64).

Technological adaptation and regional dynamics

Big-game hunting and the use of trapping systems in the three investigated areas seem to undergo one common change in the period discussed here: it seems as if the organised snow-patch hunting with the use of scaring-sticks ends at the same time as the systems of pitfall traps and the mass trapping in funnel-shaped systems are being operated most intensively. It therefore appears as if the effort invested in organised hunting was transferred from the snow patches to the large-scale trapping systems. For the mountain areas (areas 2 and 3) two additional features should be emphasised. One is that the ^{14}C-dates from house remains and midden layers provide evidence of the existence of well-established hunting stations going back to the seventh to ninth century AD, long before the most intensive mass trapping. They must have functioned as more or less permanent 'site camps', strategically placed in the hunting ground, where the hunters could recurrently return. These were conveniently placed in the landscape with regard to both the harsh mountain climate and efficient hunting. A stable seasonal occupation should be seen as a form of adaptation and organisation of hunting and trapping, and this shows that the areas were particularly attractive, since people chose to invest time and resources in constructing and maintaining the houses over several hundred years. The second feature is the presence of graves, so-called 'mountain graves' (Skjølsvold 1980; Fossum 1996). The position of the graves in the landscape varies (see i.a. Hougen 1947; Hofseth 1980; Skjølsvold 1980), but several lie close to trapping systems, such as a male grave with weapons and arrowheads dated to the eighth century close to the hunting station Tøftom in Grimsdalen (Wangen 2006).

The review of the three areas also shows that varying technology and skills have been used in the exploitation of the same type of resource. The variation appears to be widest in the hunting and trapping of wild reindeer, and has changed over time. Although we have suggested that some types of trapping replaced others, it is important to emphasise that instead of a successive development from hunting with bow and arrow, pitfall traps and snow-patch trapping to funnel-shaped systems, it is obvious that the different technologies existed side by side after they had been put into practice. One common feature of trapping in the three areas is that it was established gradually and has persisted over a relatively long period of time. This may suggest that hunting and trapping took place within the scope of well-established and long-lasting social institutions.

In a broader context, it seems as if resource exploitation in wooded and mountainous landscapes was becoming part of regional dynamics. When the pitfall trap systems in the Gråfjell/Rødsmoen area went out of use and the area was 're-aligned' to intensive iron production, the mass trapping in the high mountains appears to be intensified. When mass trapping in the high mountains and intensive iron production in the Gråfjell/Rødsmoen area ceased in the latter half of the thirteenth century, elk trapping in the Gråfjell areas was taken up again, in addition to small-scale trapping/hunting in the other areas.

Specialist knowledge of the use of the resources has obviously been present over a very long period of time, and the entire landscape – even the deepest forests and highest mountains – have been taken into possession. This indicates that exploitation must have been an incorporated part of socio-economic systems on both a local and a supra-regional level, and furthermore that this has at certain times largely been exercised as surplus production with consequences for the distribution, circulation and trade of goods.

Surplus production in a local perspective

It is not possible to draw any clear line between self-sufficiency and surplus production. Extensive and organised surplus production, however, requires a coordinated and substantial labour capacity seen in relation to the available local population, in regard to the production itself, the processing of the products, their distribution and exchange (cf. Martens 1988: 123). Regardless of the volume of surplus production, the premise is that there existed an external demand for such non-agricultural products and that the exchange and trade of the products relied on networks that stretched beyond the local societies and production areas. Nonetheless, it is important at the same time to take into account that the local communities could, on their own initiative, have been in charge of production exceeding their own consumption, *both* on a small scale to obtain products/goods they could not produce themselves *and* on a large scale for more regular trading. Even surplus production on a small scale could make a big difference in such a context. As with the 'peasants' iron bloomery', an example of iron extraction known from Ole Evenstad's book of 1782 (1960 [1790]), modest annual production could also imply a surplus for sale (Larsen 2009: 190).

Eva Svensson (2007: 189) considers that a prevailing view of the rural population or the 'ordinary' peasant in the Middle Ages is to a large degree marked by an image produced by historians based on written sources, where the rural population is seen as an historical factor of less importance than the clergy, nobility and the crown. The notion of the 'self-sufficient' farmer, where the underlying premise is that the rural society basically did not have any special need to exchange products or engage in trade on a large scale, enhances this impression (Martens 1992: 2). Generally, local surplus production is not considered to have been an aim in itself but a result of feudalistic demands and urban needs, not originating from local initiatives (Svensson 2007: 194). By studying so-called 'marginal' regions like wooded and mountainous areas it may, however, be possible to nuance this understanding of local communities, and point to the inhabitants' initiatives and active participation in the surplus production of raw materials and products of the wooded and mountainous landscapes.

The local communities must have played a significant role in surplus production in the three areas. First, the diverse forms of exploitation show that there existed specialised knowledge about where in the landscape the resources could be located: where the bog ore could be found, and to which places in the landscape the big game migrated. The proximity to the landscape that this requires can only be met by a local population. This specialised knowledge can be seen in the continual use of the areas, independent of different resource utilisation or the technology used. Second, it is reflected in the organisation and labour effort that must form the basis of the different forms of resource exploitation. One factor that should be noted is that both the iron production in the Gråfjell/Rødsmoen area and the large-scale trapping of wild reindeer in the high mountains may be described as proto-industrial or industrial (cf. Rundberget 2012: 30; Indrelid 2013). The scale of the operation presupposes an ability and willingness to engage in organised collaboration, and must have demanded a lot of local working capacity when these activities took place. This implies both labour differentiation and specialisation.

174   Kathrine Stene and Vivian Wangen

Even though the larger trapping systems may have been operated by a relatively small number of users and gradually extended over time, the construction of the systems – particularly maintenance and trapping itself – requires a great deal of work effort. Thus, the large-scale trapping required organised driving of animals into and through the kilometres-long systems, then the prepared killing, butchering and carving of the animals, and appropriate handling of the pieces of meat. Meat, skins and antlers had to be transported down from the mountain (cf. Fossum 1996: 35), preserved and finally transported out of the local areas and distributed. The large-scale iron production in the Gråfjell area required similar organisation and work effort. The intensive and well-organised production indicates that the intention was to obtain a higher yield than what the local community itself needed, and that there existed opportunities to exchange and trade such a surplus. This suggests established forms of collaboration and stable settlements at the production sites or in neighbouring areas already from the Bronze Age, and that such a demanding operation must have been integrated into well-functioning social and economic networks.

New perspectives on settlement and farming in the Uplands

To understand the use of the wooded and the mountainous areas, it is necessary to see the organisation in connection with the settlement in the nearby but lower-lying areas that today constitute more central agricultural areas (cf. Martens 1997: 9). Previously, it has been assumed that the establishment of permanent farm settlements (the *landnám*/inner colonisation) took place relatively late in the Iron Age (fourth to fifth century AD) in the middle parts of Østerdalen and in Gudbrandsdalen (Hougen 1932; Brøgger 1942; Hougen 1947; Hofseth 1980; Mikkelsen 1994). This prevailing view is mainly based on grave finds, of which only very few can be dated to the Early Iron Age. Due to the paucity of archaeological investigation in these parts of the country as well as the lack of more recent synthesising analyses (cf. Jacobsen and Larsen 2005), this concept of settlement history in the main valleys has not been problematised to any considerable extent. New investigations, however, show that there is a major potential for new source material that can shed light on early agrarian activities and settlements in these valleys, as shown for the middle part of Østerdalen (Gråfjell/Rødsmoen), where an agrarian way of life and thereby a more permanent farm settlement was established at the transition to the Roman Iron Age.

In connection with the development of a new highway (E6) along Gudbrandsdalen, thorough investigations in the middle parts of the valley were carried out in 2011 and 2012. The excavations unearthed traces of settlements in the form of buildings dated to the Roman Iron Age, the Migration Period and also the Merovingian Period. The discovery of layers with clear indications of extensive farming, both pasture and cereal cultivation, dating back to the Early and Late Bronze Age, respectively, points to an established agrarian settlement in the valley at this time (Gundersen 2016). Such early settlement

The Uplands: exploitation and management 175

has also been demonstrated in a vegetation-historical study based on analyses of pollen from a selection of bogs in North Gudbrandsdal. The pollen analysis indicates that a settlement based on agriculture, both livestock and grain cultivation, can be traced as far back as c. 1250 BC. Farming seems to be established during the pre-Roman Iron Age, and agricultural activity intensified around AD 200 (Gunnarsdóttir 1999: 139–40).

Together with the increasing numbers of new dateable finds and sites in mountain areas from the Early Iron Age and also the Bronze Age, this gives a quite different impression of the settlement in the valley. What we have underlined above as an important condition for both the organisation of the extensive trapping in the mountainous areas and the establishment of livestock grazing in Grimsdalen, namely a relatively permanent settlement in the nearby areas, is confirmed by the results from the E6 project. In this perspective it is therefore possible to assume that it is only a question of time before corresponding settlements further north in the valley are uncovered. Putting together the new excavations along the highway E6, the pollen analyses and the results from investigations in the mountain areas (areas 2 and 3), we obtain a more multifaceted picture of the general features of the settlement history of North Gudbrandsdal.

Irmelin Martens (e.g. 1988, 1992) has several times emphasised the significance of the specialised way of life in the inner valley communities of South Norway in the Iron Age. She finds it likely that a sedentary population inhabited the majority of South Norway's valley districts and mountains, with a form of economy that comprised hunting, fishing and livestock husbandry and also some grain cultivation in the Bronze and Early Iron Age (Martens 1988). This is confirmed in the above review of the Uplands, which shows an established settlement based on some farming (animal husbandry and cereal cultivation) together with organised trapping in the form of larger pitfall trap systems from the Bronze Age onwards, and later iron production on a large scale. This implies that those who participated in establishing permanent settlement in the valleys were well acquainted with varied exploitation of the mountain and woodland resources in addition to farm work (Martens 1988: 116), and 'that settlement depends upon the total resources available for exploitation, and not only on the conditions for farming' (Martens 1992: 2).

In studies of rural areas, it is necessary to distinguish between permanent settlement and its economic basis. The traditional concept of the *farm* implies an economy based on agriculture, and this is what in the majority of cases is regarded as the prerequisite for *permanent* settlement (*landnám*). As we have attempted to emphasise above, intensive big-game trapping and iron production also presuppose a nearby permanent settlement. It is therefore possible to maintain that permanent Iron Age settlement in the inner and upper parts of the Uplands seems to have had its economic basis in the woodland and mountain resources, where agriculture can rather be regarded as a supplement. In a long-term perspective, *farm = agriculture* is therefore not necessarily the foremost prerequisite for permanent settlement in the inner valley districts.

176 *Kathrine Stene and Vivian Wangen*

This might be how the settlements in Gråfjell/Rødsmoen, Grimsdalen and the valleys connected with the mountainous areas in the south-western part of North Gudbrandsdal should be understood. From the time when agriculture was established, changes took place over time, in terms of the intensity of utilisation as well as ownership rights and farm structures. Factors relating to seasonal settlements, mixed farming and agriculturally based farmsteads, in addition to studies of resource exploitation in the outlying areas, could thus nuance the settlement history of the Uplands.

Who governed the surplus production?

The review of the three areas suggests several circumstances that show how land use and surplus production may have been organised. Within both historical and archaeological research, the interpretations are traditionally based on the idea that chieftains, the king and the aristocracy, as well as the emerging ecclesiastical administration, were the prime movers for social development in the Viking Age and early Middle Ages. The intensive and at times almost industrial surplus production in wooded and mountainous areas has thus been explained as a direct consequence of the requirements of chieftains and the royal administration, and later also the ecclesiastical administration, and of the demand in central areas. It has been claimed that it was possible to appropriate and maintain regional power over large areas of land through personal associations between small and large chieftain families, and thus control the exploitation of the outfield resources (e.g. Skre 1998; Myhre 2002: 170, 185, 212–13; Øye 2002, 2005). The surplus production was consequently an important economic base for the elite. Within such a framework, operations in the resource areas seem to be intensified on the initiative of the royal power, or as a form of entrepreneurship controlled by the crown, in the Viking Age and the Middle Ages (Mikkelsen 1994; Stene 2011; Rundberget 2012; Baug 2013; Indrelid 2013; Stene 2014a).

As regards the mass trapping at Einsethø in Grimsdalen, Egil Mikkelsen (1994) has suggested that the system was initiated by the crown, by farmers with large holdings or by collaboration between these two actors well before AD 1000. Both the king and the landowning farmers are impliedly the only ones able to establish such large-scale trapping, almost as a necessity connected with the concurrent establishment of trading places and towns along the coast. Later, the clergy, represented by the Archbishop of Trondheim and the Bishop of Hamar, is assumed to have obtained a share in the relevant farms that organised mass trapping. The actual trapping itself is presumed to have been carried out and organised by farmers from the sizeable freehold farms in the district (Mikkelsen 1994: 137–8, 173). Corresponding interpretations have been put forward for the iron production in the Gråfjell area. Bernt Rundberget (2012) considers the activity to have been subject to political control, at first probably by chieftains and later by the crown. These actors encouraged groups to clear land and start iron extraction in the same areas, and thus there is a connection

The Uplands: exploitation and management   177

between the *landnám* in the Late Iron Age and the development of iron production in Østerdalen. It is presumed that royal control was established across all of Østerdalen from around AD 1050, thus indirectly controlling iron production (Rundberget 2012: 291, 306; see also Stene 2011, 2014a).

Production was not carried out under duress or direct control, neither by chieftains nor the royal power in the Middle Ages, but through the provision of 'encouragements' in the form of privileges and benefits. In the Middle Ages, the distribution and turnover of goods were controlled by the royal administration, where chieftains or magnates functioned as intermediaries between the iron producers and the crown (Rundberget 2012: 311–15). This interpretation and the models that have been put forward are interesting, and refer to relational dynamics between local communities in rural areas, and a central administration and distribution network in the last part of the Viking Age and early Middle Ages. Nevertheless, how this comprehensive local collaboration was actually organised, and how the resources were managed, is still an open question.

Questions have also been raised concerning the real significance of royal power, what areas of civic life could be governed by the central authorities and what other social factors were active at all times (Ekrem and Boje Mortensen 2003; Orning 2008; Bagge 2010; Glørstad 2012; Rundberget 2012). Viewed in this light, it has been claimed that a 'general perspective suggests that production and trade grow out of natural conditions, social relationships, cultural norms and an economic agency – all of which lay well beyond the range of control of the earliest kings' (Skre 2008: 340). It is therefore possible to assert an understanding of pre-state societies as more complex and dynamic than the impression given by more one-dimensional economic models. Several aspects of social life have to be considered as heterogeneous social arenas. As regards the outfield 'industries', questions have been raised as to whether they were controlled and managed by a central authority (Svensson 2007). A relatively modest research effort has, however, been directed towards the local arenas and how these functioned in their age. When trade in outfield products is continually emphasised as central to the development of distribution networks, increasing specialisation, growing urbanisation and social development at large, more attention should also be given to the question of what went on in the rural areas of that time.

Surplus production, both on a large and a small scale, must have been of central importance to the local economy. The yield may have been of great value for the provision of attractive gifts and payment of tax duties. Outfield products have also been a prerequisite for obtaining goods the rural communities themselves could not produce – goods necessary for the sustenance of life as well as goods that marked cultural affiliation to the larger community (Martens 1989). To produce non-agrarian goods for trade and sale may also have been part of a social strategy to strengthen local identity. By building up an economic surplus to keep up with socially acceptable consumption, they were able to participate in the wider society while at the same time maintaining their local affiliation

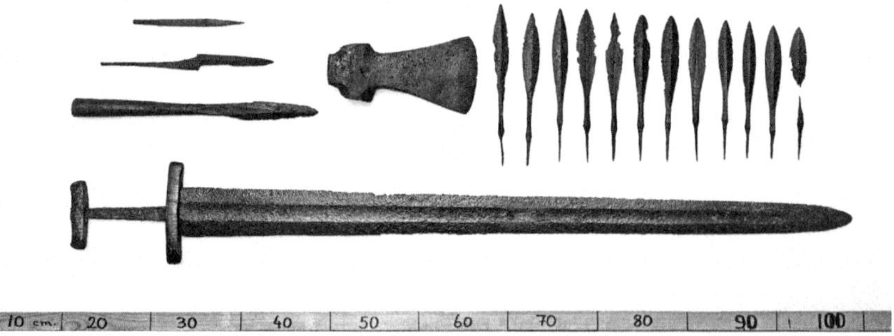

Figure 9.11 Grave finds from mountainous areas.

(a) Grave goods from a male grave, Grimsdalen (area 2), dated to the second half of the tenth century, the Late Viking Age (sword length: 92.5 cm).

(b) An oval brooch, probably from a female grave, found in Grimsdalen. The brooch is dated to c. AD 900, the Viking Age (dimensions: 11.5 × 7 cm). The find-spot is situated close to an unmarked grave, a cremation of an adult and a child. The grave included, among other things, a sword, an axe and 11 arrowheads. The grave is dated to the same period as the brooch.

(c) Grave goods from a male grave from Læshøe (in area 3), dated to the tenth century (sword length: 88.5 cm).

Source: © Museum of Cultural History, University of Oslo.

(Svensson 2007: 197). Maybe this, in part, is how the graves in the mountains in the Late Iron Age can be understood (Figure 9.11). Both the grave goods and burial customs fit the variation of type and form as those found in the nearest agricultural districts and in a large part of Scandinavia.

It is, among other things, interesting to see that the presumed symbolic and identity-bearing jewellery from the Viking Age is also found in female graves high up in the mountains (Hofseth 1980; Mikkelsen 1994; Fossum 1996). This corresponds to finds of weaponry in the male graves. The surplus seems to have been invested in prestige objects, and these objects show that the population in rural areas used the same cultural symbols and social markers as society at large (Martens 1989; Magnus 2005; Martens 2009; Røstad 2012). Thus, the local surplus can be regarded as both economic and cultural capital, because symbols used like this can also be related to formalised personal and political alliance networks, and also to gift-giving practices and economic systems that may be connected with super-regional social structures (cf. Sigurðsson 2008; Glørstad 2010: 254–79; Sindbæk 2011).

Outline of local landscape management

The resource exploitation and surplus production, as described for the three above-mentioned areas, suggest that a form of agreement existed concerning what resources and how much of these resources could be used from these land-scapes. Intensification of a specific type of resource exploitation or a change in land use must either have been based on someone's claimed rights to certain resources or parts of the landscape, or on a common consensus or social acceptance of the changes. This must particularly have been the case where one operational system excluded another. But periods of joint operation have been demonstrated, as has the use of different forms of technology for concurrent exploitation of the same resources. The presence of different systems of operation in the same areas of land may suggest that there was a common understanding of rights to the wooded and mountainous areas, and how they were to be managed.

Furthermore, the diverse and long-standing use of the woodlands and mountains indicates well-established social practices within the local population. At the same time, it is likely that the possibilities of building up a surplus may have resulted in conflicts of interests between various groups' and actors' desire to make use of these landscapes. The work effort and knowledge that demonstrably have been invested in the various forms of operation must in addition have generated a form of ownership of permanent structures. The demonstrated changes in resource exploitation may be indications of both a common understanding of rights and management, and a result of conflicts, but these conditions are precisely the ones that make it possible to discuss whether changed operational systems in an area also entailed the establishment of new social structures, and whether different actors used the resources in different ways and with differing intensity.

This means that production and resource exploitation in the woodlands and the mountains were at all times part of a multifaceted interaction between a number of different social relations and institutions on several levels. In the Viking Age and early Middle Ages, there are two possible arenas for disentangling conflicts and clarifying rights. One is the local *thing*/assembly site (Bagge 2008; Sanmark et al. 2013); the other is the institution of commons (Solem 2002; Lindholm et al. 2013). In this context, the latter institution is of specific interest. In local communities, the institutions of commons have been of greater importance for the regulation of the exploitation of land, for clarifying users' rights to landscape areas and for the division of the yield. The commons (Norw. *allmenning*, translated as 'common land') are delimited areas outside the defined farm territories, which have not been included in the right of ownership (Stenseth 2005). But the commons are not only areas of land and resources; they are also operative institutions for collective action (Ostrom 1990). Within the institutions of commons, established rules and procedures regulate land use and cooperation within the common land.

We would also like to claim that commons are one of the most significant institutions in the Viking Age, forming a stable, local basis for social interaction in rural communities and thereby also in the (re)formation of wider social networks (Wangen in prep.). In the wooded and mountainous areas of the Uplands there are three circumstances in particular that may reveal well-organised institutions of commons. First, extensive, organised collaboration within areas of land outside what can be defined as farm territory with property rights. All three areas presented above lie within large, coherent stretches of commons in present-day South Norway, which are remains of former, much larger areas of common land (Sevatdal 1985: 12). Second, there is a sedentary population with established knowledge and experience of the landscape, which creates the framework for the defining of *specific* areas for a *certain* use. This means that local communities have a common practice, and that social acceptance of how the areas ought to and can be used has been established. Third, there is a purely rational principle, based on the acknowledgement that joint effort can generate a larger or more secure yield than is possible for single individuals (Ostrom 1990: 39).

In all three landscape zones, there are resources that make a large yield possible, but this potential is not used at all times, and moreover is used with varying intensity. This is most likely due to changes in society on both a local and a super-regional level, and we suggest that local, well-established social institutions can form the basis for how resource exploitation has been structured. In cases where intensive and organised surplus production was carried out, and where it is possible to assume that external, individual actors or stronger groups were claiming special privileges, the existing social structure was probably subject to negotiation or overturned. The regional dynamics and the changes in management that are seen within these specific areas can therefore be the result of such flexible local institutions. Varied use of technology and management forms, changes in management towards regular surplus production as well as

The Uplands: exploitation and management   181

changes in types of resource exploitation may all be based on local adaptations and local initiatives. This means that the inner wooded and mountain areas were being managed both on the basis of local conditions and through interaction with super-regional institutions and structures.

Conclusion

The Uplands consist of several different landscape zones and contain a number of varied cultural remains and sites, which shows that *the Uplands* is not a uniform entity. Different forms of resource exploitation, management forms and institutions characterise the use of the landscape at all times, and must therefore be seen in connection with the practices that existed in local districts. This practice has been embodied in the landscape, in the archaeological sources. In the above, we have sought to emphasise that even 'the deepest of forests and the highest of mountains' probably were regulated and subjected to local management, but that this did not exclusively work on the local level, as surplus production necessarily requires interaction beyond the local community. We have also suggested that management of the resources and organisation of the work may have taken place within the framework of local regulation of the available areas of land. The establishment of a new kind of institutional regulation on the basis of royal as well as ecclesiastical power entails pursued adaptations and changes in the management of the landscapes. Circumstances *both* in the local community and on the socio-political level have in this way formed the conditions of opportunities for resource exploitation in the Viking Age and early Middle Ages.

The results from the presented areas show that surplus production is a mutable 'dimension'. The degree of production varied, both within each district and on the regional level. There is a coherent dynamic between the use of different local areas and the kinds of resources and commodities which were made available for distribution and trade through organised surplus production. It has been our aim, by adopting a local perspective, to emphasise the variation and diversity that exists. The rural population does not necessarily represent merely 'the ordinary farmer' in an agrarian economic sense. The varied and at times intensive exploitation of resources in the wooded and mountainous areas in the Uplands indicates permanent settlement which based its economy on non-agrarian products. This implies that local communities were not only capable of organising production, but also developed forms of collaboration that may have contributed to the establishment and maintenance of stable barter and trade networks. Organised management of the outfield resources, regulated division of the yield and arranged circulation and distribution of the surplus were perhaps what made it possible to maintain sedentary settlements in these areas. By emphasising resource exploitation as a locally based and specialised enterprise, it is possible to nuance the agrarian economic models. The rural districts constituted, through organised surplus production and local management, an integrated part of the economic system of the time.

182 *Kathrine Stene and Vivian Wangen*

Notes

1 Please note that both the terminology and the delimitation of archaeological periods used in Scandinavia may differ from the practice on the Continent and the British Isles. See Figure 9.8 for clarification of terms and datings.
2 The Museum of Cultural History has carried out archaeological investigations over several years in connection with the establishment of training areas and a firing range for the Norwegian Armed Forces in the years 1993–7 (*Rødsmoprosjektet*) and 2003–9 (*Gråfjellprosjektet*) in Hedmark County (Bergstøl 1997; Boaz 1997; Narmo 1997; Amundsen 2007; Rundberget 2007; Stene 2010, 2014a).
3 As part of the research project 'DYLAN – How to manage dynamic landscapes?' supported by the Norwegian Research Council, interdisciplinary investigations were carried out in Grimsdalen, Oppland County, including archaeological excavation and pollen analysis (Risbøl et al. 2011; Stene et al. 2015).
4 Climate changes have resulted in a rapid melting of glaciers and snow patches in the high mountains, and since 2009 comprehensive registration and systematic collection of objects from find-bearing snow patches have been carried out in Oppland County. This work has been organised within the ongoing project 'Glacier Archaeology Program in Oppland', which is a collaboration between the Oppland County Municipality and the Museum of Cultural History (Finstad and Pilø 2010).
5 The construction of the railway and highway (E6) over the Dovre massif north of Grimsdalen during the twentieth century has led to fragmentation of the wild reindeer's habitat.
6 The dates in the table are based on the widespread use of ^{14}C-dates of archaeological structures in wooded and highland areas. The discrepancy between these and the archaeological periods points out the challenges connected with comparability between the typological-chronological dating systems and the use of radiocarbon dates. The historical use of the landscapes illustrated in the table is in any case made visible in this manner, and shows that changes in resource exploitation or in technology do not always fit with the traditional periods and vice versa, and that utilisation of the landscape extends over longer or varied time spans.

References

Amundsen, Tina (ed.) 2007: *Elgfangst og bosetning i Gråfjellområdet. Gråfjellprosjektet. Bind 2.* Varia 64. Fornminneseksjonen, Kulturhistorisk museum, Universitetet i Oslo. Oslo.

Bagge, Sverre 2008: Division and unity in medieval Norway. In: Garipzanov, Ildar H., Patrick J. Geary and Przemyslaw Urbanczyk (eds): *Franks, Northmen, and Slaves: Identities and State Formation in Early Medieval Europe*, pp. 145–66. Brepols. Turnhout.

—— 2010: *From Viking Stronghold to Christian Kingdom: State Formation in Norway, c. 900–1350.* Museum Tusculanum Press. København.

Barth, Edvard K. 1996: *Fangstanlegg for rein, gammel virksomhet og tradisjon i Rondane.* Stiftelsen for naturforskning og kulturminneforskning, NINA-NIKU. Trondheim.

Baug, Irene 2013: *Quarrying in Western Norway: An Archaeological Study of Production and Distribution in the Viking Period and the Middle Ages.* University of Bergen. Bergen.

Bergstøl, Jostein 1997: *Fangstfolk og bønder i Østerdalen. Rapport fra Rødsmoprosjektets delprosjekt 'marginal bosetning'.* Varia 42. Universitetets Oldsaksamling. Oslo.

—— 2008: *Samer i Østerdalen? En studie av etnisitet i jernalderen og middelalderen i det nordøstre Hedmark.* Unipub forlag. Oslo

Boaz, Joel 1997: *Steinalderundersøkelsene på Rødsmoen.* Varia 41. Universitetets oldsaksamling. Oslo.

The Uplands: exploitation and management 183

Brink, Stefan and Neil Price (eds) 2008: *The Viking World*. The Routledge worlds. Routledge. London.

Brøgger, A. W. 1942: *Glåmdalen i oldtiden*. Norske bygder, vol. 5. John Griegs forlag. Bergen.

Callanan, Martin 2010: Northern snow patch archaeology. In: Westerdahl, Christer (ed.): *A Circumpolar Reappraisal: The Legacy of Guttorm Gjessing (1906–1979)*. BAR International Series, vol. 2154: 43–54. Archaeopress. Oxford.

Einbu, Tor 2005: Verket på Slådalen i Lesja. *Lesja historielag Årsskrift*, 2005: 38–63.

Ekrem, Inger 1998: *Nytt lys over Historia Norwegie: mot en løsning i debatten om dens alder*. IKRR, Seksjon for gresk, latin og egyptologi, Universitetet i Bergen. Bergen.

Ekrem, Inger and Lars Boje Mortensen 2003: *Historia Norvegie*. Museum Tusculanum Press. København.

Evenstad, Ole 1960 [1790]: *Afhandling om jern=Malm som findes i Myrer og Moradser i Norge og Omgangsmaaden med at forvandle den til jern og Staal, af Ole Evenstad, lensmand og Bonde af Aamods Præstegield i Østerdalen i Norge. Et Priisskrift som vandt det Kongelige Landhuusholdnings=Selskabs 2den Guldmedaille, i Aaret 1782*. Kongl. Danske Landhuusholdnings=Selskabs Skrifter D.3, pp. 387–449, pl. 1–11. København 1790. Faksimileutgave Trondheim 1960.

Finstad, Espen and Lars Pilø 2010: *Kulturminner og løsfunn ved isbreer og snøfonner i høyfjellet. Økt sårbarhet som følge av nedsmelting: global oppvarming*. Kulturhistoriske skrifter, vol. 2010-1. Oppland fylkeskommune. Lillehammer.

—— 2011: Historien. In: Finstad, Espen, Reidar Marstein, Lars Pilø, Jan Stokstad and Arne Brimi (eds): *Jotunheimen. Historien, maten, turene*, pp. 9–63. Gyldendal Norsk Forlag. Oslo.

Finstad, Espen and Marianne Vedeler 2008: En bronsealdersko fra Jotunheimen. *Viking*, VIII: 15–27.

Fossum, Anitra 1996: *Vikingtids jakt og fangst på rein i Nord-Gudbrandsdal: var de alle menn?* Norsk fjellmuseum. Lom.

Glørstad, Ann Zanette Tsigaridas 2010: *Ringspennen og kappen: kulturelle møter, politiske symboler og sentraliseringsprosesser i Norge ca. 800–950*. Universitetet i Oslo. Oslo.

—— 2012: Sign of the time? The transfer and transformation of penannular brooches in Viking-Age Norway. *Norwegian Archaeological Review*, 45(1): 30–51.

Gundersen, Ingar M. 2016: Jordbruksbosetninger i dalbunnen. Fellestrekk. In: Gundersen, Ingar M. (ed.): *Gård og utmark i Gudbrandsdalen. Arkeologiske undersøkelser i Fron 2011–2012*: 121–30. Portal forlag. Kristiansand.

Gunnarsdóttir, Helga 1999: Postglasial vegetasjonshistorie i Nord-Gudbrandsdalen, sentrale Sør-Norge. In: Selsing, Lotte and Grete Lillehammer (eds): *Museumslandskap. Artikkelsamling til Kerstin Griffin på 60-års dagen*. AmS-Rapport 12A: 113–44. Arkeologisk museum i Stavanger. Stavanger.

Høeg, Helge Irgens 1996: *Pollenanalytiske undersøkelser i 'Østerdalsområdet' med hovedvekt på Rødsmoen, Åmot i Hedmark*. Varia 39. Universitetets Oldsaksamling. Oslo.

—— 2011: Vegetasjonshistorie. Pollenanalytsiske undersøkelser i Grimsdalen og Haverdalen. In: Risbøl, Ole, Kathrine Stene and Anne Sætren (eds): *Kultur og natur i Grimsdalen landskapsvernområde. Sluttrapport fra DYLAN-prosjektet*. NIKU Tema 38: 111–54. Norsk institutt for kulturminneforskning. Oslo.

Hofseth, Ellen Høigård 1980: *Fjellressursenes betydning i yngre jernalders økonomi: sammenlignende studie av bygdene øst og vest for vannskillet i Nord-Gudbrandsdal = Importance of Mountains Resources in Younger Iron Age Economy: A Comparative Analysis of Communities East and West of the Water-Shed in Nord-Gudbrandsdal*. AmS-skrifter 5. Arkeologisk Museum i Stavanger. Stavanger.

184 *Kathrine Stene and Vivian Wangen*

Holm, Ingunn, Kathrine Stene and Eva Svensson 2009: *Liminal Landscapes: Beyond the Concepts of 'Marginality' and 'Periphery'*. Oslo Archaeological Series, vol. 11. Unipub and Institute for Archaeology, Conservation and History, University of Oslo. Oslo.

Hougen, Bjørn 1932: Jaktfunn fra dalbygdenes folkevandringstid. *Universitetets Oldsaksamling Årbok* 1930: 51–87. Oslo.

—— 1947: *Fra seter til gård. Studier i norsk bosetningshistorie*. Norsk arkeologisk selskap. Oslo.

Indrelid, Svein 2013: 'Industrial' reindeer hunting in the south Norwegian mountains in the Viking Age and Early Middle Ages. In: Grimm, Oliver and Ulrich Schmölcke (eds): *Hunting in Northern Europe until 1500 AD: Old Traditions and Regional Developments, Continental Sources and Continental Influences*. Schriften des archäologischen landesmuseum, vol. 7: 55–74. Wachholtz. Neumünster.

Jacobsen, Harald and Jan Henning Larsen 2005: Hundorp og Gudbrandsættens maktsymboler. In: Engen, Arnfinn and Rasmus Stauri (eds): *Hundoro: Tursenårsstaden i Oppland*, pp. 14–52. Samlaget. Oslo.

Jordhøy, Per 2007: *Gamal jakt- og fangstkultur som indikatorar på trekkmønster hjå rein: kartlagde fangstanlegg i Rondane, Ottadalen, Jotunheimen og Frollhogna. Førebels utkast*. NINA Rapport 246. Norsk institutt for naturforskning. Trondheim.

Jordhøy, Per, Kari Støren Binns and Stein Arild Hoem 2005: *Gammel jakt- og fangstkultur som indikatorer for eldre tiders jaktorganisering, ressurspolitikk og trekkmønster hos rein i Dovretraktene*. NINA Rapport 19. Norsk institutt for naturforskning. Trondheim.

Jordhøy, Per, Raymond Sørensen, Stig Aaboen, Johan Berge, Bjørn Dalen, Einar Fortun, Knut Granum, Rolf Rødsvol and Olav Strand 2011: *Villreinen i Ottadalen Kunnskapsstatus og leveområde*. NINA Rapport 643. Norsk institutt for naturforskning. Trondheim.

Larsen, Jan Henning 2009: *Jernvinneundersøkelser*. Varia 78. Fornminneseksjonen, Kulturhistorisk museum, Universitetet i Oslo. Oslo.

Lindholm, Karl-Johan, Emil Sandström and Ann-Kristin Ekman 2013: The archaeology of the commons. *Journal of Archaeology And Ancient History*, 10: 2–49.

Magnus, Bente 2005: Et etnisk signal? Noen tanker om vikingtidens kvinnedrakt. *Frá haug ok heidni*, 2005(2): 9–11.

Martens, Irmelin 1988: *Jernvinna på Møsstrond i Telemark*. Norske oldfunn, vol. 13. Kulturhistorisk museum, Universitetet i Oslo. Oslo.

—— 1989: Bosetningsvilkår og ressursutnyttelse i Norge. Et marginalitetsproblem? *Universitetets Oldsaksamling Årbok*, vol. 1986–8: 73–80. Universitetets Oldsaksamling, Universitetet i Oslo. Oslo.

—— 1992: Some aspects of marginal settlement in Norway during the Viking Age and Middle Ages. In: Morris, Christopher D. and D. Rackham, James (eds): *Norse and Later Settlement and Subsistence in the North Atlantic*. Occasional paper series, vol. 1. Department of Archaeology, University of Glasgow. Glasgow.

—— 1997: Jern fra Vidda til kongens skip. In: Carlstrøm, Sissel (ed.): *Hardangervidda som råstoffkjelde: ein seminarrapport*, pp. 9–20. Hallingdal Folkemuseum. Nesbyen.

—— 2009: Vågå og Tinn: to bygder med mange praktvåpen fra vikingtiden. *Viking*, 72: 183–96.

Mikkelsen, Egil 1994: *Fangstprodukter i vikingtidens og middelalderens økonomi. organisering av massefangst av villrein i Dovre*. Universitetets Oldsaksamlings Skrifter. Ny rekke, vol. 18. Universitetets Oldsaksamling, Universitetet i Oslo. Oslo.

The Uplands: exploitation and management   185

Moen, Asbjørn, Arvid Odland and Arvid Lillethun 1998: *Vegetasjon.* Nasjonalatlas for Norge, Norges geografiske oppmåling. Hønefoss.

Mølmen, Øystein 1988: *Jakt- og fangstkulturen i Skjåk og Finndalsfjellet.* Skjåk kommune. Bismo.

Myhre, Bjørn 2002: Landbruk, landskap og samfunn. 4000 f.Kr.–800 e.Kr. In: Myhre, Bjørn and Ingvild Øye (eds): *Norges landbrukshistorie I, 4000 f.Kr.–1350 e.Kr. Jorda blir levevei,* pp. 11–213. Det Norske Samlaget. Oslo.

Myhre, Bjørn and Ingvild Øye 2002: *Jorda blir levevei: 4000 f.Kr.–1350 e.Kr.* Norges landbrukshistorie, vol. 1. Samlaget. Oslo.

Narmo, Lars Erik 1997: *Jernvinne, smie og kullproduksjon i Østerdalen: arkeologiske undersøkelser på Rødsmoen i Åmot 1994–1996.* Varia 43. Universitetes Oldsaksamling. Oslo.

—— 2000: *Oldtid ved Åmøtet: Østerdalens tidlige historie belyst av arkeologiske utgravinger på Rødsmoen i Åmot.* Åmot historielag. Rena.

Nesje, Atle, Lars Holger Pilø, Espen Finstad, Brit Solli, Vivian Wangen, Rune Strand Ødegård, Ketil Isaksen, Eivind N. Støren, Dag Inge Bakke and Liss M. Andreassen 2012: The climatic significance of artefacts related to prehistoric reindeer hunting exposed at melting ice patches in southern Norway. *The Holocene,* 22(4): 485–96.

Orning, Hans Jacob 2008: *Unpredictability and Presence: Norwegian Kingship in the High Middle Ages.* Brill. Leiden.

Østmo, Einar and Lotte Hedeager 2005: *Norsk arkeologisk leksikon.* Pax. Oslo.

Ostrom, Elinor 1990: *Governing the Commons: The Evolution of Institutions for Collective Action.* Cambridge University Press. Cambridge.

Øye, Ingvild 2002: Presset på utmarka. In: Myhre, Bjørn and Ingvild Øye (eds): *Norges landbrukshistorie I. 4000 f.Kr.–1350 e.Kr. Jorda blir levevei.* pp. 361–94. Det Norske Samlaget. Oslo.

—— 2005: Introduction. In: Holm, Ingunn, Sonja Innselset and Ingvild Øye (eds): *'Utmark': The Outfield as Industry and Ideology in the Iron Age and the Middle Ages,* vol. 1: 7–20. University of Bergen. Bergen.

Risbøl, Ole 2005: Kulturminner i Gråfjell: kulturhistoriske resultater fra registreringsprosjektet. In: Stene, Kathrine, Tina Amundsen, Ole Risbøl and Kjetil Skare (eds): *'Utmarkens grøde': mellom registrering og utgravning i Gråfjellområdet, Østerdalen.* Varia 59: 5–26. Fornminneseksjonen, Kulturhistorisk museum, Universitetet i Oslo. Oslo.

Risbøl, Ole, Kathrine Stene and Anne Sætren (eds) 2011: *Kultur og natur i Grimsdalen landskapsvernområde: Sluttrapport fra DYLAN-prosjektet.* NIKU Tema 38. Norsk institutt for kulturminneforskning. Oslo.

Røstad, Ingunn Marit 2012: En fremmed fugl: 'Danske' smykker og forbindelser på Østlandet i overgangen mellom vikingtid og middelalder. *Viking,* LXXV: 181–210.

Rundberget, Bernt (ed.) 2007: *Jernvinna i Gråfjellområdet. Gråfjellprosjektet. Bind 1.* Varia 63. Fornminneseksjonen, Kulturhistorisk museum, Universitetet i Oslo. Oslo.

—— 2012: *Jernets dunkle dimensjon: Jernvinna i sørlige Hedmark, sentral økonomisk faktor og premiss for samfunnsutvikling c. AD700–1300.* Det humanistiske fakultet, Universitetet i Oslo. Oslo.

Salvesen, Astrid 1969: *Norges historie. Historien om de gamle norske kongene. Danenes ferd til Jerusalem. (Historia Norvegiae. Historia de antiquitate regum Norvagiensium. Profectio Danorum in Hierosierosolymam.).* Thorleif Dahls Kulturbibliotek. Aschehoug. Oslo.

186 Kathrine Stene and Vivian Wangen

Sanmark, Alexandra, Sarah Semple, Natascha Mehler and Frode Iversen 2013: Debating the thing in the north. In: Introduction and Acknowledgments, *Journal of the North Atlantic, Special Volume*, 5: 1–4.

Sevatdal, Hans 1985: *Offentlig grunn og bygdeallmenninger*. Nasjonalatlas for Norge. Hovedtema 8: Jord- og skogbruk. Norges geografiske oppmåling. Hønefoss.

Sigurðsson, Jón Viðar 2008: *Det norrøne samfunnet. Vikingen, kongen, erkebiskopen og bonden*. Pax forlag. Oslo.

Sindbæk, Søren Michael 2011: Urban crafts and oval brooches style, innovation and social networks in Viking Age towns. In: Svavar, Sigmundsson (ed.): *Viking Settlements and Viking Society. Papers from the Proceedings of the Sixteenth Viking Congress, Reykjavík and Reykholt, 16–23 August 2009*. Árbók Íslenzka fornleifafélag, vol. 2011: 407–21. Ísafoldarprentsmiðja. Reykjavík.

Sindbæk, Søren Michael and Bjørn Poulsen 2011: *Settlement and Lordship in Viking and Early Medieval Scandinavia*. Brepols. Turnhout.

Skjølsvold, Arne 1980: Refleksjoner omkring jernaldersgravene i sydnorske fjellstrøk. *Viking*, XLIII: 140–60.

Skre, Dagfinn 1998: *Herredømmet: bosetning og besittelse på Romerike 200–1350 e. Kr.* Acta Humaniora, vol. 32. Det humanistiske fakultet, Universitetet i Oslo. Oslo.

—— 2008: Post-substantivist towns and trade AD 600–1000. In: Skre, Dagfinn (ed.): *Means of Exchange: Dealing with Silver in the Viking Age*. Kaupang Excavation Project Publication Series, vol. 2. Norske Oldfunn, vol. 23: 327–41. Aarhus University Press. Århus.

Solberg, Bergljot 2000: *Jernalderen i Norge. Ca. 500 f.Kr.–1030 e.Kr.* Cappelen Akademisk. Oslo.

Solem, Jon 2002: 'Sem verit hafa fyrr at fornu fari'?: norsk allmenningslovgivning i høymiddelalderen. Hovedfag. Historisk institutt, NTNU. Trondheim.

Solem, Tyra 2004: Pollenanalyse av torvkjerne fra nedre Glesåtjern. Arkeologisk museum i Stavanger. Stavanger.

Solli, Brit and Vivian Wangen 2011: The archaeology of ice. Finds from the Frozen Past. Exhibition in Historical Museum, September 2011–February 2012. http://www.khm.uio.no/tema/utstillingsarkiv/isens-arkeologi/english/, read 25.04.2016.

Stene, Kathrine 2011: Utmarka: en 'arena' for samfunnsutvikling i middelalder. Massefangst av villrein og jernproduksjon i Øst-Norge. In: Håkansson, Anders and Christina Rosén (eds): *Landskaparna*. Utskrift, vol. 11: 225–44. Stiftelsen Hallands Länsmuseer, kulturmiljö Halland. Halmstad.

—— 2014a: *I randen av taigaen: bosetning og ressursutnyttelse i jernalder og middelalder. Gråfjellprosjektet. Bind 4*. Portal forlag. Kristiansand.

—— 2014b: Rapport: arkeologisk utgravning. Grav fra vikingtid. Grimsdalen statsallmenning, 86/1, Dovre kommune, Oppland. Kulturhistorisk museum, Universitetet i Oslo. Oslo.

Stene, Kathrine and Lil Gustafson 2011: Arkeologiske undersøkelser. In: Risbøl, Ole, Kathrine Stene and Anne Sætren (eds): *Kultur og natur i Grimsdalen landskapsvernområde. Sluttrapport fra DYLAN-prosjektet*. NIKU Tema 38: 39–107. Norsk institutt for kulturminneforskning. Oslo.

Stene, Kathrine, Anne Sætren, Lil Gustafson, Helge Irgens Høeg, Kristian Hasseland and Magne Samdal 2015: Grimsdalen: et skattet landskap for villreinfangst og seterbruk. In: Austerheim, Gunnar, Kari Loe Hjell, Per Sjögren, Kathrine Stene and Aud Tretvik (eds): *Fjellets kulturlandskap. Arealbruk og landskap i Norge gjennom flere tusen år*. DKNVS Skrifter, pp. 49–80. Museumsforlaget. Trondheim.

The Uplands: exploitation and management 187

Stenseth, Geir 2005: *Almenningens janusansikt: En sammenlignende rettslig analyse av almennings- og sameieforhold i norsk utmark.* Gyldendal akademisk. Oslo.

Svensson, Eva 2007: Before a world-system? The peasant-artisan and the market. In: Klápsté, Jan and Petr Sommer (eds): *Arts and Crafts in Medieval Rural Environment. Ruralia VI, 22nd–29th September 2005, Szentendre – Dobogókó, Hungary*, pp. 189–99. Brepols. Turnhout.

Wangen, Vivian 2006: Gravfunn i Grimsdalen. *Dovre historielag – Dovrebygde*, pp. 32–3.

—— [in prep.]: Allmenninger i høyfjellet: En diskusjon av allmenninger som organiserende prinsipp for ressursutnyttelse og landskapsforvaltning i Nord-Gudbrandsdalens høyfjellsområder, ca 200–1200AD. (Transl.: High-alpine commons: A discussion of commons as a principle for resource exploitation and landscape management structures in the mountain region of North Gudbrandsdal, c. 200–1200AD.). PhD thesis, University of Oslo.

Weber, Birthe, Irmelin Martens and Einar Østmo (eds) 2007: *Vesle Hjerkinn: kongens gård og sælehus.* Norske oldfunn, vol. 21. Universitetetets kulturhistoriske museer, Universitetet i Oslo. Oslo.

Figure 9.2 Landscape photos from the Gråfjell area and Rødsmoen (area 1).

a) Aerial photograph of the shieling Deset Nordseter, ca. 815–845 masl., situated in the north-western part of the Gråfjell area.

b) "Road through the forest", the road runs from the river Rena and Rødsmoen to Osen, just south of the Gråfjell area.

Photo: © Museum of Cultural History, University of Oslo/Gråfjellprosjektet.

a

b

Figure 9.3 Landscape photos from the mountain valley Grimsdalen (area 2).

a) The eastern part of Grimsdalen. The river Grimsa meanders in the bottom of the valley.
b) The shieling Tollevshaugen situated ca. 1000 masl. The mountain area Rondane can be seen in the background.

Photo: © Museum of Cultural History, University of Oslo/Kathrine Stene.

a

b

Figure 9.4 The high mountain area on the south-western side of Gudbrandsdalen (area 3). The highest peaks are ca. 2400 masl. (a), but there are also alpine plateaus with lakes and streams were there are good pastures for reindeers (b). Notice the settlement and fields in the bottom of the river valley Ottadalen c. 400 masl. (the village of Bismo to the left), and the Ice-patch Åndfonne in the foreground c. 1800-2000 masl.

Photo: © Museum of Cultural History, University of Oslo/Vivian Wange.

a

b

Figure 9.9 All production of iron in prehistoric and medieval Norway is based on bog ore. The method is generally termed the direct process of iron making: the iron was extracted from ore directly in a malleable state. Ore was heated in a furnace fuelled with wood or charcoal. The photos show important structures related to iron production in the Viking Period and Middle Ages, from the Gråfjell area.

a) A furnace.
b) A charcoal pit.

Photo: © Museum of Cultural History, University of Oslo/Gråfjellprosjekte.

Figure 9.10 Large-scale trapping systems and pitfall trap systems.

a) A stone built collecting pen (a total length of 19 m, a width of 3 m and a height of 1.1–1.8 m) at Gravhø, Grimsdalen. The collecting pen is part of a large-scale trapping system for wild reindeer.
b) A pitfall trap for wild reindeer in (Haverdalen) Grimsdalen. It is an earth-dug pit with an oval embankment around it.

Photo: © Museum of Cultural History, University of Oslo/Kathrine Stene.

a

b

Figure 10.4 a–b A selection of weights, coin and silver fragments, and imported beads found with the Langeid burials.

Photo: © Museum of Cultural History, Oslo/Ellen C. Holte.

Figure 10.5 One side of the restored, lavishly ornate hilt of the sword found in grave 8.

Photo: © Museum of Cultural History, Oslo/Ellen C. Holte.

Figure 10.6 Overview across Langeid, towards the Otra river.
Photo: © Museum of Cultural History, Oslo/Camilla C. Wenn.

Figure 12.4 Hallingskeid, Ulvik in Hardanger.
Photo: © Kjetil Loftsgarden.

Part III

Sites of trade

10 A view from the valley

Langeid in Setesdal, South Norway – a Viking-Age trade station along a mercantile highway

Zanette T. Glørstad and Camilla Cecilie Wenn

Introduction

In the transitional phase between the Viking Age and Middle Ages, a radical reorganisation of the economy took place, with an increase in the extraction of raw material and bulk goods directed towards long-distance trade, leading to stronger economic integration between remote rural areas and central markets. The importance of including commodity exchange and bulk goods to gain a more comprehensive understanding of the Viking and medieval economy has been increasingly emphasised (Skre 2007). Studies of the intensified extraction of resources like fish and grain have presented new perspectives on how North Atlantic communities reorganised their economic activity towards long-range market trade, with new economic relationships between 'peripheries' and 'cores' emerging during the eleventh century (Barrett 1997; Barrett et al. 2000; Simpson et al. 2005). An orientation towards large-scale trade systems with utilitarian products can also be discerned in Norway, where archaeological investigations indicate that the latter half of the Viking Age saw an explosive increase in extensive trapping systems (Mikkelsen 1994), large-scale iron production sites (Martens 1987, 1988; Larsen 1991, 2009; Narmo 1997; Loftsgarden 2007; Rundberget 2007) and comprehensive extraction of raw materials like soapstone for vessels and schist for whetstones (Resi 1987; Risbøl 1994; Baug 2015).

Still, it has proven difficult to grasp the nuances of the correspondence between inland resource extraction, emerging trade routes and budding urbanism (Sindbæk 2007; Ashby et al. 2015). Methodologically, there are challenges in combining archaeological material derived from traditional excavations with more recent statistical approaches directed towards the scope of resource utilisation (Larsen and Rundberget 2009). In Norway, there have also been difficulties in localising inland trading or production sites, although in the past few years indications of such sites have been discovered (Maixner 2014; Loftsgarden et al. this vol.).

Recent perspectives have emphasised the dynamic and fluctuating aspects of exchange networks, with varying integration and connectivity with local as well as international networks, depending on geographical conditions as well as local entrepreneurs (Sindæk 2007). In this chapter, a recently excavated site pointing to the correspondence between the growth of regional trade routes and local resource extraction in the tenth to twelfth century will be presented. During the summer of 2011, the Museum of Cultural History in Oslo excavated a Viking-Age cemetery at Langeid, located far up the narrow Setesdal Valley in southern Norway (Loftsgarden and Wenn 2012; Wenn et al. 2016). In addition to a large array of weapons, jewellery and tools, the burials surprisingly contained a large number of trade-related objects, in particular weights and coin fragments. The site presents one of the largest concentrations of such objects in Norway, next to the markets of Heimdalsjordet and Kaupang in Vestfold (Skre 2007; Bill and Rødsrud this vol.), prompting questions of whether Langeid represented a junction in a transactional network, and if so, the scale and type of transactions. In the first part of the chapter, an overview of the Langeid site and its finds will be presented, before the broader topographical context of the Langeid finds is considered, comparing the finds with Iron Age finds from other upper-valley regions and mountain areas in eastern Norway. The extensive new finds provide, in our view, a window into the general development of inland networks and trade routes in the tenth and eleventh centuries, and illustrate the research potential being opened up by current surveys and excavations.

The Langeid cemetery in the Setesdal Valley

The Setesdal Valley is located in south-central Norway, starting at the mountain plateaux around Hovden in the north and stretching more than 145 km south to the farming community at Evje. It is a narrow and mostly U-shaped valley, with steep mountain sides leading up to the highlands of Setesdalsheiene, and with the Otra River flowing along the valley floor (Figure 10.6, see colour plate section, and Figure 10.1). At the time of the earliest census of the area, in 1769, there were approximately 3,450 registered inhabitants in the entire valley, and population density is still low. Most people live on small farms in the valley's agricultural pockets, often separated by large distances. The valley is thus often considered isolated and inaccessible, and has until recently been subjected to few archaeological investigations. The present-day community of Langeid occupies a series of terraces in one of the larger agricultural zones in the mid to lower part of the valley.

The Viking-Age cemetery stretched along the edge of a river terrace, with the floodplain and the Otra River just below. Altogether 18 graves had been dug into the sandy subsoil right at the edge of the terrace (Figure 10.2). In addition, three smaller, near-empty pits may possibly constitute a further three graves, as they were aligned with the other graves, and the fill was similar. A circular foot ditch was also uncovered on the terrace, as well as a second foot ditch on a terrace further south. The foot ditches originally encircled grave mounds of considerable size, which have later been removed.

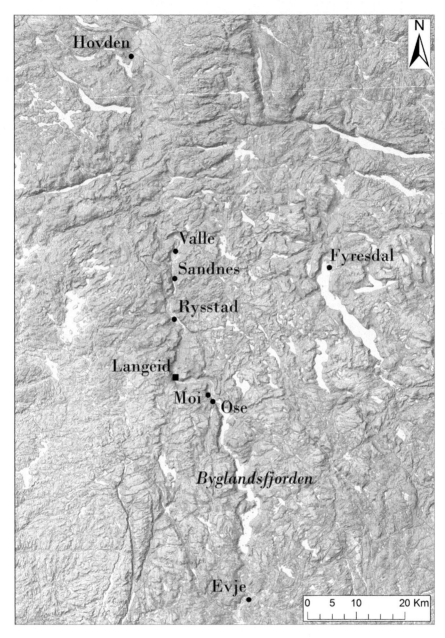

Figure 10.1 Map of the Setesdal Valley. Places referred to in the text are shown on the map.

The layout of the Viking-Age cemetery was probably planned in relation to the older grave mound. The entire cemetery was excavated, and none of the

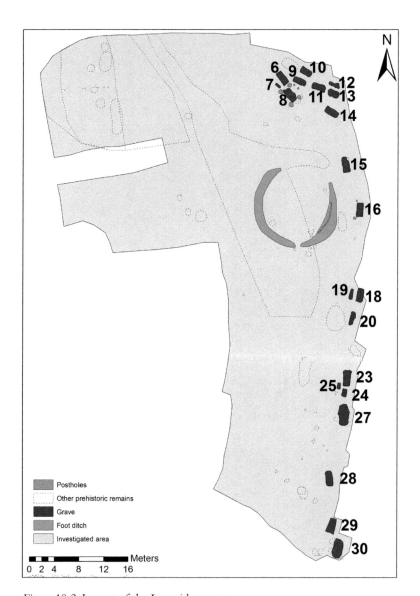

Figure 10.2 Layout of the Langeid cemetery.
Source: © Museum of Cultural History, Oslo/C. C. Wenn.

graves were visible before removal of the topsoil. Their close proximity to each other makes it unlikely that they were originally covered by a mound or cairn, as are many Viking-Age graves. It is, however, plausible that at least some originally had a marker on the surface, as all the graves apparently relate to each other. The graves showed a variety of internal and external construction features, including large stones or stone slabs, placed either as stone linings or in the upper layers, possibly having stood upright or formed part of a cover. Others had considerable amounts of small stones in their top fill, seemingly forming a type of cobbled structure which may have been visible on the surface (Table 10.1).

The 18 graves consisted of rectangular pits, measuring about 175–265 cm in length and about 60–150 cm in width (for a full presentation, see Wenn et al. 2016; Wenn in prep.). The depth varied greatly, from 4 cm to 75 cm. The variation was partly caused by erosion; nevertheless, it is obvious that some graves were originally fairly shallow. Only three graves contained human bones, all of them from cremations, and two of these are most likely secondary burials. Otherwise there were no preserved skeletal remains, and the rest of the burials are presumed to have been inhumations. A number of graves had remains of thin organic layers. In some cases these presented a rectangular or trapezoidal shape, occasionally with wood fibres, and thus seem to represent a base or platform on which the deceased had been placed, without any indications of walls. However, in at least three graves (nos. 8, 23 and 30) the dead had been placed in a coffin. In a number of other graves the fill strongly indicated some kind of physical demarcation, perhaps of wood, or even cloth or furs for swaddling.

The gender of the deceased and the number of burials in each grave have been cautiously inferred from the grave goods (Table 10.1). Many of the burials were richly furnished and/or contained high-quality items, while others contained relatively few objects of a more ordinary, everyday character. Knives were frequent, as were flints and/or fire strikers and axes. Seven swords were recovered, though only two complete ones. The swords included three of Petersen type Q, one of type Y and one richly decorated variant of type Æ. The Petersen (1919) type K axe was the most common, but axes of types E/F, I and M were also found. Only two spearheads were found, and the eight arrowheads all came from one grave. Two graves contained pairs of oval brooches, one of which also had four glass and amber beads; a third grave contained a circular silver brooch with a triquetra, and a necklace with 47 glass and amber beads. Small nails from combs were found in eight graves, needle boxes in two graves and scissors in three. Sets of two spindle whorls appeared in three graves, one of which also had a weaving sword and two wool combs. Seven or eight sickles were found, and seven whetstones, two of which were very large (50–60 cm).

Signs of trade and exchange at Langeid

The most notable aspect of the Langeid burials, however, is the clear evidence of trade-related activities, with five of the 18 burials containing fragments of coins, weights, hacksilver and a set of scales, making it one of the largest concentrations of objects of this type at a single site in Norway, outside of Kaupang and Heimdalsjordet in Vestfold County.

Four graves (nos. 6, 8, 15 and 20) held a total of 21 separate fragments of coins. Grave 6 contained eight fragments, probably from six coins, together with small pieces of hacksilver and silver wire. Three of the fragments turned

Table 10.1 The Langeid burials. The table also includes the three small pits, tentatively interpreted as graves, nos. 7, 24 and 25. In addition to the finds listed, most of the graves contained unidentified iron fragments

Grave no.	Pit size (L × W)	Construction elements	Coffin/ Platform	Male/ Female/Child	Objects in grave	Date
6	238 × 102	Stone lining, small 'cairn'		M + F	Set of scales, 6 coins, silver fragments, 5 weights, 2 sickles, 2 whetstones, 2 flints/fire strikers, 2 beads, wooden box, lock, keys, needle box, tweezers, knife, axe	t.p.q. AD 983
7	102 × 40			C?	Sherd of soapstone vessel	Late Iron Age?
8	237 × 120	4 post holes	C	M	Sword, axe, 2 coins	t.p.q. AD 975/ AD 1010–30
9	233 × 98	2 slabs on top, 2 post holes		M	Sword, knife, flint/fire striker, comb	10th–early 11th cent.
10	190 × 97		P?	M?	Knife, sickle, flint/fire striker, comb	10th–early 11th cent.
11	240 × 126		C/P?	M	Sword, axe, nails	AD 850–1000
12	183 × 70		?	F	Weaving sword (?), 2 spindle whorls, part of wool comb	Iron Age
13	181 × 106			F	2 spindle whorls, bead	Iron Age
14	223 × 108		C/P?	M	Sword, axe, knife, flint/fire striker, nails	10th–early 11th cent.
15	244 × 110	Stone lining (?)	C/P?	M	Axe, knife, 6 coins, silver wire, comb, nails, flint	t.p.q. AD 975
16	232 × 100	2 post holes		F?	Part of wool comb, flint	Iron Age

18	223 × 122	Possible lining, large stones in centre	C/P?	M + F	2 oval brooches, sword, axe, 3 weights, scissors, knife, sickle, whetstone, fire striker/2 flints	AD 985–1015
19	174 × 61		?	?	Iron fragments	AD 1065–1210
20	218 × 85		?	M	5 coins, silver wire, 2 weights, whetstone, knife, fire striker	t.p.q. AD 991
23	250 × 120	Large white stone on top	C	F?	Axe, sickle, knife, needle box, tweezers, chain, iron fittings	10th cent.
24	118 × 82			C?	Knife	Iron Age
25	90 × 50			C?	-	Iron Age
27	220 × 106	Large stones, small 'cairn', slab lining		?	2 beads, comb, flint, nails	Iron Age
28	225 × 134	Slab lining and bottom	?	M	Sword, spearhead, axe, 8 arrowheads, knife, fire striker/2 flints, comb, iron fittings, 2 beads	10th–early 11th cent.
29	246 × 125	Stone lining	P	F + M	2 oval brooches, bronze pin, weaving sword, 2 wool combs, 2 spindle whorls, 4 beads, scissors, sword, 2 axes, 2 sickles, 5 knives, 2 flints/fire-strikers, comb, 2 whetstones	Late 10th cent.
30	266 × 150	Stone lining, 'cairn', slabs on top	C	F + M?	Circular silver brooch, 47 beads, silver fragments, spearhead, 2 knives, 3 flints, scissors, sickle, comb, nails	c. 950–70

Source: Adapted from Wenn et al. (2016).

out to belong to one originally complete coin (Figure 10.4a, see colour plate section). This is a pfennig minted under Otto III in Dortmund, Germany, dated to AD 983–96 (see Hellan 2014 in Wenn et al. 2016 for full report). The fact that the three fragments had not been separated suggests that the coin was cut up a short time before the burial, indicating that non-fragmented coins also circulated and reached the inner parts of the valley. The remaining fragments are from Abbasid dirhams, minted c. 800–50. The coins were found together with silver fragments and five weights of different sizes in an area consisting of highly organic material, probably the remains of a purse. Grave 6 also contained a set of foldable copper-alloy scales of type R.476. The scales had been placed in a wooden case with a cover made of birch bark. Although the wooden case was badly preserved, it was possible to recognise the contours of an interlacing circle décor (Figure 10.3), perhaps imitating the circular design known from other scales and cases (Vegard Vike pers. comm.). The grave also contained an axe (type unknown), two whetstones, two sets of flints/fire strikers and two sickles, two glass beads, as well as the likely remains of a box, a lock and keys that may have belonged to the box, a needle box and tweezers. It is interpreted as a double male/female burial.

Grave 20 was in some respects very similar to grave 6. The grave held five coin fragments, among them two dirhams as well as a coin possibly minted under Otto-Adelheid, dated to c. 991–1035. The coins were found with two weights and fragments of silver wire. As in grave 6, these items were all

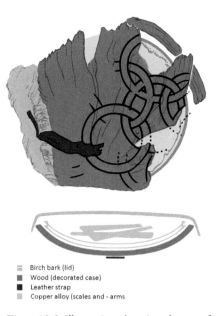

- Birch bark (lid)
- Wood (decorated case)
- Leather strap
- Copper alloy (scales and - arms)

Figure 10.3 Illustration showing the case for the set of scales from grave 6.
Source: © Museum of Cultural History, Oslo. Illustration by Vegard Vike.

A view from the valley   199

recovered from a bundle of organic material in the middle of the grave, indicating a purse. In addition, a large whetstone, a knife and a fire striker were found. Grave 8 contained an English penny minted under Ethelred II, dated to 978–1016, and a probable German coin from the same period (Hellan 2014). In grave 15, a type K axe and a knife were recovered, together with fragments of at least six coins and small fragments of silver wire. The coins included three dirhams, one half-bracteate of the late tenth century, possibly from Denmark/Skåne, and another possibly of Otto-Adelheid. Graves 8, 15 and 20 are all interpreted as male burials. Three of the graves thus contained similar combinations of fragmented coins, giving a glimpse into the stock of circulating coins: graves 6, 15 and 20 held ninth-century Abbasid or Samanid dirhams, as well as late tenth to early eleventh-century Northern European coins (Hellan 2014). The same three burials also contained other silver fragments of various types, found close to the coins and/or weights. The coins as well as the other silver fragments should probably be interpreted as hacksilver.

Altogether ten weights were found in three graves, with five separate weights from grave 6, three from grave 18 and two from grave 20 (Figure 10.4a, see colour plate section). Grave 18, the only grave with weights but no coins, is interpreted as a double burial – a male inhumation with a secondary, presumably female, cremation. A type Y sword, a small whetstone and a flint with a fire striker are associated with the male burial, as are the three weights found in the middle of the grave in a cluster of organic remains, again possibly a small leather purse. The female burial is indicated by a collection of cremated bones west of the inhumation burial. Placed on top of the burnt bones were two oval brooches wrapped in bark as well as in fur and textiles. A bear's claw was found among the burnt human bones, possibly indicating that the person had been cremated together with a bearskin. An uncommonly small type K axe, a pair of scissors, a sickle and a knife may belong to either burial.

The ten weights vary greatly, from 0.9 g to 26.19 g, and indicate that the burials may have held carefully composed sets of weights. The five weights in grave 6 vary from 1.48 g to 26.19 g, while the three weights from grave 18 are 3.4, 13.5 and 21.9 g, respectively. Grave 20 holds two of the smallest ones at Langeid, weighing only 0.9 and 1.4 g. The calculation of weight standards from Viking period weights has been widely applied and discussed (for a thorough review, see Pedersen 2008: 138–48). A.W. Brøgger's (1921) work on weight standards is still highly influential, although later studies have criticised Brøgger's work and revised details (e.g. Steinnes 1927; Sperber 2004). Several studies have demonstrated the existence of different weight standards and systems, although it is possible that these were calibrated in relation to each other (Pedersen 2008: 140–2). Due to their general state of preservations, the precise mass of the Langeid weights and their calibration to known weight standards are, however, not possible to determine accurately.

Although no typical imported objects of the era, such as Continental or Insular metalwork, were recovered, other objects testify to the way Langeid was interconnected with large-scale networks. The 47 beads from a beautiful

200 Zanette T. Glørstad and Camilla Cecilie Wenn

necklace in grave 30 consist mostly of transparent single- and double-segmented blue beads (Figure 10.4b, see colour plate section). There are also a large number of silver- and gold-foiled single-segmented beads, as well as occasional mauve single-segmented beads.

The segmented beads originate in the Islamic Caliphate, or possibly the Eastern Mediterranean, and seem to belong to the second import wave of segmented beads, dated to the mid-tenth century, the first wave occurring around AD 800 (see e.g. Callmer 1977: Tab. 1; Ambrosiani 1995; Wiker 2013). The same necklace also contained a triangular amber bead. Another amber bead was found in grave 29, both most likely made from Baltic material.

While the weapons and utensils could largely be characterised as being of standard quality, the weapons from grave 8 should be mentioned, as they stand out as being of exquisite workmanship. The upper haft of the type M battleaxe had been fitted with a thin brass sheet. A few finds with similar fittings have been recovered in London and in Birka (Vegard Vike pers. comm.). The grip of the late type Æ sword was covered with twisted silver wire. Most striking is, however, the richly decorated pommel and lower guard. The surfaces are coated in flat-hammered silver wire with decorative elements in flat-hammered gold, bordered by thin copper-alloy wire. The decorations include letter-like figures, crosses and spirals, and on the pommel, quite surprisingly, a right hand holding a cross (Figure 10.5, see colour plate section). The same type of spiral occurs on the richly decorated hilt of a type Z sword from Sollerö, Sweden (Androshchuk 2014: Dr. 12, plate 134). The closest parallel to the particular décor on the Langeid sword might be an eleventh-century sword from Kvelperud, Buskerud (C36640) which features spiral designs as well as a similar shape of the hilt. The Langeid sword was most likely produced in a foreign workshop by highly specialised craftsmen, and indicates the range of networks and resources available for what might be considered a particularly wealthy or well-travelled member of the Langeid community.

All in all, 11 burials can be dated to the tenth to eleventh century, and at least eight of the graves are later than AD 975 (Table 10.1). The remaining graves can only be given a general dating to the Iron Age/Viking Age. The graves dated on the basis of swords and/or axes tend to fall into the period AD 900–1050, according to Petersen's (1919) chronology, with one exception of AD 850–1000. Two graves (18 and 29), with a combination of oval brooches (type R.652/654) and late swords (types Y and Q), can be dated to the late tenth century on typological grounds. In the case of grave 18, this corresponds well with the radiocarbon date of the cremation, AD 985–1015 (1 sigma cal.). Four graves have a *terminus post quem* established from coins, coinciding with the dates of other objects in the graves. Graves 8 and 15 were constructed later than AD 975, grave 6 later than AD 983 and grave 20 later than AD 991. Grave 8 has an additional radiocarbon dating from a post hole: AD 1010–30. The Petersen type Æ sword is a late variant and should be placed in the first half of the eleventh century. Grave 30 has the narrowest time span. The secondary burial at the top was radiocarbon dated to AD 885–960 (1 sigma cal.). However,

A view from the valley 201

some of the beads in the primary burial are unlikely to have appeared before
c. AD 950 (Wiker 2013). Both burials thus seem to have taken place just after
the mid-tenth century.

Beyond Langeid: a regional perspective

But what form of economic activity do the deceased at Langeid and their
objects represent, and how did the activity at Langeid, a small and seemingly
isolated valley community, relate to similar environments in the region? To
bridge the apparent gap between the lack of discovered trading/production
sites and the evident growth in inland resource utilisation during the Viking
Age, the distribution of scales and weights, coins and hacksilver, as well as
objects acquired through long-distance networks is often highlighted as indicative of a more intensified and formalised exchange economy (cf. Pedersen
2008). Still, scales and weights outside of the trading sites at Kaupang and
Heimdalsjordet all come from burials or uncertain contexts. Their find contexts do not, then, indicate their primary use context, and one cannot rule out
the possibility that the placement of weighing equipment, exchange curren-
cies and likewise hacksilver in graves had metaphorical aspects. The fact that
at Langeid these objects were placed in the graves as sets strongly suggests that
their primary use and context was known, and that this pattern reflects their
actual use in trade and exchange.

There seems to be no doubt that these are graves of members of a community actively engaged in regional exchange networks, connected to larger
networks of exchange and embracing impulses and items that drew on foreign
contact and inspiration. The suggestion of trade routes and commercial activity
in Viking-Age Setesdal was first made by Jan Henning Larsen, based mainly
on finds from Valle, some 25 km north of Langeid (cf. Figure 10.1; Larsen
1980, 1984: 143–6, 2000). Here, a large number of coins and weights have
been found in at least four burial contexts, mainly dated to the early eleventh
century. A number of Celtic and Anglo-Saxon objects are known from other
funerary monuments in the area. Similarly, the only five Frankish spearheads
in Aust-Agder County have been found in Setesdal, and at least three of them
come from Valle (Larsen 2000: 45). Furthermore, before the Langeid excavations, Valle had the only finds of imported beads of glass and amber in Setesdal
(Larsen 1980).

Larsen points out that a large network of old trails and roads crossing the
highlands and mountains is known in and around Valle, some of which may
well date back to the Viking Age. From the twelfth century, furs and hides
passed through the area as tax payments to the bishop in Stavanger (Larsen
1980), giving the name to one of the known old trails in the area, the 'Hide
Road' (Norw. *Skinnvegen*). The 'Hide Road' starts at Fyresdal in Telemark
County and passes through Valle towards Lysefjord in Rogaland on the west
coast of Norway (cf. Figure. 10.7). Archaeological finds from rock shelters
along the road, for instance, suggest that the route has been used considerably

longer, as it forms a natural access route through the mountains to the west coast (Rolfsen 1977; Mikkelsen 1980). Another well-known passage is the 'Bishop's Road' (Norw. *Bispevegen*), which runs along the now desolated Finndalen from Fyresdal to Valle. It is assumed that the road dates back at least to the thirteenth century, although this route might also be considerably older (Langstrøm et al. 1984).

Valle is regarded as a likely candidate for a transshipment centre for the distribution of raw materials, particularly iron, but products like furs and hides could also have been common. Investigations at Hovden in the northern part of the Setesdal Valley attest to large-scale iron production from the late tenth century, gradually increasing and reaching industrial proportions in the thirteenth century (Larsen 2009: 163–8). It has been suggested that production averaged more than 8 tonnes of iron annually, although this estimate is most likely too low (Larsen 2009: 147). A large number of iron extraction-related sites are also known from the highlands above the valley further south, although not indicating production on such a large scale as at Hovden (Larsen 2009: 168). A transshipment centre with local, perhaps seasonal, fairs in Valle would make sense, given its proximity to communication routes leading towards other inland networks, which headed further into the wealthy agricultural lowlands of eastern Norway and to the rich agricultural communities on the west coast facing the North Sea. But could Langeid be a second such site with similar functions? The wide valley floor does give room for assembling people, but as far as the evidence goes today, there are no other distinct factors supporting the idea of a trading site at Langeid, though the distance to the 'Hide Road' is actually no further from Langeid than from central Valle. However, the new evidence from Langeid suggests as strong a connection to trade in the lower part of the valley as in the upper part.

Another striking concentration of artefacts associated with exchange is found in Fjære in the municipality of Grimstad, situated by the coast about 95 km south-east of Langeid. Grimstad has produced four of the six known Viking-Age sets of scales in the county, as well as showing a marked concentration of weights, some with mounted Anglo-Saxon coins. A number of Insular and Continental objects have been found in graves in the area (Larsen 1986). Several hoards with gold and silver objects have been discovered along the coastline in the same region. In Fjære, other factors also come into play, such as a sheltered coastline offering a relatively short and convenient passage to the Continent across the sea, and roads going along the coast and heading inland. The area is characterised by fertile agricultural conditions, but even more important were probably the many soapstone quarries accessible from Fjære, which seem to have been exploited extensively from the tenth century (Risbøl 1994: 130–1). Soapstone vessels may have been regularly exported to Denmark and to markets along the Norwegian coast, such as Kaupang (Skjølsvold 1961: 120; Larsen 2000: 42; Schou 2007). The coins, weights and imported finds seem to be concentrated to the main agricultural areas, where many of the historically known farms were the homesteads for clerical and royal representatives in the Middle Ages, and where there are large burial grounds, some dating back to the Early Iron Age, the third to fourth century AD (Larsen 2000: 41). Together, these aspects indicate an area with strong economic activity and substantial resources – political, financial and communicative – possibly including a regional emporium in the Grimstad area with sailing routes to Kaupang and/or Heimdalsjordet in Vestfold (Larsen 1986).

A word of caution should, however, be issued concerning the scale of distribution of trade-related objects in Langeid, Valle and Fjære/Grimstad, respectively. Apart from one previously collected weight, all the finds in the Langeid area are concentrated in the fairly restricted area of the cemetery, whereas the Valle finds come from graves in a much larger area, from different farms at different locations, and the same applies to the overall picture of finds in the Grimstad region. Finds of scales, weights and coins could thus represent different types of activity and varying temporal intensity. The graves in the Fjære/Grimstad area with trade-related material are hardly later than the tenth century, while the finds from the Setesdal Valley represent a later phase, mostly belonging to the tenth or early eleventh century. This could be explained by the influence of the Christianisation process on the coastal regions of southern Norway from the late tenth century, with pagan burial rites apparently fading out during the middle of the tenth century. Only one exception is found: a rich and apparently pagan early eleventh-century male burial from Bringsvær/ Fjære with a set of scales and six weights (Rolfsen 1981). This allows the formulation of several questions concerning the relationship between the two apparent economic centres of Fjære and Valle. Do they signify a shift in how and where trade was performed? Does the Bringsvær grave point to the continuation of the marketplace or node in an economic network in Fjære, of which we have evidence from the tenth century, or does it indicate a change in the organisation of regional exchange and trade routes?

Stationary and mobile entrepreneurs

One clue to the trade-related activities at Langeid might lie in the noticeable constraints presented by the natural topography, which largely dictates the location of feasible communication routes and meeting places. According to descriptions from the late eighteenth and early nineteenth century, land-based travel down and out of the valley was confined to trails and paths before the main road was built in the 1840s. These trails, like the 'Hide Road' and the 'Bishop's Road', connected Setesdal to Lysefjord and Rogaland in the west, and with the Telemark valleys and the coastal areas in the east via Fyresdal (Bull 1928: 46; Midttun 1928: 134; Kaland 1972: 169). The steep hillsides and narrow roads meant that any transportation of goods had to be by pack animal, which limited the amount of goods that could be transported (Skar 1909: 151). It is therefore no wonder that the two large lakes Byglandsfjorden and Åraksfjorden, linked by the Otra River, were also used as a vital transport route in the early nineteenth century. Traffic from Byglandsfjorden up to the

204 *Zanette T. Glørstad and Camilla Cecilie Wenn*

next inland fjord, Åraksfjorden, and to its end at Ose was possible in the middle of summer, when currents were manageable. It is possible to travel up from Ose to Langeid by boat; during the summer the river here is wide and flows fairly smoothly, and in the early twentieth century a ferry stop existed directly across the river from Langeid (Helland 1904: 117; Rysstad 1928: 11). Continued river transport was impossible northwards from Langeid, as the river becomes considerably narrower at this point, with a series of small rapids. There are, however, areas further north, notably at Rysstad, along Lake Flåni, and at Valle, where the river grows wider and calmer, and boating is easy. In between, it would have been necessary to use other forms of transport.

The topographical situation at Langeid presents it as a suitable place for transshipment and transactions. According to the archaeologist Oluf Rygh (1905: 84, 197), who compiled the still widely applied lexicon of Norwegian place names and their meanings, Langeid simply means 'the long isthmus' and alludes to how the river was no longer passable, and the boats had to be pulled over land for a while from this point. Langeid represents the northern extreme of feasible continuous boat transport on the inland lakes in summer, thus serving much of southern Setesdal. A plausible suggestion is, thus, that Langeid constituted a natural last stop for the transshipment of goods coming along the lakes from the south, as well as for goods from the surrounding farms and mountains awaiting shipment southward across the lakes. It would have provided a good opportunity for producers, local landlords and traders to meet for gossiping, bargaining and negotiating the distribution of bulk goods. The occurrence of imported beads and luxury weapons indicates that the economic activity was not limited to the transshipment and exchange of raw materials and bulk commodities. The establishment of a fairly predictable transport route could have made possible other types of trade, for example for travelling salesmen moving their goods, such as minor household items and affordable exotic goods into some of the small valley communities. Similar scenarios are probably reflected in the smaller rural communities on the Continent from the eighth and ninth centuries, where it has been suggested that travelling merchants, 'chapmen' or 'peddlers' undertook the distribution and exchange of goods from emporia to the rural population further inland (Loveluck 2013: 209–10).

Setesdal Valley and the inland expansion

In addition to the Viking-Age cemetery, the Langeid excavations also revealed settlement activity, with a large number of post holes, cooking pits and waste pits, remains of iron production as well as agricultural activities, with dates ranging from the Mesolithic to the medieval period, but with a strong prevalence of activities in the Roman Iron Age. A similar chronological situation, pointing to the intensive long-term use of the limited agricultural resources and suitable settlement sites in the valley, is reflected in other recent excavations in Setesdal Valley, not far from Langeid (Moi, approximately 7.5 km south-west of Langeid, cf. Reitan 2011; Sandnes in Valle, about 20 km north

A view from the valley   205

of Langeid, cf. Wenn et al. 2015). These locations all paint a similar picture of how small farming communities with iron production as an important additional activity were established during the Roman Iron Age in the agricultural enclaves in the valley, their activity and population probably expanding in the Viking Age. This interpretation is supported by a marked increase in stray finds from the Viking period compared with the Roman Age and Migration Period (Låg 1999; Larsen 2000), and the gradual growth of iron production in the highlands and mountain areas towards massive production in the eleventh to twelfth century.

This situation is not, however, unique to Setesdal. Assuming that settlement intensity, at least to a certain extent, is indicated by the frequency of finds, surveys of graves and stray finds point towards a strong increase in settlement in the central upper valleys in East Norway during the Viking Age. Although a number of new finds have been acquired since these surveys were compiled, the proportional relationship between the periods remains largely unchanged (Table 10.2; see also Figure 10.7). The data suggest that a major settlement expansion took place in the upper valleys and mountainous areas in the western part of Scandinavia during the late Viking Age, in the period from the late

Table 10.2 The number of burials and stray finds from the Iron Age in some of the largest valley regions in East Norway, with data for specific parts of Telemark County

	Roman–Migration Period (1st–late 6th cent.AD)		Merovingian Period (late 6th–late 8th cent. AD)		Viking Age (late 8th–mid 11th cent. AD)	
	Burials	Stray finds	Burials	Stray finds	Burials	Stray finds
Central valleys in Eastern Norway:						
Glåmdalen	3	16	9	11	86	65
Gudbrandsdalen	11	34	20	6	115	139
Valdres	53	67	47	27	106	139
Hallingdal	6	20	8	3	36	63
Sigdal-Eggedal	4	1	2	-	13	1
Numedal	9	3	4	5	34	22
Valleys in Telemark County:						
Kviteseid	3	4	1	2	48	6
Fyresdal	2	3	1	-	22	5
Lårdal	6	-	2	1	27	3
Seljord		9	4	2	56	50
Vinje	2	-	-	2	18	18
Rauland	-	7		2	12	33
Tinn	5	8	3	8	36	66

Source: Data extracted from Hougen (1947: 108, 117, 125, 141, 150); Munch (1965: 161); Kaland (1972: 180–215).

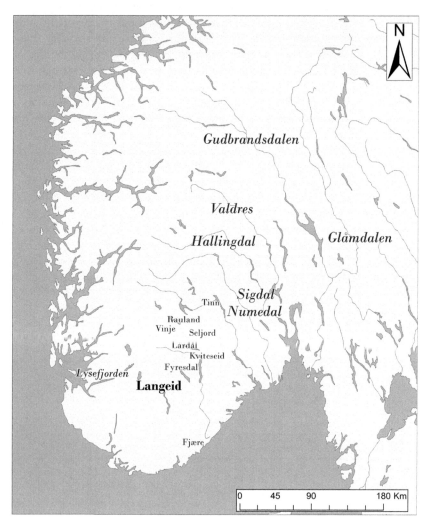

Figure 10.7 The main valley in East Norway, and main valley regions in Telemark County, referred to in Table 10.2.

ninth to early eleventh century. The upper valleys in Telemark County are particularly interesting in this regard, as they are connected with Setesdal by numerous paths and small roads across the mountains, and these, in turn, provide access towards the more fertile agricultural communities along the coastal zone. A closer look at the chronology of the Viking-Age finds in the Telemark valleys shows that, although there is a significant increase in finds from the ninth century, the major boom occurs in the tenth century (Kaland 1972: 175), coinciding with the assumed regional intensification of resource exploitation.

The Langeid graves show a noteworthy variety in burial customs associated with pagan praxis, at a remarkably late stage. This is not unique in Setesdal, where at least 16 other non-Christian graves can be dated to the eleventh century (Larsen 1984). Although relatively few, compared to the considerable number of graves from the previous centuries, they indicate a notable preservation of pagan practices to a far greater extent than what seems to be the case in the coastal districts, where pagan burials largely disappear from c. 950 (Larsen 1984). As in Setesdal, the upper regions of the valleys in Telemark have a number of late pagan burials dating from the late tenth and eleventh century. Among these is a male burial from Tinn containing a set of scales, two weights and a type Z sword, as well as other objects (Kaland 1972: 133). Still, the find from Tinn is an exception to the rule concerning grave contents: while the burials in Valle and Langeid display numerous finds of weighing equipment and imported objects, these hardly occur at all in the Telemark valleys, even though several fine-quality swords, some of them probably made abroad, have been found.

Apart from the burial in Tinn, weights and a set of scales only occur in one other place: a small concentration of weighing equipment found in two late tenth/early eleventh-century burials in Fyresdal (Kaland 1972: 133). One of these weights is very similar to the ones found in Valle, and might be indicative of how the two communities participated in regular trade, possibly even along the same trade routes. The late dating of the three burials with weighing equipment, together with the noticeable number of late pagan burials in upper Telemark in general, mirrors to some extent the situation in Setesdal. This underlines the impression of a significant economic upsurge from the late tenth century onwards in the region, as well as of a common ideological stronghold in these areas. The strong emphasis on pagan burial rituals may possibly be interpreted as reflecting an increased need to underline a local identity or as a common denominator of upper-valley identities during a period of more intensive contacts with other regions. The apparent close connection between communities in Setesdal and Telemark suggests that at this point a regular and well-developed route existed between different expanding inland communities, which made further economic expansion possible and allowed it to be effectively implemented.

Conclusion

The excavation at Langeid underlines how little information we have from Setesdal – and most likely also from other parts of Norway – and exemplifies the potential that many areas still hold. The excavation at Langeid provides a new perspective on trade in the area, as it suggests that communication was not confined to trails across the moorland and mountains, but that in the tenth century a vital and structured route existed, or was established, along the valley and the inland fjords. This should most likely be seen as part of a general process towards a more dynamic inland transport system, caused by a considerable

208   *Zanette T. Glørstad and Camilla Cecilie Wenn*

economic upsurge in the region through the increasing utilisation of hinterland resources, for example a growth in the extraction of iron from the latter half of the tenth century in large parts of East Norway, which rapidly increased at the transition to the Middle Ages. The datings of burials from Valle and Langeid coincide, strongly indicating that the two areas were interconnected in the same regional network. Further contours of fine webs of contacts towards similar inland communities can also be discerned, for instance in the neighbouring Fyresdal in Telemark County.

The development, coordination and at least temporary consolidation of these routes was most likely dependent on local entrepreneurs functioning as key intermediaries on a local scale, who seized the opportunity and potential within their area at a given time. The development of these routes should, however, not necessarily be seen as solely an effect of increased hinterland exploitation and growth in raw-material extraction. There is no direct causal link between the sharp increase in the use of resources from uncultivated land and the development of transport routes and transshipment sites. The gradual development of more stable networks linking different regions may itself have acted as an incentive to further production and investment in outlying areas.

References

Ambrosiani, Björn 1995. Beads of glass and semi-precious stone. In: Ambrosiani, Björn and Helen Clarke (eds): *Excavations in the Black Earth 1990*. Birka Studies, vol. 2. Riksantikvarieämbetet / Statens Historiska Museer. Stockholm.

Androshchuk, Fedir 2014: *Viking Swords*. The Swedish History Museum, Studies 23. Stockholm.

Ashby, Steven P., Ashley N. Coutu and Søren M. Sindbæk 2015: Urban networks and Arctic outlands: craft specialists and reindeer antler in Viking towns. *European Journal of Archaeology*, 18(4): 679–704.

Barrett, James H. 1997: Fish trade in Norse Orkney and Caithness: a zooarchaeological approach. *Antiquity*, 71: 616–38.

Barrett, James H., Roelf P. Beukens, Ian A. Simpson, Patrick Ashmore, Sandra Poaps and Jacqui Huntley 2000: What was the Viking Age and when did it happen? A view from Orkney. *Norwegian Archaeological Review*, 33: 1–39.

Baug, Irene 2015: *Quarrying in Western Norway: An Archaeological Study of Production and Distribution in the Viking Period and the Middle Ages*. Archaeopress. Oxford.

Brøgger, Anton Wilhelm 1921: *Ertog og Øre: Den gamle norske vekt*. Vitenskapsselskapets Skrifter II Hist.-Filos. Klasse 1921. No. 3. Dybwad. Kristiania.

Bull, Edvard 1928: Økonomisk og administrativ historie. In: Aall, Hans, Anton Wilhelm Brøgger, Edvard Bull, Knut Liestøl and Gisle Midttun (eds): *Norske bygder 1: Setesdalen*, pp. 46–85. Alb. Cammermeyers forlag. Bergen.

Callmer, Johan 1977: *Trade Beads and Bead Trade in Scandinavia ca. 800–1000 A.D.* Acta Archaeologica Lundensia. Series in 4°, no. 11. Gleerup. Lund.

Hellan, Terje Masterud 2014: Oppdragsrapport: Mynter fra Setesdalen. In: Wenn, Camilla Cecilie, Kjetil Loftsgarden and Zanette T. Glørstad (eds): *Rapport fra arkeologisk utgravning. Gravfelt fra vikingtid, bosetningsspor fra mesolitikum, bronsealder, jernalder og middelalder, produksjonsspor fra romertid og dyrkningsspor fra jernalder. Langeid øvre,*

A view from the valley   209

2/1, 2. *Bygland k., Aust-Agder.* Unpublished excavation report, Museum of Cultural History. Oslo.

Helland, Amund 1904: *Topografisk-statistisk beskrivelse over Nedenes amt. Første del. Den almindelige del, band 1.* H. Aschehoug and Co. (W. Nygaard). Kristiania.

Hougen, Bjørn 1947: *Fra seter til gård. Studier i norsk bosetningshistorie.* Norsk Arkeologisk Selskap. Oslo.

Kaland, Sigrid Hillern-Hansen 1972: Studier i Øvre Telemarks Vikingtid. *Universitetets Oldsaksamling Årbok,* 1969: 70–215.

Låg, Torbjørn 1999: *Agders historie 800–1350.* Agder historielag. Kristiansand.

Langstrøm, Hannelore W., Rolf Langstrøm and Øystein Lønn 1984: *Bispevegen gjennom Finndalen.* Dreyer Bok. Stavanger.

Larsen, Jan Henning 1980: Vikingtids handelsplass i Valle, Setesdal. In: Johansen, Øystein Kock, Lyder Marstrander, Egil Mikkelsen and Perry Rolfsen (eds.): *Festskrift til Sverre Marstrander på 70-årsdagen.*Universitetets Oldsaksamlings Skrifter. Ny rekke, nr. 3: 143–8. Universitetets Oldsaksamling. Oslo.

—— 1984: Graver fra sen hedensk tid i Aust-Agder. *Universitetets Oldsaksamling Årbok,* 1982/3: 173–81.

—— 1986: En mulig handelsplass i Grimstadsområdet i vikingtiden. *Universitetets Oldsakssamling Årbok,* 1984/5: 111–20.

—— 1991: *Jernvinna ved Dokkfløyvatn: De arkeologiske undersøkelsene 1986–1989.* Varia 23. Universitetets Oldsaksamling. Oslo.

—— 2000: Agder i fjern fortid. In: Seland, Bjørg (ed.): *Artikler fra høgskolens sommerseminar i historie, Farsund 1999.* Skriftserie, nr. 72: 21–57. Høgskolen i Agder. Kristiansand.

—— 2009: *Jernvinneundersøkelser: Faglig program band 2.* Varia 78. Museum of Cultural History. Oslo.

Larsen, Jan Henning and Bernt Rundberget 2009: Raw materials, iron extraction and settlement in South-Eastern Norway 200BC–AD1150. *58th Sachsensymposium i Trondheim.* Vitark: Acta Archaeologica Nidrosiensia, nr. 7: 38–50. NTNU-Vitenskapsmuseet. Trondheim.

Loftsgarden, Kjetil 2007: *Jernframstilling i raudt land: Jernvinna på Rauland i vikingtid og mellomalder.* Unpublished Master's thesis. Department of Archaeology, History, Cultural Studies and Religion, University of Bergen.

Loftsgarden, Kjetil and Camilla Cecilie Wenn 2012: Gravene ved Langeid: Foreløpige resultater fra en arkeologisk utgraving. *Nicolay arkeologisk tidsskrift,* 117: 23–32.

Loveluck, Christopher 2013: *Northwest Europe in the Early Middle Ages, c. AD 600–1150: A Comparative Archaeology.* Cambridge University Press. Cambridge.

Maixner, Birgit 2014: Pløyejord som kontekst: pilotprosjekt Missingen. http://www. khm.uio.no/tema/fagomradene/arkeologi/ployejord-som-kontekst/10_birgit-maixner—-pilotprosjekt-missingen—-28042014.pdf, read 10.05.16.

Martens, Irmelin 1987: Iron extraction, settlement and trade in the Viking and early middle ages in South Norway. In: Knirk, James E. (ed.): *Proceedings of the Tenth Viking Congress, Larkollen, Norway, 1985.* Universitetets Oldsaksamlings Skrifter. Ny rekke, nr. 9: 69–80. Universitetets Oldsaksamling. Oslo.

—— 1988: *Jernvinna på Møsstrond i Telemark.* Norske Oldfunn, vol. 13. Universitetets Oldsaksamling. Oslo.

Midttun, Gisle 1928: Gamle veger. In: Aall, Hans, Anton Wilhelm Brøgger, Edvard Bull, Knut Liestøl and Gisle Midttun (eds): *Norske bygder 1: Setesdalen,* pp. 30–46. Alb. Cammermeyers forlag. Bergen.

210 Zanette T. Glørstad and Camilla Cecilie Wenn

Mikkelsen, Egil 1980: 'Skinnvegen' Setesdalen-Lysebotn arkeologisk belyst. *Den norske Turistforeningens årbok*, 112: 81–6.

—— 1994: *Fangstprodukter i vikingtidens og middelalderens økonomi: Organisering av masse-fangst av villrein i Dovre*. Universitetets Oldsaksamlings Skrifter. Ny rekke, nr. 18. Universitetets Oldsaksamling. Oslo.

Munch, Jens Storm 1965: Borg og bygd: Studier i Telemarks eldre jernalder. *Universitetets Oldsaksamling Årbok*, 1962: 7–175.

Narmo, Lars Erik 1997: *Jernvinne, smie og kullproduksjon i Østerdalen*. Varia 43. Universitetets Oldsaksamling. Oslo.

Pedersen, Unn 2008: Weights and balances. In: Skre, Dagfinn (ed.): *Means of Exchange*. Kaupang Excavation Project. Publication Series, vol. 2. Norske Oldfunn, vol. 23: 119–78. Aarhus University Press. Aarhus.

Petersen, Jan 1919: *De norske vikingesverd: en typologisk-kronologisk studie over vikingetidens vaaben*. Videnskapsselskapets Skrifter II. Historisk-filosofisk klasse 1919: 1. Jacob Dybwad. Oslo.

Reitan, Gaute 2011: Moi: ett jorde, én gard, mange faser? Fra bronsealder til vikingtid og middelalder i Bygland, Setesdal. *Viking*, 74: 165–91.

Resi, Heid Gjøstein 1987: Reflections on Viking Age local trade in stone products. In: Knirk, James E. (ed.): *Proceedings of the Tenth Viking Congress, Larkollen, Norway, 1985*. Universitetets Oldsaksamlings Skrifter. Ny rekke, nr. 9: 95–102. Universitetets Oldsaksamling. Oslo.

Risbøl, Ole 1994: Socialøkonomiske aspekter ved vikingetidens klæberstenshandel i Sydskandinavien. *LAG*, 5: 115–61.

Rolfsen, Perry 1977: En fjellgård fra jernalderen i Bykle. *Viking*, XL: 79–128.

—— 1981: Den siste hedning på Agder. *Viking*, XLIV: 112–28.

Rundberget, Bernt 2007: *Jernvinna i Gråfjellrådet. Gråfjellprosjektet. Bind I*. Varia 63. Museum of Cultural History. Oslo.

Rygh, Oluf 1905: *Norske Gaardnavne, bd. VIII Nedenes Amt*. Amund B. Larsen/W.C. Fabritius. Kristiania.

Rysstad, Gunnar 1928: Natur og folkekarakter. In: Aall, Hans, Anton Wilhelm Brøgger, Edvard Bull, Knut Liestøl and Gisle Midttun (eds): *Norske bygder 1: Setesdalen*, pp. 30–46. Alb. Cammermeyers forlag. Bergen.

Schou, Torbjørn Preus 2007: *Handel, produksjon og kommunikasjon: en undersøkelse av klebersteinsvirksomheten i Aust-Agders vikingtid med fokus på Fjære og Landvik*. Unpublished Master's thesis. Department of Archaeology, History, Cultural Studies and Religion, University of Bergen.

Simpson, Ian A., James H. Barrett, and Karen B. Milek 2005: Interpreting the Viking Age to medieval period transition in Norse Orkney through cultural soil and sediment analyses. *Geoarchaeology*, 20: 357–79.

Sindbæk, Søren M. 2007: The small world of the Vikings: Networks in early medieval communication and exchange. *Norwegian Archaeological Review*, 40(1): 59–74.

Skar, Johannes 1909: *Gamalt or Sætesdal, band. 4*. Norli. Kristiania.

Skjølsvold, Arne 1961: *Klebersteinsindustrien i vikingetiden*. Universitetsforlaget. Oslo.

Skre, Dagfinn 2007: Commodity money, silver and coinage in Viking-Age Scandinavia. In: Graham-Campbell, James, Søren M. Sindbæk and Gareth Williams (eds): *Silver Economies, Monetisation and Society in Scandinavia, AD 800–1100*, pp. 67–91. Aarhus University Press. Aarhus.

Sperber, Erik 2004: Metrology of the weights from the Birka excavation 1990–1995. In: Ambrosiani, Björn (ed.): *Eastern Connection, Part Two. Numismatics and Metrology*.

Birka Studies, vol. 6: 66–91. Riksantikvarieämbetet / Statens Historiska Museer. Stockholm.

Steinnes, Asgaut 1927: *Ymist um norsk vekt fyrre år 900*. Den norske Videnskapsakademi Avhandlinger II. Hist—Filos. Klasse 1926, no. 5. Dybwad. Oslo.

Wenn, Camilla Cecilie [in prep.]: The late Viking Age cemetery at Langeid, Setesdal. In: Roberts, Howell and Morten Ramstad (eds): *Buried Things: Recent Discoveries of Viking Graves in Iceland and Western Norway*. Universitetet i Bergen Arkeologiske Skrifter (UBAS). Institutt for arkeologi, historie, kultur- og religionsvitenskap. Bergen. To be published 2017.

Wenn, Camilla Cecilie, Óskar Arnarsson and Grethe Bjørkan Bukkemoen 2015: Hus, haug og det omkring: Arkeologiske undersøkelser langs rv. 9 i Setesdal. *Nicolay arkeologisk tidsskrift*, 126: 29–36.

Wenn, Camilla Cecilie, Kjetil Loftsgarden and Zanette T. Glørstad 2016: *Rapport fra arkeologisk utgravning. Rv. 9 Krokå-Langeid. Langeid øvre, 2/1, 2. Bygland k., Aust-Agder*, I–III. Unpublished excavation report. Museum of Cultural History. Oslo.

Wiker, Gry 2013: Oppdragsrapport: Perler fra vikingtidsgraver i Setesdal. In: Wenn, Camilla Cecilie, Kjetil Loftsgarden and Zanette T. Glørstad (eds): *Rapport fra arkeologisk utgravning. Rv. 9 Krokå-Langeid. Del III: Vedlegg. Langeid øvre, 2/1, 2. Bygland k., Aust-Agder*. Unpublished excavation report. Museum of Cultural History. Oslo.

11 Heimdalsjordet

Trade, production and communication

Jan Bill and Christian Løchsen Rødsrud

Introduction

Only 500 m south of the famous Gokstad mound outside the town of Sandefjord in Vestfold, in a field called *Heimdalsjordet*, a new trade and production site from the Viking Age was partly excavated in 2012 and 2013. It is situated in a valley at what was in the Viking Age a well-hidden natural harbour, located by a small strait that connected the inner reaches of the two fjords Mefjorden and Sandefjord behind the island of Vesterøya (Figures 11.1, 11.2). This newly discovered site is bound to have a substantial impact on our understanding of Viking-Age trade in south-eastern Norway and beyond, in particular because it demonstrates that the renowned International marketplace at Kaupang in Larvik municipality, only 15 km to the south of Gokstad, was not as dominating as previously thought (Skre 2007, 2008a, 2011). The goal of this chapter is to provide a first preliminary report and discussion of the site for an international readership (see Bill and Rødsrud 2013 for a presentation in Norwegian). It will include presentations of structures and find groups, as well as deliberations about the dating and function of the site, as far as is possible at a time when many analyses remain to be done.

The excavations at Heimdalsjordet were conducted within the framework of the research project 'Gokstad Revitalised' (GOREV), which is a collaboration between the Museum of Cultural History in Oslo, the Section of Cultural Heritage Management at Vestfold County Council and Vestfold Museums (an inter-communal company). The project aims to contextualise the extraordinary but under-researched Gokstad ship burial, dated to the years around AD 900, through a varied series of investigations (Bill 2013). One important focus area is the economy and structure of the settlement landscape in which the monumental burial mound was placed, and how this landscape developed in the decades and centuries before and after the construction of the mound. The excavations at Heimdalsjordet are a key component in this study, since they have documented the presence of significant economic activities both before and after the construction of the Gokstad mound. The site has yielded material remains of trade in the shape of hacksilver and large amounts of cut-up coins, in combination with exotic items such as imported weights and beads. Abundant production waste and fragments from fine metalworking as well as

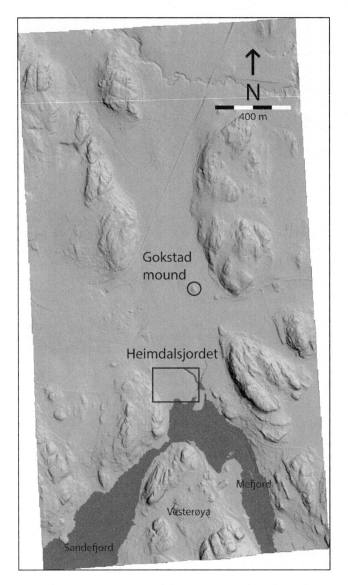

Figure 11.1 LIDAR image of the area surrounding the Gokstad mound and Heimdalsjordet. The approximate sea level at around AD 900 is indicated in dark grey.

slag from ironworking and waste from whetstone-making and amber-working indicate significant craft production on the site, probably intended for trade.

Heimdalsjordet was not, archaeologically speaking, virgin ground before excavation started in 2012. The area had attracted archaeological attention on several earlier occasions. In 1943 the archaeologist Erik Hinsch (1945) and his

Figure 11.2 Panoramic view of the Gokstad-Heimdalsjordet site.

team excavated a rather big but plundered boat grave that could be dated no more precisely than to the Viking Age. In the 1980s several other mounds were detected in aerial survey from the differential growth of vegetation. In connection with plans for road construction in 1995, the site was again surveyed with four test trenches and metal detector surveys. During this campaign a considerable number of archaeological features and finds from handicraft activities were discovered (Gansum and Garpestad 1995).

The structures

The area of Heimdalsjordet was therefore given high priority when the geophysical campaigns of the GOREV project were carried out in 2011 and 2012. More than 60 ha in the surroundings of the Gokstad mound were surveyed using magnetometry and high-resolution georadar (Bill et al. 2013). The surveys were conducted by the LBI (Ludwig Boltzman Institute for Archaeological Prospection and Virtual Archaeology at the University of Vienna) and NIKU (Norwegian Institute for Cultural Heritage Research), and resulted in the finding of several new burial mounds and possible house constructions, as well as providing a good understanding of the palaeolandscape. By far the most promising results, however, came from a 26,000 m^2 plot of arable land on Heimdalsjordet (Figure 11.3).

Here the surveys resulted in the discovery of a substantial system of ditches enclosing rounded rectangular plots that were located on either side of an apparent road or walkway oriented east–west. The western end of the 2-m-wide roadway, now disappearing under a modern house and garden, seemingly connected the investigated area with the higher ground on the western side of the valley. The eastern end of the road is not precisely defined, but it seems to terminate on a slightly raised sand and gravel spit in the centre of the valley, just next to the mouth of a small creek that enters the natural harbour. On the northern, landward site of the street the plots were mostly placed orthogonally to it, sometimes with several plots, one behind the other, while on the southern, seaward side they were in some cases arranged parallel

Figure 11.3 Graphic presentation of the GPR data from Heimdalsjordet, with preliminary interpretations.

to it. Along the long sides, each plot had its own ditch, which was not shared with the neighbouring plot. To the east, excavation has demonstrated that there are similar ditches also in areas in which the geophysical survey revealed no such structures, but it is still possible that part of the raised area on the sand spit was not divided up by ditches.

The excavations in 2012 and 2013 showed that there were significant differences in the ditches found in the western, more clayey parts of the site, and those found further to the east, on the higher, better-drained ground. To the west the ditches had been dug deep – sometimes up to 80 cm – and often had remains of wood near the bottom. They were also interconnected across the street, and it can be suggested that they functioned as drainage ditches, conducting water away from the plots of land in between. This interpretation is supported by the observation that to the east, where the soil is naturally well drained, the ditches were in general shallower and narrower. Here it could also be clearly observed that the ditch system consisted of several phases, something which was not obvious further west.

The pattern can be interpreted as reflecting a division of the site into workshop plots, the parcel boundaries being located between the drainage ditches of neighbouring plots. This seems to be a variation of the system found on other Viking-Age trading posts in Northern Europe (Jankuhn 1986; Ambrosiani and Erikson 1991; Clarke and Ambrosiani 1991; Feveile 2006; Skre 2007; Kalmring 2011).

216   *Jan Bill and Christian Løchsen Rødsrud*

Rather than using ditches as boundaries, as for instance at Ribe (Feveile and Jensen 2000; Feveile 2006, 2010) or Sigtuna (Roslund 2007; Ros 2009), some other type of border marker must have been in place, and the drainage ditches were strictly related to the activities on the individual plots. It has to be noted that very few traces of structures have been discovered on or between the parcels, probably since the site has been seriously disturbed by modern agriculture. With the exception of a few patches in the east, all the excavated areas have revealed modern plough-marks in the surface of the sterile subsoil. This does not preclude the existence of hearths or buildings on the parcels, or fences between them. The finds of wood chips in the bottoms of the ditches shows that wooden construc-tions were erected on the plots at the same time as the ditches were dug, but it is not possible to estimate the extent or character of this activity. More substantial, post-based structures must have been rare or non-existent, but it is possible to understand the drainage ditches as necessary to create dry ground for the building of corner-timbered structures, as well as for tents.

North-east of the parcelled area, the vestiges of several burial mounds have been identified in the geophysical prospection, most of them identical to those known from Hinsch's 1943 excavation and the later aerial photos. However, the initial interpretation of the geophysical data did not reveal all the burials in this area. In 2012 a find of a sword hilt during a metal detector survey led to the excavation of a previously unknown boat grave on the eastern outskirts of the burial site, a ditch surrounding the grave demonstrated that in this case, too, there had originally been a mound. The only datable artefact was a sword of Petersen's (1919) type H, a type that was in use during the period AD 800–950, albeit only rarely towards the end of the period (Hjardar and Vike 2011: 167–9; Androshchuk 2014). The find demonstrates that there may well exist more graves in the area than those observed until now. It also suggests the possibility that the burial ground on Heimdalsjordet was predominantly for boat graves, a hypothesis supported by the observation of a boat-shaped discolouration of the subsoil in one of the 1995 trenches (Gansum and Garpestad 1995).

Several other burial grounds are known from the area surrounding Heimdalsjordet, including one located on the southern tip of Vesterøya (Figure 11.2). This resembles the situation at Kaupang, where separate, spe-cialised cemeteries were placed at the outskirts of the settlement area, includ-ing one on the island of Lamøya (Stylegar 2007). The numbers of graves on the various burial sites at Kaupang are, however, much larger than at Heimdalsjordet.

The artefactual material

About 2,000 artefacts were found during the excavation of approximately 1,300 m^2, by the use of metal detectors on the entire site and by systematic sieving of topsoil samples from most of the parcelled area but not the burial ground. The artefacts are fairly typical of what can be expected at a market and production site, and will be discussed below. It should be noted, however, that

Heimdalsjordet 217

the find material is biased. Due to extensive use of metal detectors, in contrast to a rather limited degree of excavation (c. 5 per cent of the site), sieving (less than 1 per cent of the site) and field survey (not completed), fine metal finds are strongly over-represented compared to finds of organic materials, ceramics, glass and stone. Also, iron objects will tend to be under-represented, since the metal detectors were generally set to discriminate against iron because of the large amounts of modern metal waste in the topsoil.

Imports, trade and artisan crafts: coins, weights, fine metals, beads, amber and ceramics

A total of 173 coin fragments have been unearthed at Heimdal, only three of which are almost complete. The majority of the remaining coins are highly fragmented, with weights ranging from 0.03 g to 2.66 g. Most fragments represent 1/8 of the coin or less, and the fragmentation appears to be intentional. The coins are evenly distributed within the allotment area and spread further out in the eastern part (Figure 11.3). Only some 40 coins have so far been identified and dated more precisely, and these results are preliminary. Still, it is clear that dirhams dominate overwhelmingly. The identified coins show that the minting dates are predominantly from the eighth and ninth centuries, up to the mid-800s. The oldest identified coin is an Umayyad dirham minted in AD 710/11 under Caliph Walid Al-N (668–715) in Wasit (Iraq), while the youngest dirhams so far appear to be from around AD 910. The coins came from areas in today's Afghanistan, Armenia, Uzbekistan, Iran, Iraq and possibly Syria. Apparently, only three of the coins in the whole assemblage have been minted in Western Europe. One has been identified, with some uncertainty, as a denier of Louis the Pious, minted during the period AD 820–40, while the other two are currently undetermined.

Hacksilver and ingots of various materials follow more or less the same pattern as the coins. There are examples of fragments of various types of jewellery as well as bullion. Both coins and hacksilver can be cut up as payment in commercial transactions, but we assume that some of the silver may have been cut up to be melted down and converted into local products by craftsmen on the site. This is indicated by abundant finds of crucibles and other production waste from fine metalworking of lead, copper alloys, silver and gold.

Several pieces of metalwork also have a foreign origin, and it is evident that the Heimdalsjordet site received materials from both the British Isles and the Frankish/Carolingian areas in addition to the Caliphate. At least two mounts of copper alloy have insular motifs, while two strap ends and two strap slides are Carolingian types. The latter four all have parallels in the Kaupang material, and are dated by Egon Wamers (2011: 71–4, 91, Tab. 4.1, Fig. 4.23) to the period AD 820–80. Also of Continental origin are a linen-smoother of black-blue glass and three sherds of Badorf pottery. Other pottery sherds might be of Jutlandic origin; they are thought to be imported, because previous research indicates that pottery was not being produced in Norwegian areas during the

218 *Jan Bill and Christian Løchsen Rødsrud*

Viking Age (Hougen 1993). However, the pottery needs to be studied more carefully before conclusions are drawn.

A total of 147 weights have been found, representing a variety of shapes and materials. Seventy-six are made of lead and come in cylindrical, segmental, conical, biconical and square, flat forms. In addition, there are 44 copper alloy cubo-octahedral weights (shaped like dice with truncated corners, having 14 sides) and 27 oblate-spheroid weights that consist of an iron core with a thin coat of copper alloy (spherical with a flat top and bottom). The latter are assumed to originate in the Islamic world, but were subsequently produced in Scandinavia (Kruse 1992: 80–1; Sperber 1996; Steuer 1997: 460; Gustin 2004: 251). Also interesting is the decoration of three of the spheroid weights with so-called pseudo-Arabic inscriptions, i.e. imitations of Arabic script. These weights indicate a fascination for the East and perhaps a connection to the weighing of Arabic coins, as Unn Pedersen (2008: 170) has proposed. Christoph Kilger (2008: 309) suggests that these inscriptions imitate or relate to the Arabic word *bakh* – good quality – found on some dirhams and thereby playing on the authenticity of the Arab silver. These inscribed weights could thus be associated with notions of quality and reliability in the weighing of metal. Weighing equipment has often been considered a definite indicator of trading activities, but research has shown that it was a practical tool that could also be used in connection with other types of transactions, like measuring out fines or gift exchange. It could, furthermore, be a useful tool in metal casting, in composing alloys and in the production of standardised units of weight (Pedersen 2001; Gustin 2004; Pedersen 2008: 167–8, 178).

The corpus of beads is much smaller than at Kaupang, but the little collection of 59 beads from Heimdalsjordet nevertheless illustrates far-reaching contacts. Segmented beads and tubular glass beads originate in the Byzantine areas; an eye bead is from the Mediterranean; and two black beads are probably made of jet or jet-like materials from the British Isles. There are also a few examples of Western European and Scandinavian products, but no signs of large-scale glass bead production on the site. However, a few of the glass beads of Scandinavian origin may have been produced on the site. Some of the undecorated white beads are of low quality. On these pieces the glass that has been wound around a steel wire or mandrel has not completely fused into one solid piece; fragments of glass thread can be torn apart in layers. These beads were found in a plot division ditch and might have been thrown away as waste material.

A selection of the beads points towards connections to the Far East and the Caliphate. Beads of cornelian were imported to Scandinavia from areas in the Caucasus, Iran and India (Resi 2011a: 145). Rock crystal occurs naturally over a wider area, including Scandinavia. Although some beads are believed to be locally produced, most rock crystal beads have been shaped into the same forms as the cornelian beads and should thus be regarded as imports from more or less the same areas (Resi 2011a: 52–3, 143–5). The most interesting aspect of the occurrence of these beads is, however, that they constitute such a high proportion of the collection. At Kaupang, it is estimated that beads of materials other than glass or amber make up less than 2 per cent of the total collection of beads at the site (Wiker 2007: 137). At Heimdalsjordet, however, 14 beads, or 24 per cent, are of cornelian and rock crystal. The high proportion of exotic beads can be explained in terms of chronological differences. The beads of cornelian and rock crystal become more common in the period AD 860–950 and even later (Callmer 1977: 77, 91). This may point to the production and trade at Heimdalsjordet having its peak somewhat later than Kaupang, or simply that most of the bead trade there took place when the exotic beads were widely available. It may also indicate that the beads were not necessarily meant for necklaces but may be understood as liquid assets with fixed value for transactions, in conjunction with the Arab coin fragments and hacksilver (Kleingärtner and Williams 2014: 53–4).

In addition to the imported products, there is massive evidence that imported raw materials like lead, copper alloys and amber were worked on the site. These include raw material waste as well as numerous remains of crucibles, which indicate another possible import to the site, namely kaolin clay used for crucibles. This clay has special refractory properties, allowing the crucibles to withstand the heat from repeated forging (Pedersen 2010). Kaolin is not found in the Oslofjord area and is rare in Norway. However, it can be found at several places on the Continent, in the British Isles, in Scania and elsewhere in the world. Kaolin clay is comparatively similar in most places, so the exact origin was not traceable for the Kaupang material (Pedersen 2010).

Probably also related to fine metalworking are large amounts of intensely heated animal bone fragments, found in the sieved samples over most of the sampled area but particularly along the east–west-oriented street. The bone material may have been used as fuel but may also represent the production of bone ash to be used as a reactant in fine-metal processing, where it can fulfil a number of functions (see, e.g. Karageorghis and Kassianidou 1999: 180–3).

Local production: iron, whetstones, textiles and food

Traces of production based on local resources are not dominant on the site, but they are present. Most important are perhaps the concentrations of slag and sintered clay in the north-western part of the site, which seem to indicate iron-working. These traces of production go together with finds of a few important iron objects, including a crescent-shaped piece of iron or bloom from the topsoil. Such pieces of raw material are usually found only in conjunction with central iron production areas but might in this case be associated with further processing or trade. Irmelin Martens (Martens and Rosenqvist 1988) has previously listed 18 pieces from the neighbouring Telemark County, and if it can be demonstrated that this specimen belongs to the Viking Age, it will be interesting to attempt to determine its provenance (Larsen et al. 2011).

When it comes to slate and whetstone/hone production, there are examples of light-grey slate from southern Norway (probably Eidsborg stone from

220   *Jan Bill and Christian Løchsen Rødsrud*

Telemark) as well as a dark type that has been determined at Kaupang as muscovite-quartz schist originating in western Norway (Resi 2011b). Whole whetstones, large blanks and small fragments suggest that whetstones were manufactured on the site.

Wool and perhaps also vegetable fibres are another group of raw materials worked at Heimdalsjordet. This is demonstrated by 19 spindle whorls and a significant number of loom weight fragments made of burnt clay. There are as many as 18 spindle whorls made of lead and one made of steatite. Some fragments of burnt clay may be parts of spindle whorls, but they are too fragmented for secure identification. Compared with the nearby Kaupang material, the lead spindle whorls may be over-represented due to the focus on metal detecting rather than fieldwalking as the surveying method. At Kaupang, 34 per cent of the spindle whorls were made of burnt clay, 34 per cent of stone, 30 per cent of lead and 2 per cent of bone (Øye 2011: 343). The linen-smoother mentioned above also belongs to the textile-working equipment from the site.

Finally, foodstuffs form an important part of the material excavated on Heimdalsjordet. Small amounts of unburned or only lightly burned bones and teeth were found through sieving across the site. More important, however, is the discovery of large amounts of food waste in parcel ditches in the eastern, higher-lying part of the site. These mainly consisted of charred grain – as much as a small fistful from every 10 litres of soil – but also included significant numbers of fish bones. In the eastern part of the parcelled area elevated phosphate values were observed, possibly also indicating the processing or consumption of foodstuffs in the area. It should also be mentioned that a few trades that could have been expected to be present at Heimdalsjordet are suspiciously absent, since both preservation conditions and excavation methodology should have ensured the recovery of their waste products, had they been present. These include the working of soapstone, as well as of bone and antler, activities that seemingly were not carried out at all, or only to a very small extent, at Heimdalsjordet.

Dating of the site

The chronology of the site is not yet settled, but a preliminary overview of the dating evidence is presented in Figure 11.4. It clearly demonstrates that the site was in use throughout the ninth and tenth centuries AD, but there are indications of use during a longer time span and of changes in use over time. More detailed examination of the various datable find groups can elucidate this further, not the least through comparison with the material from the nearby Kaupang site.

Weights

The lead weights, which are the most common on Heimdalsjordet, have a relatively wide dating frame. Such weights are found in Norway already in

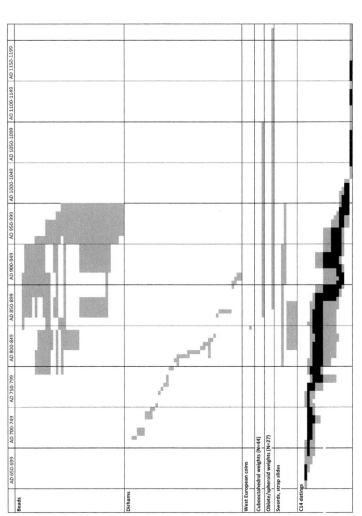

Figure 11.4 Preliminary overview of datings from the Heimdalsjordet site, with dating intervals sorted according to *terminus post quem*. The upper section shows dating intervals for individual datable beads; the coin sections give the minting dates for individual coins; the weight sections give the number and dating intervals of two datable weight types from the site; and the 'Swords, strap slides' section gives dating intervals for individual metal finds. The radiocarbon datings provided in the last section are the dates of individual samples of charred grain and hazelnut shells. One sigma probability intervals for the ¹⁴C datings are marked in black; two sigma is marked in grey. The bead chronology (Callmer 1977) does not include bead use after AD 1000, but it may be assumed that several of the bead types present were also in use in the eleventh century.

222 *Jan Bill and Christian Løchsen Rødsrud*

Table 11.1 Frequencies of different weight types at Heimdalsjordet and Kaupang

Weights (shape, metal)	Heimdalsjordet (N = 147)	Kaupang settlement and graves (N = 410)
Various, lead	52%	81%
Oblate/spheroid, copper alloy and iron	30%	5%
Cubo-octahedral, copper alloy	18%	11%
Others, copper alloy	0%	3%
	100%	100%

Source: Kaupang data: Pedersen (2008).

the Early Iron Age and continue in use in the Middle Ages (Pedersen 2008: 131–2). Other weights offer closer dating opportunities. The cubo–octahedrals occur for the first time in Scandinavia at about AD 860/70, while the oblate-spheroid weights with flat poles occur in Scandinavian contexts about ten years later (Steuer 1997: 320; Gustin 2004: 314). The cubo–octahedrals go out of use in the early twelfth century AD, while some subtypes of the oblate-spheroid weights are used into the thirteenth century AD (Steuer 1997: 320). The relative frequencies of lead weights compared to cubo–octahedrals and oblate-spheroid weights at Heimdalsjordet differ markedly from the corresponding distribution at Kaupang (see Table 11.1). This may indicate that, compared to Kaupang, a higher proportion of the activity at Heimdalsjordet took place in the late ninth century and later.

Beads

The bead material points to a dating frame that extends from the second half of the ninth and through the tenth century AD, despite the fact that there are individual beads that could be from the late eighth century. The reason for suggesting this relatively late dating is the composition of the material. The number of tubular beads of blue glass is relatively modest (N = 3), although these are generally very numerous in finds from the period AD 810/20–40 (Callmer 1977). From approximately AD 860/75, just as the white/pale turquoise ring-shaped beads disappear (also only represented by one bead at Heimdalsjordet), cornelian and rock crystal beads become common (Callmer 1977: 77, 91). These occupy a central place in the inventory of graves in the first half of the tenth century AD. The relatively high proportions of cornelian and rock crystal beads (cornelian: N = 6, rock crystal: N = 8) are significant and can point to the time from AD 860 to 950, but also later. The four silver-foil beads possibly indicate a date closer to the mid-tenth century AD, like the three colourless tubular glass beads and a blue polyhedral bead, which is dated by burial material to the mid-tenth century AD (Callmer 1977: 77, 88–90).

Heimdalsjordet 223

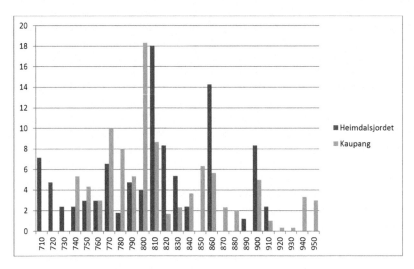

Figure 11.5 A comparison in percentages of the minting dates for 42 identified dirhams from Heimdalsjordet and 75 identified dirhams from Kaupang, following the date contribution method described in Blackburn (2008).

Coins

The 43 preliminarily identified coins (42 dirhams and one West European coin) provide further dating evidence, not the least when compared with the Kaupang material (Figure 11.5 and Blackburn 2008: Fig. 3.21). Considering the small number of coins involved, the correspondence between the two chronological distribution patterns is striking. The decline in use of money that has been suggested for Kaupang between 890 and 920 (Blackburn 2008: 52–3) also seems to have taken place at Heimdalsjordet, even if there are indications that several of the unidentified coins are Samanid, and thus may produce further tenth-century dates. What is clear, however, is that the group of pre-740 dirhams in the Heimdalsjordet assemblage constitutes a significant difference to Kaupang. In the case of Kaupang it has been suggested that all the dirhams were deposited at the site after AD 840 (Blackburn 2008: 52–3); if this is true, it might be suggested that deposition at Heimdalsjordet started some decades earlier, as pre-740 dirhams made up a larger proportion of the circulating coinage than they did from 840 onwards. For Uppåkra, a similar explanation for the presence of early dirhams has been suggested (Blackburn 2008: 54–6). As illustrated by the Loftahammar Hoard in Småland, Sweden (Blackburn 2008: 52–3), such an assumption should, however, be treated with care – among the 623 identified dirhams in this hoard more than 11 per cent are pre-750 dirhams, and its approximate *terminus post quem* date is AD 865. It thus demonstrates the significant inflow of early dirhams to Scandinavia even at this late date.

An alternative interpretation could be that Kaupang and Heimdalsjordet were supplied by slightly different bullion sources, where one of those providing silver for Heimdalsjordet consisted to a higher degree of older coins. That this could be the case is perhaps indicated by the apparent lack or scarcity of African dirhams on the site – none have been identified so far, while at Kaupang six of the 76 identified dirhams have been recognised as Tunisian or Moroccan (Rispling et al. 2008: Cat. nos. 26–9, 31, 102A). Also, the sparse representation of West European coins at Heimdalsjordet, compared to Kaupang, may indicate a different pattern of silver acquisition at the Heimdalsjordet site. This difference could either reflect true differences in the orientation of the trade networks of the two sites, a chronological difference between them or both. Mark Blackburn (2008: 57–8) has suggested that the West European coins at Kaupang represent the bullion influx before the arrival of dirhams from around AD 840. In that case the scarceness of such coins at Heimdalsjordet could be an indication of a later starting point for the use of bullion there. This would not, however, explain the apparent absence of African dirhams. An explanatory model suggesting that Heimdalsjordet was based on a more easterly oriented and perhaps complementary trading network, compared to that of Kaupang, could explain the observed differences without indicating a later starting point for the use of bullion at Heimdalsjordet.

Metalwork

Most of the metalwork from Heimdalsjordet has not been analysed yet, and cannot at present contribute to the chronological analyses. However, two sword pommels of Petersen's types H and X were found in 2013. Type H – to which the sword found in the boat grave excavated in 2012 also belongs – can be dated to the period from AD 800 to 950, while type X was in use in the period AD 900–1000 (Petersen 1919: 65, 89–101). The Carolingian strap ends and strap slides mentioned above have parallels in the Kaupang material, where they are dated to between AD 820 and AD 880 (Wamers 2011: 71–4, 91, Tab. 4.1, Fig. 4.23). A gold pendant from Heimdalsjordet has its closest parallel in the Hoen Hoard, dated to the last quarter of the ninth century (Wilson 2006: 16).

Radiocarbon dates

Hazelnut shells and grains from various stratigraphically secure contexts across the site have been ^{14}C-dated. So far, 18 datings in total have been carried out, and even if the characteristics of the radiocarbon calibration curve for the Viking Age preclude very precise interpretation, it is clear that the main phases of activity on the site fall within the ninth and tenth centuries AD. However, three datings indicate activities on the site as early as the eighth century AD, and two or three others that it was still in use in the late tenth or early eleventh century. A date from the late seventh century and one eleventh/twelfth-century dating can probably be considered outliers. However, further radiocarbon measurements are planned to elucidate the early and late phases of the site.

Preliminary conclusion on the dating of the site

In sum, the dating evidence from the site points to a prolonged period of probably varied use. Activities seem to have started already in the eighth century but apparently were of a character not leading to the loss of beads, and not necessarily including the use of bullion. It is unclear whether the ditches were dug already at that time, or whether old materials were re-deposited in the ditches at a later date. The coin evidence seems to point to trading activities at the site at the latest from the middle of the ninth century onwards, but probably somewhat earlier. Beads, coins and metalwork all demonstrate activity on the site throughout the ninth century, and from an isolated point of view this might be considered its heyday. From the early tenth century onwards – shortly after the Gokstad ship burial – the coins apparently show a decline in silver use, while beads and possibly also weights demonstrate continued activity. Only around AD 1000 does the site seem to fall completely out of use, which is somewhat later than the date for the destruction of the Gokstad ship burial, and also the one at Oseberg – between AD 953 and AD 975 (Bill and Daly 2012).

Discussion

Although incomplete and preliminary, the above presentation may serve as basis for a first discussion of what type of locality Heimdalsjordet represents. That the manufacture of iron and fine metal products was of major importance is well attested, and so is trade, although the selections of beads, dirhams and weights indicating trade oriented particularly towards the Baltic and beyond. But was the site permanently or only temporarily occupied – was it a town or a market? The evidence is not conclusive, and hopefully ongoing analyses of the deposits in the ditches will help to elucidate the question. As for now, evidence points in both directions. The drainage ditches, so obviously intended to protect structures on the plots rather than to define their boundaries, seem to us to be indicative of some kind of permanent buildings; the same is also indicated by the fact that many ditches have been re-dug on several occasions and thus demonstrate a high degree of permanency. The findings of fish bone and large quantities of charred grain on the drier, eastern part of the parcelled area may also indicate a more permanent settlement.

On the other hand, the low-lying parts of the site were prone to flooding as late as the nineteenth century (Nicolaysen 1882: 1), which was certainly the case in the Viking Age as well – and thus not an obvious choice for a permanent settlement. Another observation may also speak against permanent occupation. Although there are several burial grounds in the close vicinity of the site, the number of identified or reported burials (from old reports, stray finds, excavations and aerial and geophysical prospection) can be counted in tens rather than hundreds. Further excavation would certainly increase their numbers, but it seems unlikely that hundreds of graves would be found – as could be expected, had Heimdalsjordet housed a round-the-year population for any significant period. Scandinavian Viking-Age emporia with presumed permanent settlements have produced vast cemeteries; at Kaupang, the current estimate is 1,000 graves, at Birka 2,300–3,400 and at Hedeby 7,000–12,000 (Stylegar 2007: 75–8 and refs. therein). Was Heimdalsjordet perhaps permanently built-up, but only seasonally populated?

The discussion of Heimdalsjordet also has to take into consideration its location close to and its concurrency with Kaupang, as well as the fact that during its lifetime an undoubtedly royal monument, the Gokstad ship burial, was constructed only 500 m away from the site. It is clear that many of the activities that took place and many of the goods that could be acquired at Kaupang could also be found at Heimdalsjordet. Is the major difference between the two sites simply one of scale, with Heimdalsjordet as a satellite or a less successful competitor to Kaupang? The indication from the dirham identifications made so far is that Heimdalsjordet was at least not entirely supplied from Kaupang – the coins reaching the site were not a subset of types found on Kaupang but had a more easterly provenance. Also, other eastern imports – cornelian and rock crystal beads, as well as cubo-octahedral and spheroid weights – are much more frequent at Heimdalsjordet than at Kaupang. In contrast, find groups like glass beads, imported ceramics and soapstone objects are extremely underrepresented when the two sites are compared. The overall impression is that Heimdalsjordet's trade network was more focused on the easternmost trade routes than that of Kaupang, and that iron and fine metalworking made up a larger part of its production, while other handicrafts were less important. The two sites clearly differed not just in scale, but in other ways, too.

The fact that the Gokstad mound was erected so that it was well visible from Heimdalsjordet indicates that the visitors there probably constituted an important audience for its message, and the existence of the two sites is undoubtedly interconnected. This does not mean, however, that the burial owes its construction necessarily or solely to the presence of the market site. A third component of the complex may not have been detected archaeologically yet. Cadastral sources shows that in the Middle Ages the Gokstad farm was by far the largest in the parish (Nicolaysen 1882: 2), and a look at the landscape shows that it was placed at a marked topographical bottleneck where land transport could be easily controlled. Here the only convenient passage is found through a rock outcrop cutting across the large end-moraine deposits that provide Outer Vestfold with good conditions for agriculture and land transport (see Skre 2007, Fig. 1.1). It would not be surprising if the Gokstad farm's impressive size in the Middle Ages turned out to be a reflection of former grandeur – namely, that a power centre of some scale had earlier been situated here, benefitting from the control of landward communications in a rich agricultural landscape. In that case we may see Heimdalsjordet as a manifestation of a trade network established by the possessors, perhaps primarily to secure

Heimdalsjordet 227

the supply of luxury goods and bullion necessary for its own maintenance. How would such an interpretation comply with present ideas about Viking-Age trade in Scandinavia and in South-East Norway in particular?

A current suggestion for the classification of Viking-Age trading sites, based on Richard Hodges's (1982: 50–2) division of emporia into seasonal and resident sites, has been presented by Dagfinn Skre (2008b: 337–8). He divides the trading sites into four categories, each with its own set of characteristics:

1 central-place markets, which are seasonal, perform inter- and intraregional trade, and are located at and administered by central places;
2 local markets, which are seasonal, perform intraregional trade, and may be independent;
3 nodal markets, which are seasonal, perform long-distance and inter-/ intraregional trade, are possibly located in border areas, and possibly stand under royal protection;
4 towns, which are permanent, perform long-distance and inter-/intraregional trade, and are located (under royal protection) in border areas.

On the basis of the discussion above, it is not evident how the Heimdalsjordet site should be classified within this system. If it is accepted that the import finds from Heimdalsjordet to a large degree arrived through a different long-distance trading network than those from Kaupang, then the site should be placed in category 3 or, if regarded as permanent, in 4 (see also Sindbæk 2005: 97; Skre 2008b: 340–1). The presence of plot divisions also supports such an interpretation. However, the proximity to Kaupang makes Heimdalsjordet a puzzling case: how could Heimdalsjordet continue to exist in competition with the much larger Kaupang? The answer is obviously that competition was not fierce enough, and one reason for this could be that the two sites were separated by a political power. Before Heimdalsjordet was known, Skre suggested, in his analysis of the political situation in Vestfold in the ninth and tenth centuries, the presence of a political border between Kaupang and more northerly areas. Following his analyses, Kaupang could have been Danish up to around AD 900, while Heimdalsjordet could have been under the control of the Norwegian Yngling kings (Skre 2007: 463–8).

It could also be, however, that the two sites served different functions. Kaupang was clearly closely connected with the Continental and western trade network, a network populated with traders of many different origins, only some of them being Scandinavians. The eastern network, towards which Heimdalsjordet seems to have been more oriented, probably consisted to a higher degree of Scandinavians, many of whom undoubtedly had various bonds of loyalty and kinship back to their homelands. The social position of the traders at Heimdalsjordet and at Kaupang may thus have been quite different; especially if, as suggested above, Gokstad represents a seat of power of sorts. If the people visiting Heimdalsjordet were not (only) traders and craftsmen who were free to go where they wanted, but (also) dependents of the power

228 *Jan Bill and Christian Løchsen Rødsrud*

resting at Gokstad, we may understand Heimdalsjordet as the terminal of a trade network reaching out from Gokstad and designed to provide it with metals and other imports, at the same time as it housed the craftsmen who could convert the imports into the weapons, jewellery and other items needed to maintain Gokstad's position. In such a scenario one could see Heimdalsjordet not as a town or a nodal market in the sense described above, but perhaps as a modernised central-place market, shaped to fulfil the needs of the elite at a time when international trade was becoming increasingly important, also for the uppermost strata in society. Such an interpretation will also contribute to a discussion of the difference between an exchange site of South Scandinavian origin, as suggested for Kaupang, and a more locally based counterpart.

At present, any interpretation of Heimdalsjordet and the finds made there will, of course, be extremely tentative and liable to be proven wrong in the light of the more thorough analyses still to be carried out. Nevertheless, the process of formulating and discussing such preliminary ideas is of paramount importance for future work, since it can help to identify research potentials and needs which may otherwise remain undetected. It also helps to identify with more precision similarities and differences in the composition of finds from Heimdalsjordet and Kaupang. The current discussion has highlighted the importance of comparing not only find frequencies, but also excavation methods and volumes. Also pivotal in illuminating Heimdalsjordet's relationship to Kaupang and the Gokstad burial will be attempts to trace evidence of connections. A particularly promising perspective in this direction is the study of metal supply and techniques used by the fine-metal craftsmen of the site, compared to those of Kaupang (Pedersen 2010) and those represented in the Gokstad burial equipment. Other core activities will be: to complete the analyses of the numismatic and other datable find material, to complete the radiocarbon-dating programme for the site and to understand in more detail its chronology. These steps will – hopefully – allow us in the future to understand more of what was happening when trade and handicrafts blossomed and Norway's largest ship burial was erected at a beach in Vestfold some 1,100 years ago.

References

Ambrosiani, Björn and Bo G. Erikson 1991: *Birka: vikingastaden*. Bind 1–5. Wiken. Stockholm.

Androshchuk, Fedir 2014: *Viking Swords: Swords and Social Aspects of Weaponry in Viking Age Societies*. Statens historiska museum. Stockholm.

Bill, Jan 2013: Revisiting Gokstad: Interdisciplinary investigations of a find complex investigated in the 19th century. In: Sebastian Brather and Dirk Krausse (eds): *Fundmassen. Innovative Strategien zur Auswertung frühmittelalterlicher Quellenbestände.* Materialhefte zur Archäologie in Baden-Württemberg/Landesdenkmalamt Baden-Württemberg, vol. 97: 75–86. Konrad Theiss Verlag. Stuttgart.

Bill, Jan and Aoife Daly 2012: The plundering of the ship graves from Oseberg and Gokstad: an example of power politics? *Antiquity*, 86(333): 808–24.

Heimdalsjordet 229

Bill, Jan and Christian Løchsen Rødsrud 2013: En ny markeds- og produksjonsplass ved Gokstad i Vestfold. *Nicolay*, 120: 5–12.

Bill, Jan, Erich Nau, Wolfgang Neubauer, Immo Trinks, Christer Tonning, Lars Gustavsen, Knut Paasche and Sirri Seren 2013: Contextualising a monumental burial: The Gokstad Revitalised Project. In: Neubauer, Wolfgang, Immo Trinks, Roderick B. Salisbury and Christina Einwögerer (eds): *Archaeological Prospection: Proceedings of the 10th International Conference – Vienna, May 29th–June 2nd 2013.* Austrian Academy of Sciences Press. Wien.

Blackburn, Mark 2008: The coin-finds. In: Skre, Dagfinn (ed.): *Means of Exchange: Dealing with Silver in the Viking Age.* Kaupang Excavation Project. Publication Series, vol. 2. Norske Oldfunn, vol. 23: 29–74. Aarhus University Press. Århus.

Callmer, Johan 1977: *Trade Beads and Bead Trade in Scandinavia ca. 800–1000 A. D.* Acta Archaeologica Lundensia. Series in 4°, no. 11. Gleerup. Lund.

Clarke, Helen and Björn Ambrosiani 1991: *Towns in the Viking Age.* Leicester University Press. Leicester.

Feveile, Claus 2006: *Ribe studier: Det ældste Ribe. Udgravninger på nordsiden af Ribe Å 1984–2000.* Jysk Arkæologisk Selskab. Aarhus.

—— 2010: *Vikingernes Ribe: handel, magt og tro.* Sydvestjyske museer. Ribe.

Feveile, Jens and Stig Jensen 2000: Ribe in the 8th and 9th century. A contribution to the archaeological chronology of North West Europe. *Acta Archaeologica*, 71: 9–24.

Gansum, Terje and Hilde Garpestad 1995: *Arkeologisk forundersøkelse for FV265 Hegnaveien: Nilsesvingen.* Sandefjord kommune i Vestfold. Vestfold fylkeskommune. Tønsberg.

Gustin, Ingrid 2004: *Mellan gåva och marknad: handel, tillit och materiell kultur under vikingatid.* Institute of Archaeology, University of Lund. Lund.

Hinsch, Erik 1945: En ny båtgrav på klassisk grunn. *Viking*, IX: 163–84.

Hjardar, Kim and Vegard Vike 2011: *Vikinger i krig.* Spartacus. Oslo.

Hodges, Richard 1982: *Dark Age Economics: The Origins of Towns and Trade A.D. 600–1000.* St. Martin's Press. New York.

Hougen, Ellen-Karine 1993: *Kaupangfunnene bind IIIB. Bosetningsområdets keramikk.* Kulturhistorisk museum, Universitetet i Oslo. Oslo.

Jankuhn, Herbert 1986: *Haithabu: ein Handelsplatz der Wikingerzeit.* Wachholtz. Neumünster.

Kalmring, Sven 2011: The harbour of Hedeby. In: Svavar Sigmundsson (ed.): *Viking Settlements and Viking Society: Papers from the Proceedings of the Sixteenth Viking Congress, Reykjavík and Reykholt, 16–23 August 2009*, pp. 245–59. University of Iceland Press. Reykjavík.

Karageorghis, V. and V. Kassianidou 1999: Metalworking and recycling in Late Bronze Age Cyprus: the evidence from Kition. *Oxford Journal of Archaeology*, 18(2): 171–88.

Kilger, Christoph 2008: Wholeness and holiness: counting, weighing and valuing silver in the early Viking period. In: Skre, Dagfinn (ed.): *Means of Exchange: Dealing with Silver in the Viking Age.* Kaupang Excavation Project. Publication Series, vol. 2. Norske Oldfunn, vol. 23: 253–325. Aarhus University Press. Århus.

Kleingärtner, Sunhild and Gareth Williams 2014: Contacts and exchange. In: Williams, Gareth, Peter Pentz and Matthias Wemhoff (eds): *Vikings: Life and Legend*, pp. 28–75. British Museum. London.

Kruse, Susan E. 1992: Late Saxon balances and weights from England. *Medieval Archaeology*, 36: 67–95.

230   *Jan Bill and Christian Løchsen Rødsrud*

Larsen, Jan Henning, Jan Bill, Bernt Rundberget and Lena Grandin 2011: Distinguishing iron production sites by chemical signature of bloomery slag in south-eastern Norway: the iron clench nails in the Gokstad ship – only local production or of various origin? In: Hauptmann, Andreas, Diana Modarressi-Tehrani and Michael Prange (eds): *Archaeometallurgy in Europe III. Abstracts. Deutsches Bergbau-Museum Bochum, Germany June 29th–July 1st 2011*, p. 183. Metalla, vol. 4. Deutsches Bergbau-Museum. Bochum.

Martens, Irmelin and Anna M. Rosenqvist 1988: *Jernvinna på Møsstrond i Telemark.* Varia 13. Kulturhistorisk museum, Universitetet i Oslo. Oslo.

Nicolaysen, Nicolay 1882: *The Viking-Ship Discovered in Norway/Langskipet fra Gokstad ved Sandefjord*. Alb. Cammermeyer. Kristiania.

Øye, Ingvild 2011: Textile-production equipment. In: Skre, Dagfinn (ed.): *Things from the Town: Artefacts and Inhabitants in Viking-Age Kaupang*. Kaupang Excavation Project. Publication Series, vol. 3. Norske Oldfunn, vol. 24: 339–72. Aarhus University Press. Århus.

Pedersen, Unn 2001: Vektlodd: sikre vitnesbyrd om handelsvirksomhet? *Primitive Tider,* 4: 19–36.

—— 2008: Weights and balances. In: Skre, Dagfinn (ed.): *Means of Exchange: Dealing with Silver in the Viking Age*. Kaupang Excavation Project. Publication Series, vol. 2. Norske Oldfunn, vol. 23: 119–95. Aarhus University Press. Århus.

—— 2010: *I smeltedigelen: finsmedene i vikingtidsbyen Kaupang*. Institutt for arkeologi, konservering og historie, Det humanistiske fakultet, Universitetet i Oslo. Oslo.

Petersen, Jan 1919: *De norske vikingesverd: En typologisk-kronologisk studie over vikingetidens vaaben*. Skrifter II, Hist.-filos. klasse, vol. 1. Videnskapsselskapet i Kristiania. Kristiania

Resi, Heid Gjøstein 2011a: Gemstones: cornelian, rock crystal, amethyst, fluorspar and garnet. In: Skre, Dagfinn (ed.): *Things from the Town: Artefacts and Inhabitants in Viking-Age Kaupang*. Kaupang Excavation Project. Publication Series, vol. 3. Norske Oldfunn, vol. 24: 143–66. Aarhus University Press. Århus.

—— 2011b: Whetstones, grindstones, touchstones and smoothers. In: Skre, Dagfinn (ed.): *Things from the Town: Artefacts and Inhabitants in Viking-Age Kaupang*. Kaupang Excavation Project. Publication Series, vol. 3. Norske Oldfunn, vol. 24: 373–93. Aarhus University Press. Århus.

Rispling, Gert, Mark Blackburn and Kenneth Jonsson 2008: Catalogue of the coins. In: Skre, Dagfinn (ed.): *Means of Exchange: Dealing with Silver in the Viking Age*. Kaupang Excavation Project. Publication Series, vol. 2. Norske Oldfunn, vol. 23: 75–94. Aarhus University Press. Århus.

Ros, Jonas 2009: *Stad och gård: Sigtuna under sen vikingatid och tidlig medeltid*. Societas Archaeologica Upsaliensis. Uppsala.

Roslund, Mats 2007: *Guests in the House: Cultural Transmission between Slavs and Scandinavians 900 to 1300 A.D.* Brill. Leiden.

Sindbæk, Søren Michael 2005: *Ruter og rutinisering: vikingetidens fjernhandel i Nordeuropa*. Multivers Academic. København.

Skre, Dagfinn (ed.) 2007: *Kaupang in Skiringssal*. Kaupang Excavation Project. Publication Series, vol. 1. Norske Oldfunn, vol. 22. Aarhus University Press. Århus.

—— 2008a: *Means of Exchange: Dealing with Silver in the Viking Age*. Kaupang Excavation Project. Publication Series, vol. 2. Norske Oldfunn, vol. 23. Aarhus University Press. Århus.

—— 2008b: Post-substantivist towns and trade: AD 600–1000. In: Skre, Dagfinn (ed.): *Means of Exchange: Dealing with Silver in the Viking Age*. Kaupang Excavation Project.

Publication Series, vol. 2. Norske Oldfunn, vol. 23: 327–41. Aarhus University Press. Århus.

—— 2011: *Things from the Town: Artefacts and Inhabitants in Viking-Age Kaupang*. Kaupang Excavation Project. Publication Series, vol. 3. Norske Oldfunn, vol. 24. Aarhus University Press. Århus.

Sperber, Erik 1996: *Balances, Weights and Weighing in Ancient and Early Medieval Sweden*. Theses and papers in scientific archaeology, vol. 2. The Archaeological Research Laboratory. Stockholm.

Steuer, Heiko 1997: Waagen und Gewichte aus dem mittelalterlichen Schleswig: Funde des 11. bis 13. Jahrhunderts aus Europa als Quellen zur Handels- und Währungsgeschichte. *Zeitschrift für Archäologie des Mittelalters*, vol. 10. Rheinland-Verlag. Köln.

Stylegar, Frans-Arne 2007: The Kaupang cemeteries revisited. In: Skre, Dagfinn (ed.): *Kaupang in Skiringssal*. Kaupang Excavation Project. Publication Series, vol. 1. Norske Oldfunn, vol. 22: 65–126. Aarhus University Press. Århus.

Wamers, Egon 2011: Continental and insular metalwork. In: Skre, Dagfinn (ed.): *Things from the Town: Artefacts and Inhabitants in Viking-Age Kaupang*. Kaupang Excavation Project. Publication Series, vol. 3. Norske Oldfunn, vol. 24: 65–97. Aarhus University Press. Århus.

Wiker, Gry 2007: Monochrome blue Kaupang-beads: local manufacture or import? In Innere Strukturen von Siedlungen und Gräberfeldern als Spiegel gesellchaftlicher Wirklichkeit? In: Grünewald, Christoph and Torsten Capelle (eds): *Akten des 57. Internationalen Sachsensymposions vom 26. bis 30. August 2006 in Münster*, pp. 137–44. Aschendorff. Münster.

Wilson, David M. 2006: Introduction and summary. In: Fuglesang, Signe Horn and David M. Wilson (eds): *The Hoen Hoard: A Viking Gold Treasure of the Ninth Century*, pp. 13–25. Kulturhistorisk museum, Universitetet i Oslo. Oslo.

12 The *skeid* and other assemblies in the Norwegian 'Mountain Land'

Kjetil Loftsgarden, Morten Ramstad and Frans-Arne Stylegar

Introduction

The mountainous regions and valleys of southern Norway are sparsely populated, with relatively few villages or urban centres. This must have been even more so in the Viking Age and Middle Ages. In this chapter we argue that seasonal meeting places were therefore of great importance. From historical times a number of such places are known. Place names, written sources and oral tradition indicate the prevalence of assembly sites during a time span stretching from the Late Iron Age up to the nineteenth century. They go by different names, such as *skeid*, *stevne*, *ting* or *marked*, which evidently pertain to a fairly broad spectrum of seasonal meetings with somewhat different focuses. However, they share a number of common features, serving as an arena for social interaction, competitive games (*leik*) and feasting as well as exchange of commodities.

We argue that the seasonal meeting places in the outfield and mountain regions must be viewed in both a social and economic perspective. Furthermore, we regard the evolution of such sites as an important field of research. A challenge posed by this point of departure is the scant attention these sites have received in archaeological and historical research. The sites are often located in remote areas of mountainous regions, and as the assemblies only lasted for a limited period of time each year, the accumulated archaeological material will be correspondingly limited, with few or no remaining structures. Consequently, this has led to an under-communication of interaction between inland and coastal regions in the Viking Age and medieval period, and thus the significance of this contact has been underestimated.

This is not to say that no research has been conducted on seasonal assembly sites (e.g. Brendalsmo et al. 2009). However, in general the focus has to a large degree been on sites pertaining to international or interregional trade, such as Kaupang, Birka or Ribe, or on the medieval towns. In a political sense the attention has been on *thing* sites and administrative control (cf. Iversen et al. 2013). To the extent that the seasonal sites of the Norwegian inland have been examined, the focus has been on the exotic elements of the assemblies, especially the ritualistic and competitive aspects (Solheim 1956, 1961; Vallevik

1961; Stylegar 2006). We acknowledge this as an important feature of these assemblies; however, it is just one of several.

With this chapter we aim to give a brief introduction to the multifaceted small-scale seasonal meeting places; places where goods could be exchanged, alliances and friendships established, and scores settled or physical prowess displayed through competitions. Variations of such assemblies have been in use up until recent times, and how these were organised and perceived in the eighteenth and nineteenth centuries will constitute the backdrop for this text. Based on the archaeological data from a few selected sites, we will also discuss the dating of such assemblies. Subsequently, we will give an in-depth example from the Viking site of Bjørkum in Sogn. Our intention in combining sites as diverse in time and space as these is to indicate the lasting importance of such places, and we contend that this approach can give a broader perspective on the multi-functional gathering places of the past.

The sites discussed in this chapter all lie within the 'Mountain Land' (Figure 12.1), as described in the *Historia Norvegiae* (Ekrem and Mortensen 2006). Written during the latter half of the twelfth century, this work divides Norway into three geographical areas: the Coastal Land (*Zona itaque maritime*), the Central or Mountain Land (*Mediterranea zona/De montanis Norwegie*) and the land of the Sami people (*De Finnis*). In the area outlined as the Mountain Land a number of excavations and research projects have shown extensive exploitation of outfield resources in the Viking Age and Middle Ages, such as iron production from bog ore, and hunting and trapping (Indrelid 2009; Larsen 2009). This exploitation seems to a large extent to have surpassed local demand, which indicates that these resources constituted exchange commodities. To a certain degree the utilisation of outfield resources must have been at the expense of the cultivation of land and animal husbandry. Yet the short summers and long winters of the 'Mountain Land' provided little room for risky initiatives in sustenance strategies. We therefore postulate that stable and lasting social and economic networks were a prerequisite for the increase in specialised resource utilisation that takes place throughout the Viking period and up until c. AD 1300. This also implies increased interaction between different local communities in different regions, which in turn led to extended integration between people from inland and coastal areas. In other words, seasonal assemblies seem to have been instrumental in making possible regional specialisation in resources as well as increased social interaction between regions.

Assemblies as inland tradition

> Coming from the west, the people from Hallingdal had roamed to Raudalsknatten, and the people from Valdres had come from the east. In the early part of the day, they had exchanged horses, and some had been racing. The fastest horse this year came from Svenkerud in Hallingdal, and this was a credit to the person who owned it.
>
> (Fønhus 1924: 18–19)

234 *Loftsgarden, Ramstad and Stylegar*

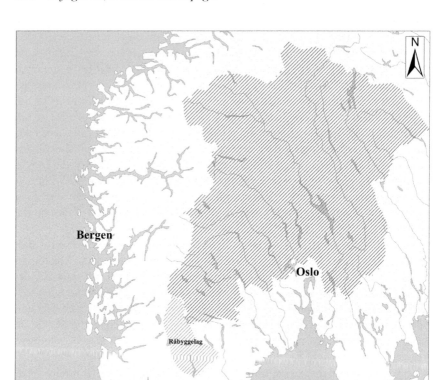

Figure 12.1 Map showing the 'Coastal Land' and the 'Mountain Land', as described in *Historia Norvegiae* c. AD 1150–75 (Storm 1880; Iversen this volume).
Source: Background map by Kartverket (Norwegian Mapping Authority).

This is how the novelist Mikkjel Fønhus describes *Raudalsdansen* (the 'Raudal Dance'), one of the many traditional yearly gatherings in the mountain and fjord areas on both sides of the Langfjella mountain range, as well as the Dovre mountain plateau. There were several different aspects to these assemblies, which played a vital role in the culture of the Uplands. Written accounts show that gatherings like *Raudalsdansen* were widespread in the eighteenth century, and some of them are even mentioned as early as the sixteenth, but we know little about when they came into being (Øverland 1891; Øverland 1898; Solheim 1952). *Raudalsdansen* on Norefjell was, as the name implies, a dance, but not just that. In Fønhus's fictional description, racing, fighting and – not least – trading are also part of the picture, offering a number of arenas for displaying oneself, acquiring status and prestige. The same applies to the majority of other traditional assembly places. They brought together people from different rural districts, and were important arenas for young people seeking spouses and for kinship alliances.

A large number of similar assemblies are known from the mountain regions in southern Norway, where inlanders from districts like Gudbrandsdalen, Valdres, Hallingdal and Numedal gathered, in addition to which they met people from the coastal and fjord areas of western Norway. The richest tradition is probably found in Valdres, where several assembly sites of this kind are known (Solheim 1956).

In accounts of the seventeenth to the nineteenth century we find a form of assembly site called a *skeid* (skeið, *n.*), which can be characterised as a seasonal meeting place with a particular focus on competitions, such as horse-fighting or horse-racing (Skar 1909; Solheim 1952, 1956, 1961; Stylegar 2006, 2014). Although the *skeid* in historical times are mostly known in the districts of Telemark and Setesdal, place names, sagas and medieval law texts indicate that they were common both in Norway and Iceland in the Viking Age and Middle Ages.

One of the most prominent *skeid* in Setesdalen and Telemark was the one in Valle. This was described in the 1770s by the vicar Reier Gjellebøl (1800: 55–8). His account of the *skeid* consists of two main elements: horse-fights and

Figure 12.2 An artist's rendition of a *skeid*.
Source: © Centre for Educational Texts, University College of Southeast-Norway.

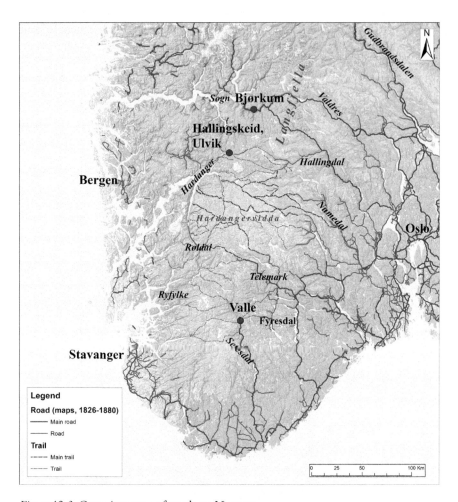

Figure 12.3 Overview map of southern Norway.
Source: Background map by Kartverket (Norwegian Mapping Authority).

horse-racing. On a fixed day in August, a crowd of people gathered together with their horses on the *skeid* field in the immediate neighbourhood of the vicarage. There, stallions were brought to an excited state and encouraged to fight each other, in pairs. It was a great honour to own the horse that remained standing in the arena, the *skeid* colt. Later, people gathered to watch horse-racing on another field. Gjellebøl highlights several characteristics of the *skeid* that he obviously found exotic and strange. The race took place without the use of a saddle, and at full gallop, in a rough manner. Both horses and people often suffered injuries.

Aspects of the exchange of goods at the assemblies

There are two particular aspects of the *skeid* and other assemblies in the 'Mountain Land' that stand out and are often brought up. One is the almost carnivalesque element that Gjellebøl emphasises; the other is the competitiveness expressed by phenomena like horse-racing and horse-fights. Both aspects are undoubtedly important, and the competitive aspect has certainly played an important part in the inland culture. In accordance with social anthropologist Jan-Petter Blom's (1969) treatment of the theme, the traditional mountain farmer population stands out in that it has developed certain cultural traits or ways of living. While the coastal and lowland population had a stable life, bound to the farm, the mountain farmers were always on the move, and this meant exploitation of extensive areas. The mountain farmer was a hunter, a cowboy and a horse-trader. As a result, Blom writes, the mountain farmer is often attributed a certain type of character: he is a gambler, an artist and a ruffian, in contrast to the easy-going coastal farmer. The more the people living in the mountains became involved in competition and social intercourse with the coastal population, the more their style and way of living came to diverge from that of people living in other tactical positions. Through this specialisation, distinctive regional cultures emerge. Blom paints a picture of a very competitive inland culture.

It is understandable that many scholarly observers have noticed the more exotic aspects of the annual social gatherings, while the more ordinary exchange of goods that took place in connection with them has rarely been the focus of attention. But the fact remains that the exchange of various products seems to have been an integral part of the majority of these gatherings. This applies not least to the large assemblies in the mountains. The Norwegian folklorist Svale Solheim, who carried out extensive studies on assemblies of this type, repeats the words of an informant about a gathering in Valdres, who said it was 'more or less (like) a market':

> On the outskirts of the assembly place, a lively small-scale trade took place. Scythes, sickles, billhooks and ordinary knives were traded. The people from Hallingdal in particular had scythes and other sharp-edged tools made of iron to sell. Some sold frieze and other types of clothing, mittens, socks and other knitted things. Some traded or exchanged horses. Peddlers were present with other types of women's adornments, which they were selling.
> (Solheim 1952: 559–60)

There is a rich oral tradition referring to this pattern of mobile trade and gatherings. There were horse-traders from the fjord areas of western Norway who brought horses, hops and other merchandise that they either exchanged or sold, while they bought skins to bring back home.

There is a partial overlap between the *skeid* of the Setesdal tradition and the mountain markets. The exchange of goods took place at the *skeid*, and

238 *Loftsgarden, Ramstad and Stylegar*

horse-fights and racing at the mountain markets. The question is: what are we actually dealing with – an exchange of goods centred around rituals or a ritualisation of the exchange of goods?

The Uplands as a transportation zone

The inland districts of South Norway, the Uplands (*Upplond*) of the sagas, have always played an important part in the traffic between the different parts of the country. The mountains certainly do divide Norway into a number of natural regions. The Langfjella mountain range divides eastern Norway from western Norway, and eastern Norway itself consists of several extensive smaller valleys, in addition to the flat countryside communities along the Oslo Fjord and around larger inland lakes. Western Norway is divided into distinct fjord districts through the natural conditions. Further north, Dovre divides eastern Norway from Trøndelag, while the latter, in its turn, is delimited from the historical Hålogaland by Helgelandsfjella. Overland traffic between these parts of the country has followed natural corridors, and this has made the Uplands particularly important in a transport context. Historian Sverre Steen writes:

> The inland districts of Norway played a role in the old communication that we nowadays have a tendency to overlook, because their products no longer play the same role in the community economy as they did in the Middle Ages.
>
> (Steen 1929: 68–9)

In accordance with the way Steen and others interpret the sagas of the Norwegian kings, there were four main routes over the Norwegian mainland. The most important one was the road that ran between Oslo and Nidaros (present-day Trondheim). The three other routes connected eastern and western Norway: the *Filefjellsveg* between Valdres and Sogn, the ancient trails across Hardangervidda known as *Nordmannsslepene*, and the trail that goes via Røldal (Figure 12.3). These trails over the mountain plateaux were of great importance. Goods were transported by packhorse, and the visible traces of this traffic are to all appearances very old (Roland 2001: 5).

The significance of this east–west traffic should not be underestimated. In many of the inland districts of southern and south-western Norway, the traffic across the valleys and over the low mountains would have been on a much larger scale than the traffic along the valleys going northwards and southwards, where the road connections were poor. This was certainly the case for Setesdal and large parts of Telemark. The traffic arteries to the east and west thus connected Telemark to the inland districts further east.

Quite how far back in time the extensive contact between the different parts of the country goes is uncertain. A hypothesis is that the increasingly regular use of the above-mentioned main traffic arteries is connected with an increased division of labour between the regions, where each produced 'what paid off best', to quote the agrarian historian Stein Tveite (1959: 31). This is where the assemblies and the other gathering places enter the picture.

The dating and archaeology of the assemblies

As mentioned, the horse-fights and horse-races are described in the sagas (see *Viga-Glums saga, Njåls-saga, Arons saga Hjǫrleifssonar* or *Þorsteins þáttr stangarhoggs*), as well as in the Frostathing Law and subsequently the rural law of Magnus the Lawmender. The similarities between how they are described in the seventeenth to nineteenth century and how they are described in the Middle Ages are remarkable and seem to indicate a long continuity in rules of conduct.

The dating of *skeid* and other assemblies in the Norwegian inland is difficult. From the aforementioned *skeid* in Valle there are no known archaeological structures. However, in Fyresdal in Telemark there are four standing stones which are mentioned in the eighteenth century in regard to the *skeid* that were held there. A priest, Hans Jacob Wille, gives the following description in 1786:

> At Molandsmoen, a couple of kilometres from the vicarage, there is a level plain, where four pointed stones have been standing in a upright position, and formed a square for a fighting ground for fighters in the old days. Nowadays, however, a small horse market is held there on 14 August, when one rides in order to test one's horse and finally releases them to fight over a mare that is held by a man protecting it with a long rod in the middle of the square, until one of them has gained power over them all. One of the remaining stones has a runic inscription.
>
> (Wille et al. 1881: 27–8)

The runic inscription has been interpreted as follows: *þórolfr reit. Sá skal ráða rú(nar), er lér stigreips.* This translates as 'Torolv wrote. He that comprehends (these) runes lends a pair of stirrups (to another one)'. The runes are thought to be from the tenth or eleventh century (Olsen 1951: 234). This may indicate that the *skeid* in Fyresdal dates back at least to the Middle Ages.

Providing a further testament to the prevalence of such gatherings are the many place names containing *skeid*. Of particular interest in this context is the place name *Hallingskeid*. There are four known places with the name *Hallingskeid* in Norway, all located in the mountains of western Norway. The term *Halling* points to people from Hallingdal, east of Langfjella. Thus, Hallingskeid signifies 'the *skeid* of the Halling', or rather 'with the Halling', and is an indication of who met at the *skeid*. One Hallingskeid is in Ulvik at approximately 1000 m above sea level in the mountain region between Hardanger and Sogn. As is the case with the other places with this name, there exists an oral tradition regarding the assembly, but the *skeid* is not mentioned in any text, either from the medieval period or from historical times. Hallingskeid is situated at a crossing point between Hardanger and Sogn, with routes going east and west.

240 *Loftsgarden, Ramstad and Stylegar*

The exact location of the *skeid* is not known; however, one place clearly stands out in the surrounding landscape, namely a flat island, free from stone, surrounded by a river, with a waterfall as a backdrop to the south and mountains on both sides (Figure 12.4, see colour plate section). In this mountainous region it is hard to find a place more suited as a venue for horse-racing or a meeting place. There is also archaeological data which may suggest this. Several cooking pits have been found here, two of which are dated to the Roman period (Gustafson 2005a: 208). In August 2015 seven additional cooking pits where excavated as part of an archaeological field course organised by the University of Bergen. The area has also been surveyed using a metal detector. These surveys resulted in finds of five horseshoes, several horseshoe nails and two knives. Although difficult to date, the horseshoes and knives seem to be from the later Middle Ages. These findings may indicate a meeting place, as there are no shielings in the immediate vicinity, and the shielings that do exist in the area were established in the eighteenth century (Ohnstad et al. 1991: 37).

Before moving on, we wish to return to Valle in Setesdalen and briefly refer to the archaeological finds from the late Viking Age in the area. As mentioned, there are no structures indicating a *skeid* in Valle; however, relatively numerous objects have been found relating to trade, such as weights, coins and imported goods. These finds stand out in the Norwegian inland and have provided the basis for the argument that there was a marketplace in Valle in the Viking Age (Larsen 1980, 1981; Stylegar 2009). The recent excavations at Langeid in Setesdal seem to confirm that trading was commonly practised at Setesdal in the Viking Age (Loftsgarden and Wenn 2012; Glørstad and Wenn this volume).

Archaeological investigations at Bjørkum in Lærdal

By comparing historical sources, traditional material and the few archaeological investigations that have been carried out, we are well on the way to understanding the different assemblies in the 'Mountain Land' and their role in the community in other respects. To extend these perspectives to the possible function and character of these sites in the Viking Age and early Middle Ages, we will here draw attention to Bjørkum, a multi-functional site dating to the period from the eighth to tenth century, excavated by the University Museum of Bergen in 2009 (Ramstad 2011; Ramstad et al. 2011).

Bjørkum lies at an altitude of 130 m above sea level in Tønjum Parish, about 20 km upstream from the village in Lærdal. The site is situated in a border area between inland valley systems, mountains and fjord landscapes. The geographical position of Bjørkum places it in close spatial relationship with a number of historical paths leading east, west, north and south, supporting complex networks of communication linking inland regions and coastal areas. Moreover, the generally fast-flowing Lærdal river runs quietly past Bjørkum, and one of few natural fords in the Lærdal valley is found here.

The historical settlement at Bjørkum consists of marginal farms. There were no records of prehistoric remains or grave monuments from the locality prior to the excavations, and it seems likely that there was no central farm at Bjørkum during prehistoric times. Botanical analyses testify that the area was cleared as early as the transition between the late Neolithic and the Bronze Age, and cultivated up to the Roman period. There is little or no evidence of cultivation during the Late Iron Age. However, it is first during this period that archaeological features appear in the area. It is thus interesting to note that cereal remains have been found in several of the Late Iron Age structures, suggesting that grain was brought to the site from outside. In the same period, there is a relative decrease in grazing indicators and fungal spores indicative of manure, concurrent with macrofossil samples containing sclerotia (oogonia, oospores) as well as other spores that testify to a good oxygen supply in the deposits, which can be associated with a lot of trampling and other disturbance of the soil. Furthermore, the sediments from the Late Iron Age have very high values of charcoal dust, taken as indicating a considerable amount of activity around open fires on the site (Halvorsen 2012).

During the excavation a relatively confined central area of about 1,500 m^2 was discovered, with a greasy cultural layer containing bone, or black earth. The favourable preservation conditions at Bjørkum are puzzling. In general, the preservation of bone is extremely poor at Norwegian Late Iron Age sites. For instance in the Lærdal valley itself, over the last 30 years there have been several large-scale surveys and excavations of sites dating from late Neolithic times and onwards, where, with the exception of a few fragments of burnt bone, there have been no finds of organic material. However, at Bjørkum the preservation conditions for skeletal material were extremely good. A likely explanation is that relatively extensive activities have taken place during a fairly short period, so that the organic components have not had time to decompose and a more basic soil has formed.

Apart from the fact that all the architectural features are located within a small area along the riverbank, it is not possible to recognise any strict overall plan or spatial organisation of buildings and activity areas. Altogether, nine definite post-built houses have been documented along the riverbank. Some smaller post-built structures could represent sheds or other types of lighter constructions (Figure 12.5). There was no evidence for division into smaller rooms or activity areas within any of the buildings. Neither is there any definite building for animals, indicated by traces of stables or cowsheds. There are structural similarities to contemporaneous houses from the Late Iron Age. At the same time, the buildings at Bjørkum seem to be smaller, lighter and more temporary. This is underpinned by the fact that the post holes are in most cases very shallow, with very little or no stone lining, and there are few indications of replacement.

Perhaps more surprising was the identification of at least 13 pit houses in addition to imprints of six lighter house structures, possibly tent-like. Even though the number of pit houses is not impressive compared to many localities

Figure 12.5 A visualisation of the Bjørkum site in approximately AD 750.
Source: Produced by Arkikon.

in South Scandinavia (i.e. Birkedahl and Johansen 2000; Nørgård Jørgensen et al. 2010: 103–8), this is in fact the largest concentration of pit houses known from western Norway (see also Øye 2006: 445–56). In earlier research, pit houses have been interpreted as handicraft and production units (Mortensen 1997; Øye 2006; Nørgård Jørgensen et al. 2010; Milek 2012). The majority of the pit houses in western Norway (like those at Osen in Gaular, Henjum in Leikanger, and Kvåle and Stedje in Sogndal) seem to represent permanent and solid post-built structures with many similarities to the ones found on the typical Late Iron Age farms in South Scandinavia. The pit houses at Bjørkum appear to be lighter and less permanent structures (Ramstad 2011). In the outdoor areas between the houses, large hearths and some 40 cooking pits were documented.

The 60 radiocarbon dates that have been obtained from Bjørkum all fall within the eighth to tenth century, and appear to be grouped in two phases: a small set fall within the period AD 850–1030, and may possibly be linked to the reuse of old buildings. The establishment of the Bjørkum site and the main phase lie within the time interval AD 700–850, thus corresponding to a period of about 150 years.

The total number of finds within the area investigated is fewer than 1,200 objects. The material consists of everyday objects, personal belongings like fragments of dress ornaments and beads, and whetstones. Dominant among the metal tools are relatively small and probably multi-functional knives (Wahlborg 2012). Some of the raw materials would have been available locally, while the acquisition of other raw materials may be linked geographically to more comprehensive distribution networks. Spindle whorls and loom weights can be related to the outfield and shieling activities in the mountain regions, and can be taken as reflecting the increased importance of secondary products and woollen fabrics during the Viking Age. Some of the textiles that have been produced on the sites seem to have been of very high quality (Cartwright 2012). A find of an unfinished rock crystal bead also testifies to the practising of more specialised crafts and may be linked to the mountainous areas around Lærdal, as these have rich deposits of rock crystal.

At Bjørkum, a number of objects made from bone and antler, like needles and game pieces, were found. Of particular importance are cut reindeer antlers, as well as other small chips and fragments of antler that may have been linked to the manufacture of articles for daily use and comb-making. Altogether, the material probably contains traces of up to ten combs in a typical Viking-Age style. Neither ordinary workshops nor specific production areas were found. In the surrounding mountain regions, trapping systems and bowmen's hides bear witness to the significance of reindeer hunting in the Viking Age and early medieval period. It is worth noting that bones of reindeer are lacking in the osteological material. An obvious explanation for this phenomenon is that the antlers were transported to the location as raw material, as opposed to more comprehensive exploitation of wild reindeer by humans on the site.

Bjørkum: a Viking-Age multi-functional meeting place

The remains from handicraft production as well as the existence of a large number of cooking pits and pit houses make Bjørkum stand out as an exceptional site in Norwegian Viking-Age archaeology. The inland location of the site, surrounded by mountains, also distinguishes Bjørkum from other localities of this type. Approximately 20 km into the mountains south of Bjørkum one reaches a place called Hallingskeid, separate from the one previously mentioned. Without going too far in the direction of connecting the site directly with assembly places that are so far known only through written sources and oral traditions from the Middle Ages and later, it should be permissible to take into consideration that Bjørkum exhibits several of the characteristics which one would, at the outset, expect to find on this type of site.

In relation to this it is worth mentioning a more recent study linked to pit houses, seasonal gathering places and communication centres in South Scandinavia in the Late Iron Age, where parallels are drawn to the North Scandinavian 'church villages' (Nørgård Jørgensen et al. 2010). These represent gathering places connected with religious holidays and market activities, as well as with political and legal institutions. The visiting families had their own cabins or huts where they spent the nights for as long as the gatherings lasted. Secondary activities included different types of handicraft and production. In that sense, the shift from 'church villages' to well-known seasonal marketplaces in the far north, like the Skibotn market in Troms, seems to have been gradual

(Hage 1985). A corresponding scenario seems to fit better with the pit houses and the other small and lighter housing structures at Bjørkum, rather than viewing them as remains of more permanent handicraft activity and settlement (Ramstad 2011: 47). The seasonal character of the Bjørkum site also brings up associations with localities interpreted as *thing* sites and other types of multi-functional gathering places (cf. Sanmark 2009).

It is also interesting to note the presence of many cooking pits, a phenom-enon otherwise primarily connected with farm settlements of the Early Iron Age (Gustafson 2005b: 105). During the transition to the Late Iron Age, they become much rarer, and assemblages of cooking pits seem to be limited to more 'special' contexts, for instance courtyard sites (Olsen 2005: 338). It seems rea-sonable to link the large exterior hearths and cooking pits at Bjørkum to social gatherings with feasts and sharing of food to sustain and strengthen social bonds. A third of the structures contained unburnt bones and/or objects of bone. In a small pit, all bones except the head and the lower limbs of a decapitated lamb were found. The seemingly intentional deposition of unburned bones in cook-ing pits and in outdoor hearth features may indicate sacrifices, as well as com-plex ritual actions linked to the disposal of animal bones.

It may prove difficult to form a true picture of the functions Bjørkum had in the Late Iron Age. It does not seem to have been an ordinary farming settlement; to recognise any clear organisational principle behind the place-ment of the buildings is problematic, and obvious activity areas are lacking. Furthermore, both the range of production activities and their scale appear to have been relatively limited, and there are none of the traces one would expect of the handling of precious metals, such as are found at Viking-Age trading places. Finds of, among other things, a lead weight may, however, indicate some use of standardised weight units and barter. Maybe the answer is that Bjørkum had a number of different and overlapping functions. The problem of interpretation is therefore of a rather analytical nature. We lack clear concepts and models to describe a place like Bjørkum, and its relation to other places in the social, political and economic landscape of the Viking Age (Ramstad 2011; Ramstad et al. 2011).

Inner Sogn together with Lærdal represents a border area between the coast and the inland, a central 'crossroads' where communication routes over the mountains have always been seen as important (cf. Hougen 1944). In the archaeological material, this connection can be traced at least as far back as the Roman Iron Age. In historical times and in the medieval period there were several seasonal markets in Inner Sogn, the best known being the *Lusakaupang* and later on the *Lærdalsmarknad*. These markets attracted large crowds of peo-ple from inland communities in eastern Norway as well as from the agrarian settlements along the Sognefjord (Espe 1983). As we have tried to convey, less light has been shed on the smaller-scale meeting places, the *skeid* and other seasonal gathering places, where people from the east and the west met. We believe that such assemblies may be just as appropriate as models for the interpretation of the locality at Bjørkum as the better-known marketplaces down by the fjord.

Regionalisation and markets in the Viking Age

During the Viking Age and early medieval period there is an increase in the utilisation of outfield resources (Mikkelsen 1994; Baug this volume; Tveiten and Loftsgarden this volume). This indicates intensified resource specialisation and must in turn have entailed new forms of cooperation and exchange. We argue that stable political, economic and social networks were a prerequisite for this development, in that they made outfield resources a viable subsistence alternative for settlements in a marginal agricultural area. The seasonal assemblies or markets can be viewed as an embodiment of these networks. If one looks at iron production in isolation, we see limited production in the Late Iron Age, which develops into a production that far surpasses local demand in the early Middle Ages (Larsen 2009; Rundberget 2012). However, this extensive iron production took place almost exclusively in eastern parts of South Norway, the iron production in western Norway being modest at best (Tveiten and Loftsgarden this volume). Thus, the iron that was needed in western Norway most likely had to be imported from the east, from the 'Mountain Land'. Similarly, it is likely that at least from the twelfth century Denmark was dependent on iron from the Norwegian inland as well as from southern Sweden (Elsøe Jensen 2010).

The increased significance and value of products from the 'Mountain Land' may have created new opportunities for a number of different actors. We therefore have to envisage a situation in which the mountain plateaux functioned as an arena where different local communities from east and west were to a greater degree oriented towards exploiting the same geographic areas and resources. In addition, recent research indicates a more complex picture, in which the mountainous areas were apparently also being exploited by more mobile communities based on hunting and fishing, linked to people with a Finno-Ugric tradition and Sami identity (Bergstøl 2008; Gjerde 2010). While this naturally created new economic and socio-political opportunities, the intensified interaction between people from different landscapes and traditions also involved the potential for increased social tension and stress.

In communities with few or no urban centres, the most likely opportunity for extensive communication would have been assemblies where large groups of people met at regular intervals. Assemblies such as *skeid* would have been essential for extensive social interaction, making efficient distribution of innovations and ideas possible. Because assemblies of this kind gathered people from a wide array of regions together at one and the same time, they should be regarded as potentially decisive in connection with the development of cultural norms, including norms for material culture. Likewise, they may be regarded as an essential mechanism for regionalisation and the development of a common culture and identity in the Viking Age and the medieval period.

246   *Loftsgarden, Ramstad and Stylegar*

So, what about Bjørkum? The establishment of the locality coincides with a transitional period where the societies experienced profound structural changes. A good 200 years later, the end of the main phase coincides with a period when the West-Norwegian societies were involved in new and complex networks with the surrounding world, when raids and migrations westwards started and, somewhat later, the first processes connected with the emergence of super-regional government and the formation of a kingdom began.

The suggested parallels between Bjørkum and the assemblies known from later tradition shed an interesting light on the site and seem to open up a broader spectrum of interpretations than those founded on more abstract and formalised socio-political models. They bring forth some of the complexity one faces when trying to characterise or define different forms of gathering places and corresponding multi-functional sites – places and situations where there were not necessarily any strict divisions between ritual activities, alliance building, feasting and consumption, production and trade, games and competitions, or entertainment and recreation.

When we put all the pieces together, it is not hard to imagine that Bjørkum may have played a vital role in a social and economic landscape that not only included Lærdal and parts of Inner Sogn, but may also have had lines of communication to the mountain regions and further eastwards. Hypothetically, one could envisage Bjørkum as part of a larger network of similar places that were established during the transitional period leading to the Viking Age. In a landscape with scattered settlements, like Sogn and inland areas in South Norway, such places may have functioned as centres of communication or multi-functional meeting places: important institutions for maintaining and strengthening social relations.

References

Bergstøl, Jostein and Gaute Reitan 2008: Samer på Dovrefjell i vikingtiden: et bidrag til debatten omkring samenes sørgrense i forhistorisk tid. *Historisk Tidsskrift*, 87(1): 9–27.

Birkedahl, Peter and Erik Johansen 2000: The eastern Limfjord in the Geramanic Age and Viking Period. Internal Structures and External Relations. *Acta Archaeologica*, 71(1): 25–33.

Blom, Jan-Peter 1969: Ethnic and cultural differentiation. In: Barth, Fredrik (ed.): *Ethnic Groups and Boundaries: The Social Organization of Culture Difference*, pp. 74–86. Universitetsforlaget. Oslo.

Brendalsmo, Jan, Finn-Einar Eliassen and Terje Gansum 2009: *Den Urbane underskog: strandsteder, utvekslingssteder og småbyer i vikingtid, middelalder og tidlig nytid.* Novus forlag. Oslo.

Cartwright, Ben 2012: Shimmering cloth, like the river by this path. *Archaeological Textiles Review*, 54: 39–43.

Ekrem, Inger and Lars Boje Mortensen 2006: *Historia Norwegie.* Museum Tusculanum Press. København.

Elsøe Jensen, Jørgen 2010: *Gensidig afhængighed: en arv fra fortiden. Danmarks middelalderbyer - et vidnesbyrd om spredningen af vestlig civilisation.* Syddansk universitetsforlag. Odense.

Espe, Alfred 1983: Den gamle Lærdals-marknaden. In: 'Dæ va are tie dao': i Lærdal og Borgund: lokalhistorie, hermer, forteljingar, prologar og dikt, pp. 15–22. Lærdal Mållag. Lærdal.

Fønhus, Mikkjel 1924: Raudalsdansen: to fortellinger fra Valdres. Aschehoug. Kristiania.

Gjellebøl, Reier 1800: Beskrivelse over Sætersdalen i Christiansands Stift. Topographisk Journal For Norge, 26: 1–177.

Gjerde, Hege Skalleberg 2010: Tilfeldig? Neppe: finsk-ugriske smykker i Sør-Norge. Viking, LXXIII: 49–60.

Gustafson, Lil 2005a: Kokegroper i utmark. In: Gustafson, Lil, Tom Heibreen and Jes Martens (eds): De gåtefulle kokegroper. Varia 58: 207–14. Fornminneseksjonen, Kulturhistorisk Museum. Oslo.

—— 2005b: Om kokegroper i Norge. In: Gustafson, Lil, Tom Heibreen and Jes Martens (eds): De gåtefulle kokegroper. Varia 58: 103–7. Fornminneseksjonen, Kulturhistorisk Museum. Oslo.

Hage, Ingebjørg 1985: Skibotn: markedsplass og landsby. In: Mellem, Reidun (ed.): Menneske og miljø i Nord-Troms. Årbok 1985: 40–55. Nord-Troms Historielag.

Halvorsen, Lene Synnøve 2012: Vegetasjons- og jordbrukshistorie på Bjørkum (gbnr.3/2), Lærdal, Sogn og Fjordane. Prosjekt: E16 Stuvane–Seltun. De Naturhistoriske samlinger, Universitetsmuseet i Bergen. Bergen.

Hougen, Bjørn 1944: Gamle fjellstuetufter. Viking, VIII: 183–214.

Indrelid, Svein 2009: Arkeologiske undersøkelser i vassdrag: faglig program for Sør-Norge. Riksantikvaren. Oslo.

Iversen, Frode, Sarah Jane Semple, Natascha Mehler and Alexandra Sanmark 2013: The Assembly Project: Meeting-places in Northern Europe AD 400–1500 (TAP): Final report. https://dl.dropboxusercontent.com/u/44707393/TAP%20uploads/Nettversjoner/TAP%20final%20report%202013%20web.pdf, read 01.03.16

Larsen, Jan Henning 1980: Vikingtids handelsplass i Valle, Setesdal. In: Marstrander, Sverre and Øystein Kock Johansen (eds): Festskrift til Sverre Marstrander på 70-årsdagen. Universitetets Oldsaksamling skrifter. Ny rekke nr. 3: 143–8. Universitetets Oldsaksamling. Oslo.

—— 1981: Førhistoria i Valle kommune, Setesdal. Nicolay skrifter, vol. 1. Oslo.

—— 2009: Jernvinneundersøkelser. Varia 78. Fornminneseksjonen, Kulturhistorisk Museum. Oslo.

Loftsgarden, Kjetil and Camilla C. Wenn 2012: Gravene ved Langeid: Foreløpige resultater fra en arkeologisk utgraving. Nicolay, 117: 23–31.

Mikkelsen, Egil 1994: Fangstprodukter i vikingtidens og middelalderens økonomi: organiseringen av massefangst av villrein i Dovre. Universitetets Oldsaksamlings skrifter. Ny rekke nr. 18. Universitetets Oldsaksamling. Oslo.

Milek, Karen 2012: The roles of pit houses and gendered spaces on Viking-Age farmsteads in Iceland. Medieval Archaeology, 56(201): 85–130.

Mortensen, Mona 1997: For women only? Reflections on a Viking Age settlement at Stedje in Sogndal in Western Norway. Studien zur Sachsenforschung 10: 196–206.

Nørgård Jørgensen, Anne, Lars Jørgensen and Lone Gebauer Thomsen 2010: Assembly sites for cult, markets, jurisdiction and social relations. historic-ethnological analogy between North Scandinavian church towns, Old Norse assembly sites and pit house sites of the Late Iron Age and Viking Period. In: Boye, Linda, Per Ethelberg, Lene Lutz Heidemann, Pernille Kruse and Anne Birgitte Sørensen (eds): Det 61: Internationale Sachsensymposion 2010 Haderslev, Danmark, pp. 95–112. Wachholtz Verlag. Neumünster.

248 *Loftsgarden, Ramstad and Stylegar*

Ohnstad, Anders, Andreas Bjørkum and Jarle Bondevik 1991: *Djup fjord og høg himmel: festskrift til Anders Ohnstad på 80-årsdagen 27. juni 1991*. Norsk bokreidingslag. Bergen.

Olsen, Asle Bruen 2005: Et vikingtids tunanlegg på Hjelle i Stryn: en konservativ institusjon i et konservativt samfunn. In: Bergsvik, Knut Andreas and Asbjørn Engevik (eds): *Fra funn til samfunn: jernalderstudier tilegnet Bergljot Solberg på 70-årsdagen*. UBAS Nordisk, vol. 1: 319–56. Arkeologisk institutt, Universitetet i Bergen. Bergen.

Olsen, Magnus 1951: *V. Buskerud fylke; VI. Vestfold fylke; VII. Telemark fylke*, vol. 2. Norsk historisk kjeldeskrift-institutt. Oslo.

Øverland, Ole Andreas 1891: Thomaskirken paa Filefjeld. *Folkebladet*, 4.

―― 1898: Hestekampe i Norden. In: Øverland, Ole Andreas (ed.): *Norske historiske Fortællinger*, pp. 1–30. Cammermeyer. Kristiania.

Øye, Ingvild 2006: Kvinner som tradisjonsformidlere: Rom og redskaper. In: Barndon, Randi, Sonja M. Innselset, Kari Klæbo Kristoffersen and Trond Lødøen (eds): *Festskrift til Gro Mandt på 70-årsdagen*. UBAS nordisk, vol. 3: 439–53. Arkeologisk institutt, Universitetet i Bergen. Bergen.

Ramstad, Morten 2011: Bjørkum: Et innblikk i nye økonomiske og sosiale strukturer i tidlig vikingtid. *RISS*, 8(2): 40–53.

Ramstad, Morten, Lene Synnøve Halvorsen and Asle Bruen Olsen 2011: Bjørkum: feasting, craft production and specialisation on a Viking Age rural site in Norway. http://antiquity.ac.uk/projgall/ramstad328/ read 01.03.16.

Roland, Hilde 2001: *Prosjekt Nordmannsslepene*. Buskerud fylkeskommune. Drammen.

Rundberget, Bernt 2012: *Jernets dunkle dimensjon: jernvinna i sørlige Hedmark, sentral økonomisk faktor og premiss for samfunnsutvikling c. AD 700–1300*. Universitetet i Oslo, Det humanistiske fakultet. Oslo.

Sanmark, Alexandra 2009: The case of the Greenlandic assembly sites. *Journal of the North Atlantic*, 2: 178–92.

Skar, Johannes 1909: *Gamalt or Sætesdal*. Norli. Kristiania.

Solheim, Svale 1952: *Norsk sætertradisjon*. Aschehoug. Oslo.

―― 1956: Horse-fight and horse-race in Norse tradition. *Studia Norvegica Ethnologia and Folkloristica*, vol. III: 1–173. Aschehoug. Oslo.

―― 1961: Hestekamp. I Kulturhistorisk leksikon for nordisk middelalder, vol. VI. Gyldendal. Oslo.

Steen, Sverre 1929: *Ferd og fest: reiseliv i norsk sagatid og middelalder*. Frydenlunds bryggeri. Oslo.

Storm, Gustav 1880: *Monumenta historica Norvegiæ: latinske Kildeskrifter til Norges Historie i Middelalderen*. Brøgger. Kristiania.

Stylegar, Frans-Arne 2006: Skeidfoler og blothester. Hingestekamp og døderitualer i yngre jernalder. In: Glørstad, Håkon, Birgitte Skar and Dagfinn Skre (eds): *Historien i forhistorien. Festskrift til Einar Østmo på 60-årsdagen*. Kulturhistorisk museum Skrifter 4: 207–20. Kulturhistorisk museum, Universitetet i Oslo. Oslo.

―― 2009: Kaupangs omland og urbaniseringstendenser i norsk vikingtid In: Brendalsmo, Jan, Finn-Einar Eliassen and Terje Gansum (eds): *Den Urbane underskog. Strandsteder, utvekslingssteder og småbyer i vikingtid, middelalder og tidlig nytid*. Novus forlag. Oslo.

―― 2014: Horse-fights and cow-fights in Norwegian folk tradition. In: Teichert, Matthias (ed.): *Ergänzungsbände zum Reallexikon der germanischen Altertumskunde: Sport und Spiel bei den Germanen Nordeuropa von der römischen Kaiserzeit bis zum Mittelalter*, vol. 88: 457–66. De Gruyter. Berlin.

Tveite, Stein 1959: *Jord og gjerning: trekk av norsk landbruk i 150 år: Det Kongelige selskap for Norges vel, 1809–1959*. Bøndenes forlag. Kristiansand.

Vallevik, O.P. 1961: Grøndalsmarknaden, Hallingskeid-leikane og anna. *Hardanger historielag tidsskrift*, vol. III: 7–18.

Wahlborg, Anders S. 2012: Knivløs mann er livløs mann 'Knívleysurmaður er lívleysurmaður'. En analyse av knivene fra Bjørkum i Lærdal, Sogn og Fjordane. Unpublished Master's thesis. Universitetet i Bergen. Bergen.

Wille, Hans Jacob, Ludvig Daae and Hans Jacob Wille 1881: *Utrykte Optegnelser om Thelemarken*. A.W. Brøgger. Kristiania.

13 The urban hinterland

Interaction and law-areas in Viking and medieval Norway

Frode Iversen

Introduction

While previous research on urbanisation in Scandinavia has focused upon the role of the king and the Church as founders and developers of towns, less attention has been directed towards the economic and legal preconditions and ramifications of this development, in particular the way trade in the rural hinterlands of towns developed and was regulated in relation to an urban market. The legal assembly through which administrative and economic changes were channelled – the *thing* – was a particularly strong institution in Scandinavian societies compared to Central Europe (Taranger 1898; Imsen 1990, Iversen 2013). This may have played a crucial role in the economic development of urban hinterlands and control over inland markets, in particular regarding the surplus production of important commodities such as hunting produce and iron from the 'Mountain Land' (Holm et al. 2005; Rundberget 2012). What effect did urbanisation and emerging market power have on inland regions and law administration in the Viking Age and Middle Ages?

During the thirteenth and fourteenth centuries most of the Norwegian rural *lawthings* were relocated to coastal towns. Both urban and rural *lawthings* were administered by a lawman who, although situated in the town, nevertheless also actively participated in important *things* and legal meetings in the rural hinterland. Hence, legal matters drew people to certain towns. Previous research on Norse legal organisation has mainly addressed the internal administrative organisation of the medieval towns (Helle 2006: 114–18), to a lesser degree discussing the towns as legal centres for a greater hinterland. Here, I will investigate the impact relocating *lawthings* from rural to urban locations had on the organisation of rural jurisdictions and urban hinterlands. Were the jurisdictions adapted to the towns' need for greater hinterlands, and what was the role of the *thing* in these processes?

Before Christianity, in the Norse world the *thing* was the most important societal meeting place, both locally and regionally. The *thing* was the Archimedean point in Norse cosmology as well as the human world. Everything revolved around it. The Norse gods resolved their disputes at the *thing* (Løkka 2010). In the human world, delegates travelled great distances to annual meetings at *lawthings* (*lagting*). These had judicial and legislative authority over vast regions – the so-called provincial law-areas, of which there were about 20 in Scandinavia prior to the mid-thirteenth century (Iversen 2015).

The pre-Christian *thing*, however, was not purely a legal body, as it is in modern times. It also held political, economic and cultic authority. Separate trade laws, *Bjarkøyretter*, developed at the latest from around AD 1000 (Hagland and Sandnes 1997). Towns became, or were from the start, separated from the rural jurisdiction and obtained their own laws and courts (*mót*). Beyond the town boundary (*takmark*), rural law (*heraðs rett*) applied. In medieval Norway, the urban bailiff (*gjaldker*) was the head royal official in the town and also held the rights of prosecution. He led or took part in legal meetings at the town assembly (*mót*), and no doubt collected fines, taxes and tributes on behalf of the king. He was equivalent to the rural bailiff (*sýslumaðr/fogd*).

Compared to Europe, the degree of urbanisation in Scandinavia was low, particularly in Norway (Holt 2009). In 1135 the English chronicler Ordericus Vitales knew only six *civitas* in the Kingdom of Norway: Konghelle, Borg, Oslo, Tønsberg, Bergen and Nidaros. By the end of the Middle Ages there were only 16 towns in Norway, compared to more than a hundred in Denmark and 40–50 in Sweden (Jensen 1990; Helle 2006). In Norway most medieval towns were royal foundations (Brendalsmo and Molaug 2014). According to written sources of the thirteenth century, Nidaros was founded by Olaf Tryggvasson (995–1000), Bergen by Olaf Kyrre (1066–93), Borg by Olaf Haraldsson (1015–28) and Oslo by Harald Hardrada (1046–66). There has been much discussion on the time of foundation, comparing written and archaeological evidence (Molaug 2007), but recent research tends to highlight consistency between the sources, in particular for Nidaros (Christophersen and Nordeide 1994) and Oslo (Schia 1991: 122–32). This is not quite so clear for Bergen (Hansen 2005). The saga phrase *setja kaupstad* may indicate when an existing market or 'embryo town' became a judicial entity and achieved formal trading rights (Christophersen 1998). It has, for instance, been argued that Harald Bluetooth established Oslo, while Harald Hardrada empowered it with certain judicial rights (Schia 1991).

Only one Norwegian town, Skien, seems to have been founded on aristocratic initiative, while Stavanger and Hamar developed and grew when bishops' seats were established there in the twelfth century (Brendalsmo and Molaug 2014). Concerning Tønsberg, the sagas give no foundation history, but recently the archaeologists Jan Brendalsmo and Petter Molaug (2014) have concluded that here, too, the king played a major role in the initial phase. The Norwegian kings seem to have had a relatively stronger grip on trade and towns compared to their European counterparts. There were few towns, and most of them were subordinated to the king. The initiative behind the archeologically known trading sites predating the medieval towns of Norway is debated. Dagfinn Skre (2007) has suggested that the Danish king Gorm founded Kaupang in Vestfold in the early ninth century, while this is more

252   *Frode Iversen*

uncertain for the newly discovered, contemporary trading site of Heimdal, near Gokstad in Vestfold.

Legal assemblies must have been a propelling factor for processes of territorialisation. At the *thing* attendees from different communities met. Both the royal and ecclesiastical administrative landscape echoed the hierarchy of the *thing* institution, with local, supra-local and regional meetings. My point of departure is thus to (a) reconstruct the rural jurisdictions of Norway in the Viking Age and early Middle Ages (AD 800–1150), and (b) investigate how they changed in the High and late Middle Ages (AD 1150–1537), when the majority of Norwegian towns reached their peak. The hypothesis is that these areas were also the main inland trading areas for the medieval towns. The precise state of the juridical division and organisation in the twelfth and thirteenth centuries is still to some extent unresolved and has been the subject of debate. By reconstructing the judicial areas I hope to shed light on the changing hinterland of the towns. Obviously, towns became jurisdictions in their own right, but what was their impact on the organisation of provincial law territories? This will lay the foundation for subsequent discussion of changes in how people interacted within the emerging Kingdom of Norway. I will focus on South Norway, as this area had more towns in the Middle Ages, and the changes in administrative organisation were profound. I will also concentrate on the interaction between coastal areas with towns, and the interior valleys without urban centres.

Background: law–areas and trade regulations

According to *Historia Norwegie* (1150–75), Norway was divided into three main geographic areas: The Coastal Land (*Zona itaque maritime*), the Central or Mountain Land (*Mediterranea zona / De montains Norwegie*) and the land of the Sami people (*De Finnis*), a division I shall retain in this context (Ekrem and Mortensen 2003: 54–64) (Figure 13.1). There were four provincial law-areas (*patriae*) in the Coastal Land, and four in the Mountain Land. These were further subdivided into provinces, 30 in the Coastal Land and 12 in the Mountain Land. These 42 regions in eight law-areas were the fundamental regions of human interaction, judicially speaking, in Norway in the twelfth century. These were further divided into about 550 local *thing* districts. The main law-areas and their divisions are listed in Table 13.1. These differ considerably from the territorial organisation that emerges during the period 1250–1350, as first pointed out by historian Gustav Storm (1880) and discussed by Gustav Indrebø (1937: 41–3), Asgaut Steinnes (1946) and Eyvind Fjeld Halvorsen (1995), among others. The question is how towns influenced the administrative 'legal landscape'.

Regarding South Norway, my hypothesis is that the axes of human interaction prior to urban development followed the topographic, economic and climatic zones, which had similar legal requirements. Coastal areas connected with other coastal areas, and mountain and upland communities with each

The urban hinterland 253

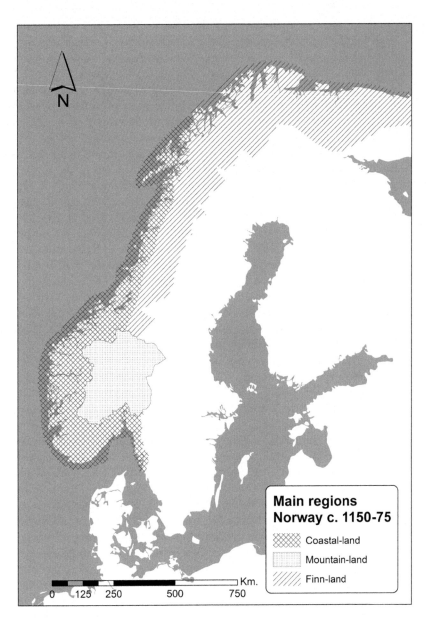

Figure 13.1 The major divisions of Norway, according to *Historia Norwegie* (c. 1150–75).

other. There was less interaction between the coast and the interior, which may have changed with the rise of towns and trading centres during the Viking Age and Middle Ages. Coastal towns stimulated increased trade with inland

254 *Frode Iversen*

areas, and thus had a 'civilising' impact. This evolved along vertical axes of identity and economy, perpendicular to older law territories and topography. In the High Middle Ages, the law-parish system was redefined, which expresses the underlying socio-economic development, where inland resources were increasingly drawn into the market economy of the coastal towns.

In *Historia Norwegie*, the maritime zone is described as a *Decapolis*, an area with ten towns. Gustav Storm (1880: 76) identified these as Nidaros, Bergen, Oslo, Borg, Tønsberg and Konghelle, together with Stavanger, Veøy, Skien and Kaupanger in Sogn (Figure 13.5). However, the precise number may have been somewhat unimportant for the anonymous author. He alludes to the 'learned' concept of the ten cities of the Decapolis. Two of the gospels mention the Decapolis; it was the core area of Christianity (Matt. 4: 25; 2 Macc. 5: 20). Furthermore, the Decapolis is mentioned by the Roman historian Pliny the Elder (AD 23–79) in *Naturalis Historia* (N.H. 5.16.74). The towns of the Decapolis have traditionally been seen as bridgeheads for both Greek and Roman culture in the Semitic areas of Judea and Syria, and these towns also represented strongholds on the Roman Empire's eastern border. The author of *Historia Norwegie* may have associated the Decapolis with a form of Christian 'civilising' power, radiating from the coastal towns. In reference to the interpretation of the prose Edda *Gylfaginning*, which explains the creation and destruction of the Norse gods' world, both archaeologist Frans-Arne Stylegar (2004) and religious historian Gro Steinsland (1991: 24) have pointed out differences in cosmological concepts regarding the coast and the inlands in Norse mythology. Therefore, it is tempting to ask: did the coastal towns have a 'civilising' force? Was the 'wild' inland territory – the Mountain Land with its rich resources – amalgamated into the Norwegian realm as a result of urbanisation?

In 1384 the child-king Olav IV Håkonsson of Norway and Denmark, under the guardianship of his mother, Queen Margrete Valdemarsdotter, declared that all trade within certain areas north of Bergen should take place in old towns with jurisdiction, *takmark* (NgL III: 121; RN VII: 1191). Competition from the Hanseatic towns, such as Lübeck, Hamburg and Bremen, increased in the Holy Roman Empire, and stock fish from northern Norway and timber from eastern Norway were important commodities on the European market. In this competitive situation, the kings of Norway tried to reinforce Norwegian towns by granting them a trade monopoly within certain areas. This may only have represented confirmation and enforcement of existing customary rights, but clearly the intension was to secure royal rights and income from trade on the home market (Blom 1967).

The trading territories listed in 1384 coincided with customary rural jurisdictions, namely law-parishes and counties. All trade within Finnmark and Helgeland (= Hålogaland law-parish) was to take place in the town of Vågan. Trondheim received similar rights with respect to Namdalen, Nordmøre and Trøndelag, which is equivalent to the Frostathing area, apart from the southernmost county, Romsdal, where the old royal villa, trading and assembly site of Veøy had a monopoly. The same applied to Borgund in the case of Sunnmøre – the northernmost county in the law-area of the Gulathing. Trade elsewhere, in fjords and fishing villages, was declared illegal (NgL III: 121; RN VII: 1191).

We lack direct information on the trade monopoly and the rural hinterlands of towns in South-East Norway before the fifteenth century. Trade in timber increased from the thirteenth century, and many 'loading sites' for timber purchase evolved along the coast, such as Son and Drøbak in the district of Follo; Koppervik, Bragernes and Strømsø by the estuary of the Drammen river; Sandefjord, Snekkestad and Melsomvik in Vestfold; and Langesund at Skien. The historian Knut Helle claims the trade contravened the monopolies of the old towns (Helle 2006: 129). In 1299 a royal ban was imposed on all traders against the sale of goods outside the towns, while farmers were still allowed to trade with each other (NgL III: 42; RN II: 1011). Later, in 1302, this ban was explicitly directed against foreign traders (Bagge et al. 1973: 218). The earlier town privileges, for example that of Oslo from 1358 (RN VI: 469), do not specify the primary hinterland, while in 1358 Skien renewed its rights to trade 'hard stone' (hone stones), grain and other commodities in the area of Skienssyssel (RN VI: 489). During the fifteenth century several towns obtained formalised exclusive trading rights: Stavanger received exclusive rights within Stavanger Diocese (1425), Marstrand in Båhuslen (1442), Oslo in Oslo Diocese (1445) and Skien in the county of Telemark and interior areas (1473).

The origin and organisation of *lawthings*

It is attested that Norwegian kings moved rural *lawthings*, for example the Eidsivathing and Gulathing, from one location to another, and established new ones, such as the Borgarthing (Taranger 1898). However, it is unlikely that royal power dealt directly with the geographical organisation of jurisdictions in the early phases. The development towards larger law-areas cannot be understood purely from a power perspective, with the king as the sole instigator. I regard this as a process where both *bottom-up* and *top-down* forces worked together. The population had its legal needs. Local communities and societies could benefit from being part of a larger law-area. The emergence of larger regions could, for example, increase mobility and trade. On the other hand, royal power required an institution that could legitimise the king's power and negotiate on behalf of the people.

It is often claimed that there was just one *lawthing* per law-area in Norway in the Middle Ages: the Eidsivathing, Gulathing, Frostathing and Borgarthing. However, in 1223 there were two lawmen and two *lawthings* in each of the major law-areas in Norway (Table 13.2; Figures 13.2 and 13.3). The exception was the Frostathing area, where there were three *lawthings*, including one in Jämtland (Seip 1934; Indrebø 1936).

The German legal historian Kondrad Maurer (1907: 8) proposed that the law-parish system (*lagsogn*) appeared in the late Middle Ages. A law-parish is a

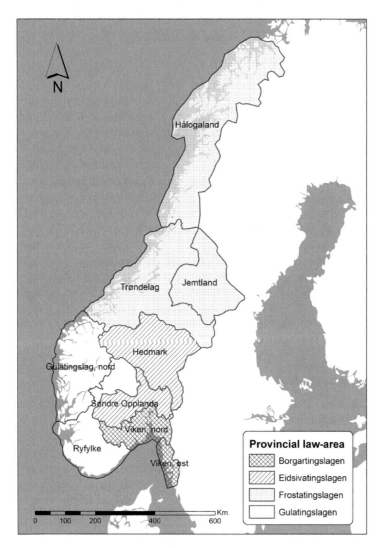

Figure 13.2 The law-parishes of Norway in 1223, according to the Saga of Håkon Håkonsson.

subdivision of a law-area. However, Maurer did not include the evidence of Håkon Håkonsson's Saga, which specifies nine lawmen in Norway in 1223 and the law-parishes for most of them. The historians Jens Arup Seip (1934) and Gustav Indrebø (1936) were the first to discuss the law-parish system in detail. Indrebø suggested that it was established in the twelfth century, when lawmen became royal officials. On the other hand, Seip was not convinced that all the lawmen from the eastern provinces participated in the *hofdingiafundr* in Bjørgvin in 1223, a political meeting where the leading men of the kingdom met. He believed there were even more lawmen in earlier periods, as indicated by the administrative geography stated in *Historia Norwegie* (Seip 1934: 12).

I contend that the law-parish system may have an earlier origin. There are several arguments for this. First, this appears to have been the situation in both Denmark and Sweden. There were four or five *lawthings* (*landsting*) in each of the three Danish provincial law-areas in the thirteenth century (Jørgensen 1940; Lerdam 2001; Vogt and Tamm 2009; Andersen 2010). Similarly, in Sweden there were multiple *lawthings* within the same law-area. Snorri Sturluson's description of the Kingdom of Svitjod is illustrative (Hkr, King Olav Haraldsson's Saga: 77). Here, we gain insight into a formation process where several autonomous territories amalgamated into a 'legal cooperative'. Many of the regions had their own laws and legislative *things*. The cooperative had decided that, when two laws were in conflict, one law should override the other as *lex superior* – the Uppsala Law. The lawman from the 'weightiest' area, Tiundaland ('Land with Ten Hundreds'), outranked the other lawmen from less weighty areas, such as Attundaland ('Land with Eight Hundreds') and Fjärdrundaland ('Land with Four Hundreds') (Iversen 2013). A market was held in Uppsala for a week in connection with the annual assembly (Hkr, King Olav Haraldsson's Saga: 77).

To summarise: I do not envisage the situation in Norway in 1223 as something new or associated with royal organisation, as Indrebø has suggested. On the contrary, I find it plausible that, for instance, Ranrike (Båhuslen) in present-day Sweden had its own *lawthing* prior to its integration into the Borgarthing area in the eleventh century. I see the law-parish division of 1223 as a remnant of this. The question is how these law-parishes changed as urban influence increased.

Methods and materials: the scheme of the study

The first stage of investigating this hypothesis is to identify and reconstruct the 'legal landscape' in Norway during the Viking Age and Middle Ages (800–1537). Four main sources are available for this purpose: *Historia Norwegie*, c. 1150–75, Håkon Håkonsson's Saga for the year 1223, a mid-sixteenth-century legal manuscript (AM: 94 4°) and Christian IV's law of 1604. The latter two provide lists of the Norwegian *lawthings* of the time. Together with charter evidence from c. 1250–1550, this enables a discussion of the changes in the 'legal landscape' of Norway before and after c. 1250–1300.

The dating and purpose of *Historia Norwegie* is much debated. Recently, Lars Boje Mortensen (Ekrem and Mortensen 2003) has convincingly argued that Inger Ekrem's (1998) classic hypothesis must be reconsidered. She claimed that *Historia Norwegie* was written prior to the foundation of the Norwegian Church Province (1152/3). The aim was to convince the Pope and the cardinals that

258   *Frode Iversen*

Norway was well organised, mature and deserved the status of an independent church province, seceding from the Danish Church Province (*Prouincia danorum*), with its centre at Lund (Nyberg 1991). However, as Mortensen has pointed out, this is not very likely. According to *Historia Norwegie*, Iceland paid tribute to Norway, which did not occur before 1264 in secular terms. Therefore, the passage probably refers to the tithes the bishops of Iceland paid to the archbishop in Nidaros. This suggests that *Historia Norwegie* was written after 1152/53, when the Nidaros Church Province was established. Furthermore, since Jämtland is not mentioned as part of the Kingdom of Norway, which it was from 1177, Mortensen dates the saga to c. 1150–75.

The identification of the regions in *Historia Norwegie* is relatively unproblematic, and is discussed at length by Gustav Storm (1880). In more recent times, this has been studied by, among others, Frans-Arne Stylegar (2004). *Historia Norwegie* states that there were 30 *prouinciae* in the Coastal Land. P.A. Munch believed the number 30 ('XXX') was incorrect and considered Hålogaland as a single shire (*fylke*) (Munch 1850: 30). Munch's authority overruled the actual statement in the source; surprisingly, Storm followed his lead and corrected 30 to 22 in his source-critical edition (Storm 1880: 76), something which has been repeated in later translations. Even the newest source-critical edition, from 2003, gives this figure (Ekrem 1998: 33, note 113; Ekrem and Mortensen 2003: 179, note 105).

In my opinion, such an error is unlikely. The coastline from Hålogaland to Karløy stretches for over 600 km. From Vennesund to Vegestav it must have been over 1500 km, and a further subdivision of this large area seems probable (Iversen 2015). Twenty-one provinces are specified for the remaining Coastal Land. If there are indeed 30 provinces in total, Hålogaland must, therefore, have had nine provinces. This seems to equate with the known historical divisions of 'half-shires' and counties or *syssel* (*sýsla*) in Hålogaland, extending northward up to Troms (Indrebø 1935). I have, therefore, chosen to follow the primary source, and propose nine provinces in Hålogaland, as shown in Table 13.1.

The historian Eyvind Fjeld Halvorsen (1995) has pointed out how little Snorri and other thirteenth-century saga writers knew about people and the former administrative organisation of *Upplǫnd*. In the Kings' Sagas *Upplǫnd* almost always refers to the Eidsivathing area, but the Icelandic authors knew little about events here in the eleventh and tenth centuries (Halvorsen 1995: 51, 54). This is one of the reasons why *Historia Norwegie* is an especially important source for this particular area (Robberstad 1951). In regard to the Mountain Land, my interpretations differ somewhat from Storm's (1880: 81) suggestions. I believe Land, Hadeland and Tverrdalene were the neighbouring provinces to Ringerike, and Toten to Gudbrandsdalen. Toten was connected to the *lawthing* at Hamar in 1337, and therefore probably part of the northern law-parish in 1223 (DN III: 191). This law-parish may have comprised *patriae* 3 and 4 in the Mountain Land, according to the division in *Historia Norwegie* (see below). This area probably coincided with the land held by the 'rebel leader' Sigurd Erlingsson Ribbung in the early 1220s. He established a seat on the little island of Frognøy, central to the area, and close to the bishop's residence at Storøya

The urban hinterland 259

and the royal villa of Stein. According to Håkon Håkonsson's Saga, most people from Telemark to Vardal submitted to Sigurd (HH: 75).

I do not consider Råbyggelag as part of Telemark, as Storm believed and Stylegar also suggests (Stylegar 2004). The description *remotis ruribus*, 'remote or far-flung rural areas', fits well with the elongated valley of Numedal. There are further arguments for this, such as that Numedal was subject to the Skien *lawthing* in the late Middle Ages (Taranger 1915). In the *Landnåmabok* (*Hauksbok*), a 'Telemark-*thing*' is mentioned (ch. 314). This was allegedly located near a mountain pass, close to *Tinz dal*, which is probably identifiable as present-day Tinn. A 'Telemark-*thing*' at Tinn would only have been central to the province if it included Numedal. Furthermore, Råbyggelag was neither part of the Skien *lawthing* nor of the Diocese of Hamar, but was subject to the Gulathing from 1274 at the latest. The suffix *-lag* (ON *lög*) in the name *Råbyggelag* means law, which indicates that Råbyggelag was originally an independent law-area. If Råbyggelag was, however, part of the Mountain Land, I would expect it to have been labelled a province, or preferably a *patria*, which is not the case. In other respects, I follow Storm and share his viewpoint that the four *patriae* in the Mountain Land were *separate legislative districts* (Storm 1880: XXVII).

Håkon Håkonsson's Saga is the main source for the law-parishes in the early thirteenth century. As previously mentioned, this saga records that nine lawmen met at the *hofdingiafundr* in Bjørgvin in 1223 (HH: 85–95; Helle 1972: 248). The subject of this important political meeting was the right to the Norwegian throne. The lawmen's opinion was given considerable importance in the conflict between Håkon Håkonsson and Earl Skule.

In addition to charters, I have used two other sources concerning *lawthings* from 1300–50. Evidence is drawn from Christian IV's 1604 law, which provides a detailed overview of the *lawthings* in Norway, in addition to a mid-sixteenth-century manuscript which also lists the country's *lawthings* (AM94 4°; Ngl III: 4–6; Hallanger and Brandt 1855: 7, note 1; Indrebø 1935: 74). It is a copy of a manuscript from c. 1320 of the 1274 rural law of Magnus the Lawmender (AM: 322fol; NgL IV: 502). However, the list itself is a postscript, probably added by Peder Claussøn Friis (1545–1614), according to Anna Catharina Horn at the University of Oslo (correspondence via email 1 March 2012). These sources have to be used retrospectively and compared to the older charter evidence.

The two later sources show 12 or 13 *lawthings* in Norway, not the nine mentioned in 1223. There was a new rural *lawthing* at Agdesiden and two new town *lawthings*. In addition, several rural *lawthings* were relocated to towns.

The source AM: 94 4° indicates three *lawthings* within the Frostathing area: Steigen, Trondheim and Jämtland. There were three in the Gulathing area, namely Bergen, Stavanger and Agdesiden, and four in the Eidsivathing area – Oslo, Skien with Telemark, Tønsberg and Hedmark with Oppland. Finally, there were also two *lawthings* in the Viken area: Fredrikstad and Båhus. It is worth noting that Foss *lawthing* is not mentioned, despite the fact there were assemblies at Foss in 1450, 1558 and 1604 (see below). Another curiosity is that the town *lawthings* in Skien, Tønsberg and Oslo are listed under the

260 *Frode Iversen*

Eidsivathing area, and not the Borgarthing area, as their locations would suggest. However, it is clear that parts of the earlier Eidsivathing district were now under the jurisdiction of lawmen in these very towns: thus, Upper Telemark and Numedal were subject to Skien, Tverrdalene to Tønsberg, and Ringerike and Romerike to Oslo, an issue I will return to later.

The charters issued by lawmen have previously been catalogued by Eivind Vågslid (1930). Indrebø's (1936) article on the Norwegian lawmen and his critique of Seip's (1934) interpretation of the law-parish system have been useful. These two works diverge on some points, and my conclusions also differ somewhat from these, something that will be explained as we proceed. A review of the Swedish charters indicates that Aslak Petersson, the lawman in Viken, issued a charter from Foss, Båhuslen on a Wednesday after 23 June 1450 (SDHK: 26289). The letter was not published in *Diplomatarium Norvegicum*. Another charter dated 25 June 1444 was issued at Foss by the same lawman, in *Laghmanz stadh*, the lawmans-place (DN XI: 178). According to the law of 1604, one of the two fixed *lawthings* at Foss was to be held on the first working day after St Hans's Day (St John's Eve), namely 24 June, which fits well with both letters. Foss is centrally located in Båhuslen, and it is reasonable to assume it was both the seat of the lawman and location of the *lawthing*. This was an old assembly site. There is mention of a *thing* by Foss Church in the Sverris Saga (SS: 167) for the year c. 1200, concerning a battle between King Sverre and his rivals during the civil wars. Only archaeological excavation could help date the Foss *lawthing* more precisely.

There is no written evidence to say Tjølling was a *lawthing*. Both the name, ON *þjóðalyng* or 'People's Heath', and the archaeological discoveries in 2010 indicate that Tjølling was an important *thing* site, as previous research has also suggested. I consider it the likely *lawthing* for Vingulsmark, Vestfold and Grenland, a subject I will return to later.

I have reconstructed the law-areas with a GIS application, using land registers and tax records to reconstruct the exact areas. I assume that the Mountain Land was identical to the Eidsivathing and the Diocese of Hamar, with the exception of Valdres and Hallingdal, which were under the Gulathing and also the Diocese of Stavanger. Neither was Solør part of Hamar Diocese (DN XXI: 130). Jørgen H. Marthinsen's map of the law-parishes c. 1320 in *Norsk historisk leksikon* (Imsen and Winge 2004) has been useful for seeing concurrences with Seip's and Indrebø's results.

Results

The Coastal Land was composed of four *patriae*: Viken in the east (*Sinius orientalis*), the south and west coast (*Gulacia*), Trøndelag in Middle Norway (*Trondheimia*) and Hålogåland, north of Trøndelag (*Halogia*). This matches the areas of the Borgarthinglag, Gulathingslag and Frostathingslag, including Hålogaland, respectively. The Gulathing area was subdivided into six provinces, while in Trøndelag there were eight provinces surrounding the Trondheim Fjord and three along the open seacoast.

The Mountain Land also consisted of four *patriae*, with 12 provinces in total, corresponding to the area of the Eidsivathing. Their identification is somewhat vague, as previously discussed. Toten is, as mentioned, assigned to the fourth *patria* (see Table 13.1).

How does this fit with the well-informed Saga of Håkon Håkonsson? At the Bjørgvin meeting in 1223, three lawmen from the Frostathing area attended, while the Gulathing, Viken and 'Upland' areas were each represented by two. The lawmen from Frostathing represented the areas Trøndelag, Hålogaland and Jämtland. Both the *þingasaga* and the Frostathing Law consider Hålogaland as part of the Frostathing law-area (F X: 3; F XVI: 2; Storm 1877: 15; Indrebø 1935: 75).

Dagfinn Bonde was a lawman of Gulathing, and Amunde Remba represented Ryfylke. There were also two lawmen from *Eidsivathing* (the Uplands) at the meeting in 1223. Tore Lagmann (Gudmundsson) was the lawman for the southern 'Uplands' (Seip 1934: 12). Sakse of Haug was the lawman for Hedmark, and the *lawthing* was located in the vicinity of Hamar. Moving on, Tord Skolle was the lawman for the area east of the Svinesund, namely Båhuslen. It appears his father and forefathers had previously also been lawmen here. It is reasonable to associate them with the *lawthing* at Foss or Baholm near Konghelle. Øystein Roesson was probably the lawman for the remainder of the Borgarthing law-area, more specifically the law-parishes of Vingulsmark, Vestfold and Grenland (Indrebø 1936: 492). Tjølling is central to this area, which makes it a likely candidate for the location of the *lawthing*. Around 1200, a man called Simon at the Tomb in Råde is mentioned as a lawman (DN I 3; Indrebø 1936: 492), potentially for this law-parish.

When this picture is compared to younger sources, interesting patterns appear. King Christian IV's law of 1604 gives detailed information on the *lawthings* in Norway, including the meeting dates (see Table 13.3). In total, 13 *lawthings* are mentioned, including the town *lawthings* at Tønsberg and in Oslo. Båhuslen had been divided into two law-parishes, with *lawthings* at both Båhus and Foss. There appears also to have been a *lawthing* at Agdesiden, which was 'held on rotation' between four counties (*syssel*). The urban *lawthings* in Oslo, Fredrikstad, Tønsberg and Skien met four to five times a year. The frequency of meetings was somewhat less for the other *lawthings*, down to once or twice a year. The king's bailiff (*fogd*) had an obligation to attend the *lawthing*. The attendees of the *lawthings* were appointed by the bailiffs at the local *things* (*syssel*) on Laetare Sunday (the fourth Sunday in Lent) (C IV: ch. 1).

Discussion: towns and *things*

I will now discuss the changing administrative division of legal matters in Norway, in relation to towns and trading areas. Which areas changed, and were these changes due to increased urban impact on the organisation of rural law-areas?

The Eidsivathing law-area was reorganised after the civil wars (c. 1130–1240), when its outer parts (Øvre Telemark, Numedal, Tverrdalene and Ringerike)

Table 13.1 Proposed subdivision of districts and provinces in Norway in *Historia Norvegie*, c. 1150–75

Main area	District (patria)	Municipality (province)	Identification
Zona itaque maritime The Coastal Land 10 towns (Decapolis) • 4 *patriae* • 22 or 30 provinces	**Sinus orientalis** Borgarthing (Viken)	4 provinces from the border with Denmark to Rygjabit	Ranrike, Vingulsmark, Vestfold, Grenland **4 provinces**
	Gulacia Gulathing (south and west coast to the island of Mien)	6 provinces. More was most remote (= northerly). Valdres and Hallingdal were subject to the Gulathing	Agder, Rogland, Hordland, Sogn, Firda, Sunnmore **6 provinces**
	Trondhemia Frostathingslag (Trondelag)	11 provinces (8 by the fjord and 3 beyond)	Orkdalen, Gauldalen, Strinda, Stjordalen, Skaun, Verdalen, Sparbuen, Inneroya, Romsdalen, Nordmore, Namdalen **11 provinces**
	Halogia Frostathingslag (Hålogland, north to Vegestav, bordering Bjarmeland)	30 provinces in total, and therefore nine provinces in Hålogaland	Herøy half-shire (Alstadhaug *syssel*), Rødøy half-shire, Bodo *syssel*, Steigar *syssel*, Lofoten *syssel*, Ulvoy *syssel* (Vesterålen), Andenes *syssel*, Senja, Troms **9 provinces**
Mediterranea zona/De montains Noruegie (Eidsivathing/the Uplands) The Mountain Land • 4 *patriae* • 12 provinces	*Patria 1*	Romerike and Ringerike plus unnamed neighbouring provinces (plural)	Romerike, Ringerike, Neighbour 1 (Land), Neighbour 2 (Hadeland), Neighbour 3 (Sigdal, Modum, Krodsherad) **5 provinces**
	Patria 2	Telemark and unnamed remote rural areas (*remotis ruribus*)	Upper Telemark and Numedal. Telemark without Grenland and parts that were under Oslo Diocese (DN IX: 186), Brunkeberg was under Hamar Diocese in 1357 (DN III: 291). **1 province**
	Patria 3	Hedmark with Elvdalene	Hedmark and Østerdalen with Solor/Vinger **2 provinces**
	Patria 4	Gudbrandsdalen with Loar and unnamed neighbouring provinces (plural). The Dovre range marks the boundary.	Gudbrandsdalen Lom (Loar) Neighbour 1 (Lesja) Neighbour 2 (Toten) (see DN III: 191) **4 provinces**
	Borders Götaland in Sweden and stretches north to Trondheim.		

Table 13.2 A suggestion for the law-parish divisions in Norway in 1223

Provincial law-area	Lawman in 1223	Law-parish	Lawthing	Provinces in Historia Norwegie (HN)
Frostathing	Gunnar Grjonbak Bonde	Trøndelag	Frosta	11 provinces (see Table 13.1)
	Bjarne Mårdsson	Hålogaland	Steigen	9 provinces (see Table 13.1)
	Torstein Åsmundsson	Jämtland	Jamtamót	Not part of Norway when HN was written
Gulathing	Dagfinn Bonde	Gula	Gulathing	Hordaland, Sogn, Firda, Sunnmøre
	Åmunde Remba	Ryfylke	Avaldsnes	Rogaland, Agder (+ Valdres, Hallingdal)
Borgarthing	Øystein Roesson	Borgarthing	(Tjølling?)	Vingulsmark, Vestfold, Grenland
	Tord Skolle	Viken, east of Svinesund	Foss	Vika (= Ranrike/ Båhuslen)
Eidsivathing	Tore Lagmann	Søndre Opplanda	(Stein?)	*Patriae* 3 and 4 (see Table 13.1)
	Sakse of Haug	Hedmark	Åker	*Patriae* 1 and 2 (see Table 13.1)

Source: Håkon Håkonsson's Saga.

Table 13.3 *Lawthing* and meeting dates according to Christian IV's law of 1604

Region	Location in 1604	Time as of 1604	Date
Båhuslen *lawthing* (town)	Båhus	1) the Monday before St Bottolf's/ Botwulf of Thorney's Day	17 June (St Bottolf)
		2) the Monday after *Fastelaven* Sunday	the Sunday before Ash Wednesday
Viken *lawthing*	Foss	1) the first working day after the Feast of the Conversion of St Paul	25 January (St Paul's Day)
		2) the first working day after St John's Eve (St Hans's Day)	24 June (St John's Day)
Borgarthing (town)	Fredrikstad	1) the first day after Twelfth Night	6 January
		2) the Monday after Laetare Sunday	the Monday after the fourth Sunday in Lent
		3) the second Tuesday after Easter (*Tokketirsdag*)	the second Tuesday after Easter
		4) the day after St Vitus and Modesti	15 June (St Vitus's Day)
		5) the first Sunday after Winter Night	14 October

(continued)

Table 13.3 (continued)

Region	Location in 1604	Time as of 1604	Date
Oslo *lawthing* (town)	Oslo	1) three days before and after St Paul's Day 2) three days before and after Laetare Sunday 3) three days after *Tokketirsdag* 4) three days before and after St John's Eve 5) Three days before and after Winter Night	25 January (St Paul's Day) three days before and after the fourth Sunday in Lent three days after the second Tuesday after Easter 24 June 14 October
Eidsvoll *lawthing*	Eidsvoll	1) St. Bottolf's Day	17 June
Tønsberg *lawthing* (town)	Tønsberg	1) the first Monday after Twelfth Night 2) the Monday after Laetare Sunday 3) *Tokketirsdag* 4) three days after St Bottolf's Day 5) Autumn Feast of the Cross	6 January the Monday after the fourth Sunday in Lent the second Tuesday after Easter three days after 17 June (St Bottolf's Day) 14 September
lawthing in Oppland	Not named (Hamar/ Åker?)	1) *Tokketirsdag* 2) Martinmas	the second Tuesday after Easter 11 November
Skiens *lawthing* (town)	Skien	1) three days before and after Laetare Sunday 2) three days before and after St Bottolf's Day 3) three days before and after Martinmas 4) *Tokketirsdag*	the fourth Sunday in Lent 17 June (St Bottolf's Day) 11 November the second Tuesday after Easter
lawthing in Agdesiden	Mandal Lista Nødnes Råbyggelag	1) the Monday after Trinity Sunday 2) Nativity of Mary Feast Day 3) the next working day after Michaelmas 4) the next working day after St John's Eve	the second Monday after Pentecost 8 September 30 September 25 June
Stavanger *lawthing* (town)	Stavanger	1) St Bottolf's Day 2) Autumn Feast of the Cross	17 June (St Bottolf's Day) 14 September
Bergen *lawthing* (town)	Bergen	1) St Bottolf's Day	17 June (St Bottolf's Day)
Trondheim *lawthing* (town)	Trondheim Jemtland	1) St Bottolf's Day 2) 14 days before St John's Eve	17 June (St Bottolf's Day) 10 June
Steigen *lawthing*	Steigen The fishing villages in Finnmark	1) St Bottolf's Day 2) every third year	17 June (St Bottolf's Day)

The urban hinterland   265

came under the jurisdiction of the Borgarthing. Stronger links were established with the royally controlled coastal towns of Skien, Tønsberg and Oslo. The reorganisation of the Mountain Land may be seen in the context of the civil wars. The last 'rebel leader' of the 'Mountain Land', Sigurd Erlingsson Ribbung, died in 1226, and when the powerful Duke Skule Bårdsson from Trøndelag was killed in 1240, internal resistance was weakened. King Håkon Håkonsson strengthened his position and kingdom.

I distinguish nine probable law-parishes in Norway in 1223, in four law-areas: the Borgarthing area, consisting of two law-parishes (Figure 13.2) – (1) Viken/ Ranrike (Båhuslen) and (2) Vingulsmark, Vestfold and Grenland; the Gulathing area, with another two – (3) the southern (Ryfylke) and (4) the northern law-parish; three in the Frostathing area – (5) Hålogaland, (6) Trøndelag and (7) Jämtland; and two in the Eidsivathing area – (8) the southern and (9) the northern law-parish (cf. Table 13.2). These divisions coincide with Indrebø's (1936: 491–3) interpretation. I shall review the known and possible *lawthings*, and compare these to the urban *lawthing* assemblies and the areas of jurisdiction of the town lawmen. I will follow the law-parish divisions specified above, and discuss each in turn. In Table 13.2 and Figures 13.2 and 13.3, I suggest the connection between law-parish, lawmen and *lawthing*, and the provinces of *Historia Norwegie*.

Charters, place names and archaeological evidence indicate the following *lawthings* in the Borgarthing area: (1) the Foss *thing* (1450, SDHK: 26289; 1558, DN XII: 493) and the Båholm *thing* (1396, DN IV: 670), indicating that *lawthings* were held at both urban and rural locations in Båhuslen/Vika law-parish; (2) Tjølling, as mentioned previously, may have been the *lawthing* site for the northern law-parish. At Lunde in Tjølling, a site consisting of over 1,000 cooking pits has been discovered. These sites have been interpreted as testifying to large, seasonal gatherings, possibly in connection with legal/cultic assemblies. Radiocarbon dates from 30 of these pits indicate activity from the Pre-Roman Iron Age to the Merovingian Period (Iversen and Ødegaard in prep). This may point to an early assembly site at Tjølling, which also has the largest stone-built medieval church in Vestfold, dating from the twelfth century (Brendalsmo 2003). There is no evidence that Tjølling Church held a particularly high position in the Church hierarchy. The construction of such a spacious building here is perhaps best explained in the context of the *lawthing*, which, of course, occasioned large gatherings. In 1557 a 'half-shire' assembly was arranged at Tjølling for the Brunla county (*syssel*), corresponding to the southern half of the shire of Vestfold (DN I: 1118). This is rare evidence for the continuity of the *thing* location. However, the *lawthing* at Tjølling seems to have been reduced to a county-*thing*, possibly when the *lawthings* and law-men in Tønsberg and Skien took over the highest level of law enforcement in rural districts.

Only a fragment of the secular Borgarthing Law is preserved (Halvorsen and Rindal 2008). The fragment concerns the *thing* organisation in the law-area. It states that cases could be moved from so-called third- or half-shire-*things*

266 *Frode Iversen*

(*tredingting/halvfylkesting*) to a shire-*thing* (*fylkesting*) or to a *thing* with final authority (*ályktaþing*), as well as from shire-*things* to a three-shire-*thing* (NgL II: 523). Seip interpreted *ályktaþing* as meaning the highest *thing* (Seip 1934: 14). The Gulathing Law has a similar provision, describing the procedures for moving non-consensus cases to courts of higher rank (G: 35). I would suggest that the three shire-*things* in the law refer to the *lawthing* for the western law-parish, including the three shires of Vingulsmark, Vestfold and Grenland, and that the *ályktaþing* refers to the *lawthing* of the eastern law-parish (Båhuslen). The Borgarthing at Borg, close to the border between the two law-parishes, had the highest rank in the law-area.

Lawmen are mentioned in Tønsberg and Oslo in 1266. Together with the lawman from Romerike, they would pass judgement in cases in the rural district of Frogn (Indrebø 1936: 494). This shows that, even in this early phase, 'urban' lawmen acted beyond their urban areas. The lawmen from Skien and Tønsberg are also mentioned in a document from 1294 (Vågslid 1930: 13, 58, 65). In my opinion, this can be interpreted as indicating that Tjølling had ceased to function as the *lawthing* for Vingulsmark, Vestfold and Grenland, and that the lawmen from Tønsberg and Skien had taken over legal matters in the hinterlands.

There were two lawmen from the Gulathing area in 1223, one of whom represented Ryfylke. This fits well with the rural *lawthing* territories here: (3) At Avaldsnes on 24 June 1322 (DN I: 168; RN IV: 169), Ryfylke law-parish comprised Agder and Rogaland, and more tentatively, Valdres and Hallingdal. Already prior to 1150–75, Valdres and Hallingdal were under the Gulathing Law. In the late Middle Ages they were part of the Diocese of Stavanger, indicating an association with the southern law-parish. The *lawthing* was moved to the town of Stavanger before 1351 (DN III: 275). Then there is (4) the Gulathing itself. According to Egil's Saga, a *thing* was held at Gulen in spring c. 930 (Egs: 56; Helle 2001: 25–7). The case concerned a dispute between parties in the shires of Hordaland and Firda. A law court (*lagrett*) of 36 men reached a verdict in the case. This has been interpreted as indicating 12 men from each of the shires of Firda, Sogn and Hordaland, and further, that the Gulathing law-area originally comprised only these three shires (Helle 2001: 26). However, we should keep in mind that the thirteenth-century Egil's Saga is not very reliable, and also uses the anachronistic term *lendmaðr* in this particular case. Furthermore, this interpretation does not consider the possibility that the subdivisions and law-parishes could be of great age.

The Gulathing was moved to Bergen around 1300 (DN I: 147) and was amalgamated with the town *lawthing*. The last known date when two lawmen, one urban and one rural, were simultaneously serving in Bergen was in 1348 (DN II: 295). In 1366 a lawman with the title of 'Gulathing and Bergen lawman' appears (DN II: 387; Seip 1934: 20, note 1).

In the Frostathing area there were important assemblies both at Frosta and Øyra (5). The relationship between them has been extensively discussed. The Frostathing Law, from c. 1260, describes an annual *thing* at Øyra, half a month

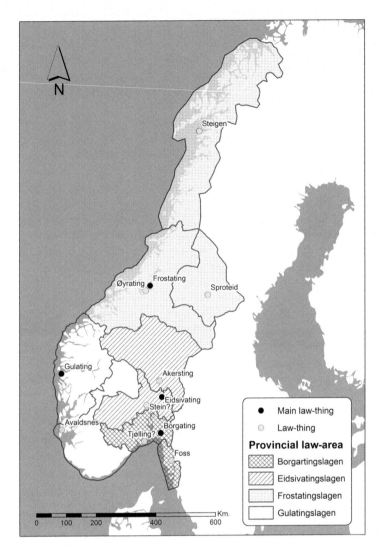

Figure 13.3 The *lawthings* of Norway, 1223.

before St John's Eve. From the eight provinces, all farmers with labourers had a duty to attend the Øyrathing (F: 1, 4; NgL I: 122, 128). It has been suggested that the Øyrathing was the *lawthing* for the eight provinces by the Trondheim Fjord before the law-area was expanded to include the three coastal provinces to the west (Indrebø 1935). However, it may be significant that the Øyrathing was not a representative *thing*, such as all the other *lawthings* we know. In the 1260s the Øyrathing had two main functions: to endorse laws and to choose the king. A royal charter from 1260 unequivocally states that the king was to

268   *Frode Iversen*

be chosen at the Øyrathing in Nidaros (RN I: 1974). According to the Sverris Saga, only kings received by the Øyrathing were the rightful, *rett tekin*, kings of Norway (Sverris Saga: ch. 12). On this basis, Jørn Sandnes (1967) claimed the *Øyrathing* was established by royal decree when Nidaros was founded (Sandnes 1967: 1–19). I concur, and see the *Øyrathing* as the younger *thing*, connected with the founding of the town, and the Frostathing as the prime *lawthing* of the law-area.

Eilif, lawman of Nidaros, is mentioned in 1297, and Indrebø believes his functions applied to both the town and the rural hinterland (Indrebø 1936: 496–7). If this is the case, it is only an interlude, because in 1346 the urban and rural lawmen had separate roles in Trondheim (DN V: 186). However, by 1422, the lawmen were being referred to by the title 'Frostathing and town lawman' (DN III: 66).

Steigen *lawthing* for the Hålogaland law-parish (6) is mentioned on 23 June 1404 (DN II: 580; Falkanger 2007: 20). The relationship between the *lawthing* at Steigen and a *thing* at Vågan has been discussed. Narve Bjørgo (1982: 50) surmises that the Vågan *thing* at Brudberget was a town *thing*, and does not regard Steigen as a younger, superseding *lawthing*, as Seip considers it to be, an opinion I share.

Jamtamót (7) was the main *thing* assembly for Jämtland, and was located at Fröson in Storsjön (near Östersund). It was held at Sproteid in the late Middle Ages. Jamtamót was held the week after St Gregory's Feast Day, 12 March, while the date of the *thing* in 1604 was 14 days before St John's Eve. This perhaps had its origins in the trade and cultic activities around Fröson (Scand. *Frøys Øy*, 'Frey's Island').

The original extent of the Eidsivathing law-area is unclear. Most likely, it coincided with the Diocese of Hamar and much of the Mountain Land (Figure 13.4). The border between the dioceses of Hamar and Oslo fell between Brunkeberg (Hamar) and Kvitseid (Oslo) (DN IX: 186; DN III: 291). In all likelihood, this mirrors the border between the Eidsivathing and Borgarthing areas. It was divided into four *patriae* in 1150–75 and two law-parishes in 1223. Two surviving fourteenth-century manuscripts of the Eidsivathing Christian law from the eleventh century mention lawmen in the plural, indicating an older division into several law-parishes (E: 30, 44; Halvorsen and Rindal 2008: 49, 90; Storm 1880: XXVII). To resolve this problem, I would simply suggest that two and two *patriae* shared a lawman. According to this logic, the southern law-parish includes (a) Upper Telemark with remote settlements in Numedal, and (b) Ringerike, Romerike and surrounding provinces, while the northern law-parish consisted of (a) Hedmark with Østerdalen and (b) Gudbrandsdalen and neighbouring provinces.

We do not know where the *lawthing* for the southern law-parish (8) took place. In around 1240, a lawman lived at the farm Hov, a day's ride from Eidsvoll (HH: 235, 238; Indrebø 1936: 494). The Bishops of Hamar had two residences within the diocese, at Hamar in the north and at Storøya in Hole, Ringerike, in the south. This was for the purpose of administering the two

The urban hinterland 269

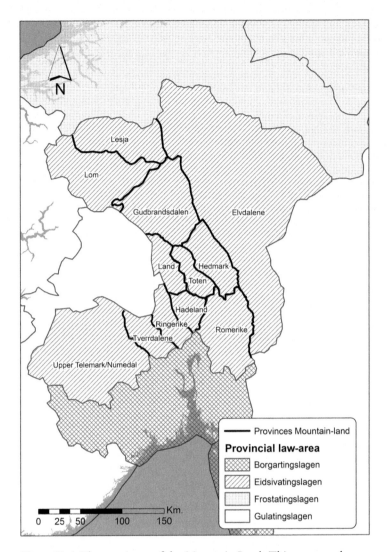

Figure 13.4 The provinces of the Mountain Land. This area may have corresponded to the Eidsivathing law-area before the latter was reorganised during the reign of Håkon Håkonsson (1217–63).

parts of the diocese (Hommedal 1999). The *lawthing* for the northern law-parish was at Hamar and therefore near the bishop's palace. If we assume a parallel ecclesiastical and secular organisation, then a *lawthing* for the southern law-parish may be sought near Storøya.

Archaeological evidence suggests the bishop's palace on Storøya existed in the thirteenth century but may go back to the foundation of the diocese in the mid-twelfth century (Hommedal 1999: 13). A verdict (*domsbrev*) from 1389 shows clearly that the bishop executed his power of prosecution from Storøya (DN IV: 561). Storøya borders the royal manor at Stein, where Halfdan the Black was reputedly buried in around 850. The archaeologists Perry Rolfsen and Jan Henning Larsen conclude, after a thorough review of historical and archaeological sources regarding the phenomena of 'Halfdan's burial mounds'

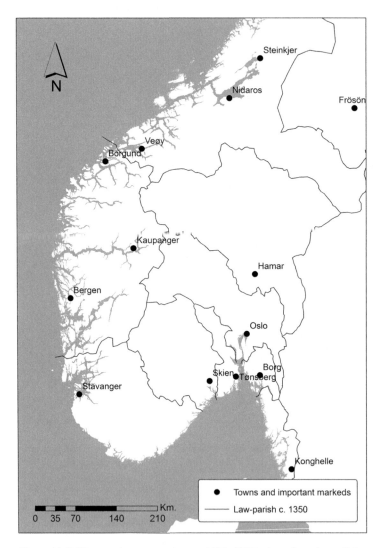

Figure 13.5 New regions emerging c. 1250–1350: the relocation of the rural *lawthings* to urban centres laid the foundation for the new cooperative law-regions of Norway, and gradually the inland was included in the 'urban economy' of the kingdom.

The northern law-parish in the Eidsivathing area (9) may have encompassed
(a) Hedmark with Østerdalen, and (b) Gudbrandsdalen and the provinces. The
'people' of Gudbrandsdalen, Hedmark and Østerdalen supported the inaugura-
tion of King Christian I in Oslo in 1450 (DN III: 812). This area appears to
coincide with the northern law-parish of 1223, where Sakse was the lawman.

Skien's *lawthing* was established in the mid-thirteenth century, and its juris-
diction comprised the fringe parts of both the law-areas of Borgarthing and
Eidsivathing; that is, Grenland from Borgarthing, and Upper Telemark and
Numedal from Eidsivathing.

A combined urban and rural Oslo lawman is known from the 1260s onwards
and served the areas of the southern law-parish that were not under the new
law-parishes of Skien and Tønsberg. As late as 1604, the Oslo lawman went
annually to the Eidsivathing. He was also the lawman for Oslo county (*syssel*),
which together suggests that the northern part of the shire of Vingulsmark
had been transferred from 'Tjølling law-parish' to the new Oslo jurisdiction.
Indrebø (1936: 498) considers that the whole of Vingulsmark was under the
Oslo lawman, but this is difficult to substantiate. Later, the southern part of
Vingulsmark lay under the jurisdiction of the lawman in Tønsberg. Therefore,
it seems most reasonable that Vingulsmark was divided in two, and that only
the northern part came under the lawman in Oslo (together with Marker).

Conclusion: the urban impact and the alteration of
the legal landscape

We can see a clear development, where co-dependent regions were significantly altered around 1250–1300, especially in South Norway (Figure 13.5).
During King Håkon Håkonsson's reign (1217–63) the 'Mountain Land' was
reorganised in accordance with strategic economic interests, namely exploitation of inland resources. The Kingdom of Norway gained a common law
for the whole kingdom in 1274 during the reign of his son, Magnus the
Lawmender, and this was a major step towards a unified kingdom.

The first town, Kaupang in Tjølling, lay centrally in a law-parish that
included Vingulsmark, Vestfold and Grenland. This was perhaps the primary
hinterland for Kaupang. The *thing* at Tjølling also attracted people to the
area. The next generation of towns in the Borgarthing area were deliberately
adapted to the established provinces: Skien in Grenland, Tønsberg in Vestfold,

Oslo in Vingulsmark and Konghelle in Vika. A town in each province, all centrally located, with the exception of Konghelle, which bordered Sweden and Denmark. The establishment of Borg early in the eleventh century breaks this pattern. It is feasible that Borg was created primarily to support the political and legal integration of Ranrike under Olaf Haraldsson's rule.

There were great changes to the boundary between the Borgarthing and Eidsivathing law-areas. Prior to c. 1250, Grenland was under Borgarthing, and Upper Telemark under Eidsivathing. Skien's hinterland was amalgamated under a new jurisdiction, and the *lawthing* located within the town. This change encouraged greater interaction across the older law-regions, which was formative for the modern Telemark County (except Numedal). The lawman of Tønsberg was active in the countryside from at least the 1260s. In the later Middle Ages the law-parish also included Tverrdalene, which had originally been under the Eidsivathing area, as well as part of Borgar *syssel* on the far shore of the Oslo Fjord. Consequently, Tønsberg and Borg may have competed as chief legal centres. The lawman in Tønsberg received a relatively large law-parish and part of the Mountain Land.

Regardless, ultimately the winner was Oslo. The town gained a large share of the southern law-parish of the Eidsivathing area, specifically Romerike, Ringerike, in addition to Marker and half of Vingulsmark. In c. 1350 Valdres and Hallingdal were added to this list. This must have had great significance for the development of Oslo as one of the foremost towns in Norway in the fourteenth century. In reality, the former law-parishes connected with the *lawthings* at Tjølling and Ringerike (location unidentified) were subsequently split between Skien, Tønsberg and Oslo, each receiving their share. These new jurisdictions changed the axes of human interaction from 'horizontal' to 'vertical' interchange, as each town gained a part of both the Coastal Land and the Mountain Land. In the towns of Stavanger and Hamar, each with a bishop's see, the changes were less marked, and they remained central to their respective law-parish. In secular affairs, Stavanger lost the Mountain Land of Valdres and Hallingdal to Oslo, while Hamar lost the southern law-parish of Eidsivathing to the three coastal towns. This, though, was a compromise. The areas remained connected to their original diocese. This dual connection is also seen in Jämtland, which in secular terms was under Frostathing and in ecclesiastical terms under Uppsala. This special category, in terms of cultural geography, is worthy of a study in its own right.

Significant changes occurred after 1223. Rural *lawthings* were relocated to the towns, and the lawmen's roles in the town and countryside became fused together (Seip 1934: 16–24). Gulen and Avaldsnes (*Gulathingslag*) were absorbed by Bergen and Stavanger in the fourteenth century. Two ancient law-parishes were divided between Skien, Tønsberg and Oslo. The Frostathing moved to Trondheim. In this process the Borgarthing lost its overall function as a *thing*, since the western law-parish was broken up. While there were at least nine rural *lawthing* sites in 1223, only Foss, Steigen and Eidsvoll remained in rural areas in 1604. Konghelle was a border town that was too impractically

The urban hinterland   273

located to be the central *lawthing* for Båhuslen. Foss was more central, and perhaps remained the location of the *lawthing* for this reason. In scantily urbanised Hålogaland, Steigen remained the *thing* site, and Vågan did not have the gravity as a town to attract the *lawthing*. Altogether, seven or eight coastal towns in Norway partly or wholly attracted the functions of the rural *lawthing*. This applies to Konghelle (Bahus) (partly), Borg, Oslo, Tønsberg, Skien, Stavanger, Bergen and Trondheim, as well as Hamar in the Mountain Land. The changes on the western shore of the Oslo Fjord and the southern Mountain Land were the most extensive, as jurisdictions were altered to meet the needs of the coastal towns.

Despite the fact that all the towns were not equally successful as legal centres, the Decapolis metaphor in *Historia Norwegie* did contain a prophetic element. Even though the Decapolis did not have the direct 'civilising influence' that the concept alludes to, the coastal towns did influence the regional network of Norway. The changes were due to political developments and the power of the market.

References

AM = Arnamagnæanske håndskriftsamling. http://nfi.ku.dk/om_instituttet/arnamag naeansk/ read 12.05.16.

Andersen, Per 2010: *Studier i dansk proceshistorie: Tiden indtil Danske Lov 1683*. Bibliotek for ret og kultur 2. Jurist- og Økonomforbundets Forlag. København.

Bagge, Sverre, Knut Helle and Synnøve Holstad Smedsdal 1973: *Norske middelalderdokumenter: I utvalg ved Sverre Bagge, Synnøve Holstad Smedsdal, Knut Helle*. Universitetsforlaget. Bergen.

Bjørgo, Narve 1982: Vågastemna i mellomalderen. In: Imsen, Steinar and Gudmund Sandvik (eds): *Hamarspor. Eit festskrift til Lars Hamre, 1912 – 23 januar 1982*, pp. 45–60. Universitetsforlaget. Oslo.

Blom, Grethe Authén 1967: *Kongemakt og privilegier i Norge inntil 1387*. Universitetsforlaget. Oslo.

Brendalsmo, Jan 2003: Tjølling kirke: Om en basilika, en kaupang og en storgård. In: Skarvang, Ingar (ed.): *Tjølling kirke. Veien, sannheten og livet i bygda gjennom 850 år*, pp. 22–38. Tjølling kirke. Tjodalyng.

Brendalsmo, Jan and Petter Molaug 2014: To norske byer i middelalderen: Oslo og Tønsberg før ca. 1300. *Collegium Medievale*, 27: 136–202.

C = see Hallanger and Brandt 1855.

Christophersen, Axel 1998: "Setja", "efla" or "reisa" kaupstad? A critical reading of the Sagas on the origin of Trondheim in light of archaeological evidences. *Hikuin*, 25: 61–78.

Christophersen, Axel and Sæbjørg Walaker Nordeide 1994: *Kaupangen ved Nidelva: 1000 års byhistorie belyst gjennom de arkeologiske undersøkelsene på folkebibliotekstomten i Trondheim 1973–1985*. Riksantikvarens skrifter 7. Riksantikvaren. Oslo.

DN = *Diplomatarium Norvegicum*: C.C.A. Lange and C.R. Unger (eds) 1847–1990. P.T. Mallings Forlagshandel. Christiania/Oslo.

E = Eidsivatingslagens kristenrett, see Halvorsen and Rindal 2008.

Egs = *Egilsoga*: Leiv Heggestad (transl.) 1950: Norrøne bokverk 15. Oslo.

274 *Frode Iversen*

Ekrem, Inger 1998: *Nytt lys over Historia Norwegie: Mot en løsning i debatten om dens alder?* IKRR, Seksjon for gresk, latin og egyptologi, Universitetet i Bergen. Bergen.

Ekrem, Inger and Lars B. Mortensen (eds) 2003: *Historia Norwegie.* Museum Tusculanum Press, University of Copenhagen. Copenhagen.

F = *Frostatingslova:* Jan Ragnar Hagland and Jørn Sandnes (transl.) 1994. Norrøne bokverk. Samlaget. Oslo.

Falkanger, Thor Aage 2007: *Lagmann og lagting i Hålogaland gjennom 1000 år.* Universitetsforlaget. Oslo.

G = *Gulatingsloven:* Bjørn Eithun, Magnus Rindal and Tor Ulset (eds) 1994: *Den eldre Gulatingsloven.* Riksarkivet. Oslo.

Hagland, Jan Ragnar and Jørn Sandnes 1997: *Bjarkøyretten: Nidaros eldste bylov. Norrøne bokverk.* Samlaget. Oslo.

Hallanger, Fr. and Fr. Brandt 1855: *Kong Christian den Fjerdes norske Lovbog af 1604 / efter Foranstaltning af Det akademiske Kollegium ved Det Kongelige Norske Frederiks Universitet udgiven af Fr. Hallager og Fr. Brandt.* Carl Werner. Christiania.

Halvorsen, Eyvind Fjeld 1995: Inland Norway in the Middle Ages. *Collegium Medievale,* 1: 51–61.

Halvorsen, Eyvind Fjeld and Magnus Rindal 2008: *De Eldste østlandske kristenrettene, tekst etter håndskriftene, med oversettelser.* Norrøne tekster 7. Riksarkivet. Oslo.

Hansen, Gitte 2005: *Bergen c. 800–c. 1170: The Emergence of a Town.* The Bryggen papers. Main Series, no. 6. Fagbokforlaget. Bergen.

Helle, Knut 1972: *Konge og gode menn i norsk riksstyring ca. 1150–1319.* Universitetsforlaget. Bergen.

—— 2001. *Gulatinget og Gulatingslova.* Skald. Leikanger.

—— 2006: *Norsk byhistorie: Urbanisering gjennom 1300 år.* Pax. Oslo.

HH = *Håkonar saga Håkonarsonar.* Finn Hødnebø (transl.) 1979. Norges kongesagaer 4. Oslo.

Hkr = Sturluson, Snorri [1979]: *Heimskringla.* Norges kongesagaer 1–2. Translated by Anne Holtsmark and Didrik Arup Seip. Gyldendal Norsk Forlag. Oslo.

Holm, Ingunn, Sonja M. Innselset and Ingvild Øye (eds) 2005: *'Utmark': the outfield as industry and ideology in the Iron Age and the Middle Ages.* UBAS International, vol. 1. Department of Archaeology, University of Bergen. Bergen.

Holt, Richard 2009: Medieval Norway's urbanization in a European perspective. In: Brendalsmo, Jan, Finn-Einar Eliassen and Terje Gansum (eds): *Den Urbane underskog: Strandsteder, utvekslingssteder og småbyer i vikingtid, middelalder og tidlig nytid,* pp. 231–46. Novus. Oslo.

Hommedal, Alf Tore 1999: Hamarbiskopens gard på Storøya i Tyrifjorden: På sporet av et monumentalanlegg. In: Pedersen, Ragnar (ed.): *Historien om historien,* pp. 7–22. Hedmarksmuseet og Domkirkeodden. Hamar.

Imsen, Steinar 1990: *Norsk bondekommunalisme: fra Magnus Lagabøte til Kristian Kvart 1, Middelalderen.* Tapir. Trondheim.

Imsen, Steinar and Harald Winge 2004: *Norsk historisk leksikon,* 2. utg. Cappelen. Oslo.

Indrebø, Gustav 1935: Fjordung: granskingar i eldre norsk organisasjons-soge. Bergens museums aarbok, 1935: 1. Bergen.

—— 1936: Spreidde merknader um dei norske logmannsebæti i millomalderen. *Historisk Tidsskrift,* 30: 489–526.

—— 1937: *Den gamle norske fylkesskipnaden.* Norsk Rikskringkasting. Oslo.

Iversen, Frode 2013: Concilium and Pagus: Revisiting the Early Germanic Thing System of Northern Europe. *Journal of the North Atlantic,* Special Volume 5: 5–17.

—— 2015: Community and Society – the Thing at the Edge of Europe. *Journal of the North Atlantic*, Special Volume 8: 5–21.

Iversen, Frode and Marie Ødegaard [in prep.]: Excavation at Lunde, Tjølling, Vestfold. Report, Museum of Cultural History, University of Oslo.

Jensen, Jørgen Elsøe 1990: Danske middelalderbyer: Middelalderlig byplanlægning i Danmark. *Fortid og nutid*, 4: 233–48.

Jørgensen, Poul Johs 1940: *Dansk retshistorie*. Gads Forlag. København.

Lerdam, Henrik 2001: *Kongen og tinget: Det senmiddelalderlige retsvæsen 1340–1448*. Museum Tusculanums Forlag. København.

Løkka, Nanna 2010: *Steder og landskap i norrøn mytologi: En analyse av topografi og kosmologi i gudediktene av Den eldre Edda*. Det humanistiske fakultet, Institutt for lingvistiske og nordiske studier, Universitetet i Oslo. Oslo.

Maurer, Konrad 1907: *Altnorwegisches Gerichtswesen: Vorlesungen über altnordische Rechtsgeschichte, aus dem Nachlaß des Verfassers herausgegeben von der Gesellschaft der Wissenschaften in Kristiania*. Deichert'sche Verlagsbuchhandlung. Leipzig.

Molaug, Petter 2007: *Occupying Town Plots on the Early Development of Habitation in Norwegian Medieval Towns*. NIKU. Oslo.

Munch, Peter Andreas 1850: *Symbolae ad historiam antiquiorem rerum Norvegicarum*. Typis excuderunt Carolus C. Werner and Socii. Christiania.

NgL = *Norges gamle Love indtil 1387*: Gustav Storm and Ebbe Hertzberg (eds) 1846–95. Christiania.

N.H. = Plinius Secundus, Gaius [1942]: *Naturalis historia*, Libri III–VII. Translated by H. Rackham: Natural history. Harvard University Press. Cambridge, MA.

Nyberg, Tore 1991: Adam av Bremen och Flolrenslistan. *Scandia*, 57(2): 153–89.

RN = *Regesta Norvegica*. http://www.dokpro.uio.no/dipl_norv/regesta_felt.html read 12.05.16.

Robberstad, Knut 1951: Ordet patria i Historia Norvegiæ. *Historisk Tidsskrift*, 35: 187–91.

Rolfsen, Perry and Jan Henning Larsen 2005: Er det flere Halvdanshauger? *Viking*, LXVIII: 101–30.

Rundberget, Bernt 2012: *Jernets dunkle dimensjon: Jernvinna i sørlige Hedmark, sentral økonomisk faktor og premiss for samfunnsutvikling c. AD 700–1300*. Det humanistiske fakultet, Universitetet i Oslo. Oslo.

Sandnes, Jørn 1967: Trøndelags eldste politiske historie. *Historisk Tidsskrift*, 46: 1–20.

Schia, Erik 1991: *Oslo innerst i Viken: Liv og virke i middelalderbyen*. Aschehoug. Oslo.

SDHK = Svenskt Diplomatariums huvudkartotek över medeltidsbreven. http://sok. riksarkivet.se/SDHK read 12.05.16.

Seip, Jens Arup 1934: *Lagmann og lagting i senmiddelalderen og det 16de århundre*. Det Norske videnskaps-akademi i Oslo. II, Historisk-filosofisk klasse no. 3. Oslo.

Skre, Dagfinn 2007: *Kaupang in Skiringssal. Kaupang Excavation Project*. Publication Series, vol. 1. Norske Oldfunn, vol. 22. Aarhus University Press. Århus.

Steinnes, Asgaut 1946: Ikring Historia Norvegiæ. *Historisk tidsskrift*, 34: 1–61.

Steinsland, Gro 1991: *Det hellige bryllup og norrøn kongeideologi: En analyse av hierogamimyten i Skírnismál, Ynglingatal, Háleygjatal og Hyndluljód*. Solum. Oslo.

Storm, Gustav 1877: *Sigurd Ranessøns proces, udgivet efter Haandskrifterne af Gustav Storm*. Malling. Kristiania.

—— 1880: *Monumenta Historia Norvegiæ. Latinske kildeskrifter til Norges historie i middelalderen utgivne efter offenlig foranstalting*. Kristiania.

Stylegar, Frans-Arne 2004: "Upplond". *Arkeologi i Nord*. http://arkeologi.blogspot.no/ 2004/08/upplond.html read 12.05.16.

276 Frode Iversen

SS = *Sverris Saga*: Þorleifur Hauksson (ed.) 2007: Norges kongesagaer. Hið íslenzka fornritafélag. Reykjavík.

Taranger, Absalon 1898: *Udsigt over den norske rets historie. Forelæsninger I.* Kart- and Litograferingskontoret. Kristiania.

—— (ed.) 1915: *Magnus Lagabøtes Landslov.* Cammermeyers boghandel. Kristiania.

Vågslid, Eivind 1930: *Norske logmannsbrev frå millomalderen: Ei skrifthistorisk etterrøking av logmannsbrev frå Oslo, Uppland, Skien, Tunsberg, Borgarting og Bohuslän.* Det Norske videnskaps-akademi. Oslo.

Vogt, Helle and Ditlev Tamm 2009: *Dansk retshistorie og vestlig forfatningsudvikling.* Studieudgave. Jurist- og Økonomforbundets Forlag. København.

Index

Note: the following abbreviations have been used – f = figure; n = note; t = table

Adelsö (Sweden) 135
aDNA 9, 71
Africa: coinage 224
Agder 16
Agdesiden (Norway) 261, 264t
agency: economic/social 2, 3, 16–19, 36
agricultural economy 6, 17, 18, 147;
    Coastal Land 237; Denmark; exchange
    systems 46, 51, 52, 53–4; iron and iron
    production 113, 120, 121, 205, 208,
    245; Mountain Land 237, 241, 244, 245;
    Norway 163, 165, 169, 173, 174–6;
    summer farming system (shielings)
    163–4, 165, 167, 169, 240, 243; Sweden
    6; tariffs 96, 99, 101–2, 106; tithes 119;
    trade stations 192, 202–3, 204; see also
    animal husbandry; grain cultivation; rural
    economy
Åhus (Sweden) 13
amber 15, 18, 195, 200–1; production sites
    213, 217, 219
amulets see armrings
Amunde Remba (lawman) 261
Anglo-Saxon lands 3; grave-goods 201
animals: bone 199, 241, 243, 244;
    ornament 4; sacrifice 244
animal husbandry 241; coinage and 96–7,
    98, 99, 100; iron production and 120,
    121; livestock grazing 163, 165, 167, 169,
    170–1, 175; see also agricultural economy;
    grain cultivation; rural economy
antler production 3, 4, 5, 9, 10, 11, 21;
    comb production 70–1; everyday objects
    243; procurement of raw materials 82t,
    149, 174; see also hunting and trapping
Arabic (Islamic): coinage 198, 199, 217,
    223f, 226; jewellery 200, 218, 219; silver
    13, 52, 55$n4$; trade and trading systems 3

Åraksfjorden (lake) 203–4
Archaeological Prospection and Virtual
    Archaeology, Ludwig Boltzman Institute
    for (LBI) (University of Vienna) 214
archaeological sites and regions: **map** 7
Århus (Denmark) 12, 143, 151, 155
aristocracy 6, 176; control over production
    16–19
armrings 130, 131, 132, 133, 134
Arnamagnæanske håndskriftsamling
    (manuscript) 257, 259
arrowheads 170, 171, 172
artisanal production 3, 5–6, 13, 18–19, 21,
    87; excavation finds 217–19
Ashby, S. et al. 22
Askvik, H. 75
Aslak Petersson 260
Aslanian, S.D. 35
assemblies of people see skeid; thing and
    thingmen
Attundaland ('Land with Eight Hundreds')
    (Sweden) 257
aura (weight unit of silver) 52
axes 195, 198, 199, 200

Båhuslen (Norway/Sweden) 261, 263t,
    265, 273
bailiffs 96, 251, 261
bakestones 73t, 76–7, 82t, 84, 86
Baltic Sea 79, 80, 80t, 81, 86, 200
barrows see burial mounds
Baug, I. 12, 14, 15, 16, 17, 18
beach markets 13
beads 18, 46, 200, 201, 204, 212; dating
    221f, 222, 225, 242; see also jewellery
Belgium 80, 80t, 81, 85, 86
Bergen (Norway) 10, 12, 106, 156$n1$;
    bakestones 84; ceramics 84, 85–6;

278 *Index*

comb production 71, 72; consumption of domestic products 74, 76, 78, 79, 80*t*; consumption of iron 68–9, 120; *lawthings* 251, 254, 264*t*, 266, 272, 273; production of domestic products 63, 63*t*, 64, 83; reconstruction of central settlement areas 65*f*, 66; trade and trading systems 151–2, 153

bespoke production 4, 5, 128, 130, 131

Birka (Sweden) 6, 135, 226; silver 42, 44, 46, 50, 51

'Bishop's Road' (*Bispevegen*) 202, 203

Bjørgo, N. 268

Bjørkum (Lærdal, Norway) 14, 240–1, 242*f*, 243–5

black earth 241

Black ware cooking pots 79, 80*t*, 80–1, 85

Blackburn, M. 224

blinds (hunting) 171

Blom, J.-P. 237

boats *see* ships and boats

bog ore *see* iron and iron production

Bohuslän (Sweden) 10, 99, 107*n1*

bóndafé (payment from farmers) 96, 99

bone (animal) 199, 241, 243, 244

bone ash 219

Borg (Norway) 64, 251, 254, 272, 273

Borgarthing (Norway): coinage 95, 96, 99; law-parishes 263*t*, 265–6, 268, 271–2; *lawthings* 255, 257, 259

Borgund (Norway) 255; domestic and exotic materials 63, 64, 71, 78, 80*t*, 85

Borgundkaupangen (Norway) 14

Borre ship-burial (Norway) 129, 132–3

bow and arrow hunting 170, 172, 243

bracteates (coins) 99–100, 107, 199

Brendalsmo, J. 251

bridge building 201

Britain: domestic and exotic materials 15, 79, 80, 80*t*, 84; excavation finds 217, 218, 219

Broberg, B. 59, 86

Brøgger, A.W. 199

bronze castings 49, 111

brooches 135, 178*f*, 185, 199, 200; equal-armed 125*f*, 126, 127, 131, 132; penannular 46, 130, 131, 132, 133–4; silver 44, 49

Bücher, K. 32

building and construction materials 151, 215, 216; procurement 81, 82*t*; rural economy 241, 242*f*, 243, 244; urbanism and urbanisation 60, 63–4, 65*f*, 66; *see also* domestic and exotic materials

bullion 42, 217, 224, 225

burial mounds 18, 129; *lawthings* 270, 271; trade and production sites 212, 214, 216, 225, 226

burials 101, 54, 208, 225–6; boats 18, 129, 212, 214, 216; cairns 44, 194, 196*t*, 197*t*; chamber graves; Christian 70, 203; customs 44, 47*t*, 51, 203; Denmark; double 198, 199; Iron Age 205*t*; male 46, 51, 53, 154, 203, 207; mountain graves 172, 178*f*, 179, 195, 200, 207; pagan 203, 207; ships 18, 129, 224, 225, 226; *see also* cemeteries; grave goods; hoards

burnt mark silver 96, 97, 106, 107

butter 6

Bygland (Norway) 17

Byglandsfjorden (lake) (Norway) 203–3

Byzantium 218

cairns 44, 194, 196*t*, 197*t*; *see also* burial mounds

Caledonian hones 74, 75, 76, 83, 86

Caliphate *see* Arabic

Callmer, J. 2, 124, 125, 128

Carelli, P. 147, 149

Carolingian Empire 150, 217, 224; coinage 95

Celestine III, Pope 106–7

Celtic grave-goods 201

cemeteries 18; grave-goods 196*t*, 197*t*; signs of trade and exchange 194*f*, 195, 198*f*, 199–201; *see also* burials, grave-goods, hoards

Central Land *see* Mountain Land

central-place markets 227, 228

Central-Place Theory 34–5

ceramics and pottery 13, 15, 149; consumption 18, 84–6; procurement 63, 79, 80, 80*t*, 81–2, 82*t*, 217–18; soapstone 140, 145, 146–7

chamber graves *see* burial mounds; cairns

charcoal pits 115–16, 117, 167, 169, 241; **maps**: distribution in Norway (Viking Age and Middle Ages) *114*; recorded medieval sites/charcoal pits in Gravfjellet (Norway) *118*; *see also* iron and iron production

charters 259, 260, 265, 267–8

chieftains and chiefdom 18, 34, 36, 53; gift exchange economy 257; redistributive economy 36; surplus production 176–7

Christaller, W. 34–5

Christian I (king of Norway) 271

Christian IV (king of Norway) 96, 257, 261, 263*t*

Christianity: blending with Norse beliefs 254; burials 70, 203; conversion to 2, 3, 268; Sweden 2

chronology 4, 8, 9, 10, 11, 60, 111; trade and trading systems 200, 206, 220, 221*f*, 228

churches 20, 34, 62, 64, 265; 'church villages' 243–4; sites 14, 265; **map**: agrarian settlements and parish churches (c12/13th) *45*; *see also* ecclesiastical administration

'circulation society': polycentric model 35

clay moulds 125–6

Cnut (king of Denmark and England)

Coastal Land 5, 12, 13, 17, 19, 237; Christianisation of 203; compensation schemes 98–9; economy 19, 20–1; law-parishes 262*t*, 265, 272; *lawthings* 250, 252, 253–4, 258, 260; trade and trading systems 202, 206, 255

coinage 69; African 224; Anglo-Scandinavian 201, 202; animal husbandry and 96–7, 98, 99, 100; Arabic (Islamic) 198, 199, 217, 223*f*, 226; Carolingian Empire 95; compensation schemes 95, 99–100, 107; dating 223*f*, 224, 225; ecclesiastical law and money 106–7; excavation finds 217; expenses and travel routes 95–6, 97*t*, 98*t*, 99; grave-goods 198, 199; hoards 14, 17, 19, 20, 195, 212; royal families control of minting 101–2, 106, 107; silver 3, 13, 19–20, 42, 44, 52; *thing* and *thingmen* 95, 100–2, 105–6; **maps**: travel compensation/geographical zones in Gulathing/Frostathing law-areas *103, 104*

colonization 174

comb production 58–9, 10, 11, 195, 243; consumption 66, 67*t*, 70–1, 74; procurement 81, 82*t*, 87

commission production 4, 5

commodity production: local/regional/interregional trade and 4–6, 8, 16, 20, 21–2; long-distance trade 8–12; as payment method 42

common land 180

communication centres *see* seasonal markets; *skeid*; trading routes

compensation schemes 95, 99–100, 107; **maps**, travel compensation/geographical zones in Gulathing/Frostathing law-areas *103, 104*

complex societies 1, 16, 18; pre/early-state 31, 32, 33, 34, 38

'consumer towns' 5, 21, 120

consumption patterns 18; domestic and exotic materials 63–4, 66, 68–72, 74–9, 80*t*, 81, 82–3, 87

Continental grave-goods 199, 202

Cook, S. 32

cooking pits 240, 242, 243, 244, 265

copper alloy 49*f*, 198, 217, 218; jewellery 125, 128, 129, 130, 131–2, 134; urbanism and urbanisation 69, 70–1, 81–2, 86

cornelian 218–19, 222, 226

counterfeiting (coins) 106

Coutu, A.N. *see* Ashby, S. et al.

craft industries *see* fine-metalworking; jewellery; shoe production; weaponry; weaving

crafts-people: housing 134; pit houses 241, 242*f*, 243, 244

cremation 44, 47*t*, 195, 199, 200

Cultural Heritage Research, Norwegian Institute for (NIKU) 214

Curtin, P. 35

cut-up silver 19–20, 52

Daae, L. *see* Wille, H.J. et al.

Dagfinn Bonde (lawman) 261

Dalton, G. 1

dark schist *see* whetstone

De Finnis *see* Sami people

De montanis Norwegie *see* Mountain Land

de-evolution of technology: iron 115–16

decapolis 254, 273

Denmark 4, 10, 12, 15, 96, 199; agricultural economy; burials 140, 149, 199; ceramics 86; fortifications 8; *lawthings (landsting)* 257, 262*t*, 272; long-distance trade 15, 245; metalworking 111–12, 114, 245, 254; quernstones 140, 143, 145, 148–9; settlement patterns 12, 251; shoe production 87; soapstone 10, 140, 145, 147–9, 152, 202; trade and trading systems 224, 225

destroyed graves 44

dirhams 198, 199, 217, 218, 223*f*, 226

distribution maps 37

domestic and exotic materials 59–60, 63; ceramics 79, 80*t*, 81–2; production 63*t*, 81, 82*t*, 83–7; small-scale crafts 66*t*, 67*t*, 68–72, 73*t*, 74, 81; **map**: non-agrarian activities and urbanisation *61*; *see also* building and construction materials; hones; quernstones; whetstones

double burial 198, 199

'DYLAN – How to manage dynamic landscapes' (Norwegian Research Council) 182*n3*

280 *Index*

Earl Skule 259
Early Viking Age (700–950) 3, 15, 18, 19, 21; commodity production 6, 9–10; non-ferrous metalworking 54, 124; soapstone 139, 140, 148, 155; urbanisation 12, 13
ecclesiastical administration 6, 8, 21, 181, 258; iron and iron production 119, 120*t*; law and money 102, 106–7; *lawthings* and 260, 268, 269–70, 272; power and 181, 270; silver 60, 64; trade and trading systems 154; *see also* churches
economy 1–4, 22, 32; Coast Land 20–1; commodity production for local/regional/interregional trade and 4–6, 8; commodity production for long-distance trade 8–12; evolutionary model 2, 115; redistributive 35, 36, 38; subsistence-oriented/status-driven 32–3; subsistence/commission production 4; trade routes and monetisation 14–20; urbanisation and seasonal markets 12–14
Eddas 254
Edict of Pitres (AD 864) 95
Egil's Saga 105, 266
Eidsborg (Norway) 14, 220; production/procurement 74, 75, 76, 83, 86
Eidsivathing (Norway); coinage 95, 96, 98*t*, 99; law-parish divisions 263*t*, 265, 268, 271, 272; *lawthings* 255, 258, 259, 260, 261
Eidsvoll (Norway) 264*t*, 272
Ekrem, I. 257
elites 38, 53, 134, 176; tribute 36, 37, 131, 154, 251
elk hunting/trapping 163, 167, 169
embroidery/sewing threads 72, 81, 82*t*, 86, 87
equestrian equipment *see* horses
Erling Skakke 106
Europe: historical time designations *ixt*
Evenstad, O. 173
everyday products 4, 19, 154, 195, 217; *skeid* 242, 243; small-scale crafts 66*t*, 67*t*, 68–72, 73*t*, 74
evolutionary model of economy 2, 115
exchange systems 5, 6, 173, 201; agricultural economy 46, 51, 52, 53–4; coinage 100–1; non-ferrous metalworking 126, 131, 134; pre-state/early state 31, 35, 37, 38; silver 42, 53, 54; *skeid* (assembly of people) 237–8; soapstone 145, 153
exotic materials *see* domestic and exotic materials

Færden, G. 11
fairs 52, 202
Far East 218
farm settlements *see* agricultural economy; animal husbandry; grain cultivation; rural economy
Faroe Islanders' Saga 105
Faroe Islands 95, 140, 144, 145
fehird 153, 156*n1*
félag 154
female burials/graves 46, 55*n2*
fencing systems 12
festivals *see* fairs
Feveile, C. 125
fieldwalking 220
Filefjellsveg (trading route) 238
final authority *thing* (*ályktaþing*) 266
fine-metalworking 213, 217, 219, 228
Finley, M.I. 1, 32, 34
fishing and fishermen 13, 147, 152, 191, 225, 245
Fjære (Norway) 13–14, 202, 203
Fjärdrundaland ('Land with Four Hundreds') (Sweden) 257
Flodin, L. 11
Fønhus, M. 233, 234–5
foodstuffs 6–7, 149–50, 154, 220, 224, 225; coinage and 96–7, 98, 99
foresty *see* Uplands (Norway)
formalism 32, 33, 34, 36, 38
Forsa (Hälsingland, Sweden) 52
fortifications 8
Foss *lawthing* (Norway) 259, 260, 265, 272, 273
France 80, 80*t*, 85
Frankish trade 3, 126, 149, 201, 217
Fredrikstad (Norway) 261
Frisia 5, 9, 15–16, 126, 149
Frösön (formerly Kråksta) (Jämtland, Norway/Sweden) 52
Frostathing Law 52, 239, 266
Frostathing (Norway): coinage 95, 96, 97, 99, 105; law-parishes 263*t*, 265, 266–7, 272; *lawthings* 255, 259, 261; **maps** *103, 104*
Frostatingslova 119
Fuglesang, S.H. 127, 132
funeral and burial customs 44, 47*t*, 51, 203
funnel-shaped trapping systems 170–2
fur and hide 4, 5, 6, 71, 243; procurement 82*t*, 174, 201
furnaces 11, 113, 114–15, 119, 121, 163
Fyn (Denmark) 15
Fyresdal (Norway) 207, 208, 239
Fyrkat fortress (Jylland) 8

Index 281

gathering places *see* seasonal markets; *skeid*
geographical nodes 37–8
geophysics 14
Germany 34, 113, 147; domestic and
 exotic materials 80*t*, 81, 85, 86;
 maps, quernstone regions in southern
 Scandinavia 148
gift exchange economy 1, 35, 177,
 179, 218; chieftains 177; hierarchical
 relationships 130, 131, 132, 133, 134
Gjellebøl, R. 235, 236, 237
glass-bead makers 5
Glørstad, Z. 130, 132
'Gokstad Revitalised' (GOREV) 212, 214
Gokstad ship burial (Norway) 18, 129, 212,
 214, 225, 226–8
gold and goldsmiths 128, 130, 134, 202, 217
Gorm (King of Denmark) 251
government *see* kings; royal families and
 administration; *skied*, ecclesiastical
 administration
Gråfjell area (Norway) 163, 172, 173, 174;
 maps, archaeological sites *164*; resource
 exploitation 167, 168*t*, 169
grain cultivation 53, 169, 175, 191, 241;
 trade/production sites 220, 224, 225;
 see also agricultural economy; animal
 husbandry; rural economy
grave-goods 9, 17, 18, 20; jewellery
 178*f*,195, 200; mountain areas 170,
 178*f*, 179, 195, 200, 207; Norway *178*;
 in ship burials 18, 29, 212, 225, 226;
 silver weighs/balances 44, 46, 47*t*, 48*f*,
 49*f*; trade-related 194*f*, 195, 196*t*, 197*t*,
 198*f*, 199–201, 203; weaponry 18, 53,
 204, 216, 224, 228; *see also* burials;
 cemeteries; hoards
Gravfjellet (Norway) 111, 116, 117, 118,
 119; **maps**: recorded early Iron Age sites
 in Gravfjellet (Norway) *117*; recorded
 medieval sites/charcoal pits *118*
Greco-Romano economy 32–3
Grenland (Norway) 271, 272
Grimsdalen (Norway) 163–4, 168*t*, 170,
 175, 182*n*5; **map**: archaeological sites *165*
Grimstad region (Norway) 202, 203
group-level identity markers 38
Gudbrandsdalen (Norway) 174, 268, 271
Gulathing (Norway) 95, 96, 97*t*, 99, 100;
 lawthings 255, 259, 261, 263*t*, 265, 266;
 monetarisation 105, 106; **map** *103*, *104*
Gulatingslovi 119
Gulli (Norway) 132
Gustin, I. 1
Gylfaginning (Edda) 254

hacksilver 126, 195, 199; coinage 42–3, 44,
 49, 53, 55*n4*; excavation finds 212, 217,
 219; *see also* silver
Håkon Håkonsson (king of Norway) 257,
 259, 261, 265, 269, 271; **map**: law-
 parishes of Norway according to saga
 (1223) *256*
half-shire-*thing* (*tredingting/halvfylkesting*)
 265–6
Halfdan the Black 270, 271
Halland (Sweden) 10
Hällesjö (Jämtland, Norway/Sweden) 55*n4*
Hallingdal (Norway) 266, 272
Hallingskeid (Norway) 239, 243
Hålogaland (Norway) 95, 261, 268, 273
Halvorsen, E.F. 252, 258
Hamar (Norway) 62, 64, 251, 261, 273;
 Bishops of 176, 268, 269, 272
Handelstorget (excavation) 78
handicrafts 195, 220, 243
Hansen, I.L. 1
Harald Bluetooth (king of Denmark) 251
Haraldr Finehair (king of Norway) 130
Haraldr Hardrada (king of Norway) 251
Härjedalen (Norway/Sweden) 51*t*
Hasebroek, J. 32
Hasselmo, M. 59, 86
Hedeby (Denmark) 6, 19, 44, 135, 150,
 155; burials 226; quernstones 12, 15,
 144; soapstone 10, 11, 13, 140, 147;
 whetstone 9
Hedmark (Norway) 271
Hedmarken (Norway) 17–18, 20
Heimdal (Norway) 252
Heimdalsjordet (seasonal market)
 (Norway) 12, 13, 14, 20, 225–8;
 artefactual material 216–20; dating of
 the site 220, 221*f*, 222*t*, 223*f*, 224–5;
 excavation of 212, 213*f*, 214*f*; site
 structures 214, 215*f*, 216
Helle, K. 255
'Hide Road' (*Skinnvegen*) 201–2, 203
high-resolution georadar 214
Hinsch, E. 213, 214, 216
hinterland 35, 63, 69, 82, 208, 250–2;
 impact of alteration of legal landscape
 271–3; law-areas (*patriae*) and
 trade regulations 252, 253–5; legal
 administrative divisions 261, 262–4*t*,
 265–6, 267–8, 269–70, 271; origin and
 organisation of *lawthings* 255, 256–61;
 seasonal markets 12–13, 14, 15, 16;
 maps: law-parishes (*lagsogn*) of
 Norway (1223) *256*; *lawthings* of
 Norway (1223) *267*; major divisions of

282 Index

Norway (*Historia Norvegie*) 253; new regions emerging (c.1250–1350) 270; provinces of Mountain Land 269; *see also* urbanism and urbanisation

Historia Norvegie (*Norvegiae*) 20, 54, 161, 233; *lawthings* 252, 254, 257–8, 262*t*, 263*t*, 265, 273; **map**: major divisions of Norway 253

hoards 14, 17, 19, 20, 132, 202; silver 42–3, 52, 53, 55*n4*, 102; *see also* burials; cemeteries; grave goods; weaponry

Hodges, R. 227

hofdingiafundr (political meeting) 257, 259

Höggärde (Jämtland, Norway/Sweden) 48*f*, 50*f*, 53

Holm, O. 17

hones 73*t*, 74–6, 82*t*, 83, 86, 219–20; *see also* domestic and exotic materials; quernstones; soapstone; whetstones

Horn, A.C. 259

horses 6, 53; racing/fighting 235, 236, 237, 238, 239, 240

Hougen, B. 170

housing 6, 21, 171, 172, 214, 241; crafts-people 134; organic growth 54, 177; pit houses 241, 242*f*, 243, 244, *see also* urbanism and urbanisation

Hovden (Norway) 202

hunting and trapping 21, 175, 245, 250; large-scale hunting 170–2, 176, 191; resource exploitation 163, 165, 167, 169; technological adaptation 171–2, 173, 174, 182*n5*; *see also* antler production

Hyllestad (Norway) 11, 12, 15, 21, 74, 83; quernstones/soapstone 144, 145, 147, 148, 149, 150; trade and trading systems 151, 152–3, 154; **map**: distribution of quernstones from Hyllestad 143

Iceland 140, 144, 145, 258

imports 15, 17, 114, 132, 144, 202; domestic and exotic materials 79, 80*t*, 81, 82*t*; foreign traders 255; rural economy 217–9, 226, 228; *see also* long-distance trade

in casu metal-casters 5

Indrebø, G. 252, 256, 260, 265, 268, 271

inductively coupled plasma mass spectrometry (ICP-MS) 146

inhumation graves 47*t*, 49, 50, 52, 195, 199

inland transport: the homelands 201, 202, 204, 207–8

Inner Sogn (Norway) 244, 246

Insular grave-goods 199, 202

interior economy 20–1

Ireland 15

Iron Age *viii, ix*, 2; agricultural economy 6, 241, 242, 243, 244; burials 200, 203, 204, 205*t*; hunting 163, 165, 167, 168*t*, 170; iron and iron production 4, 111, 113, 115–16, 163, 245; settlement 174, 175, 177, 179; trade and trading systems 15, 222, 232, 265; **map**: recorded sites in Gravfjellet area (Norway) 117

iron and iron production 3, 4, 5, 13, 16, 17; agricultural economy 113, 120, 121, 205, 208, 245; de-evolution of technology 115–16; long-distance trade 8, 9, 10, 202, 250; political control of 176–7; procurement of raw materials 82*t*, 149; producers 119, 120*t*; production sites 21, 111, 163, 213, 219, 226; small-scale production/smelting 66*t*, 67–8, 69, 81; technological innovation/changes 11, 115–16, 117, 118, 119, 121; trade stations 202, 204; Uplands 167–8, 169, 172, 173, 174, 175; weights 49*f*; **maps**: all recorded iron production sites (Norway/Sweden) (C4th BC– AD C19th) 112; recorded early Iron Age sites in Gravfjellet (Norway) 117; *see also* charcoal pits; non-ferrous metalworking; production

isotope analysis 9

Jamtamót (Norway/Sweden) 268

Jämtland (Norway/Sweden) 17, 18, 42–3, 52–4, 99, 107*n1*; *lawthings* 255, 258, 261, 268, 272; silver and payment transactions 49, 50*f*, 51*t*; silver weights/balances as grave goods 44, 46, 47*t*, 48*f*, 49*f*, 55*n3*; **maps**: distribution of finds of weights/balances 45; position on the Scandinavian Peninsula 43

Jensen, J.E. 114

jewellery 178*f*, 217, 224, 228; Arabic (Islamic) 200, 218, 219; grave-goods 178*f*, 195, 200; silver 46, 49; urban commodity production 125*f*, 127*f*, 130–2 133; *see also* beads

Jormön (Frostviken) (Jämtland, Norway/Sweden) 53

jurisprudence *see lawthings*

Jutland peninsula (Jylland) 8, 13, 15; soapstone 140, 143, 146, 147

kaolin clay 70, 71, 82*t*, 86, 87, 219

Kattegat 11, 13

Kaupang (Norway) 5, 6, 251, 271; beads 219; ceramics 86; coinage 19, 223, 224; commodity production 124,

Index 283

125*f*, 126, 127*f*, 155; comparison with Heimdalsjordet (seasonal market) (Norway) 212, 216, 220, 223–4, 226, 227–8; jewellery 130–2, 133; long-distance trade 9, 10, 11; seasonal markets 12, 13; serial production 128, 129*f*, 130; silver 42; soapstone 146–7, 154, 202; standardization and 132–4; trade and trading systems 15–16, 18, 19

Kaupanger (Norway) 254; domestic and exotic materials 63, 64, 68, 70, 80*t*, 85

Kilger, C. 218

kings 130, 239, 268; coinage 95, 96, 100, 106; *lawthings* and 251, 254, 257, 260, 261, 263*t*; sagas 267; 257, 259, 261, 265, 269, 271; **map**: law-parishes of Norway according to Håkon Håkonsson (king of Norway) (1223) *256*; *see also* royal families and administration

Konghelle (Norway/Sweden) *see* Kungahälla

koupstad (small trading place) 60

Kresten, P. 147, 149

Kungahälla (Norway/Sweden) 62, 64, 68, 70, 71, 76; ceramics 78–9, 80*t*, 81, 254, 272–3

labour 12, 16, 161, 173, 238

Lærdal (Norway) 244, 246

Lærdalsmarknad (seasonal market) (Norway) 244

Lagabøter, M. 68

Lamøya (island) 216

land and landowners 154, 176, 180

Landnámabok (*Hauksbok*) 259

landscape management 179–81

Langeid (Norway): cemetery 194*f*, 195, 196*t*, 197*t*, 198*f*, 199–201; inland expansion of trade 204, 205*t*, 206, 207; regional trade exchange networks 201–3; stationary and mobile trade entrepreneurs 203–4, 208; **map**: Setesdal Valley *193*

Larsen, J.H. 201

Larson, L.M. 100–1

Late Viking Age (950–1100) 5–6, 10–11, 12, 14, 19; grave-goods 46, 50, 51

lawthings 255, 256–61; law-areas (*patriae*) and trade regulations 252, 253–5; law-parish divisions 263*t*, 265, 267–71; meeting dates 263–4*t*, 266, 267; proposed subdivision of districts and provinces 262*t*; **maps**: law-parishes (*lagsogn*) of Norway (1223) *256*; *lawthings* of Norway (1223) *267*; *see also* thing and *thingmen*

LBI *see* Ludwig Boltzman Institute for Archaeological Prospection and Virtual Archaeology (LBI) (University of Vienna)

lead 69, 217, 218, 220, 244; models for jewellery 124, 125*f*, 126, 127*f*, 128, 129*f*, 131

leather *see* fur and hide

legal institutions *see lawthings*

levy-fleet fund (*leiðang*) 106

LIDAR *see* Light Detection and Ranging

Light Detection And Ranging (LIDAR) 116

liūðrēttr (law of the people) 52

livestock grazing 163, 165, 167, 169, 170–1, 175

local/regional/interregional trade and 4–6, 8, 227

Löddeköpinge (seasonal market) (Øresund, Sweden) 12, 13

Lödöse (Sweden) 86

Lofoten (Norway) 18

Loftahammar Hoard (Småland, Sweden) 223

Long Eighth Century: Production, Distribution and Demand (Hansen and Wickham) 1

long-distance trade 23, 4–5, 6, 17, 72, 83–4; commodity production 8–12, 191, 201; soapstone 8–9, 10, 11, 15, 21, 154; *see also* imports

longhouses *see* housing

longphorts *see* Ireland

longships *see* ships and boats

loom weights 139, 243

Ludwig Boltzman Institute for Archaeological Prospection and Virtual Archaeology (LBI) (University of Vienna) 214

Lund (Sweden) 11, 12

Lusakaupang (seasonal market) (Norway) 14, 244

Lusakaupangen *see Lusakaupang* (seasonal market)

luxury items 18–19, 204, 227; embroidery 72, 81, 82*t*, 86–7

magnetometry 214

Magnus Lagabøters Landslov 119

Magnus the Lawmender (king of Norway) 95, 96, 100, 239, 259, 271

male burials/graves 46, 51, 53, 154, 203, 207

Malinowski, B. 35

Mann, M. 38

mannebøter (wergild) 100, 101

manufacturing *see* production

manuscripts 257, 259, 268

marginalised production 17, 53, 149, 173, 241, 245; iron and iron production 111, 114, 116

284 Index

markets *see* seasonal markets
Markets in Early Medieval Europe (Pestell and Ulmschneider) 1
Marstrand (Norway/Sweden) 255
Martens, I. 175, 219
mass production 1, 8, 126, 127
materiality 31, 37
Maurer, K. 255, 256
Mauss, M. 35
Mediterranea zona see Mountain Land
Mediterranean 80, 80*t*, 86–7, 218
Mellan gåva och marknad ('Between gift and market') (Gustin) 1
merchants 145, 152, 204; early state societies 35, 36, 37, 131
metal-detection 14, 44, 216, 217, 220, 240
metalworking *see* copper alloy; gold; iron and iron production; lead; non-ferrous metalworking; silver
Meyer, E. 32
Middle Viking Age (875–1573) 46, 50, 51, 52, 54
Mikkelsen, E. 170
Mill stone project 74
mills 34
Mindets Tomt (excavation) 69
mints and minting 101–2, 106, 107
'mixed farming' 169, 175, 176
mobile communities 233, 245, 252
Molaug, P. 69, 251
monasteries 64
monetisation 3; ecclesiastical law and 106–7; power and 95, 102; silver and payment transactions 49, 50*f*, 51*t*; *thing* and *thingmen* 102, 105–6; trade routes and 14–20
monumental building activities 60, 61, 64, 68, 81
Mortensen, L.B. 257, 258
mounds *see* burial mounds
mountain graves 172, 178*f*, 179, 195, 200, 207
Mountain Land; agricultural economy 241, 244, 245; dating and archaeology of *skeid* 239–40; exchange systems 237–8; law-parish divisions 261, 262*t*, 265, 268, 271, 272, 273; *lawthings* 250, 252, 253, 258, 259; multi-functional meeting places 14, 240–1, 242*f*, 243–5; regionalisation and markets 245–6; *skein* as inland tradition 233, 234, 235*f*, 236; transportation zones 238–9; **maps**: as described in *Historia Norvegiae 234*; provinces of Mountain Land *269*
mountains *see* Uplands (Norway)

multi-functional meeting places 14, 240–1, 242*f*, 243–5, 246
Munch, P.A. 258
Museum of Cultural History (Oslo) 182*n2:4*, 192, 212
Myrvoll, S. 72, 75
mythology 254

nation states *see* state power and formation
navigation *see* trade routes; transportation
neo-evolutionism 33, 34, 36
networks 35, 37–8, 51, 173, 199–200, 226–7; procurement 72, 79, 82*t*, 83, 84, 85, 86–7; regional exchange networks 201–3; soapstone/quernstones 147, 148–51, 153, 155; *see also* trade and trading systems
new institutional economics 36–7, 38
Nidaros (Norway) 251, 254, 258, 268
NIKU *see* Norwegian Institute for Cultural Heritage Research
nodal markets 13, 83, 86–7, 150–1, 155, 227
non-agrarian activities 60, 181; **map** *61*
non-ferrous metalworking 5, 18, 49, 135; commodity production and urbanism/urbanisation 124, 125*f*, 126, 127*f*; consumption 66, 67*t*, 69–70, 86, 87; fine-metalworking 213, 217, 219, 228; jewellery 130–2; procurement of raw materials 82*t*; production sites 224, 225, 226; serial production 124, 125, 128, 129*f*, 130, 133; standardised production 132–4; *see also* iron and iron production
Nordmannsslepene (trading route) 238
Norrland (Sweden)
Norse; burials 195, 196*t*, 216; cosmology 250
North Atlantic islands 153, 155
North, D.C. 36
North Gudbrandsdal (Norway) 163, 167, 168*t*, 171, 175, 176; map: archaeological sites *166*
Norway 20, 21, 54, 59, 62, 107*n1*; Christianisation 2, 3, 70, 203, 254, 268; colonization by 174; major divisions 252; **map**: non-agrarian activities and urbanization *61*; major divisions (*Historia Norvegie*) *253*; South Norway *162*
Norwegian Institute for Cultural Heritage Research (NIKU) 214
Norwegian Law (1604) 96
Norwegian Research Council 182*n3*
Numedal (Norway) 259, 268

Ohthere (Norse merchant) 20
Olaf/Olav Haraldsson (king of Norway)
251, 257, 272, 275
Olaf Tryggvasson (king of Norway) 251
Olav IV Håkonsson (king of Norway and
Denmark) 254
Olav Kyrre (king of Norway) 95, 96, 251
Olav the Saint (king of Norway) 100, 106
Oppland see Uplands
Oppland County Council/Municipality
(Norway) 116, 182*n4*
Ordericus Vitales (English chronicler) 251
Oseberg ship burial (Norway) 225
Oslo (Norway): bakestones 77–8, 84;
ceramics 80*t*, 84; domestic and exotic
materials 63, 64, 65*f*, 68–9, 70, 71–2;
iron and iron production 83; law-
parishes 264*t*, 265, 266, 268, 271, 272;
lawthings 251, 254, 255, 261, 273;
quernstones 74, 152; *skeid* 238; soapstone
78, 79; whetstones/hones 74–6, 83
Oslofjord (Norway)
Oslogate 6 (excavation) (Norway) 10
Østerdalen valley (Uplands (inner eastern
Norway)) 11–12, 115, 174, 177, 268, 271
Østfold (Norway) 16, 21
outfield resources *see* Uplands
oxen: as payment 52
Øyra (Norway) 266, 267–8
Øystein, Archbishop 106
Øystein Roesson (lawman) 261

packhorses 238
pagan practices 203, 207
Peder Claussøn Friis 259
Pedersen, U. 218
pendants 46, 126, 127*f*, 128, 129*f*, 131, 224
penninger (coin) 100, 107
Pestell, T. 1
Petersen, J. 200, 216, 224
Pirenne, H. 32
pit houses 241, 242*f*, 243, 244
pitfall trap systems 163, 165, 167, 169, 170;
technological adaptions 171, 172, 175
place names 204, 232, 235, 239, 265
Poetic Edda
Polanyi, K. 1, 2, 17; pre-state/early state
trade 31, 32, 34, 35–6
political power 31, 35, 38, 227–8
polycentricism 35
'port-of-trade' model 34, 83
pottery *see* ceramics and pottery
power 17, 53, 119, 226, 254; ecclesiastical
181, 270; monetarisation and 95, 102;
political 31, 35, 38, 227–8; production

and 130–1, 134, 135, 176; royal 176,
177, 255; trade and trading systems
145, 250, 273
Prästbordet (Sweden) 48*f*
Pre-Christian burials *see* burials;
grave-goods
pre-state societies 32–3, 38
pre-urbanisation 75, 150
primitivism *see* substantivism
procurement of resources 8; antler
production 82*t*, 149, 174; continuity/
variation in exploitation (Uplands) 167,
168*t*, 169–71, 182*n6*; domestic and
exotic materials 59–60, 63, 82*t*, 83–5,
85–6, 87; from hinterland 245, 250;
trade monopolies 254, 255, 265
'producer towns' 6, 21
production 2, 3, 11, 19, 21; archaeological
sites 8, 10; domestic and exotic materials
63, 63*t*, 64, 81, 82*t*, 83–7; peasant and
freeholder agency 16–19; power and
130–1, 134, 135, 176; technological
innovation 11–12; *see also* iron and iron
production
proto-urban production centres 150, 173

quarries and quarrying 8, 12, 16–17, 21;
domestic products 66, 74, 75, 78; largest
quernstone quarries (Norway) *142*; trade
and trading systems 150, 151, 153, 154,
202; **map**: location of known soapstone
quarries (Norway) *141*
quernstones 3, 6, 8, 10, 11, 19; centres
of procurement 82*t*; as a commodity
140, 143, 144; consumption 73*t*, 74;
long-distance trade 15, 83; patterns of
distribution 11–12; producers 153–5;
quarries and quarrying 14–15, 21;
shipping; trade and trading systems
144–7, 148–53; **maps**: distribution
of quernstones from Hyllestad *143*;
largest quernstone quarries (Norway)
142; quernstone regions in southern
Scandinavia *148*; *see also* domestic and
exotic materials; hones; soapstone;
whetstone

Råbyggelag (Norway) 259
radiocarbon dating 224–5, 242, 265
Ranrike (Båhuslen, Norway/Sweden)
257, 272
Raudalsdansen ('Raudal Dance') 233, 234–5
reciprocity 35, 36, 38
recoinage (*renovatio monetae*) 95, 102, 107
redistributive economy 35, 36, 38

286 *Index*

reindeer *see* antler production; hunting and trapping

Renfrew, C. 37

resource procurement *see* procurement of resources

Ribe (Jylland) 6, 9, 10, 11, 12, 13, 216; trade and trading systems 147, 155

rich graves 154

Ringerike (Norway) 268, 272

river transportation 203–4

roads and road building 201–2, 203, 214, 238

rock crystal 218–19, 222, 226, 243

Rødsmoen (Norway) 163, 167, 168t, 172, 173, 174; **map**: archaeological sites *164*

Rolfsen, P. 270, 271

Romerike (Norway) 16, 268, 272

Romsdal (Norway) 254

rope 4

Roskilde (Denmark) 12

Rostovtzeff, M. 32

royal families and administration 52, 202–3, 267–8; control of coin minting, 101–2, 106, 107; impact on rural economy 101–2, 176–8, 179, 255; impact on urbanism 6, 8, 21, 62–3, 227, 251; iron and iron production 119, 120, 176, 177, 181; *lawthings* 265, 267–8; power and 176, 177, 255; tax revenue 251; trade monopolies 254, 255, 265; tribute 251; *see also* kings

royal stewards (*ármaðr*) 105

royal/rural bailiff (*sýslumaðr/fogd*) 251, 261

Rundberget, B. 11–12, 176–7

runic inscriptions 52

rural economy 6, 9, 10, 13, 14, 15–16; commodity production 16, 20, 21–2, 191, 208; domestic and exotic materials 63, 81; royal families and administration 101–2, 176–8, 179, 255; self-sufficiency and 172–4, 181; silver as payment 17, 19–20, 42–3, 52–3; *see also* agricultural economy; animal husbandry; grain cultivation

rural law (*heraðs rett*) 251

Rural Law of Magnus the Lawmender (1274) 95, 96, 97t, 98t; **maps**: travel compensation/geographical zones in Gulathing/Frostathing law-areas *103, 104*

rural production *see* rural economy

Ruter og rutinisering ('Routes and routinising') (Sindbæk) 1

rye 8

Rygh, O. 204

saga literature 239; *lawthings* 251, 257, 258, 261, 266, 268; **map**: law-parishes of Norway (1223) *256*

Sakse of Haug (lawman) 261

Saltdal (Norway) 15, 144, 150, 152, 153

Sami people 233, 245, 252

Sandnes, J. 268

Sandvik, G. 100–1

scales *see* weighing equipment

schist *see* whetstone

Schleswig (Germany) 150

Schultzén, J. 55n3

sea trade routes 14–16

seasonal markets 3, 5, 20, 34, 121, 240; characteristics 227, 228; 'church villages' 243–4; urbanism and urbanisation 12–14; *see also* skeid; trade stations

Sebbersund (seasonal market) (Limfjord, Denmark) 12, 13, 151, 155

Section of Cultural Heritage Management (Vestfold County Council) 212

Seip, J.A. 256–7, 260

Seland, E.H. 2

self-sufficiency 173

serial production 124, 125, 126, 130, 133

Setesdal (South-Norway) 17, 18, 20, 235; cemeteries 194f, 195, 196t, 197t, 198f, 199–201; inland expansion of trade 204, 205t, 206, 207; regional trade exchange networks 201–3, 238, 240; stationary and mobile trade entrepreneurs 203–4; **map**: Setesdal Valley *193*

settlement hierarchies 34–5

settlement patterns 6, 251; Norway 170, 174–6, 180, 204, 205t, 206–7

sheep herding 100, 101

Shetland 140, 144

shielings *see* summer farming system

ships and boats: burials 18, 129, 212, 225, 226; coinage and 100, 101; trade and trading systems 150, 151, 152, 153, 154–5, 203

shire-*thing* (*fylkesting*) 266

shoe production 5, 66, 67t, 71–2; procurement and consumption 81, 82t, 86, 87

Sigtuna (Sweden) 44, 50, 51

Sigurd Erlingsson Ribbung 258–9, 265

silver 17, 69, 202; Arabic 13, 52, 55n4; coinage 3, 13, 19–20, 102, 105, 107; jewellery 126, 128, 130, 131, 134; payment transactions 49, 50f, 51t; procurement 217, 224, 225; tariffs 96, 97t, 98t, 99–100; weights/balances as grave goods 44, 46, 47t, 48f, 49f, 55n3,

195; **map**: distribution of finds of weights/balances in Jämtland (Norway/Sweden) *45*; *see also* hacksilver
silversmiths 42
Simon at the Tomb in Råde (lawman) 261
Sindbæk, S.N. 1, 15, 86, 87; *see also* Ashby, S. et al.
Sjælland (Denmark) 15
Skagerrak (Norway) 15
Skåne (Denmark) 15
skeid 232–3; dating and archaeology of 239–40; exchange systems 237–8; as inland tradition 233, 234, 235*f*, 236; multi-functional meeting places 14, 240–1, 242*f*, 243–5; regionalisation and markets 245–6; transportation zones 238–9; *see also* seasonal markets; trade stations
Skibotn (seasonal market) (Troms, Norway) 243
Skien (Norway): bakestones 84; ceramics 80*t*; domestic and exotic materials 63, 64, 68, 70, 71, 72; iron 83; law-parishes 264*t*, 265, 266, 271, 272, 273; *lawthings* 251, 254, 255, 259, 261; soapstone 78, 79; tariffs 96, 98*t*, 99; whetstones/hones 75, 76, 83
Skiringssal (Norway) 131
Skre, D. 42–3, 54, 227, 251
Skule Bårdsson, Duke 265
slag-tapping 113, 116, 119, 163
slave trade 101
small market sites 14
small-scale crafts 66*t*, 67*t*, 68–72, 73*t*, 74, 81–2
'small-world' networks 38
smiths 5, 67, 68, 69, 120, 121
Snorri Sturluson 257, 258, 271
snow-patch hunting systems 171, 172
soapstone 36, 13, 16–17, 18, 21; as a commodity 73*t*, 78, 86; long-distance trade 8, 9, 10, 11, 15, 84; monument-building 64–5; procurement of raw materials 82*t*, 83, 191; producers 153–5; trade and trading systems 144–7, 148–53, 202; **map**: location of known soapstone quarries (Norway) *141*; *see also* domestic and exotic materials; hones; quernstone; whetstone
social complexity *see* complex societies
social networks 37–8, 179–80
Solheim, S. 237
South Norway *see* Uplands

southern Scandinavia (Denmark) 45–6, 9, 10, 15; domestic and exotic materials 80*t*, 85–6; trade and trading systems 149, 155
special objects commissioned *see* bespoke production
spindle whorls 195, 220, 243
Stalsberg, A. 55*n2*
standardised production 124, 132–4, 140
standing stones 239
state power and formation 3, 32, 33, 34, 38
Stavanger (Norway) 201; domestic and exotic materials 63, 64, 71, 74, 80*t*, 81; law-parishes 264*t*, 266, 272, 273; *lawthings* 251, 254, 255
steatite *see* soapstone
Steen, S. 238
Steigen (Norway) 264*t*, 268, 272, 273
Stein 270, 271
Steinnes, A. 252
Steinsland, G. 254
stone products *see* bakestones; building and construction; hones; quernstones; soapstone; whetstones
stone settings 44
Storm, G. 252, 254, 258, 259
Storøya (Norway) 268, 269–70
strap-ends/slides 125*f*, 217, 221*f*, 224
stray finds: burials 205*t*
Stylegar, F.-A. 254, 258, 259
subsistence production 4, 5, 32, 245
substantivism 1, 32, 33, 34, 36, 38
summer farming system (shielings) 163–4, 165, 167, 169, 240, 243
surplus production 172–4, 176–7, 178*f*, 179, 180–1
Svensson, E. 173
Sverre Sigurdsson (king of Norway) 106, 260, 268
Sweden 10, 54, 200; agricultural economy 6; burials 47*t*; ceramics 85, 86; Christianisation 2; coinage 19; iron and iron production 11, 111, 113, 120, 245; *lawthings* 257; non-ferrous metalworking 135, 226; quernstones 10, 147, 149, 150; settlements 251; shoe production 86–7; silver 42, 43, 44, 46, 50, 51; soapstone 16, 139, 140, 143, 147; urbanism and urbanisation 60, 251; weights 46; **maps**: all recorded iron production sites (C4th BC– AD C19th) *112*; quernstone regions in southern Scandinavia *148*
swords 53, 216, 224; mountain graves 178*f*, 179, 195, 200, 207
symbolism: foodstuff 150; jewellery 134, 179; utensils 150

288   *Index*

tald mark (coin) 106
tannery sites 72
tar products 4
tariffs 95, 96, 99, 101–2, 106; travel
   compensation 97–8*t*
tax revenue/taxation 107, 119, 153, 156*n1*,
   177, 201
technological innovations 10, 11–12;
   hunting and trapping 171–2; iron and iron
   production 11, 115–16, 117, 118, 119, 121
Telemark County (Norway) 219, 220;
   lawthings 268, 272; *things* and *thingmen*
   235, 238, 239, 259; trading and trading
   systems 205*t*, 207, 208, 255; **map**: main
   valley regions *206*
Telemarkvassdraget (river system) 75
textiles 195, 220, 243
thing and *thingmen* 20, 96, 180, 244, 250–1;
   coinage 101–2, 105–6; compensation
   schemes 95, 99–100; ecclesiastical law
   and money 106–7; expenses and travel
   routes 95–6, 97*t*, 98*t*, 99; **map**: travel
   compensation/geographical zones in
   Gulathing/Frostathing law-areas *103*,
   104; *see also lawthings*
timber 63–4, 66, 82*t*, 255
tin 126
tingfareøret (economic compensation for
   attending *thing*) 95
Tinn (Norway) 207, 259
tithes 119, 120*t*, 258
Tiundaland ('Land with Ten Hundreds')
   (Sweden) 257
Tjølling (Norway) 260, 265, 266, 271, 272
Tøftom (Dovre, Norway) 12
Tønsberg (Norway); bakestones 84; ceramics
   80*t*; *lawthings* 251, 254, 261, 264*t*, 265,
   266, 271, 272, 273; quernstones 152;
   silver 69, 70
tools of trade 194*f*, 195, 196*t*, 197*t*, 198*f*,
   199–201, 203
Tord Skolle (lawman) 261
Tore Lagmann (Gudmundsson) (lawman) 261
town assembly (*mót*) 251
towns *see* urbanism and urbanization
'trade diaspora' 35
trade laws (*Bjarkøyretter*) 251
trade monopolies 83–4, 254, 255
trade stations 191–2, 208; inland expansion
   204, 205*t*, 206, 207; regional exchange
   networks 201–3; signs of trade and
   exchange in cemeteries 194*f*, 195, 196*t*,
   197*t*, 198*f*, 199–201; stationary and
   mobile entrepreneurs 203–4; **maps**: main

valley (East Norway)/main valley regions
   (Telemark County) *206*; Setesdal Valley
   193; *see also* seasonal markets; *skeid*
trade and trading systems 221, 31–3, 173,
   181; 'administered trade' patterns 17, 18;
   analytical models of 33–4; characteristics
   227; commodity production 4–6, 8–12;
   Denmark 140, 149; exclusive trading
   rights 255; interaction models 34–6;
   long-distance trade 2, 3, 8–12; new
   institutional economics 36–7; power and
   145, 250, 273; soapstone/quernstones
   144–7, 148–53, 150, 153, 155; travel
   expenses 95–6, 97*t*, 98*t*, 99; **maps**:
   travel compensation/geographical zones
   in Gulathing/Frostathing law-areas *103*,
   104; *see also* networks
trading routes 14–16, 87, 114, 238–9; rural
   economy 201–2, 203–4, 207–8; *see also*
   transportation
Transaction Cost Theory 36
transit trade 9, 14
transportation 6, 15, 53–4, 204, 238–9; costs
   of 35, 36; inland in homelands 203–4,
   208; soapstone/quernstones 150, 151,
   152, 153, 154–5; *see also* trading routes
transshipment centres 202, 204
tribal societies 34
tribute 258; to elites 36, 37, 131, 154, 251;
   to royal families 251
Trøndelag (Norway) 52, 69, 114, 115, 261
Trondheim, Archbishop of 176
Trondheim (Norway) 10, 11, 12;
   bakestones 84; ceramics 80*t*, 85, 86;
   domestic and exotic materials 63, 64,
   65*f*, 66, 68, 71, 72; iron production 81;
   lawthings 254, 264, 268, 273; stockfish
   152; whetstones/hones 75
Tune (Østfold, Norway) 14
Tveite, S. 238–9

ubotamål (outlawry) 106
Ulmschneider, K. 1
Ulriksen, E. 78
unica production 3, 5
University of Bergen 240
University Museum of Bergen 240
University of Oslo 259
University of Vienna 214
Uplands (Norway) 11–12, 15–16, 234,
   261, 264*t*; continuity/variation in
   resource exploitation 167, 168*t*, 169–71,
   182*n6*; geographical and archaeological
   background 163, 165, 167, 182*n2–4*;

local landscape management 179–81; settlement and agricultural economy 174–6; surplus production and local population 160–1, 172–4, 176–7, 178f, 179, 180–1; technological adaptation and regional dynamics 171–2; transportation zones 238–9; **maps**: distribution of archaeological sites (Gråfjell area/Rødsmoen) *164*; distribution of archaeological sites (Grimsdalen) *165*; distribution of archaeological sites (North Gudbrandsdal) *166*; South Norway *162, 236; see also* rural economy
Uppåkra (Sweden) 223
Uppland (Sweden) 258
Uppsala Law (Sweden) 257, 272
urban bailiff (*gjaldker*) 251
Urban Code of Bergen (1276) 151
urbanism and urbanisation 6, 10, 21–2, 227; commodity production 124, 125f, 126, 127f, 153–5; construction of buildings/infrastructure in Norway 60, 63–4, 65f, 66, 81, 82; consumption patterns 63–4, 66, 68–72, 74–9, 80t, 81, 82, 87; royal families and administration 6, 8, 21, 62–3, 227, 251; seasonal markets 3, 5, 12–14; Sweden 251; trade and trading systems 17–18, 151–3; **map**: non-agrarian activities 61; *see also* hinterland; housing
utensils 4, 19, 83, 200; soapstone 146, 150, 154

Vågan (Norway) 14, 62, 64, 152, 254, 268, 273
Vågar *see* Vågan
Vågslid, E. 260
Valdres (Norway) 235, 237, 238, 266, 272
Valle (Norway) 17, 235, 236, 239, 240; trade and trading systems 201–2, 203, 207, 208
Veblen, T. 31
Veøy (Norway) 60, 62, 64, 66, 254, 255
Veøykaupangen (Romsdal, Norway) 14, 68, 70
verdict (*domsbrev*) 270
vessel glass 18
Vesterøya (Norway) 216
Vestfold (Norway) 15–16, 21, 129, 146, 154, 271; trade and trading systems 226, 227, 228, 255

Vestfold County Council 212
Vestfold Museums 212
Vike, V. 198
Viken (Norway) 261, 263t
Viking Age *see* Early Viking Age (700–950); Late Viking Age (950–1100); Middle Viking Age (1050–1573)
Vingulsmark (Norway) 271, 272
ViS Group *vii, viii*

Wallis, J.J. 36
walrus-ivory products 4
Wamers, E. 217
ware types: ceramics 79–81, 85
wax models/moulds 124, 125f, 128–9, 133
weaponry 18, 53, 204, 216, 224, 228; mountain graves 178f, 179, 195, 200, 207
weaving 139, 195, 196t, 197t, 220, 243
weighing equipment 13, 17, 18, 19, 20, 198f; dating 220, 221f, 222t; excavation finds 212, 218, 244; jewellery 126, 131; male burials/graves 154, 207; silver 44, 46, 47t, 48f, 49f, 55n3; trade-related grave-goods 194f, 195, 196t, 197t, 198f, 199–201, 203; **map**: distribution of finds in Jämtland (Norway/Sweden) *45*
Weingast, B. 36
Western Europe 217, 218, 224
Western Scandinavia 8, 9, 10, 12, 13, 14; commodity production 4, 18, 19; hoards 20; seasonal markets 20; trade and trading systems 15, 17
whetstones 3, 6, 9–11, 13–15, 19, 21; as a commodity 149, 191, 195; consumption 74–6; grave-goods 198, 199; Mountain Land 242; production sites 213, 219–20; *see also* domestic and exotic materials; hones; quernstone; soapstone
Wickham, C. 1
Wille, H.J. et al. 239
wood *see* timber
wool 6, 220
workshops 18, 106, 200, 215, 243; non-ferrous 125, 131, 133

zinc 69
zona itaque maritime see Coastal Land
Zona Montana (Mountainous Land/Uplands) (Norway) 20, 21

Taylor & Francis eBooks

Helping you to choose the right eBooks for your Library

Add Routledge titles to your library's digital collection today. Taylor and Francis ebooks contains over 50,000 titles in the Humanities, Social Sciences, Behavioural Sciences, Built Environment and Law.

Choose from a range of subject packages or create your own!

Benefits for you
- Free MARC records
- COUNTER-compliant usage statistics
- Flexible purchase and pricing options
- All titles DRM-free.

Benefits for your user
- Off-site, anytime access via Athens or referring URL
- Print or copy pages or chapters
- Full content search
- Bookmark, highlight and annotate text
- Access to thousands of pages of quality research at the click of a button.

REQUEST YOUR **FREE** INSTITUTIONAL TRIAL TODAY

Free Trials Available
We offer free trials to qualifying academic, corporate and government customers.

eCollections – Choose from over 30 subject eCollections, including:

Archaeology	Language Learning
Architecture	Law
Asian Studies	Literature
Business & Management	Media & Communication
Classical Studies	Middle East Studies
Construction	Music
Creative & Media Arts	Philosophy
Criminology & Criminal Justice	Planning
Economics	Politics
Education	Psychology & Mental Health
Energy	Religion
Engineering	Security
English Language & Linguistics	Social Work
Environment & Sustainability	Sociology
Geography	Sport
Health Studies	Theatre & Performance
History	Tourism, Hospitality & Events

For more information, pricing enquiries or to order a free trial, please contact your local sales team:
www.tandfebooks.com/page/sales

 Routledge
Taylor & Francis Group

The home of
Routledge books

www.tandfebooks.com